The Great Age of the English Essay

The Great Age
of the English Essay

An Anthology

EDITED BY

Denise Gigante

Yale University Press ⸶ New Haven & London

Published with assistance from the Annie Burr Lewis Fund.

Designed by Sonia L. Shannon.
Set in Galos type by The Composing Room of Michigan, Inc.
Printed in the United States of America by Sheridan Books, Inc., Ann Arbor, Michigan.

Library of Congess Cataloging-in-Publication Data

The great age of the English essay : an anthology / edited by Denise Gigante.
p. cm.
"Published with assistance from the Annie Burr Lewis Fund."
Includes bibliographical references and index.
ISBN 978-0-300-11722-6 (cl. alk. paper); ISBN 978-0-300-14196-2 (pb. : alk. paper)
1. English essays.   I. Gigante, Denise, 1965–
PR1363.G73 2008
824—dc22
2008017947

A catalogue record for this book is available from the British Library.
The paper in this book meets the guidelines for permanence and durability
of the Committee on Production Guidelines for Book Longevity
of the Council on Library Resources.

10 9 8 7 6 5 4 3 2 1

Contents

Acknowledgments

SINCE THE INCEPTION OF THIS PROJECT, Lauren Caldwell has provided first-rate editorial assistance, and I am grateful to her beyond words. The anthology has also benefited greatly from previous editions of the essayists herein contained, and I am thankful for the work of Margaret Bailey, Walter Jackson Bate, Christine Blouch, Donald F. Bond, Jeffrey N. Cox, Austin Dobson, P. P. Howe, Gerard Edward Jenson, Greg Kucich, Grevel Lindop, E. V. Lucas, Daniel McDonald, Robert Morrison, Alexander Pettit, Rebecca Sayers, Patricia Meyer Spacks, Albrecht B. Strauss, David Womersley, and Duncan Wu. For insightful criticism and advice I would like to thank Harold Bloom, David Bromwich, James Engell, William Germano, John Kulka, Christopher Rovee, and Cynthia Wall. Due credit and appreciation go also to George Brown, Erik Gray, Stephen Orgel, and Fred Porta for help with classical translations; to John Bender, Ian Duncan, Kate Greenspan, Regina Janes, Seth Lerer, and Blakey Vermeule for responses to random footnote queries; to Nora Soledad Martin, Yee-Chiang Sim, and Alex Whitlyn Jacobs for research assistance; to Stanford University for financial assistance; and to the outstanding editorial team of Jennifer Banks, Susan Laity, and Lindsay Toland at Yale University Press.

Note on the Text

$\underset{\smile}{\textcolor{black}{\text{\large Y}}}$

FOR CONSISTENCY AND EASE OF READING, the texts of the essays have been modernized according to the following principles.

Typography: Words beginning paragraphs in all caps have been changed to sentence case. Block italicization of paragraphs as well as clearly unsignifying capitalization within sentences has been removed, but internal italics or capitalizations drawing attention to a word or phrase (the Ancients and the Moderns, the Town and the Country) have been left in place. Also, persons addressed according to profession or station (the Knight, the Lady, the Captain) and entities treated as proper nouns (the Republic of Letters) or deities (Virtue) remain capitalized.

Spelling: Archaic vowel patterns ("shew" for "show"; "intirely" for "entirely"; "satyr" for "satire"; "chearful" for "cheerful"; "meer" for the adjective "mere") and consonant clusters no longer in use ("politick" for "politic") have been standardized according to modern usage, with the idiosyncratic exception of Boswell's *Hypochondriack.* Potentially confusing conventions for past tenses ("eat" for "ate"; "sate" for "sat") and archaic elisions ("drop'd" for "dropped"; "darkning" for "darkening") have been updated. Standard British spellings (favour; surprize) have been left as is, as have hyphenated words (to-morrow, law-suit, back-gammon) that present no confusion. Occasionally, missing letters have been added ("canvass" for "canvas") and extra spaces removed ("herself" for "her self") for the sake of uniformity.

Punctuation: Dashes following commas or end punctuation have been removed unless they occur within sentences to set off phrases. Periods following royal numerals (Henry VIII.) have been removed.

Dates: Dates at the end of essays indicate their original appearance in print.

Annotations: All translations from classical texts, unless indicated otherwise, are from the Loeb Classical Library (Cambridge: Harvard University Press, 1900–2006). Citations to John Milton are to *John Milton: Complete Poems and Major Prose,* ed. Merritt Y. Hughes (New York: Odyssey, 1957). Act, scene, and line numbers from the works of William Shakespeare are from *Complete Works of William Shakespeare* (Oxford: Oxford University Press, 1986). All biblical citations are from the King James Bible (1611). All references to Virgil's *Eclogues* and *Aeneid* are from *Virgil,* trans. H. Rushton, rev. ed. G. P. Goold (Cambridge: Harvard University Press, 1999–2000). Notes prefaced by "see" (e.g., "See Shakespeare, *Hamlet,* IV.v.175–77") indicate paraphrases; direct citations (e.g., "Shakespeare, *Hamlet,* IV.v.175–77") indicate quotations. Editorial titles and subtitles appear in brackets.

Introduction

You should be extending your stay among writers whose genius
is unquestionable, deriving constant nourishment from them
if you wish to gain anything from your reading that will find a
lasting place in your mind. To be everywhere is to be nowhere.
—Seneca, *Letters from a Stoic,* II

THE GREAT AGE OF THE ENGLISH ESSAY offers a vibrant gallery
of personae speaking in a multiplicity of voices, from the confessional to the
critical, the familiar to the parodic, the picturesque to the grotesque. As
developed from the popular broadsides of Joseph Addison and Richard
Steele, the periodical essay tradition afforded a peculiar opportunity for an
author to create a character—more nearly, a pose or persona—who participated directly in the public sphere, thereby becoming something more
than a fictional character. Steele's Tatler thus gossiped about current events
and scandal, Addison's Spectator observed real-life rogues and politicians,
Samuel Johnson's Rambler perambulated London storing up thought for
mental meanderings, and Thomas De Quincey's Opium Eater haunted the
dark underworld of psychological obsession and physical addiction. Inhab-
iting a pseudo-fictional space somewhere between a public sphere marked
by cultural change and a more private, self-enclosed world, the essayists
took on the most contested topics of their day, pursuing them through all
the nooks and crannies of experience. In essays ranging from taste and aesthetic principles to war, from natural history to fashion and gender roles
and relations, these writers invented a number of stylistic techniques that
continue to be used in the novel and other forms of prose and that constitute some of the best moments in English literary history.

This anthology makes no claim to include all the great diversity of
voices, anonymous or otherwise, to be found in print throughout the for-
mative period of the periodical essay. As Seneca says, to be everywhere is to

be nowhere. Instead, what the book offers are complex and sustained serial representations of personality: the Tatler, the Spectator, the Rambler, the Idler, the Hypochondriack, the Lounger, and Lamb's Londoner (Elia), to name a few. The periodical essay in Britain reflects a moment when literature was less sharply distinguished from other forms of writing, such as journalism, philosophical speculation, private memoirs and letters, travel narratives, and sermons. But the distinguishing feature of the sort of "ephemera" presented here (essays published as twopenny sheets or in newspapers, journals, and reviews) is their literary dimension. Mixing personal reflections with social critique, the first British essayists, from whom today's literary critics descend, self-consciously sought to forge a "literary" tradition. Although a number of them published separate papers devoted to politics (Steele's *Guardian,* Addison's *Freeholder,* Fielding's *Patriot,* Leigh Hunt's *Examiner* and ill-fated *Liberal*), their periodical papers demanded no specialized knowledge, political or philosophical, of their readers. Instead, the essayists filtered historical and sociopolitical critique through the lenses of character and narrative voice. As James Boswell declared, "We may be in some degree whatever character we choose."[1] Occasionally they would comment directly on foreign policy or finer points of religion, but for the most part they renounced political partisanship and abstruse scholarly speculation for a broader belletristic stance within a shared "Republic of Letters." Readers in this tradition learned criticism from the critics, navigating the dynamic form of the essay with increasing care and sophistication and absorbing the principles of critical thinking.

Although it remains a relatively unexplored genre within the academy today, the English periodical essay grew up alongside the novel, like it challenging the borders between fiction and nonfiction prose. The earliest novels in English sought to straddle fantasy and fact, presenting themselves as historical accounts of real people: Daniel Defoe's *The Life and Adventures of Robinson Crusoe,* Jonathan Swift's *Travels into Several Remote Nations of the World . . . by Lemuel Gulliver, First a Surgeon, and Then a Captain of Several Ships,* Samuel Richardson's *Clarissa; or, The History of a Young Lady,* Laurence Sterne's *The Life and Opinions of Tristram Shandy, Gentleman,* and Frances Burney's *Evelina; or, The History of a Young Lady's Entrance into the World* are typical in this regard. Later in the nineteenth century, as the novel became more plainly fictional and the critical essay more plainly critical, their shared roots in the Enlightenment Republic of Letters withered and were forgotten. Nevertheless, by the mid-eighteenth century, the essay had emerged as a premier literary form in which cultural values were stated and disputed—sometimes treated seriously, with their various ramifications teased out with care, at other times subject to ridicule or satire—in which authors, aspiring or established, could contribute to the central debates of their age. From the beginning, the dual purpose of the periodical essay in reporting the news, foreign and domestic, was to entertain and to reform the reigning morals, manners, and tastes of the time. But the undeclared stylistic objective was to teach readers how to read critically and to create meaning from the fluid, freewheeling form of the essay—as well as from the historical and cultural framework in which it was set. Far more than a historical curiosity, then, the periodical essay was the forerunner of modern literary studies and cultural criticism.

How, then, did the essay form emerge as a quintessentially "literary" mode, shaping our sense of criticism and the arts? Two important strains of influence need to be taken into account: the tradition of classical rhetoric that formed part of the early liberal arts education, and the miscellaneous print world of "Grub Street" (fictional abode of literary hacks) that sprang from new printing technologies, which had produced, by the end of the seventeenth century, a number of periodicals with literary pretensions. Rhetoric, part of the medieval *trivium* (the three verbal arts), was defined as the art and technique of persuasion, and it was taught along with grammar and logic. Insofar as rhetorical techniques relied heavily upon the sequential ordering of ideas to persuade an audience of a certain argument or to inculcate a certain perspective, they might seem contrary to the aims of the periodical essayist, whose stylistic maneuvers tended to favor the digressive, associative manner of letters and personal journals. Yet the ancient Greek concept of the *rhetor* (orator) highlighted the rhetorician as a *real* person, standing in a *real* place (the courtroom, street corner, or, later, coffeehouse), speaking to a *real* audience for certain ends. And these three basic concepts—speaker, place, and audience—became foundational to the development of the periodical essay form in English.

In *The Art of Rhetoric,* Aristotle stressed the importance of the personality behind the speaking voice, and Joseph Addison opens the first number of *The Spectator* with the observation that "a reader seldom peruses a book with pleasure, till he knows whether the writer of it be a black or a fair man, of a mild or choleric disposition, married or a bachelor, with other particulars of the like nature, that conduce very much to the right understanding of an author." The adoption of a pose or persona was a necessary opening gambit in the British periodical essay. In the midst of thriving, turn-of-the century London, still spinning from the excesses of the Restoration court, Richard Steele took on the persona of Isaac Bickerstaff, Esq., an elderly gentleman of benevolent disposition and strict manners, diligently committed to writing down his "lucubrations" by candlelight for the benefit of his readers. When Addison introduced the more neutral persona of the Spectator, he related that the Spectator's mother, on the eve of her pregnancy, dreamed she would give birth to a judge—an accurate prediction of the man who would lay down the basic principles of aesthetic judgment and modern taste. Born at a small hereditary estate bounded by the same hedges and ditches that had been there since the time of William the Conqueror, the Spectator offered readers a reliable source of commentary, his dependability assured by his past. Rhetoricians recognized the human tendency to gravitate toward reliable, familiar, and trustworthy speakers and to avoid those who are inconsistent, impolite, or unreliable. Following Addison and Steele, most essayists emphasized the nature of their periodical personae, the serial personalities they chose to exhibit.

Frequently, by the same logic, a periodical essay series would fizzle out when the persona behind it was exhausted. Once the thirty-seven-year-old Steele became known as the creator of the elderly Bickerstaff, for instance, his cover was blown (or so he claimed), and his popular *Tatler* series came to an end.[2] "I never designed in it to give any Man any secret wound by my concealment," Steele explained in his farewell number (no. 271), "but spoke in the character of an old man, a philosopher, an humorist, an astrologer, and a censor, to allure my reader with the variety of my subjects, and insinuate, if I could, the weight of reason with the agreeableness of wit." The rambunctious Steele, fond of drinking and gambling, may have considered his own persona inadequate to the task of inculcating values such as self-control, reasonableness, moderation, and plain, unvarnished truth. For if the periodical essayists set out to entertain, they were equally concerned to improve the minds and manners of their audience, to instruct as well as change them.

The rhetorical concept of place was equally essential to the essay tradition. Haranguing an audience in an outdoor theater of ancient Greece may seem a far cry from identifying one's periodical paper as being written at Will's Coffee House during the reign of Queen Anne, but rhetorical technique stressed the importance of the cultural context in which a message was to appear. Wishing to reflect the diversity of "the Town," a melting pot of high and low life, wit and obscenity, turn-of-the-century literary periodicals datelined their facetious news and scandal from various locales around London. Ned Ward's *English Lucian,* for example, which ran from January through April 1698, borrowed the newspaper convention of datelines, launching its lampoons from places like Lincoln's Inn Fields, Whitechapel, the Old Bailey, Drury Lane, Lombard Street, and Saint James's coffeehouse. Many of these were socially symbolic as well as geographical locations.

In the opening number of *The Tatler,* Steele announced that all accounts of gallantry, pleasure, and entertainment would be dated from White's Chocolate-house; all discussions of poetry and the arts from Will's Coffee House; all learned commentary from the Graecian; all observations on foreign and domestic news from Saint James's; and miscellaneous thoughts from his "own apartment," whose location like its resident remained unidentified. As *The Tatler* progressed, its individual numbers tended to consolidate a smattering of stories into one essay dated from a single venue, more often than not Bickerstaff's apartment. Branching out from the coffeehouse but seeking to reflect a more polite spectrum than Ned Ward's urban haunts, Addison's Spectator culled his Speculations from visits to places like Westminster Abbey, Hay-Market Square, the Royal Exchange, and Drury Lane Theatre, describing what he found there in the manner of "a Speculative Statesman, Soldier, Merchant and Artisan." Eventually in *The Tatler* and from the start of *The Spectator,* epigraphs from the classics in Latin or Greek—headings that were also known as "places" (*topoi*) in Renaissance rhetorical tradition—edged out the more journalistic headings derived from newspapers.[3]

For periodical essayists from Steele and Addison, the classical quotation provided a thematic point of departure, which the essay circled around and often returned to at the end. Following the Roman rhetoricians, particularly Cicero and Quintilian, Erasmus delineated a model of composi-

tion based on the use of commonplace books: private storehouses of anecdotes, maxims, verses, and literary quotations, arranged under different
places, or headings. Francis Bacon, a seventeenth-century exemplar of this
model, published his essays between 1597 and 1625, ranging them under
general subject headings such as "Of Truth," "Of Death," "Of Revenge,"
"Of Adversity," and "Of Simulation and Dissimulation," to take the first
few. Bacon's French contemporary Michel de Montaigne (1533–92), the
founder of the style favored by the periodical essayists, popularized a more
familiar, less epigrammatic mode of essay writing than Bacon, but he too
organized his essays thematically, revolving around such commonplace
concerns as custom, age, glory, and the education of children. As the century wore on, the importance of place as a geographical marker diminished,
giving way to mental places in the periodical essay tradition. In his 1826 essay "On Coffee-Houses and Smoking," Leigh Hunt lamented the loss of
the clubby, coffeehouse culture available to the early essayists, fantasizing
about what it would be like to stumble into one of those legendary places
through the back door of his local tobacco shop.

Beyond speaker and place, the rhetorical concept of audience informed the periodical essay tradition. In general the essayists tended to assume a British audience familiar with a belletristic tradition in which scientific, aesthetic, economic, and sociopolitical matters freely overlapped.
This is not to say that the community forged through Enlightenment print
culture was a monolithic entity instead of an internally conflicted collection
of individuals spanning the class spectrum and holding diverse political
opinions and religious views. But far more than for today's periodicals, the
audience during the great age of the English essay assumed coherence as a
Republic of Letters, a rhetorical fiction that Jürgen Habermas has identified
with the public sphere.[4] Well through the Romantic period readers sought
an ideal of general knowledge, having not yet splintered into the specialized
interest groups that made trade publications possible.

Steele explicitly addressed his news, anecdotes, and moral censures to
the male audience of the coffeehouse milieu, though his papers often made
it back into the home. At the start of *The Tatler* he resolved "also to have
something which may be of entertainment to the fair sex." Addison went
even further than his literary partner in an effort to reach female readers. In
Spectator no. 10 he recommended his "speculations to all well regulated

families, that set apart an hour in every morning for tea and bread and butter," earnestly advising them "to order this paper to be punctually served up, and to be looked upon as part of the tea equipage." Taking this cue, a number of tea-table periodicals cropped up in the 1720s, including the anonymous weekly *Tea-Table,* which appeared from 21 February to 22 June 1724, Alan Ramsay's *The Tea-Table Miscellany* (1724–32), and Eliza Haywood's two-part *The Tea-Table* (1725–26), a precursor to her more popular *The Female Spectator.* Unlike Restoration-era periodicals (mostly bawdy forums for scandal and gossip), eighteenth-century periodical essays set out to address a polite, mixed audience of middle-class readers.

Although the periodical essay was built on basic rhetorical principles, it tended to be more conversational in tone and desultory in its wanderings than essays in strict scholastic style, rambling comfortably from personal reflection to social critique and back again. Bacon, who produced essays in the clear, concise style favored by classical rhetoricians, serves as a good point of contrast. Making use of the technique of "point" espoused by Seneca, he filled his essays with epigrammatic statements about the human condition—shrewd points and observations that could be excerpted from the whole as self-contained apothegms. Like his English peer Thomas Hobbes (1588–1679), Bacon favored a simpler, less ornamental style than Erasmus, but his essays nevertheless come down to us as condensed academic utterances. He does not slip into the chatty, relaxed attitude of Steele's Tatler, nor does he probe the darker depths of authorial subjectivity in the manner of Romantics like Hazlitt and De Quincey.

The periodical essayists preferred to address readers as confidants, taking them into the private space of the study to consider human nature and events in the more relaxed manner popularized by Montaigne, who secluded himself for roughly ten years in the tower of his château at Périgord with his voluminous library of books before publishing his collected essays in 1580. Montaigne's first English followers included Sir Thomas Browne (1605–82), Abraham Cowley (1618–67), and Sir William Temple (1628–99), whose essay "Of Ancient and Modern Learning" (1690) prompted the famous controversy of the Ancients versus the Moderns. By treating his material in a more overtly subjective manner than had been previously done, Montaigne became (as Hazlitt put it) "the father of this kind of personal authorship among the moderns, in which the reader is admitted behind the curtain, and sits down with the writer in his gown and slippers."[5] For Hazlitt, Montaigne was an undisguised egotist, but his self-reflexive, familiar style was one that he and other Romantics adopted. Yet whereas Montaigne let readers exclusively into the secret of his own affairs, the British periodical essayists starting with Bickerstaff let them into those of their neighbors as well. Adding narrative elements, including anecdotes and character sketches, to Montaigne's familiar prose, they devised forms of narration that were later used successfully in the novel, with its wider social sweep.

Among the various beaux and belles, gossips and gamblers, antiquarians, starving poets, and newsmongers populating the panorama of eighteenth-century periodical literature is one social type—the virtuoso—who mirrors the essayist and serves as a recurring object of satire. Not content to learn about nature through books, the natural philosophical aficionado known as the virtuoso was a product of the age of empiricism and inductive methodology. Much as the essayist ventured out to collect specimens of human nature, the virtuoso collected rocks, shells, botanical specimens, and other curiosities. Johnson wrote that this character is distinguished by "an unextinguishable ardour of curiosity, and an unshaken perseverance in the acquisition of the productions of art and nature." However, to avoid becoming a target of satire, virtuosos needed to proceed with caution, steering clear of that excessive zeal that would (in Addison's words) "discover the sex of a cockle, or describe the generation of a mite, in all its circumstances."[6] Like the virtuoso, the periodical essayist, it is implied, would do well to steer a middle course through the seas of experience, providing practical information and insight and avoiding the treacherous region of abstruse research. In the opening number of *The Tatler,* Steele begged his reader to put up with its one-penny price, for he had to put himself to some trouble and expense to gather information by way of empirical research. Every sally into the educated circles of the Graecian required a fresh supply of Spanish snuff, he explained, every conversation, even with the headwaiter of Saint James's, clean linen. Relying on experience as the only true path to knowledge, the virtuoso exemplified empirical pursuit after the overthrow of medieval scholasticism, just as the Connoisseur (George Colman and Bonnell Thornton's mid-century imitation of the Spectator) came to exemplify cultural pursuit in a flourishing new world of arts and letters.

Contemporary Grub Street provided another formal toolkit for the early periodical essayists. Beginning with the Parisian *Journal des sçavans,* established in Paris in 1665, periodicals began to feature synopses of books, an incipient form of the literary review. The British *History of the Works of the Learned,* which ran from 1699 through 1712, followed its French forebear, and Peter Anthony Motteux's *Gentleman's Journal* (1692–94) added letters, poetry, music, historical commentaries, and philosophical inquiries to book notices and translations.[7] From the end of the seventeenth century, the periodical press offered commentary on aristocratic habits (gambling, dueling, swindling) and fashion (hair, face patches, coquetry); helped to furnish guidelines for taste; and articulated basic principles of artistic, theatrical, and literary criticism. Two stylistic features derived from these fledgling literary productions—the letter to the editor and the editorial club—especially influenced eighteenth-century periodicals from the time of *The Tatler* and *The Spectator.*

When the English bookseller John Dunton established his *Athenian Mercury* (1691–97) as a forum dedicated to resolving "the nice and curious questions proposed by the Ingenious," he positioned himself at the head of a (fictitious) club of gentleman scholars. Just as Steele's Bickerstaff and many of his more feeble imitators would later do, Dunton instructed readers where to leave letters and questions for the club. The *Mercury*'s popularity was reflected in a number of successors, including Thomas Brown's *London Mercury* (begun 1692), the *Jovial Mercury* (begun 1693), the *Ladies Mercury* (begun 1693), John Oldmixon's *Muses Mercury* (1707–8), and Daniel Defoe's "Mercure Scandale; or, Advice from the Scandalous Club," which supplemented his weekly *Review* (1704–13) of news from the Continent by responding to letters penned by the curious.[8] One "society of Gentlemen" belonging to the *British Apollo* (1708–11), which included the poets Aaron Hill and John Gay, answered more than two thousand questions, serious and comical, allegedly posed by readers. Miscellaneous by definition, these magazines lent themselves to a patchwork-style presentation of subject matter. The question-and-answer format allowed them to broach a wide range of topics, from the biblical to the lexical, the philosophical to the practical.

In the frontispiece of one miscellany that Dunton attributed to "the Athenian Society" (responsible for the *Athenian Mercury*), a dozen gowned and bewigged gentlemen sit at a table gravely cogitating queries submitted for review, as an astrologer in their midst makes a prediction by means of a cross-staff.[9] The astrologer prefigures Steele's Tatler, named after the seventeenth-century mountebank John Partridge, whom Swift had mocked under the pseudonym Isaac Bickerstaff.[10] The society of scholars also presages the Tatler's more humorous club of old prattlers: Sir Jeoffrey Notch, a gambler who squanders the ancient estate of his family; Major Matchlock, who is obsessed with the Civil War battle of Marston Moor; Dick Reptile, dubbed an indolent fellow; and an Old Bencher who has ten distichs of *Hudibras* by memory that he never fails to impart before leaving the company of his friends. These "worthies" do not respond to questions, but they keep the Tatler company while he prepares his lucubrations.

Ned Ward's *The Weekly Comedy,* published prior to *The Tatler* from May through July 1699, expands the idea of the editorial club as a cast of characters. This periodical represented a cross-section of life "as it is dayly acted at most coffee-houses in London" and featured stock types such as Snarl, a disbanded Captain; Scribble, a newswriter; Snap, a sharper; Squabble, a lawyer; Whim, an entrepreneur; and Prim, a beau. A decade later Ward's *The Weekly Comedy; or, The Humours of the Age* (1707) followed suit with a similar cast of contemporary types: "Levy, a recruiting officer; Hazard, a gamester; Venture, a merchant; Talley, a stock broker; Querpo, a quack; Horoscope, an astrologer; Shuffle, a time server; Bays, a poet; Compass, a sailor; and Bohee, the coffee man."[11] In *The Tatler,* founded that same year, Addison and Steele brought the personality of the periodical persona and his few friends into relief, emphasizing the originality of imaginative composition.[12] Later, the Spectator's Club arrived on the scene with a Man About Town named Will Honeycomb, a Student of Law and Literature, a Churchman, a Soldier, a London Merchant, and an oddly lovable (given the Whig orientation of the journal) Tory country squire named Sir Roger de Coverly. Adapting the tradition of Ward's *London Spy* (1698–1700), in which a country gentleman follows his friend on a raucous romp through the seedy side of London, Addison and Steele's Sir Roger lead the Spectator through the squire's provincial retreats, including Sunday chapel. In this respect, the early periodical essayists were like Chaucers of their age, identifying and memorializing familiar types from burgeoning commercial society.

This society, of course, included women, and the male periodical clubs had their female counterparts. In response to Steele's claim that tattling was a characteristically female activity and that he had named his paper after the gossiping "fair sex," the parodic *Female Tatler* (published bi-weekly from 1709 to 1710) appeared to address a more explicitly female readership. In the persona of Phoebe Crackenthorpe, the Female Tatler issued advice on how to manage husbands and other domestic affairs, provided entertainment in the form of romantic tales, and offered instruction on philosophical and political matters. Some have proposed Bernard Mandeville or the playwright Thomas Baker as the mastermind behind the Female Tatler, while others have suggested Mary Delarivier Manley (a member of "the Fair Triumvirate of Wit" with Eliza Haywood and the playwright Aphra Behn) or the playwright Susannah Centlivre. But whether male or female, or a combination of both, the authors were aware that the Female Tatler would not have had access to the same public sphere as her male namesake, places where cultural affairs were typically discussed and deals as well as reputations were made. Accordingly, she gathered a fictitious biweekly assembly that spanned the social spectrum from "his grace, My Lord Duke to Mr. Sagathie, the spruce merchant," or from "the Duchess to Mrs. Topsail, the sea captain's wife at Wapping," dating all articles from her "own apartment." In this manner, the Female Tatler joined her male counterpart in cultural conversation with statesmen, beaux, lawyers, parsons, poets, and ladies of all degrees.

The coffeehouse circuit of Enlightenment London, itself a clubby environment, provided the model for the fictional clubs of the periodical papers. Addison and Steele belonged to the renowned Kit-Cat Club, which flourished between 1696 and 1720, taking its name from the mutton-pie maker Christopher Cat, proprietor of the Cat and Fiddle in Gray's-Inn Lane where the society first met. Its purpose, as the cultural historian John Brewer explains, was "to shape the arts by creating an elaborate web of influence and patronage and by creating a sympathetic climate of opinion for writers it favoured."[13] The fifty-five Kit-Cat Club members, united in sympathy for Whig policy and a desire to promote the arts, set up subscriptions for books and sponsored theatrical events, which they attended en masse. This club was exclusively male, but a few decades later Dr. Johnson founded a club of artists and leading intellectuals on the same model that was open to women. Prominent cultural figures like James Boswell, Edmund Burke, David Garrick, Edward Gibbon, Oliver Goldsmith, and Horace Walpole carried on the tradition of networking in company with female authors like Frances Burney, Elizabeth Carter, Elizabeth Montagu, and Hannah More. Women had gradually gained access to cultural conversation at such places as picture galleries and print shops, pleasure gardens and the licensed theaters, circulating libraries and social assemblies. By the middle of the century, Elizabeth Montagu, the illustrious "Queen of the Bluestockings," was inviting educated women as well as men to her Gothic home at Sandleford, sponsoring refined conversation in which both sexes could participate.

The idea of the female club as a conservative, middle-class forum for women to escape the confinements of card playing and other frivolous activities entered the periodical essay tradition around this time by way of Eliza Haywood's *Female Spectator* (1744–46). Conceptually based on Addison and Steele's Spectator Club, the Female Spectator's Club included Mira, a married wit; Euphrosine, the daughter of a merchant; and an unnamed Widow of Quality. In the frontispiece to the monthly periodical these ladies, spanning the range of female experience—married woman, virgin, widow—are shown seated at a table in a classically appointed library holding pens as well as fans in their hands, an image alluding to the Spectator Club depicted in the frontispiece to the collected editions of Addison's and Steele's papers. The Female Spectator warned her readers against the dangers of things like gambling and parental tyranny, relating cautionary tales of a romantic cast with characters named for their foibles: Tenderilla, Eageretta, Blumetta, Pompilius, and the seducer Clitander, for example. Frequently, the essays contained an obvious moral: do not run away with a lover, do not marry for mercenary reasons, do not wear your emotions on your sleeve. Reading Haywood's *Female Spectator* may well bring to mind De Quincey's complaint against *The Spectator:* "To read of their Phillises, and Strephons, and Chloes, and Corydons—names that, by their very non-reality amongst names of flesh and blood, proclaim the fantasticalness of the life with which they are poetically connected—it throws one into such convulsions of rage, that I move to the window, and (without thinking what I am about) throw it up, calling '*Police! police!*'"[14] Haywood, who had enjoyed success as a prolific novelist by the 1740s, extended the essay form to narrative lengths it had not seen before. One year following *The Female Spectator,* she took up the tattling persona of "The Parrot," whose sex now mattered less than its species. Both personae were ploys to avoid the explicitly male stance of the periodical first-person speaker.

A number of Bluestockings (a derogatory term derived from Benjamin Stillingfleet's casual blue worsted stockings, which he wore to Montagu's home instead of the more formal black silk) have gained a lasting reputation as writers, some contributing to the development of the periodical essay. Elizabeth Carter, the most learned of the Bluestockings, did not define the voice of Johnson's Rambler, though she did contribute two essays (nos. 44 and 100) to the series. Charlotte Lennox, author of *The Female Quixote* (1752), contributed in the persona of "the Trifler" to *The Lady's Museum* (1760–61), and Frances Brooke published thirty-seven numbers of a weekly in the mode of *The Spectator* entitled *The Old Maid* (1755–56). Satirized by her contemporary "Mr. Town" (from *The Connoisseur*), the fictional spinster retaliates against his "ill-bred and unexpected attack" in her second number with the wit of literary flirtation, giving her critic "permission to say whatever he pleases of me, provided he does not attempt to praise me." Like many essayists, Brooke's Old Maid addressed a range of topics, from interpersonal relations to politics.

Eventually, as more people began to earn a living as professional writers, the age of literary patronage dissolved into a market-based economy. Writers of all stripes turned increasingly to booksellers for financial support and commissioned themselves to the growing bands of periodical publications (newspapers, magazines, reviews, essay serials) associated with Grub Street. In this light, when Johnson assumes the voice of "the Idler" from 1758 through 1760, we might see his choice of persona as laden with irony. Left to his own devices, the Idler informs us, he might never have found a voice at all—though for all his idleness he was able to supply the printer's boy with incisive and often memorable prose compositions on a weekly basis for two years. Appealing to "universal patronage," Johnson's Idler serves as a figure for the struggling professional writer, seeking to make a place for what Wordsworth called "wise passiveness." In a commercial value system that rewarded economic labor and competition ("busyness" in the field of artistic production as in other forms of manufacture), imaginative activity could be viewed as idle.

Like Johnson's Idler, Oliver Goldsmith's "Bee" was a loaded figure for the writer in the second half of the eighteenth century. Derived from Seneca and imported into Renaissance rhetorical tradition, the bee gathers and synthesizes material from diverse sources. In the opening number of *The Bee* (1759), Goldsmith depicts an imaginary conversation with his publisher who makes an appearance as the author is attempting to formulate a persona for his periodical. The publisher attempts to relieve his anxiety by reducing the role of the author in periodical publication, as seen through the eyes of Grub Street: "The republic of letters is at present divided into three classes. One writer, for instance, excels at a plan, or a title-page, another works away at the body of the book, and a third is a dab at an index. Thus a Magazine is not the result of any single man's industry, but goes through as many hands as a new pin, before it is fit for the public." Prefiguring Adam Smith's account at the start of *The Wealth of Nations* of how the division of labor in a pin factory alienates workers, Goldsmith's persona resists becoming a mechanical cog in the wheel of print culture. Instead, he chooses a more self-consciously aesthetic attitude, opting like the bee to dally among the flowers, extracting whatever honey (read "beauty") he can from the bustling, workaday world of eighteenth-century London. "Like the Bee, which I had taken for the title of my paper," he says, "I would rove from flower to flower, with seeming inattention, but concealed choice, expatiate over all the beauties of the season, and make my industry my amusement." Among theater and book reviews, short stories, and moral tales, he mixed translations from Dutch and French imitators of *The Spectator*, including Justus van Effen's *The Misanthrope* (1711) and Pierre de Marivaux's *Le Spectateur français* (1721–24), typically without attribution. In the unregulated, miscellaneous world of periodical production, Goldsmith's Bee gathered all too freely.

The final decades of the century marked a transitional period in which literary tastes turned from urbane wit to sensibility, from measured prose to anguished feeling. As writers began to emphasize the authenticity and originality of the speaking subject, the genius, or spirit, behind the layered personality of the essayist came to the fore. Assuming an extreme form of the eighteenth-century Man of Feeling, the "Hypochondriack," Boswell, like Johnson before him and Henry Mackenzie after him, immersed his periodical persona in a well of introspection. For seventy monthly numbers published in *The London Magazine* from 1777 through 1783, Boswell's Hypochondriack wallowed in, rather than shied away from, "the fretfulness, the gloom, and the despair that can torment a thinking being." When Mackenzie, called by Sir Walter Scott "the Scottish Addison," began a periodical in the manner of *The Spectator,* he gave voice to a nostalgic sense of loss and a longing for a closer relation to nature that was characteristic of later Romantic writers. Mackenzie's *The Mirror,* named for the Edinburgh pub in which his literary coterie gathered to drink claret and read *The Spectator,* ran from 1779 to 1780. Five years later their *Lounger* (1785–87) followed Johnson's *Idler* in conscious rebellion against commercial busyness. Mackenzie's series of essays describing the Lounger's visit to his old-fashioned friend Colonel Caustic express anxiety about the invasion of Town manners into the country, final refuge from the shifting values accompanying commercial change that troubled Mackenzie as a Man of Feeling.

Echoing the nostalgic tone of the 1780s, the Romantic essayists reveal a heightened sense of consciousness about their relation to English literary tradition and the essay form as such. Hazlitt, whose essay "The Letter-Bell" (1825) in this volume exemplifies such nostalgia, and his fellow "Round Table" author Leigh Hunt explicitly work to shape—and escape into—individual literary canons. Hazlitt's "On Reading Old Books" (1821), Hunt's "My Books" (1823), and Lamb's "Detached Thoughts on Books and Reading" (1822), among other essays from the 1820s, contain impassioned descriptions of the practice of book collecting and reading, a fashion that involved the design of private spaces for reading, displaying, and even mutilating (unbinding, annotating, slicing engravings from) books. Together, they join the wave of bibliophilia sweeping England at the start of the nineteenth century and spreading across the Atlantic. Fans of the Romantics, American literary writers "admired Hazlitt as essayist (ignoring his radicalism), loved Leigh Hunt, worshiped De Quincey, and idolatrously adored Charles Lamb."[15] In 1834 one group of Whig high-church "Knickerbockers," as they called themselves, founded an "Original American Magazine" to continue the periodical essay tradition of Hazlitt, Hunt, Lamb, and De Quincey, attempting to reproduce their urbane elegance and "Cockney" wit in culturally up-and-coming New York.

Ultimately, the quarterlies and monthlies in which the Romantic essayists published gave way to the monthlies and weeklies of the Victorian era. Anthony Trollope poked fun in *Barchester Towers* (1857) at the ante-diluvian country squire who "possessed a complete set of the 'Idler,' the 'Spectator,' the 'Tatler,' the 'Guardian,' and the 'Rambler'; and would discourse by hours together on the superiority of such publications to any-thing which has since been produced in our Edinburghs and Quarter-lies."[16] The irony lies in the fact that quarterlies such as the Whig *Edin-burgh Review* (founded 1802) and the Tory *Quarterly Review* (founded 1809) had already lost ground by this time to the new generation of peri-odicals of which the old-fashioned squire, a literary descendant of Sir Roger de Coverly, seems wholly unaware. Trollope published something in the neighborhood of three dozen novels in the weekly and monthly format, and he recognized the need for characters to grow along with their times: "And as, here in our outer world, we know that men and women change,— become worse or better as temptation or conscience may guide them—so should these creations of [the serial novelist] change, and every change should be noted by him. On the last day of each month recorded, every per-son in his novel should be a month older than on the first."[17] In this light, we might consider Lamb's idiosyncratic Elia a precursor to the serialized characters of Victorian fiction as we experience his daily life attending the theater, vacationing in Hertfordshire, visiting a Quaker meeting, receiving no mail on Valentine's Day, recalling the elder benchers of the Inner Tem-ple, imagining the children he might have had, or memorably eulogizing his taste for roast pig.

While it has been suggested that the collected volumes of *The Specta-tor* would make a good novel, only in Lamb's essays published under the signature "Elia" do we have the opportunity to see a periodical character develop with age and even die, as Elia does before publication of the col-lected edition, *The Last Essays of Elia* (1833). In this, he anticipates the fictional characters of nineteenth-century novels, which started to appear periodically in weekly or monthly installments the following decade. Charles Dickens's *Pickwick Papers* appeared in monthly numbers from April 1836 through 1837, and by the end of that run Dickens had come into his own as the foremost novelist of the age. He was on the vanguard of this new publishing trend, and he followed the "Perambulations, Perils, Trav-els, Adventures, and Sporting Transactions of the Corresponding Members of the Pickwick Club" (as the subtitle read) with *Nicholas Nickleby* in monthly numbers from 1838 to 1839. Soon thereafter came *The Old Curiosity Shop* and *Barnaby Rudge* in weekly numbers from 1840 to 1841, *Martin Chuzzlewit* in monthly numbers from 1843 to 1844, *Dombey and Son* in monthly numbers from 1846 to 1848, and the rest is history. In January 1847, William Makepeace Thackeray's *Vanity Fair: Pen and Pencil Sketches of English Society* also began to appear in monthly numbers, for by mid-century serial novel publication had become standard practice.

This anthology concludes in the decade that Dickens took up his pen, looking forward not only to the serial publication of novels but also to the Victorian tradition of social criticism practiced by Thomas Carlyle, Matthew Arnold, and John Ruskin—and to the aestheticist form of the essay employed by Algernon Charles Swinburne, Walter Pater, and Oscar Wilde. Like Hunt, extolling the dandified accoutrement of the walking stick in 1820, Wilde would sport his green carnation as a sign of (among other things) the lingering value of beauty, a subject deftly defined by Addison in his *Spectator* series "The Pleasures of the Imagination" (nos. 411–21). Readers would do well to consider that the subjective style of criticism associated with Romanticism and culminating in the cultural credo of art for art's sake originated—however ironically—with the disinterested attitude of Addison's Spectator and his serial, seriocomic speculations.

NOTES

1. James Boswell, entry for 21 November 1762, *Boswell's London Journal, 1762–3*, ed. F. A. Pottle (New York: McGraw-Hill, 1950).

2. This explanation was Steele's fiction; as Richmond P. Bond points out, "Although the identity of Isaac Bickerstaff was immediately guessed by the cognoscenti of London he continued to function as an individual and an eidolon throughout the life of the paper, commenting on the world at large and promoting reform"; Bond, *The Tatler: The Making of a Literary Journal* (Cambridge: Harvard University Press, 1971), 20.

3. For more on the use of rhetorical "places," see Ann Moss, *Printed Commonplace-Books and the Structuring of Renaissance Thought* (Oxford: Clarendon Press, 1996).

4. Jürgen Habermas, *The Structural Transformation of the Public Sphere: An Inquiry into a Category of Bourgeois Society* (Cambridge: MIT Press, 1989).

5. William Hazlitt, "On the Tatler," in *The Complete Works of William Hazlitt,* ed. P. P. Howe, 21 vols. (London: J. M. Dent, 1930–34), 4:7–10 (quotation on p. 7).

6. See *Rambler* no. 82 and *Tatler* no. 216, respectively.

7. *The History of the Works of the Learned; or, An Impartial Account of Books Lately Printed in All Parts of Europe, with a Particular Relation of the State of Learning in Each Country* (London, 1699–1712).

8. While Defoe's *Review* ran from 1704 to 1713, the "Advice from the Scandalous Club" was dropped in 1705 and converted into its own *Little Review; or, An Inquisition of Scandal, Being a Continuation of Advice from the Scandal Club* for twenty-three numbers.

9. See *The Young Student's Library,* ed. John Dunton (London, 1691).

10. Jonathan Swift predicted that Partridge would die on the night of 29 March at eleven o'clock in his "Account of the Death of Mr. Partrige the Almanack-Maker Upon the 29th Instant," the subtitle of "The Accomplishment of the First of Mr. Bickerstaff's Predictions" from his *Predictions for the Year 1708, Wherein the Month, and Day of the Month, Are Set Down, the Persons Named, and the Great Actions and Events of Next Year Particularly Related, as They Will Come to Pass. Written to Prevent the People of England from Being Further Imposed on by Vulgar Almanack-Makers.* In another pamphlet, *'Squire Bickerstaff Detected; or, The Astrological Imposter Convicted, by John Partrige, Student in Physick and Astrology,* the astrologer speaks from the rather absurd position of insisting that he is not dead. Swift's final stab in the persona of Bickerstaff was a pamphlet printed the next year, entitled *A Vindication of Isaac Bickerstaff Esq; Against What Is Objected to Him by Mr. Partrige in His Almanack for the Present Year, 1709.*

11. Walter Graham, *English Literary Periodicals* (New York: Thomas Nelson and Sons, 1930), 52–54.

12. So too periodicals following in the vein of *The Tatler* stress the serial personality. In addition to *The Female Spectator, The Connoisseur, The Rambler,* and others included here, we might name, e.g., *The Honest Gentleman* (1718), *The Spinster* (1719), *The Old Whig* (1719), *The Lay Monk* (1713), *The Reader* (1714), *The Country Gentleman* (1726), *The Fool* (1746), *The Entertainer* (1755), *The Rhapsodist* (1757), *The Genius* (1762), *The Whisperer* (1770), *The New Spectator* (1784–86), *The Busy Body* (1787), *The Actor* (1789), *The Speculator* (1790), *The Trifler* (1795), *The Flapper* (1796), and *The Quiz* (1796).

13. John Brewer, *The Pleasures of the Imagination: English Culture in the Eighteenth Century* (New York: Farrar, Straus and Giroux, 1997), 40.

14. Thomas De Quincey, "Schlosser's Literary History" (Part I), *The Works of Thomas De Quincey,* gen. ed. Grevel Lindop, ed. Robert Morrison, 21 vols. (London: Pickering and Chatto, 2000–2003), 16:195.

15. Perry Miller, *The Raven and the Whale: The War of Words and Wits in the Era of Poe and Melville* (New York: Harvest, 1956), 29.

16. Anthony Trollope, *Barchester Towers,* ed. Michael Sadleir and Frederick Page (Oxford: Oxford University Press, 1996), 1:211.

17. Anthony Trollope, *An Autobiography,* ed. Michael Sadleir and Frederick Page (Oxford: Oxford University Press, 1980), 233.

John Rocque, *A New and Accurate Survey of the Cities of London and Westminster*, 1751
(Anne and Jerome Fisher Fine Arts Library, University of Pennsylvania Library)

Richard Steele
(1672–1729)

SWASHBUCKLING SIR RICHARD STEELE was the man behind
the mask of Isaac Bickerstaff, Esq., a fictional elderly gentleman with a propensity for moralizing who served as the mouthpiece for the first of the
great English literary periodicals, *The Tatler*. The paper ran three times
weekly as a folio-sized broadside from 12 April 1709 through 2 January
1711. The penname Bickerstaff was taken from Jonathan Swift, who adopted
it in his satires on his contemporary, the astronomer John Partridge. Steele,
having abandoned a career in the British Army, took up the name for the
first of his literary poses. In "The Round Table," William Hazlitt would
later look back fondly on Steele's Bickerstaff as "a gentleman and a scholar,
a humourist and a man of the world; with a great deal of nice easy naïveté
about him. If he walks out and is caught in a shower of rain, he makes us
amends for this unlucky accident, by a criticism on the shower in Virgil, and
concludes with a burlesque copy of verses on a city-shower." Bickerstaff
vividly portrays life in London during the reign of Queen Anne: an age of
full-bottomed periwigs, rustling hoops, and paste shoe buckles, in which
the middle classes were gaining increased socioeconomic power and the
arts were once again beginning to flourish.

Steele made his mark on the intellectual life of the Enlightenment
through his association with leading wits, poets, playwrights, and "pretty
fellows," whose contributions he solicited for his journalistic ventures. After *The Tatler* wound down, he founded *The Spectator*, which ran every day
but Sunday from 1 March 1711 through 6 December 1712 (and again thrice
weekly from 18 July through 20 December 1714), setting the pattern for the
English periodical essay and spawning numerous copycats throughout the
century. Steele invented the members of the Spectator's Club, including
the famous Sir Roger de Coverly, whom Addison fleshed out with loving
care. In the lull between the old and new *Spectator*s, Steele devoted his en-

ergies to political criticism and published *The Guardian* in collaboration with Addison, from March through September 1713. That same year he became a Whig member of Parliament, where he engaged in political controversy with Swift, the leading Tory spokesman. Although expelled in March 1714 by his political rivals (for seditious libel in pamphlets he had refused to publish anonymously), he returned within six months under the Hanoverian monarchy. After being knighted by George I and having produced his last great work, *The Conscious Lovers* (1722), Steele retired in poverty to Wales, birthplace of his recently deceased wife Mary Scurlock ("dear Prue"). With its many reversals, his colorful life reflects the exciting and volatile world in which he lived.

Selections are from *The Lucubrations of Isaac Bickerstaff, Esq.* (London, 1710–11).

The Tatler

No. 1. [Introducing the Tatler]

By Isaac Bickerstaff, Esq.

Quicquid agunt Homines nostri Farrago Libelli.[1]

TUESDAY, APRIL 12, 1709.

Though the other Papers which are published for the use of the good people of *England,* have certainly very wholesome effects, and are laudable in their particular kinds, they do not seem to come up to the main design of such narrations, which, I humbly presume, should be principally intended for the use of politic persons, who are so public-spirited as to neglect their own affairs to look into transactions of State. Now these gentlemen, for the most part, being men of strong zeal, and weak intellects; it is both a charitable and necessary work to offer something, whereby such worthy and well-affected members of the commonwealth may be instructed, after their reading, *what to think:* which shall be the end and purpose of this my Paper,

---

1. "All the doings of mankind . . . shall form the motley subject of my page"; Juvenal, *Satires,* I.85–86.

wherein I shall from time to time report and consider all matters of what kind soever that shall occur to me, and publish such my advices and reflections every *Tuesday, Thursday,* and *Saturday* in the week, for the convenience of the Post.[2] It is also resolved by me to have something which may be of entertainment to the fair sex, in honour of whom I have taken the title of this Paper. I therefore earnestly desire all persons, without distinction, to take it in for the present *gratis,* and hereafter at the price of one penny, forbidding all hawkers to take more for it at their peril. And I desire all persons to consider, that I am at a very great charge for proper materials for this work, as well as that before I resolved upon it, I had settled a correspondence in all parts of the known and knowing World: and forasmuch as this globe is not trodden upon by mere drudges of business only, but that men of spirit and genius are justly to be esteemed as considerable agents in it, we shall not upon a dearth of news, present you with musty foreign edicts, or dull proclamations, but shall divide our relation of the passages which occur in action or discourse throughout this Town, as well as elsewhere, under such dates or places as may prepare you for the matter you are to expect, in the following manner:

All accounts of *Gallantry, Pleasure,* and *Entertainment,* shall be under the article of *White's Chocolate-house; Poetry,* under that of *Will's Coffee-house; Learning,* under the Title of *Graecian; Foreign* and *Domestic News,* you will have from *St. James's Coffee-house;* and what else I shall on any other subject offer, shall be dated from my own *Apartment.*

I once more desire my Reader to consider, that as I cannot keep an ingenious man to go daily to *Will's,* under twopence each day merely for his charges; to *White's,* under sixpence; nor to the *Graecian,* without allowing him some plain *Spanish,* to be as able as others at the learned table; and that a good observer cannot speak with even *Kidney* at St. *James's* without clean linen.[3] I say, these considerations will, I hope, make all persons willing to comply with my humble request (when my *gratis* stock is exhausted) of a penny a-piece; especially since they are sure of some proper amusement, and that it is impossible for me to want means to entertain 'em, having, be-

2. These were days on which the post left London for the outlying provinces.
3. "Spanish" refers to Spanish tobacco. Humphrey Kidney was the head-waiter at Saint James's Coffee-house.

sides the helps of my own parts, the power of divination, and that I can, by casting a figure, tell you all that will happen before it comes to pass.

But this last faculty I shall use very sparingly, and not speak of any thing till it is passed, for fear of divulging matters which may offend our superiors.

WHITE'S CHOCOLATE-HOUSE, APRIL 7.

The deplorable condition of a very pretty Gentleman, who walks here at the hours when men of quality first appear, is what is very much lamented. His history is, that on the 9th of *September*, 1705, being in his one and twentieth year, he was washing his teeth at a tavern-window in *Pall-mall*, when a fine equipage passed by, and in it a young Lady who looked up at him; away goes the coach, and the young Gentleman pulled off his nightcap, and instead of rubbing his gums, as he ought to do, out of the window till about four a clock, he sits him down, and spoke not a word till twelve at night; after which, he began to enquire, If any body knew the Lady—the company asked, What Lady? But he said no more till they broke up at six in the morning. All the ensuing winter he went from church to church every Sunday, and from playhouse to playhouse all the week, but could never find the original of the picture which dwelt in his bosom. In a word, his attention to any thing but his passion, was utterly gone. He has lost all the money he ever played for, and been confuted in every argument he has entered upon since the moment he first saw her. He is of a noble family, has naturally a very good air, and is of a frank, honest temper: but this passion has so extremely mauled him, that his features are set and uninformed, and his whole visage is deadened by a long absence of thought. He never appears in any alacrity, but when raised by wine; at which time he is sure to come hither, and throw away a great deal of wit on fellows, who have no sense further than just to observe, That our poor Lover has most understanding when he's drunk, and is least in his senses when he's sober.

. . .

FROM MY OWN APARTMENT.

I am very sorry I am obliged to trouble the Public with so much discourse upon a matter which I at the very first mentioned as a trifle, *viz.* the death of Mr. *Partridge,* under whose name there is an *Almanack* come out for the year 1709.[4] In one page of which it is asserted by the said *John Partridge,* That he is still living, and not only so, but that he was also living some time before, and even at the instant when I writ of his death. I have in another place, and in a Paper by itself, sufficiently convinced this man that he is dead, and if he has any shame, I don't doubt but that by this time he owns it to all his acquaintance: for though the legs and arms, and whole body of that man may still appear and perform their animal functions; yet since, as I have elsewhere observed, his art is gone, the man is gone. I am, as I said, concerned, that this little matter should make so much noise; but since I am engaged, I take myself obliged in honour to go on in my lucubrations, and by the help of these arts of which I am master, as well as my penetration in astrological speculations, I shall, as I see occasion, proceed to confute other dead men, who pretend to be in being, that they are actually deceased. I therefore give all men fair warning to mend their manners, for I shall from time to time print Bills of Mortality; and I beg the pardon of all such who shall be named therein, if they who are good for nothing shall find them-selves in the number of the deceased.

12 April 1709

---

4. John Partridge (1644–1715) had been satirized by Jonathan Swift (under the name of Isaac Bickerstaff) as a quack. Appended to *Tatler* no. 216 (26 August 1710), written by Addison and printed in this volume, is a brief advertisement: "Whereas an ignorant upstart in astrology has publicly endeavoured to persuade the world, that he is the late *John Partridge,* who died in the 28th of *March, 1708;* these are to certify all whom it may concern, that the true *John Partridge* was not only dead at that time, but continues so to this present day. Beware of counterfeits, for such are abroad." See Introduction, n. 10.

No. 60. [Tom Wildair &c.]

WHITE'S CHOCOLATE HOUSE, AUGUST 26.

To proceed regularly in the history of my worthies, I ought to give you an account of what has passed from day to day in this place; but a young fellow of my acquaintance has so lately been rescued out of the hands of the Knights of the Industry, that I rather choose to relate the manner of his escape from 'em, and the uncommon way which was used to reclaim him, than to go on in my intended diary.

You are to know then, that *Tom Wildair* is a student of the *Inner Temple,* and has spent his time, since he left the University for that place, in the common diversions of men of fashion; that is to say, in whoring, drinking, and gaming. The two former vices he had from his father; but was led into the last by the conversation of a partizan of the *Mirmidons* who had chambers near him.[5] His allowance from his father was a very plentiful one for a man of sense, but very scanty for a modern fine gentleman. His frequent losses had reduced him to so necessitous a condition, that his lodgings were always haunted by impatient creditors, and all his thoughts employed in contriving low methods to support himself, in a way of life from which he knew not how to retreat, and in which he wanted means to proceed. There is never wanting some good-natured person to send a man an account of what he has no mind to hear; therefore many epistles were conveyed to the father of this extravagant, to inform him of the company, the pleasures, the distresses, and entertainments, in which his son passed his time. The old fellow received these advices with all the pain of a parent, but frequently consulted his pillow to know how to behave himself on such important occasions, as [to] the welfare of his son, and the safety of his fortune. After many agitations of mind, he reflected, that necessity was the usual snare which made men fall into meanness, and that a liberal fortune generally made a liberal and honest mind; he resolved therefore to save him from his ruin by giving him opportunities of tasting what it is to be at ease, and enclosed to him the following order upon Sir *Tristram Cash:*

5. The Myrmidons were the followers of Achilles; in *Tatler* no. 56, Steele refers to them as "a body who kept among themselves, and had nothing to lose; therefore never spared either *Greek* or *Trojan,* when they fell in their way, upon a party."

"*Sir*,
Pray pay to Mr. *Tho. Wildair,* or order, the sum of one thousand pounds, and place it to the account of
Yours, *Humphrey Wildair.*"

Tom was so astonished at the receipt of this order, that though he knew it to be his father's hand, and knew he had always large sums at Sir *Tristram's;* yet a thousand pounds was a trust of which his conduct had always made him appear so little capable, that he kept his note by him, till he writ to his father the following letter:

"*Honoured Father,*
I have received an order under your hand for a thousand pounds in words at length, and I think I could swear it is your hand. I have looked it over and over twenty thousand times. There is in plain letters, T,H,O,U,S,A,N,D; and after it, the letters, P,O,U,N,D,S. I have it still by me, and shall, I believe, continue reading it till I hear from you."

The old Gentleman took no manner of notice of the receipt of his letter; but sent him another order for three thousand pounds more. His amazement on this second letter was unspeakable. He immediately double-locked his door, and sat down carefully to reading and comparing both his orders. After he had read 'em till he was half mad, he walked six or seven turns in his chamber, then opens his door, then locks it again; and to examine thoroughly this matter, he locks his door again, puts his table and chairs against it; then goes into his closet, and locking himself in, read his notes over again about nineteen times, which did but increase his astonishment. Soon after, he began to recollect many stories he had formerly heard of persons who had been possessed with imaginations and appearances which had no foundation in Nature, but had been taken with sudden madness in the midst of a seeming clear and untainted Reason. This made him very gravely conclude he was out of his wits; and with a design to compose himself, he immediately betakes him to his night cap, with a resolution to sleep himself into his former poverty and senses. To bed therefore he goes at noon-day, but soon rose again, and resolved to visit Sir *Tristram* upon this occasion.

He did so, and dined with the knight, expecting he would mention some advice from his father about paying him money; but no such thing being said; Look you, Sir *Tristram,* (said he) you are to know, that an affair has happened, which———Look you, (says *Tristram*) I know Mr. *Wildair,* you are going to desire me to advance; but the late call of the bank, where I have not yet made my last payment, has obliged me———*Tom* interrupted him, by showing him the bill of a thousand pounds. When he had looked at it for a convenient time, and as often surveyed Tom's looks and countenance; Look you, Mr. *Wildair,* a thousand pounds———Before he could proceed, he shows him the order for three thousand more———Sir *Tristram* examined the orders at the light, and finding at the writing the name, there was a certain stroke in one letter, which the father and he had agreed should be to such directions as he desired might be more immediately honoured, he forthwith pays the money. The possession of four thousand pounds gave my young gentleman a new train of thoughts: he began to reflect upon his birth, the great expectations he was born to, and the unsuitable ways he had long pursued. Instead of that unthinking creature he was before, he is now provident, generous, and discreet. The father and son have an exact and regular correspondence, with mutual and unreserved confidence in each other. The son looks upon his father as the best tenant he could have in the Country,[6] and the father finds the son the most safe banker he could have in the City.

WILL'S COFFEE-HOUSE, AUGUST 26.

There is not any thing in Nature so extravagant, but that you will find one man or other that shall practice or maintain it; otherwise, *Harry Spondee* could not have made so long an harangue as he did here this evening, concerning the force and efficacy of well-applied nonsense. Among ladies, he positively averred, it was the most prevailing part of eloquence; and had so little complaisance as to say, a woman is never taken by her reason, but always by her passion. He proceeded to assert, that the way to move that, was only to astonish her. I know (continued he) a very late instance of this; for

---

6. For the estate the son will eventually inherit.

being by accident in the next room to *Strephon*,[7] I could not help over-hearing him as he made love to a certain great Lady's woman. The true method in your application to one of this second rank of understanding, is not to elevate and surprize, but rather to elevate and amaze. *Strephon* is a perfect master in this kind of persuasion: his way is, to run over with a soft air a multitude of words, without meaning or connexion, but such as do each of 'em apart give a pleasing idea, though they have nothing to do with each other as he assembles 'em. After the common phrases of salutation, and making his entry into the room, I perceived he had taken the fair nymph's hand, and kissing it, said, Witness to my Happiness ye Groves! Be still ye Rivulets! Oh! Woods, Caves, Fountains, Trees, Dales, Mountains, Hills, and Streams! Oh! Fairest, could you love me? To which I over-heard her answer, with a very pretty lisp, Oh! *Strephon*, you are a dangerous crea-ture: why do you talk these tender things to me? But you men of wit——— Is it then possible, said the enamoured *Strephon*, that she regards my sorrows? Oh! Pity, thou balmy cure to an heart o'erloaded. If rapture, so-licitation, soft desire, and pleasing anxiety———But still I live in the most afflicting of all circumstances, doubt———Cannot my Charmer name the place and moment?

> *There all those Joys insatiably to prove,*
> *With which Rich Beauty feeds the Glutton Love.*[8]

Forgive me, Madam, it is not that my heart is weary of its chain, but——— ———This incoherent stuff was answered by a tender sigh, Why do you put your wit to a weak woman? *Strephon* saw he had made some progress in her heart, and pursued it, by telling her that he would certainly wait upon her such an hour at *Rosamond's* Pond; and then———The Sylvan Deities, and Rural Powers of the Place, sacred and inviolable to *Love; Love*, the mover of all noble hearts, should hear his vows repeated by the streams and echoes. The assignation was accordingly made. This style he calls the unintelligible method of speaking his mind; and I'll engage, had this Gallant spoken plain *English*, she had never understood him half so readily: for we may take it for

7. A common name in pastoral tradition.
8. See Abraham Cowley, *Davideis*, III.1015–16.

granted, that he'll be esteemed as a very cold Lover, who discovers to his mistress that he is in his senses. . . .

27 August 1709

No. 89. [Sir Isaac Bickerstaff, Censor of Great Britain]

Rura mihi placeant, riguiq; in Vallibus Amnes,
*Flumina Amem Sylvasq; inglorius————*⁹

GRECIAN COFFEE-HOUSE, NOVEMBER 2.

I have received this short epistle from an unknown hand.

> "Sir,
>
> I have no more to trouble you with, than to desire you would in your next help me to some answer to the enclosed concerning yourself. In the mean time I congratulate you upon the increase of your fame, which you see has extended itself beyond the Bills of Mortality."
>
> "*Sir,*
>
> That the Country is barren of news, has been the excuse time out of mind for dropping a correspondence with our friends in *London;* as if it were impossible out of a Coffee-house to write an agreeable letter. I am too ingenuous to endeavour at the covering of my negligence with so common an excuse. Doubtless, amongst friends bred as we have been, to the knowledge of books as well as men, a letter dated from a garden, a grotto, a fountain, a wood, a meadow, or the banks of a river, may be more entertaining, than one from *Tom's, Will's, White's,* or St. *James's.* I promise therefore to be frequent for the future in my rural Dates to you: but for fear you should, from what I have said, be induced to believe I shun the commerce of men, I

---

9. "Let my delight be the country, and the running streams amid the dells— may I love the waters and the woods, though fame be lost"; Virgil, *Georgics,* II.485–86.

must inform you, that there is a fresh topic of discourse lately risen amongst the ingenious in our part of the world, and is become the more fashionable for the ladies giving into it. This we owe to *Isaac Bickerstaff*, who is very much censured by some, and as much justified by others. Some criticise his style, his humour and his matter; others admire the whole man: some pretend, from the informations of their friends in Town, to decipher the author; and others confess they are lost in their guesses. For my part, I must own myself a professed admirer of the Paper, and desire you to send me a complete set, together with your thoughts of the 'Squire, and his lucubrations."

There is no pleasure like that of receiving praise from the praise-worthy; and I own it a very solid happiness, that these my lucubrations are approved by a person of so fine a taste as the author of this letter, who is capable of enjoying the world in the simplicity of its natural beauties. This pastoral letter,[10] if I may so call it, must be written by a man who carries his entertainment wherever he goes, and is undoubtedly one of those happy men who appear far otherwise to the vulgar. I dare say, he is not envied by the vicious, the vain, the frolic, and the loud; but is continually blessed with that strong and serious delight which flows from a well-taught and liberal mind. With great respect to country sports, I may say, this gentleman could pass his time agreeably, if there were not a hare or a fox in his country. That calm and elegant satisfaction which the vulgar call melancholy, is the true and proper delight of men of knowledge and virtue. What we take for diversion, which is a kind of forgetting ourselves, is but a mean way of entertainment, in comparison of that which is considering, knowing, and enjoying ourselves. The pleasures of ordinary people are in their passions; but the seat of this delight is in the reason and understanding. Such a frame of mind raises that sweet enthusiasm which warms the imagination at the sight of every work of Nature, and turns all around you into picture and landscape. I shall be ever proud of advices from this gentleman; for I profess writing news from the learned as well as the busy world.

10. A pun: "pastoral letter" generally refers to a letter written by a pastor to his congregation.

As for my labours, which he is pleased to enquire after, if they can but wear one impertinence out of human life, destroy a single vice, or give a morning's cheerfulness to an honest mind; in short, if the world can be but one virtue the better, or in any degree less vicious, or receive from them the smallest addition to their innocent diversions, I shall not think my pains, or indeed my life, to have been spent in vain.

Thus far as to my studies. It will be expected I should in the next place give some account of my life. I shall therefore, for the satisfaction of the present age, and the benefit of posterity, present the world with the following abridgment of it.

It is remarkable, that I was bred by hand, and ate nothing but milk till I was a twelve-month old; from which time, to the 8th year of my age, I was observed to delight in pudding and potatoes; and indeed I retain a benevolence for that sort of food to this day. I do not remember that I distinguished myself in any thing at those years, but by my great skill at taw, for which I was so barbarously used, that it has ever since given me an aversion to gaming. In my twelfth year, I suffered very much for two or three false concords. At fifteen, I was sent to the university, and stayed there for some time; but a drum passing by, (being a lover of music) I listed myself for a soldier.[11] As years came on, I began to examine things, and grew discontented at the times. This made me quit the sword, and take to the study of the occult sciences, in which I was so wrapped up, that *Oliver Cromwell* had been buried, and taken up again, five years before I heard he was dead.[12] This gave me first the reputation of a conjurer, which has been of great disadvantage to me ever since, and kept me out of all public employments. The greater part of my later years has been divided between *Dick's* Coffee-house, the *Trumpet* in *Sheer-Lane,* and my own lodgings.

FROM MY OWN APARTMENT, NOV. 2.

The evil of unseasonable visits has been complained of to me with much vehemence by persons of both sexes; and I am desired to consider this very

11. Bickerstaff's biography here and elsewhere is modeled on Steele's.
12. Oliver Cromwell (1599–1658), Lord Protector of England from 1653 to 1658, died of natural causes and was buried in Westminster Abbey. His body was exhumed along with other regicides and hanged publicly in 1661.

important circumstance, that men may know how to regulate their conduct in an affair which concerns no less than life itself. For to a rational creature, it is almost the same cruelty to attack his life, by robbing him of so many moments of his time, or so many drops of his blood. The author of the following letter has a just delicacy in this point, and hath put it into a very good light.

> "Mr. *Bickerstaff,*   *Octob. 29.*
>
> I am very much afflicted with the Gravel, which makes me sick and peevish. I desire to know of you, if it be reasonable that any of my acquaintance should take advantage over me at this time, and afflict me with long visits, because they are idle, and I am confined. Pray Sir, reform the Town in this matter. Men never consider whether the sick person be disposed for company, but make their visits to humour themselves. You may talk upon this topic, so as to oblige all persons afflicted with chronical distempers, among which I reckon visits. Don't think me a sour man, for I love conversation and my friends; but I think one's most intimate friend may be too familiar; and that there are such things as unseasonable wit, and painful mirth."

It is with some so hard a thing to employ their time, that it is a great good fortune when they have a friend indisposed, that they may be punctual in perplexing him, when he is recovered enough to be in that state which cannot be called sickness or health; when he is too well to deny company, and too ill to receive them. It is no uncommon case, if a man is of any figure or power in the world, to be congratulated into a relapse.

WILL'S COFFEE-HOUSE, NOV. 2.

I was very well pleased this evening, to hear a gentleman express a very becoming indignation against a practice which I myself have been very much offended at. There is nothing (said he) more ridiculous, than for an actor to insert words of his own in the part he is to act, so that it is impossible to see the poet for the player: you'll have *Pinkethman* and *Bullock* helping out

Beaumont and *Fletcher*.[13] It puts me in mind (continued he) of a collection of antique statues which I once saw in a gentleman's possession, who employed a neighbouring stone-cutter to add noses, ears, arms, or legs, to the maimed works of *Phidias* or *Praxiteles*.[14] You may be sure this addition disfigured the statues much more than time had. I remember a *Venus,* that by the nose he had given her, looked like Mother *Shipton;* and a *Mercury,* with a pair of legs that seemed very much swelled with a dropsy.

I thought the gentleman's observations very proper; and he told me, I had improved his thought, in mentioning on this occasion those wise commentators who had filled up the Hemi-sticks of *Virgil;* particularly that notable poet, who, to make the *Aeneid* more perfect, carried on the story to *Lavinia's* wedding. If the proper officer will not condescend to take notice of these absurdities, I shall myself, as a censor of the people, animadvert upon such proceedings.

3 November 1709

No. 132. [The Old Prattlers' Club]

Habeo Senectuti magnum Gratiam, quae mihi Sermonis aviditatem auxit, Potionis & Cibi sustulit. Tull de Sen.[15]

SHEER-LANE, FEBRUARY 10.

After having applied my mind with more than ordinary attention to my studies, it is my usual custom to relax and unbend it in the conversation of such as are rather easy than shining companions. This I find particularly necessary for me before I retire to rest, in order to draw my slumbers upon me by degrees, and fall asleep insensibly. This is the particular use I make of

13. William Penkethman (1692–1724) and William Bullock (c. 1657–1740) were popular comic actors; Francis Beaumont (1584–1616) and John Fletcher (1579–1625) were Jacobean playwrights.

14. Phidias and Praxiteles were classical Greek sculptors. Mother Shipton, mentioned below, was a legendary seventeenth-century prophet.

15. "I am profoundly grateful to old age, which has increased my eagerness for conversation and taken away that for food and drink"; Cicero, *De senectute* (On Old Age), 46.

a set of heavy honest men, with whom I have passed many hours with much indolence, though not with great pleasure. Their conversation is a kind of preparative for sleep: it takes the mind down from its abstractions, leads it into the familiar traces of thought, and lulls it into that state of tranquility, which is the condition of a thinking man when he is but half awake. After this, my Reader will not be surprised to hear the account which I am about to give of a Club of my own contemporaries, among whom I pass two or three hours every evening. This I look upon as taking my first nap before I go to bed. The truth of it is, I should think myself unjust to posterity, as well as to the society at the *Trumpet,* of which I am a member, did not I in some part of my writings give an account of the persons among whom I have passed almost a sixth part of my time for these last forty years. Our Club consisted originally of fifteen; but partly by the severity of the law in arbitrary times, and partly by the natural effects of old age, we are at present reduced to a third part of that number: in which however we have this consolation, that the best company is said to consist of five persons. I must confess, besides the aforementioned benefit which I meet with in the conversation of this select society, I am not the less pleased with the company, in that I find myself the greatest wit among them, and am heard as their oracle in all points of learning and difficulty.

Sir *Jeoffrey Notch,* who is the oldest of the Club, has been in possession of the right-hand chair time out of mind, and is the only man among us that has the liberty of stirring the fire. This our foreman is a gentleman of an ancient family, that came to a great estate some years before he had discretion, and run it out in hounds, horses, and cock-fighting; for which reason he looks upon himself as an honest worthy Gentleman who has had misfortunes in the world, and calls every thriving man a pitiful upstart.

Major *Matchlock* is the next senior, who served in the last Civil Wars, and has all the battles by heart. He does not think any action in *Europe* worth talking of since the fight of *Marston Moor;* and every night tells us of his having been knocked off his horse at the rising of the *London* 'Prentices; for which he is in great esteem amongst us.[16]

16. The Battle of Marston Moor, in Yorkshire, took place in July 1644; the Royalists were routed by the forces of Parliament. The uprising of London apprentices refers to an event of July 1647, when petitioners forced their way into the

Honest old *Dick Reptile* is the third of our society: he is a good natured indolent man, who speaks little himself, but laughs at our jokes, and
brings his young nephew along with him, a youth of eighteen years old, to
show him good company, and give him a taste of the world. This young fellow sits generally silent; but whenever he opens his mouth, or laughs at any
thing that passes, he is constantly told by his uncle, after a jocular manner,
"Ay, ay, *Jack,* you young men think us fools; but we old men know you
are."

The greatest wit of our company, next to myself, is a Bencher of the
neighbouring inn, who in his youth frequented the ordinaries about *Char-
ing-Cross,* and pretends to have been intimate with *Jack Ogle.* He has about
ten distichs of *Hudibras* without book, and never leaves the Club till he has
applied them all. If any modern wit be mentioned, or any town frolic spoken of, he shakes his head at the dulness of the present age, and tells us a
story of *Jack Ogle.*[17]

For my own part, I am esteemed among them, because they see I am
something respected by others, though at the same time I understand by
their behaviour, that I am considered by them as a man of a great deal of
learning, but no knowledge of the world; insomuch that the Major sometimes, in the height of his military pride, calls me the Philosopher: and Sir
Jeoffrey no longer ago than last night, upon a dispute what day of the
month it was then in *Holland,* pulled his pipe out of his mouth, and cried,
What does the Scholar say to it?[18]

Our Club meets precisely at six a clock in the evening; but I did not
come last night till half an hour after seven, by which means I escaped the

---

House of Commons. The members of Bickerstaff's club live in memories of events
from the mid-seventeenth century.

17. John Ogle (1647–c. 1685), was a member of the Duke of Monmouth's
guards and a notorious prankster and rake. Samuel Butler's poem *Hudibras* (1663)
was a satire on the Puritans.

18. Although England continued to use the Julian calendar (instituted in 45
B.C. by Julius Caesar) through August 1752, most of Europe had switched by this
time to the Gregorian calendar (instituted by Pope Gregory XIII in 1582 and
dated from the traditional birth year of Christ). Because the Julian calendar
gained a day roughly every 134 years, England had fallen eleven days behind the
Continent.

Battle of *Naseby,* which the Major usually begins at about three quarters after six; I found also, that my good friend, the Bencher, had already spent
three of his distichs, and [was] only waiting an opportunity to hear a sermon spoken of, that he might introduce the couplet where *a-Stick* rhymes
to *Ecclesiastick.*[19] At my entrance into the room, they were naming a red
petticoat and a cloak, by which I found that the Bencher had been diverting
them with a story of *Jack Ogle.*[20]

I had no sooner taken my seat, but Sir *Jeoffrey,* to show his good will
towards me, gave me a pipe of his own tobacco, and stirred up the fire. I
look upon it as a point of morality, to be obliged by those who endeavour
to oblige me; and therefore in requital for his kindness, and to set the conversation a going, I took the best occasion I could, to put him upon telling
us the story of old *Gantlett,* which he always does with very particular concern. He traced up his descent on both sides for several generations, describing his diet and manner of life, with his several battles, and particularly
that in which he fell. This *Gantlett* was a game-cock, upon whose head the
Knight in his youth had won five hundred pounds, and lost two thousand.
This naturally set the Major upon the account of *Edge-hill* Fight, and ended
in a duel of *Jack Ogle's.*[21]

Old *Reptile* was extremely attentive to all that was said, tho' it was the
same he had heard every night for these twenty years, and upon all occasions, winked upon his nephew to mind what passed.

This may suffice to give the world a taste of our innocent conversation, which we spun out till about ten of the clock, when my maid came
with a lantern to light me home.[22] I could not but reflect with myself as I
was going out upon the talkative humour of old men, and the little figures

19. The Battle of Naseby marked Cromwell's victory over the Royalists in
June 1645. The couplet from Butler's *Hudibras* is: "Pulpit, Drum Ecclesiastick, /
Was beat with fist, instead of a stick" (I.i.11–12).

20. Jack Ogle, having lost his trooper's cloak gambling, appeared in review
with his landlady's scarlet petticoat tied in a bundle behind him. When the Duke of
Monmouth, having discerned Ogle's ruse, demanded the gentlemen to "Cloak,"
Ogle replied, "I can't Cloak, but I can Petticoat with the best of you." See n. 17.

21. The English Civil War began with the Battle of Edgehill on 23 October
1642.

22. London streets were poorly lighted and unsafe in the dark.

which that part of life makes in one who cannot employ this natural propensity in discourses which would make him venerable. I must own, it makes me very melancholy in company, when I hear a young man begin a story; and have often observed, that one of a quarter of an hour long in a man of five and twenty, gathers circumstances every time he tells it, till it grows into a long *Canterbury* tale of two hours by that time he is three-score.

The only way of avoiding such a trifling and frivolous old age, is, to lay up in our way to it such stores of knowledge and observation as may make us useful and agreeable in our declining years. The mind of man in a long life will become a magazine of wisdom or folly, and will consequently discharge itself in something impertinent or improving. For which reason, as there is nothing more ridiculous than an old trifling story-teller, so there is nothing more venerable than one who has turned his experience to the entertainment and advantage of mankind.

In short, we who are in the last stage of life, and are apt to indulge ourselves in talk, ought to consider, if what we speak be worth being heard, and endeavour to make our discourse like that of *Nestor*, which *Homer* compares to the flowing of honey for its sweetness.[23]

I am afraid I shall be thought guilty of this excess I am speaking of, when I cannot conclude without observing, that *Milton* certainly thought of this passage in *Homer*, when in his description of an eloquent spirit, he says, *His Tongue drop'd Manna*.[24]

11 February 1709

23. "Then among them uprose Nestor, sweet of speech, the clear-voiced orator of the men of Pylos, he from whose tongue flowed speech sweeter than honey"; Homer, *Iliad*, I.247–49.
24. John Milton, *Paradise Lost*, II.112–13.

No. 214. [The Political Barometer]

———Soles & aperta Serena
Prospicere, & certis poteris cognoscere Signis. Virg.[25]

FROM MY OWN APARTMENT, AUGUST 21.

In every party there are two sorts of men, the *Rigid* and the *Supple*. The *Rigid* are an intractable race of mortals, who act upon principle, and will not, forsooth, fall into any measures that are not consistent with their received notions of honour. These are persons of a stubborn, unpliant morality, that sullenly adhere to their friends when they are disgraced and to their principles, though they are exploded.[26] I shall therefore give up this stiff-necked generation to their own obstinacy, and turn my thoughts to the advantage of the *Supple,* who pay their homage to places, and not persons; and without enslaving themselves to any particular scheme of opinions, are as ready to change their conduct in point of sentiment, as of fashion. The well-disciplined part of a court are generally so perfect at their exercise, that you may see a whole assembly, from front to rear, face about at once to a new man of power, though at the same time they turn their backs upon him that brought them thither. The great hardship these complaisant members of society are under, seems to be the want of warning upon any approaching change or revolution; so that they are obliged in a hurry to tack about with every wind, and stop short in the midst of a full career, to the great surprize and derision of their beholders.

When a man foresees a decaying Ministry, he has leisure to grow a malcontent, reflect upon the present conduct, and by gradual murmurs fall off from his friends into a new party, by just steps and measures. For want of such notices, I have formerly known a very well-bred person refuse to return a bow of a man whom he thought in disgrace, that was next day made Secretary of State; and another, who after a long neglect of a minister, came to his levee, and made professions of zeal for his service the very day before he was turned out.

25. "Nor less after rain may you foresee bright suns and cloudless skies, and know them by sure signs"; Virgil, *Georgics,* I.394–95.
26. A reference to the imminent fall of the Whig ministry; see *Tatler* no. 190.

This produces also unavoidable confusions and mistakes in the descriptions of great men's parts and merits. That ancient lyric, Mr. *D'Urfey,* some years ago wrote a dedication to a certain Lord, in which he celebrated him for the greatest poet and critic of that age, upon a misinformation in *Dyer's* letter, that his noble patron was made Lord Chamberlain.[27] In short, innumerable votes, speeches, and sermons, have been thrown away, and turned to no account, merely for want of due and timely intelligence. Nay it has been known, that a panegyric has been half printed off, when the poet, upon the removal of the minister, has been forced to alter it into a satire.

For the conduct therefore of such useful persons as are ready to do their country service upon all occasions, I have an engine in my study, which is a sort of a Political Barometer, or, to speak more intelligibly, a State *Weather-Glass,* that, by the rising and falling of a certain magical liquor, presages all changes and revolutions in government, as the common glass does those of the weather. This Weather-Glass is said to have been invented by *Cardan,* and given by him as a present to his great countryman and contemporary *Machiavel,* which (by the way) may serve to rectify a received error in chronology, that places one of these some years after the other.[28] How or when it came into my hands, I shall desire to be excused, if I keep to myself; but so it is, that I have walked by it for the better part of a century, to my safety at least, if not to my advantage; and have among my papers, a register of all the changes that have happened in it from the middle of Queen *Elizabeth's* reign.[29]

27. Thomas D'Urfey dedicated *The Comical History of Don Quixote* (1694) to Charles Sackville, sixth earl of Dorset, as "*Best Judge of Men, and best of Poets too*" (ll. 60–65). *Dyer's Letter* was a newsletter published by the Tory journalist John Dyer (d. 1713), begun shortly after the Revolution of 1688.

28. Jerome Cardan (1501–76) was an Italian physician and astrologer. Niccolò Machiavelli was a Florentine statesman and author of *The Prince* (1515), which counseled cunning and manipulation as practical political policy.

29. This period, one of great tumult and change, saw the excommunication of Elizabeth, the institution of Stuart rule, the Civil War in which Charles I was beheaded, Puritan repressiveness under Oliver Cromwell, the restoration of Charles II and his licentious rule, a revolution that forced James II to flee the country, the emergence of the Whig and Tory Parties, and the wartime regime of William III and Queen Anne.

In the time of that Princess, it stood long at *settled Fair.* At the latter end of King *James* the First, it fell to *Cloudy.* It held several years after at *Stormy;* insomuch that at last despairing of seeing any *Clear* weather at home, I followed the royal exile, and some time after finding my Glass rise, returned to my native country with the rest of the Loyalists. I was then in hopes to pass the remainder of my days in *settled Fair:* but alas! during the greatest part of that reign, the *English* nation lay in a *dead Calm,* which, as it is usual, was followed by high winds and tempests till of late years: in which, with unspeakable joy and satisfaction, I have seen our political weather returned to *settled Fair.* I must only observe, that for all this last summer my Glass has pointed at changeable. Upon the whole, I often apply to Fortune *Aeneas's* speech to the Sybil:

———— *Non ulla Laborum,*
O Virgo, nova mi Facies inopinave surgit
Omnia praecepi, atq; Animo mecum ante peregi.[30]

The advantages which have accrued to those whom I have advised in their affairs, by virtue of this sort of prescience, have been very considerable. A nephew of mine, who has never put his money into the stocks, or taken it out, without my advice, has in a few years raised five hundred pounds to almost so many thousands. As for myself, who look upon riches to consist rather in content than possessions, and measure the greatness of the mind rather by its tranquility than its ambition, I have seldom used my Glass to make my way in the world, but often to retire from it. This is a by-path to happiness, which was first discovered to me by a most pleasing apothegm of *Pythagoras: When the Winds,* says he, *rise, worship the Echo.* That great philosopher (whether to make his doctrines the more venerable, or to gild his precepts with the beauty of imagination, or to awaken the curiosity of his disciples; for I will not suppose what is usually said, that he did it to conceal his wisdom from the vulgar) has couched several admirable precepts in remote allusions and mysterious sentences. By the winds in this apothegm, are meant State-hurricanes and popular tumults. When these

30. "For me no form of toil arises, O maiden, strange or unlooked for; all this have I foreseen and debated in my mind"; Virgil, *Aeneid,* VI.103–5.

arise, says he, worship the Echo; that is, withdraw yourself from the multitude into deserts, woods, solitudes, or the like retirements, which are the usual habitations of the Echo.[31]

    22 August 1710

31. Dr. Johnson quotes this saying of Pythagoras's, preserved by Iamblichus in his biography of the philosopher in *Rambler* no. 117, and comments: "This could not but be understood by his disciples as an inviolable injunction to live in a garret, which I have found frequently visited by the echo and the wind." In Voltaire the saying is paraphrased, "'During a tempest, worship the echo': or while civil broils endure, withdraw into retirement"; *A Philosophical Dictionary* (London, 1824), 69.

Joseph Addison

(1672–1719)

IF RICHARD STEELE WAS THE DOMINANT personality be-
hind *The Tatler,* Joseph Addison set the tone for *The Spectator,* which became the model for English periodical writing for more than a century. As
Samuel Johnson remarked in his *Lives of the English Poets,* "His prose is the
model of the middle style; on grave subjects not formal, on light occasions
not groveling; pure without scrupulosity, and exact without apparent elab-
oration. . . . Whoever wishes to attain an English style, familiar but not
coarse, and elegant but not ostentatious, must give his days and nights to
the volumes of Addison." Unlike the Tatler's lucubrations, the Spectator's
speculations convey the polish of a classically learned gentleman with little
fondness for "meddling with any practical part in life," as he says in *Spectator* no. 1. Rather than datelining his papers White's, Will's, or any of the
other leading London coffeehouses as Steele's Isaac Bickerstaff had done,
Addison chose to begin his numbers of *The Tatler* and *The Spectator* with
classical quotations, a practice that later was more widely adopted.

Whereas Steele's early literary efforts had been made in the genre of
Restoration comedy—*The Funeral* (1701), *The Lying Lover* (1703), *The
Tender Husband* (1705)—Addison, upon his return from a four-year tour
of the Continent, made his reputation with an epic poem, *The Campaign*
(1704), which celebrated the victory of the Duke of Marlborough at the
Battle of Blenheim. Like Steele, he served as a member of Parliament, from
1708 until his death. His diverse literary efforts, including an opera libretto
(*Fair Rosamond,* 1707), a prose comedy (*The Drummer,* 1716), and a neoclassical tragedy (*Cato,* 1713), were celebrated by Whigs and Tories alike.
His final publication, a political paper (*The Freeholder,* 1715–16), terminated in the year of his marriage to the Countess of Warwick, a union
marked by strained relations with his rakish stepson and his own failing
health. His friendship with Steele collapsed the year of his death in a dispute

over the Peerage Bill (1719). He was buried at Westminster Abbey among the stately tombs he memorialized in *Spectator* no. 26.

Of the 555 numbers of the original *Spectator* (before its 1714 revival for 80 additional numbers), Steele wrote 236 and Addison 274, treating the English reading public to commentaries on manners and morals and offering lively portraits of contemporary types from the rake to the coquette, the newsmonger to the pedant, the virtuoso to the parson.

Selections are from the collected *Tatler* in *The Lucubrations of Isaac Bickerstaff, Esq.* (London, 1710–11), and *The Spectator* (London, 1712–15).

The Tatler
No. 155. [The Upholsterer]
By Isaac Bickerstaff, Esq.

———*Aliena Negotia curat*
Excussus propriis———Hor.[1]

FROM MY OWN APARTMENT, APRIL 5.

There lived some years since within my neighbourhood a very grave person, an Upholsterer, who seemed a man of more than ordinary application to business. He was a very early riser, and was often abroad two or three hours before any of his neighbours. He had a particular carefulness in the knitting of his brows, and a kind of impatience in all his motions, that plainly discovered he was always intent on matters of importance. Upon my enquiry into his life and conversation, I found him to be the greatest newsmonger in our quarter; that he rose before day to read the *Post-Man;* and that he would take two or three turns to the other end of the town before his neighbours were up, to see if there were any *Dutch* Mails come in. He had a wife and several children; but was much more inquisitive to know what passed in *Poland* than in his own family, and was in greater pain and anxiety of mind for King *Augustus's* welfare than that of his nearest relations. He

1. "I have looked over other people's business, after being flung overboard from my own"; Horace, *Satires*, II.iii.19–20.

looked extremely thin in a dearth of news, and never enjoyed himself in a westerly wind. This indefatigable kind of life was the ruin of his shop; for about the time that his favourite prince left the crown of *Poland*, he broke and disappeared.[2]

This man and his affairs had been long out of my mind, till about three days ago, as I was walking in St. *James*'s Park, I heard some body at a distance hemming after me: and who should it be but my old neighbour the Upholsterer? I saw he was reduced to extreme poverty, by certain shabby superfluities in his dress: for notwithstanding that it was a very sultry day for the time of the year, he wore a loose great coat and a muff, with a long campaign-wig out of curl;[3] to which he had added the ornament of a pair of black garters buckled under the knee. Upon his coming up to me, I was going to enquire into his present circumstances; but was prevented by his asking me, with a whisper, Whether the last letters brought any accounts that one might rely upon from *Bender*?[4] I told him, None that I heard of; and asked him, Whether he had yet married his eldest daughter? He told me, No. But pray, says he, tell me sincerely, what are your thoughts of the King of *Sweden*? For tho' his wife and children were starving, I found his chief concern at present was for this great monarch. I told him, That I looked upon him as one of the first heroes of the age. But pray, says he, do you think there is any thing in the story of his wound? And finding me surprised at the question, Nay, says he, I only propose it to you. I answered, That I thought there was no reason to doubt of it. But why in the heel, says he, more than in any other part of the body? Because, says I, the bullet chanced to light there.

This extraordinary dialogue was no sooner ended, but he began to launch out into a long dissertation upon the affairs of the *North;* and after having spent some time on them, he told me, He was in a great perplexity how to reconcile the *Supplement* with the *English-Post,* and had been just

2. European news (chiefly political and military, as in the Dutch mails) came in by sailing ships, requiring an eastern wind. The Polish king Augustus II (1670–1733) was deposed by Charles XII of Sweden in 1701. The Upholsterer "broke" by going bankrupt.

3. A curled French wig worn around the time of the first Duke of Marlborough's military campaigns.

4. After his defeat at Poltava, Charles XII fled to the Turkish city of Bender.

now examining what the other Papers say upon the same subject. The *Daily-Courant*, says he, has these words, *We have advices from very good hands, that a certain Prince has some matters of great importance under consideration.* This is very mysterious; but the *Post-Boy* leaves us more in the dark, for he tells us, *That there are private intimations of measures taken by a certain Prince, which time will bring to light.* Now the *Post-Man*, says he, who use[d] to be very clear, refers to the same news in these words; *The late conduct of a certain Prince affords great matter of speculation.* This certain Prince, says the Upholsterer, whom they are all so cautious of naming, I take to be—Upon which, though there was no body near us, he whispered something in my ear, which I did not hear, or think worth my while to make him repeat.

We were now got to the upper end of the *Mall*, where were three or four very odd fellows sitting together upon the bench. These I found were all of them politicians, who used to sun themselves in that place every day about dinner-time. Observing them to be curiosities in their kind, and my friend's acquaintance, I sat down among them.

The chief politician of the bench was a great asserter of paradoxes. He told us, with a seeming concern, That by some news he had lately read from *Muscovy*, it appeared to him that there was a storm gathering in the Black Sea, which might in time do hurt to the naval forces of this nation. To this he added, That for his part, he could not wish to see the Turk driven out of *Europe*, which he believed could not but be prejudicial to our woollen manufacture. He then told us, That he looked upon those extraordinary revolutions which had lately happened in these parts of the world, to have risen chiefly from two persons who were not much talked of; and those, says he, are Prince *Menzikoff*, and the Duchess of *Mirandola*.[5] He backed his assertions with so many broken hints, and such a show of depth and wisdom, that we gave our selves up to his opinions.

The discourse at length fell upon a point which seldom escapes a knot of true-born *Englishmen*, Whether in case of a religious war, the Protestants would not be too strong for the Papists? This we unanimously determined on the Protestant side. One who sat on my right hand, and, as I found by

5. Alexander Menzikoff (1672–1729) was a prince of Russia (commonly known as Muscovy) and Mirandola was a duchy in northeast Italy.

his discourse, had been in the *West-Indies,* assured us, that it would be a very easy matter for the Protestants to beat the Pope at sea; and added, that whenever such a war does break out, it must turn to the good of the *Lee-ward* Islands.[6] Upon this, one who sat at the end of the bench, and, as I afterwards found, was the geographer of the company, said, That in case the Papists should drive the Protestants from these parts of *Europe,* when the worst came to the worst, it would be impossible to beat them out of *Norway* and *Greenland,* provided the Northern Crowns hold together, and the Czar of *Muscovy* stand neuter.

He further told us for our comfort, That there were vast tracts of land about the Pole, inhabited neither by Protestants nor Papists, and of greater extent than all the *Roman* Catholic dominions in *Europe.*

When we had fully discussed this point, my friend the Upholsterer began to exert himself upon the present negotiations of peace; in which he deposed princes, settled the bounds of kingdoms, and balanced the power of *Europe,* with great justice and impartiality.

I at length took my leave of the company, and was going away; but had not been gone thirty yards, before the Upholsterer hemmed again after me. Upon his advancing towards me, with a whisper, I expected to hear some secret piece of news, which he had not thought fit to communicate to the bench; but instead of that, he desired me in my ear to lend him half a crown. In compassion to so needy a statesman, and to dissipate the confusion I found he was in, I told him, if he pleased, I would give him five shillings, to receive five pounds of him when the Great Turk was driven out of *Constantinople;* which he very readily accepted, but not before he had laid down to me the impossibility of such an event, as the affairs of *Europe* now stand.

This Paper I design for the particular benefit of those worthy citizens who live more in a coffee-house than in their shops, and whose thoughts are so taken up with the affairs of the allies, that they forget their customers.

6 April 1710

6. Islands in the West Indies under possession of the French and Spaniards ("the Papists").

No. 158. [Tom Folio]

Faciunt nae intelligendo, ut nihil intelligant. Ter.[7]

FROM MY OWN APARTMENT, APRIL 12.

Tom Folio is a broker in learning, employed to get together good editions, and stock the libraries of great men.[8] There is not a sale of books begins till *Tom Folio* is seen at the door. There is not an auction where his name is not heard, and that too in the very nick of time, in the critical moment, before the last decisive stroke of the hammer. There is not a subscription goes forward, in which *Tom* is not privy to the first rough draft of the proposals; nor a catalogue printed, that doth not come to him wet from the press. He is an universal scholar, so far as the title-page of all authors, knows the manuscripts in which they were discovered, the editions through which they have passed, with the praises or censures which they have received from the several members of the learned world. He has a greater esteem for *Aldus* and *Elzevir,* than for *Virgil* and *Horace.* If you talk of *Herodotus,* he breaks out into a panegyric upon *Harry Stephens.*[9] He thinks he gives you an account of an author, when he tells you the subject he treats of, the name of the editor, and the year in which it was printed. Or if you draw him into further particulars, he cries up the goodness of the paper, extols the diligence of the corrector, and is transported with the beauty of the letter. This he looks upon to be sound learning and substantial criticism. As for those who talk of the fineness of style, and the justness of thought, or describe the brightness of any particular passages; nay, though they write themselves in the genius and spirit of the author they admire, *Tom* looks upon them as men of superficial learning, and flashy parts.

7. "Does not this use of their critical faculty show that they are no critics?"; Terence, prologue to *Andria* (The Girl from Andros), l. 17.
8. Tom Folio is reputedly based on Thomas Rawlinson (1681–1725), a bibliophile whose large accumulation of books compelled him to sleep in a passageway of his home.
9. Aldus Manutius (c. 1450–1515) was a famous Venetian printer; Elzivir was the name of a family of early-seventeenth-century Dutch printers. Tom Folio rates "Harry Stephens" (Henri Estienne, a sixteenth-century French printer of classics) above Herodotus.

I had yesterday morning a visit from this learned idiot, (for that is the light in which I consider every Pedant) when I discovered in him some little touches of the coxcomb, which I had not before observed. Being very full of the figure which he makes in the Republic of Letters, and wonderfully satisfied with his great stock of knowledge, he gave me broad intimations, that he did not *believe* in all points as his forefathers had done. He then communicated to me a thought of a certain author upon a passage of *Virgil's* account of the dead, which I made the subject of a late Paper.[10] This thought hath taken very much among men of Tom's pitch and understanding, though universally exploded by all that know how to construe *Virgil*, or have any relish of antiquity. Not to trouble my reader with it, I found upon the whole, that *Tom* did not believe a future state of rewards and punishments, because *Aeneas*, at his leaving the Empire of the Dead, passed through the Gate of Ivory, and not through that of Horn.[11] Knowing that *Tom* had not sense enough to give up an opinion which he had once received, that we might avoid wrangling, I told him, That *Virgil* possibly had his oversights as well as another author. Ah! Mr. *Bickerstaff*, says he, you would have another opinion of him, if you would read him in *Daniel Heinsius's* edition.[12] I have perused him myself several times in that edition, continued he; and after the strictest and most malicious examination, could find but two faults in him: one of them is in the *Aeneids*, where there are two commas instead of a parenthesis; and another in the third *Georgic*, where you may find a semicolon turned upside down. Perhaps, said I, these were not *Virgil's* thoughts, but those of the transcriber. I do not design it, says *Tom*, as a reflection on *Virgil*: on the contrary, I know that all the manuscripts *reclaim* against such a punctuation. Oh! Mr. *Bickerstaff*, says he, what would a man give to see one simile of *Virgil* writ in his own hand? I asked him which was the simile he meant; but was answered, Any simile in *Virgil*. He then told me all the secret history in the Commonwealth of Learning; of modern pieces that had the names of ancient authors

10. *Tatler* no. 154 (4 April 1710).

11. The two gates through which dreams proceeded: those from the Gate of Ivory cheat the dreamer with false hopes; those from the Gate of Horn bear truth. See Virgil, *Aeneid*, VI.893–96.

12. The classical scholar Daniel Heinsius produced a well-known edition of Virgil in 1636.

annexed to them; of all the books that were now writing or printing in the several parts of *Europe;* of many amendments which are made, and not yet published; and a thousand other particulars, which I would not have my memory burdened with for a Vatican.[13]

At length, being fully persuaded that I thoroughly admired him, and looked upon him as a prodigy of learning, he took his leave. I know several of *Tom's* class who are professed admirers of *Tasso* without understanding a word of *Italian;* and one in particular, that carries a *Pastor-Fido* in his pocket, in which I am sure he is acquainted with no other beauty but the clearness of the character.[14]

There is another kind of Pedant, who, with all *Tom Folio's* impertinencies, hath greater super-structures and embellishments of *Greek* and *Latin,* and is still more insupportable than the other, in the same degree as he is more learned. Of this kind very often are Editors, Commentators, Interpreters, Scholiasts, and Critics; and in short, all men of deep learning without common sense. These persons set a greater value on themselves for having found out the meaning of a passage in *Greek,* than upon the author for having written it; nay, will allow the passage itself not to have any beauty in it, at the same time that they would be considered as the greatest men of the age for having interpreted it. They will look with contempt upon the most beautiful poems that have been composed by any of their contemporaries; but will lock themselves up in their studies for a twelvemonth together, to correct, publish, and expound, such trifles of antiquity as a modern author would be contemned for. Men of the strictest morals, severest lives, and the gravest professions, will write volumes upon an idle sonnet that is originally in *Greek* or *Latin;* give editions of the most immoral authors, and spin out whole pages upon the various readings of a lewd expression. All that can be said in excuse for them, is, that their works sufficiently show they have no taste of their authors; and that what they do in this kind, is out of their great learning, and not out of any levity or lasciviousness of temper.

13. The Vatican Library, one of the oldest and most extensive collections of books and manuscripts.

14. Torquato Tasso (1544–95) was a Renaissance poet and the author of the epic *La Gerusalemme liberata* (Jerusalem Delivered). *Il pastor fido* (The Faithful Shepherd, 1590) was a pastoral tragicomedy by Giovanni Battista Guarini.

A Pedant of this nature is wonderfully well described in six lines of *Boileau*, with which I shall conclude his character.

Un Pêdant enyvré de sa vaine science,
Tout herisse de Grec, tout bouffi d'arrogance,
Et qui de mille Auteurs retenus mot pour mot,
Dans sa tête entassez n'a souvent fait qu'un Sot,
Croit qu'un Livre fait tout, & que sans Aristote
La Raison ne voit goute, & le bon Sens radote.[15]

13 April 1710

No. 163. [Ned Softly, Sonneteer]

Idem Infaceto est infacetior Rure
Simul Poemata attigit; neque idem unquam
Æquè est beatus, ac Poema cum scribit:
Tam gaudet in se, tamque se ipse miratur.
Nimirum idem omnes fallimur; neque est quisquam
Quem non in aliqua Re videre Suffenum
Possis.———Catul. de Suffeno.[16]

WILL'S COFFEE-HOUSE, APRIL 24.

I yesterday came hither about two hours before the company generally make their appearance, with a design to read over all the news-papers; but

15. "A pedant staggered with his vain science/All bristled up with Greek, all puffed up with arrogance/And retaining a thousand authors word for word/In his head heaped up, he often appears nothing but a fool,/He believes that a book is everything, and that without Aristotle,/Reason can have nothing to do with taste, and good sense is nonsense"; Nicolas Boileau-Despréaux, *Satires,* IV.5–10.

16. "He is more clumsy than the clumsy country, whenever he touches poetry; and at the same time he is never so happy as when he is writing a poem, he delights in himself and admires himself so much. True enough, we all are under the same delusion, and there is no one whom you may not see to be a Suffenus in one thing or another"; Catullus, *Poems,* XXII.14. Here Suffenus stands for any bad poet.

upon my sitting down, I was accosted by *Ned Softly,* who saw me from a corner in the other end of the room, where I found he had been writing something. Mr. *Bickerstaff,* says he, I observe by a late Paper of yours, that you and I are just of a humour; for you must know, of all impertinencies, there is nothing which I so much hate as news. I never read a *Gazette* in my life; and never trouble my head about our armies, whether they win or lose, or in what part of the world they lie encamped. Without giving me time to reply, he drew a paper of verses out of his pocket, telling me, That he had something which would entertain me more agreeably, and that he would desire my judgment upon every line, for that we had time enough before us till the company came in.

Ned Softly is a very pretty poet, and a great admirer of easy lines. *Waller* is his favourite: and as that admirable writer has the best and worst verses of any among our great *English* poets, *Ned Softly* has got all the bad ones without book, which he repeats upon occasion, to show his reading, and garnish his conversation.[17] *Ned* is indeed a true *English* reader, incapable of relishing the great and masterly strokes of this art; but wonderfully pleased with the little *Gothic* ornaments of epigrammatical conceits, turns, points, and quibbles, which are so frequent in the most admired of our *English* poets, and practised by those who want genius and strength to represent, after the manner of the Ancients, simplicity in its natural beauty and perfection.

Finding myself unavoidably engaged in such a conversation, I was resolved to turn my pain into a pleasure, and to divert myself as well as I could with so very odd a fellow. You must understand, says *Ned,* that the sonnet I am going to read to you was written upon a lady, who showed me some verses of her own making, and is perhaps the best poet of our age. But you shall hear it. Upon which he began to read as follows:

To Mira, *on her incomparable Poems.*

I.
When dress'd in Laurel Wreaths you shine,
And tune your soft melodious Notes,

17. The Cavalier poet Edmund Waller (1606 – 87).

You seem a Sister of the Nine,
Or Phoebus *self in Petticoats.*
2.
I fancy, when your Song you sing,
(Your Song you sing with so much Art)
Your Pen was plucked from Cupid's *Wing;*
For ah! it wounds me like his Dart.

Why, says I, this is a little nosegay of conceits, a very lump of salt: every verse hath something in it that piques; and then the dart in the last line is certainly as pretty a sting in the tail of an epigram (for so I think your critics call it) as ever entered into the thought of a poet. Dear Mr. *Bickerstaff,* says he, shaking me by the hand, every body knows you to be a judge of these things; and to tell you truly, I read over *Roscommon's* translation of *Horace's Art of Poetry* three several times, before I sat down to write the sonnet which I have shown you.[18] But you shall hear it again, and pray observe every line of it, for not one of them shall pass without your approbation.

When dress'd in Laurel Wreaths you shine.

That is, says he, when you have your garland on; when you are writing verses. To which I replied, I know your meaning: A metaphor! The same, said he, and went on:

And tune your soft melodious Notes.

Pray observe the gliding of that verse; there is scarce a consonant in it. I took care to make it run upon liquids. Give me your opinion of it. Truly, said I, I think it as good as the former. I am very glad to hear you say so, says he; but mind the next.

18. Wentworth Dillon, fourth Earl of Roscommon, wrote a blank-verse translation of Horace's *Ars poetica* (Art of Poetry; 1680), which contained a brief preface outlining his views on poetics.

You seem a Sister of the Nine.

That is, says he, you seem a sister of the Muses; for if you look into ancient authors, you will find it was their opinion, that there were nine of them. I remember it very well, said I; but pray proceed.

Or Phoebus *self in Petticoats.*

Phoebus, says he, was the god of poetry. These little instances, Mr. *Bickerstaff,* show a gentleman's reading. Then to take off from the air of learning, which *Phoebus* and the Muses have given to this first stanza, you may observe, how it falls all of a sudden into the familiar; *in Petticoats!*

Or Phoebus *self in Petticoats.*

Let us now, says I, enter upon the second stanza. I find the first line is still a continuation of the metaphor.

I fancy, when your Song you sing.

It is very right, says he; but pray observe the turn of words in those two lines. I was a whole hour in adjusting of them, and have still a doubt upon me. Whether in the second line it should be *Your Song you sing;* or, *You sing your Song?* You shall hear them both:

I fancy, when your Song you sing,
(Your Song you sing with so much Art.)

OR,

I fancy, when your Song you sing,
You sing your Song with so much Art.

Truly, said I, the turn is so natural either way, that you have made me almost giddy with it. Dear Sir, said he, grasping me by the hand, you have a great deal of patience; but pray what do you think of the next verse?

Your Pen was pluck'd from Cupid's *Wing.*

Think! says I; I think you have made *Cupid* look like a little goose. That was my meaning, says he; I think the ridicule is well enough hit off. But we now come to the last, which sums up the whole matter:

For Ah! it wounds me like his Dart.

Pray how do you like that *Ah!* Doth it not make a pretty figure in that Place? *Ah!* It looks as if I felt the dart, and cried out at being pricked with it.

For Ah! it wounds me like his Dart.

My friend *Dick Easy,* continued he, assured me, he would rather have written that *Ah!* than to have been the author of the *Aeneid.* He indeed objected, that I made *Mira*'s pen like a quill in one of the lines, and like a dart in the other. But as to that—Oh! as to that, says I, it is but supposing *Cupid* to be like a porcupine, and his quills and darts will be the same thing. He was going to embrace me for the hint; but half a dozen critics coming into the room, whose faces he did not like, he conveyed the sonnet into his pocket, and whispered me in the ear, he would show it me again as soon as his man had written it over fair.

25 April 1710

No. 216. [Nicholas Gimcrack, the Virtuoso]

—Nugis addere Pondus.[19]

FROM MY OWN APARTMENT, AUGUST 25.

Nature is full of wonders; every atom is a standing miracle, and endowed with such qualities, as could not be impressed on it by a power and wisdom less than infinite. For this reason, I would not discourage any searches that are made into the most minute and trivial parts of the Creation. However,

19. "Undue weight to trifles"; Horace, *Epistles,* I.19.42.

since the world abounds in the noblest fields of speculation, it is, methinks, the mark of a little genius to be wholly conversant among insects, reptiles, animalcules, and those trifling rarities that furnish out the apartment of a Virtuoso.

There are some men whose heads are so oddly turned this way, that though they are utter strangers to the common occurrences of life, they are able to discover the sex of a cockle, or describe the generation of a mite, in all its circumstances. They are so little versed in the world, that they scarce know a horse from an ox; but at the same time will tell you, with a great deal of gravity, that a flea is a rhinoceros,[20] and a snail an hermaphrodite. I have known one of these whimsical philosophers who has set a greater value upon a collection of spiders than he would upon a flock of sheep, and has sold his coat off his back to purchase a tarantula.

I would not have a scholar wholly unacquainted with these secrets and curiosities of Nature; but certainly the mind of man, that is capable of so much higher contemplations, should not be altogether fixed upon such mean and disproportioned objects. Observations of this kind are apt to alienate us too much from the knowledge of the world, and to make us serious upon trifles, by which means they expose philosophy to the ridicule of the witty, and contempt of the ignorant. In short, studies of this nature should be the diversions, relaxations, and amusements; not the care, business, and concern of life.

It is indeed wonderful to consider, that there should be a sort of learned men who are wholly employed in gathering together the refuse of Nature, if I may call it so, and hoarding up in their chests and cabinets such creatures as others industriously avoid the sight of. One does not know how to mention some of the most precious parts of their treasure, without a kind of an apology for it. I have been shown a beetle valued at twenty crowns, and a toad at an hundred: but we must take this for a general rule, that whatever appears trivial or obscene in the common notions of the world, looks grave and philosophical in the eye of a Virtuoso.

To show this humour in its perfection, I shall present my Reader with

20. Probably a reference to the rhinoceros beetle, which has projecting horns on its thorax and head.

the legacy of a certain Virtuoso,[21] who laid out a considerable estate in natural rarities and curiosities, which upon his death bed he bequeathed to his relations and friends, in the following words:

> *The Will of a Virtuoso.*
> I *Nicholas Gimcrack* being in sound health of mind, but in great weakness of body, do by this my Last Will and Testament bestow my worldly goods and chattels in manner following:
>
> *Imprimis,* To my dear wife,[22]
> One box of butterflies,
> One drawer of shells,
> A female skeleton,
> A dried cockatrice.
>
> *Item,* To my daughter *Elizabeth,*
> My receipt for preserving dead caterpillars,
> As also my preparations of winter *May-Dew,*
> and embryo pickle.
>
> *Item,* To my little daughter *Fanny,*
> Three crocodile's eggs.
> And upon the birth of her first child, if she marries with her mother's consent,
> The nest of an humming-bird.
>
> *Item,* To my eldest brother, as an acknowledgment for the lands he has vested in my son *Charles,* I bequeath
> My last year's collection of grasshoppers.
>
> *Item,* To his daughter *Susanna,* being his only child, I bequeath my
> *English* weeds pasted on royal paper.
> With my large folio of *Indian* cabbage.

21. The name of the virtuoso is derived from Sir Nicholas Gimcrack, the main butt of satire in Thomas Shadwell's comic play *The Virtuoso* (1676).
22. See *Tatler* no. 221, in which the widow Elizabeth Gimcrack offers to sell a parcel of dried spiders at a bargain. *Imprimis* is a legal term meaning "first."

Item, To my learned and worthy friend Dr. *Johannes Elscrikius,*
Professor in Anatomy, and my associate in the studies of Nature, as an
eternal monument of my affection and friendship for him, I bequeath
My rat's testicles, and
Whale's pizzle,
To him and his Issue male; and in default of such Issue in the said
Dr. *Elscrickius,* then to return to my Executor and his heirs for ever.

Having fully provided for my nephew *Isaac,* by making over to him
some years since
A horned *Scarabaeus,*[23]
The skin of a rattle-snake, and
The mummy of an *Egyptian* king,
I make no further provision for him in this my Will.

My eldest Son *John* having spoken disrespectfully of his little Sister
whom I keep by me in spirits of wine,[24] and in many other instances
behaved himself undutifully towards me, I do disinherit, and wholly
cut off from any part of this my personal estate, by giving him a single
cockle shell.

To my second son *Charles,* I give and bequeath all my flowers,
plants, minerals, mosses, shells, pebbles, fossils, beetles, butterflies,
caterpillars, grasshoppers, and vermin, not above specified: as also all
my monsters, both wet and dry, making the said *Charles* whole and
sole Executor of this my Last Will and Testament; he paying, or causing to be paid, the aforesaid legacies within the space of six months after my decease. And I do hereby revoke all other wills whatsoever by
me formerly made.

26 August 1710

23. A large black dung-beetle.
24. That is, a fetal embryo.

No. 220. [The Church Thermometer]

Insani sanus Nomen ferat, aequus iniqui,
Ultra quam satis est, Virtutem si petat ipsam. Hor.[25]

FROM MY OWN APARTMENT, SEPT. 4.

Having received many letters filled with compliments and acknowledg-
ments for my late useful discovery of the Political Barometer,[26] I shall here
communicate to the public an account of my Ecclesiastical Thermometer,
the latter giving as manifest prognostications of the changes and revolutions in Church, as the former does of those in State, and both of them being absolutely necessary for every prudent subject who is resolved to keep
what he has, and get what he can.

The Church Thermometer, which I am now to treat of, is supposed
to have been invented in the reign of *Henry* the Eighth, about the time
when that religious Prince put some to death for owning the Pope's su-
premacy, and others for denying Transubstantiation.[27] I do not find, however, any great use made of this instrument till it fell into the hands of a
learned and vigilant priest or minister, (for he frequently wrote himself
both one and the other) who was some time Vicar of *Bray.* This gentleman
lived in his vicarage to a good old age; and after having seen several succes-
sions of his neighbouring clergy either burnt or banished, departed this life
with the satisfaction of having never deserted his flock, and died Vicar of
Bray.[28] As this glass was first designed to calculate the different degrees of
heat in Religion, as it raged in Popery, or as it cooled and grew temperate in
the Reformation, it was marked at several distances, after the manner our

25. "Let the wise man bear the name of madman, the just of unjust, should he
pursue Virtue herself beyond due bounds"; Horace, *Epistles,* I.6.15–16.

26. See *Tatler* no. 214 in this volume, by Steele.

27. Henry VIII (1491–1547) broke from the Roman Catholic Church to establish the Church of England. His reign was marked by doctrinal contradictions.

28. In the sense that he switched allegiances, serving as a priest under Tory
High Church government and a minister under Whiggish Low Church rule, the
legendary Vicar of Bray (a real-life person who became a figure of speech) never deserted his flock.

ordinary thermometer is to this day, *viz. extreme Hot, sultry Hot, very Hot, Hot, Warm, Temperate, Cold, just Freezing, Frost, hard Frost, great Frost, extreme Cold.*

It is well known, that *Toricellius,* the inventor of the common weather glass, made the experiment in a long tube which held thirty-two foot of water; and that a more modern virtuoso finding such a machine altogether unwieldy and useless, and considering that thirty-two inches of quicksilver weighed as much as so many foot of water in a tube of the same circumference, invented that sizeable instrument which is now in use.[29] After this manner, that I might adapt the thermometer I am now speaking of to the present constitution of our Church, as divided into *High* and *Low,* I have made some necessary variations both in the tube and the fluid it contains.[30] In the first place, I ordered a tube to be cast in a planetary hour, and took care to seal it hermetically, when the sun was in conjunction with *Saturn.* I then took the proper precautions about the fluid, which is a compound of two very different liquors; one of them a spirit drawn out of a strong heady wine; the other a particular sort of rock water, colder than ice, and clearer than crystal. The spirit is of a red fiery colour, and so very apt to ferment, that unless it be mingled with a proportion of the water, or pent up very close, it will burst the vessel that holds it, and fly up in fume and smoke. The water on the contrary is of such a subtle piercing cold, that unless it be mingled with a proportion of the spirits, it will sink through almost every thing that it is put into, and seems to be of the same nature as the water mentioned by *Quintus Curtius,* which, says the historian, could be contained in nothing but in the hoof or (as the *Oxford* manuscript has it) in the skull of an ass.[31] The Thermometer is marked according to the following figure,

29. Evangelista Torricelli (1608–47), an Italian physicist, invented the barometer.

30. High Church advocates tended toward conservatism, favoring ceremonial liturgy based on the Roman Catholic model, whereas Low Church advocates were for stripping the church of ceremony and focusing on scripture and individual response.

31. In Quintus Curtius's biography of Alexander the Great, the hero is killed with poison that had been stored in the hoof of an ass. The alleged variant in the "Oxford manuscript" referring to the ass's skull is tongue in cheek.

which I set down at length, not only to give my reader a clear idea of it, but also to fill up my Paper.

Ignorance.
Persecution.
Wrath.
Zeal.
CHURCH.
Moderation.
Lukewarmness.
Infidelity.
Ignorance.

The reader will observe, that the Church is placed in the middle point of the Glass, between *Zeal* and *Moderation,* the situation in which she always flourishes, and in which every good *Englishman* wishes her who is a friend to the constitution of his country. However, when it mounts to *Zeal,* it is not amiss; and when it sinks to *Moderation,* is still in a most admirable temper. The worst of it is, that when once it begins to rise, it has still an inclination to ascend, insomuch that it is apt to climb from *Zeal* to *Wrath,* and from *Wrath* to *Persecution,* which always ends in *Ignorance,* and very often proceeds from it. In the same manner it frequently takes its progress through the lower half of the Glass; and when it has a tendency to fall, will gradually descend from *Moderation* to *Lukewarmness,* and from *Lukewarmness* to *Infidelity,* which very often terminates in *Ignorance,* and always proceeds from it.

It is a common observation, that the ordinary thermometer will be affected by the breathing of people who are in the room where it stands; and indeed, it is almost incredible to conceive how the Glass I am now describing will fall by the breath of a multitude crying *Popery;* or on the contrary, how it will rise when the same multitude (as it sometimes happens) cry out in the same breath, *The Church is in Danger.*[32]

As soon as I had finished my Glass, and adjusted it to the above-mentioned scale of religion, that I might make proper experiments with it, I carried it under my cloak to several coffee-houses, and other places of resort

32. A Tory slogan, linking the Church of England to stable rule and dissent to civil war.

about this great city. At St. *James*'s Coffee-house, the liquor stood at *Moderation;* but at Will's, to my extreme surprize, it subsided to the very lowest mark on the Glass. At the *Grœcian,* it mounted but just one point higher; at the *Rainbow,* it still ascended two degrees: *Child*'s fetched it up to *Zeal,* and other adjacent coffee-houses to *Wrath.*

It fell into the lower half of the Glass as I went further into the city, till at length it settled at *Moderation,* where it continued all the time I stayed about the *Exchange,* as also whilst I passed by the *Bank.* And here I cannot but take notice, that through the whole course of my remarks, I never observed my Glass to rise at the same time that the Stocks did.

To complete the experiment, I prevailed upon a friend of mine, who works under me in the occult sciences, to make a progress with my Glass through the whole Island of *Great Britain;* and after his return, to present me with a register of his observations. I guessed beforehand at the temper of several places he passed through, by the characters they have had time out of mind. Thus that facetious divine, Dr. *Fuller,* speaking of the Town of *Banbury* near a hundred years ago, tells us, it was a place famous for cakes and *Zeal,*[33] which I find by my Glass is true to this day as to the latter part of this description; though I must confess, it is not in the same reputation for cakes that it was in the time of that learned author; and thus of other places. In short, I have now by me, digested in an alphabetical order, all the counties, corporations and boroughs, in *Great Britain,* with their respective tempers, as they stand related to my Thermometer: but this I shall keep to myself, because I would by no means do any thing that may seem to influence any ensuing elections.

The point of doctrine which I would propagate by this my invention, is the same which was long ago advanced by that able teacher *Horace,* out of whom I have taken my text for this discourse: We should be careful not to overshoot ourselves in the pursuits even of virtue. Whether *Zeal* or *Moderation* be the point we aim at, let us keep fire out of the one, and frost out of the other. But alas! the world is too wise to want such a precaution. The terms *High-Church* and *Low-Church,* as commonly used, do not so much

33. The English clergyman Thomas Fuller (1608–61) plays on Shakespeare's line from *Twelfth Night:* "Dost thou think, because thou art virtuous, there shall be no more cakes and ale?" (II.iii.110–11). Banbury is still famous for its cakes.

denote a principle, as they distinguish a party. They are like words of battle, that have nothing to do with their original signification, but are only given out to keep a body of men together, and to let them know friends from enemies.

I must confess, I have considered with some little attention the influence which the opinions of these great national sects have upon their practice; and do look upon it as one of the unaccountable things of our times, that multitudes of honest gentlemen, who entirely agree in their lives, should take it in their heads to differ in their Religion.

5 September 1710

The Spectator
No. 1 . [Introducing Mr. Spectator]

Non fumum ex fulgore, sed ex fumo dare lucem
Cogitat, ut speciosa dehinc miracula promat. Hor.[34]

I have observed, that a reader seldom peruses a book with pleasure, till he knows whether the writer of it be a black or a fair man, of a mild or choleric disposition, married or a bachelor, with other particulars of the like nature, that conduce very much to the right understanding of an author. To gratify this curiosity, which is so natural to a reader, I design this Paper, and my next, as prefatory discourses to my following writings, and shall give some account in them of the several persons that are engaged in this work. As the chief trouble of compiling, digesting, and correcting will fall to my share, I must do myself the justice to open the work with my own history.

I was born to a small hereditary estate, which, according to the tradition of the village where it lies, was bounded by the same hedges and ditches in *William* the Conqueror's time that it is at present, and has been delivered down from father to son whole and entire, without the loss or acquisition of a single field or meadow, during the space of six hundred years. There runs a story in the family, that when my mother was gone with child of me about three months, she dreamt that she was brought to bed of a judge: whether this might proceed from a law-suit which was then depend-

34. "Not smoke after flame does he plan to give, but after smoke the light, that then he may set forth striking wondrous tales"; Horace, *Ars poetica*, ll. 143–44.

ing in the family, or my father's being a Justice of the Peace, I cannot determine; for I am not so vain as to think it presaged any dignity that I should arrive at in my future life, though that was the interpretation which the neighbourhood put upon it. The gravity of my behaviour at my very first appearance in the world, and all the time that I sucked, seemed to favour my mother's dream: for, as she has often told me, I threw away my rattle before I was two months old, and would not make use of my coral till they had taken away the bells from it.

As for the rest of my infancy, there being nothing in it remarkable, I shall pass it over in silence. I find, that, during my nonage, I had the reputation of a very sullen youth, but was always a favourite of my School-Master, who used to say, *that my parts were solid and would wear well.* I had not been long at the University, before I distinguished myself by a most profound silence: for during the space of eight years, excepting in the public exercises of the college, I scarce uttered the quantity of an hundred words; and indeed do not remember that I ever spoke three sentences together in my whole life. Whilst I was in this learned body I applied myself with so much diligence to my studies, that there are very few celebrated books, either in the learned or the modern tongues, which I am not acquainted with.

Upon the death of my father I was resolved to travel into foreign countries, and therefore left the University, with the character of an odd unaccountable fellow, that had a great deal of learning, if I would but show it. An insatiable thirst after knowledge carried me into all the countries of *Europe,* in which there was any thing new or strange to be seen; nay, to such a degree was my curiosity raised, that having read the controversies of some great men concerning the antiquities of *Egypt,* I made a voyage to *Grand Cairo,* on purpose to take the measure of a pyramid; and as soon as I had set myself right in that particular, returned to my native country with great satisfaction.

I have passed my latter years in this city, where I am frequently seen in most public places, though there are not above half a dozen of my select friends that know me; of whom my next Paper shall give a more particular account. There is no place of general resort, wherein I do not often make my appearance; sometimes I am seen thrusting my head into a round of politicians at Will's, and listening with great attention to the narratives that are made in those little circular audiences. Sometimes I smoke a pipe at

Child's; and whilst I seem attentive to nothing but the *Post-Man*, over-hear
the conversation of every table in the room. I appear on *Sunday* nights at
St. *James*'s Coffee-House, and sometimes join the little committee of politics in the inner room, as one who comes there to hear and improve. My
face is likewise very well known at the *Grœcian*, the *Cocoa-Tree*, and in the
theatres both of *Drury-Lane* and the *Hay-Market*. I have been taken for a
merchant upon the *Exchange* for above these ten years, and sometimes pass
for a *Jew* in the assembly of stockjobbers at *Jonathan*'s. In short, where-ever
I see a cluster of people I always mix with them, though I never open my
lips but in my own Club.

Thus I live in the world, rather as a Spectator of mankind, than as one
of the species; by which means I have made myself a speculative statesman,
soldier, merchant and artizan, without ever meddling with any practical
part in life. I am very well versed in the theory of an husband, or a father,
and can discern the errors in the economy, business and diversion of others,
better than those who are engaged in them; as standers-by discover blots,
which are apt to escape those who are in the game. I never espoused any
party with violence, and am resolved to observe an exact neutrality between
the Whigs and Tories, unless I shall be forced to declare myself by the hos-
tilities of either side. In short, I have acted in all the parts of my life as a
looker-on, which is the character I intend to preserve in this Paper.

I have given the reader just so much of my history and character, as to
let him see I am not altogether unqualified for the business I have undertaken. As for other particulars in my life and adventures, I shall insert them
in following Papers, as I shall see occasion. In the mean time, when I consider how much I have seen, read and heard, I begin to blame my own tac-
iturnity; and since I have neither time nor inclination to communicate the
fullness of my heart in speech, I am resolved to do it in writing; and to print
myself out, if possible, before I die. I have been often told by my friends,
that it is pity so many useful discoveries which I have made, should be in the
possession of a silent man. For this reason therefore, I shall publish a sheet-
full of thoughts every morning, for the benefit of my contemporaries; and
if I can any way contribute to the diversion or improvement of the country
in which I live, I shall leave it, when I am summoned out of it, with the secret satisfaction of thinking that I have not lived in vain.

There are three very material points which I have not spoken to in this

Paper, and which, for several important reasons, I must keep to myself, at least for some time: I mean, an account of my name, my age, and my lodgings. I must confess I would gratify my reader in any thing that is reasonable; but as for these three particulars, though I am sensible they might tend very much to the embellishment of my Paper, I cannot yet come to a resolution of communicating them to the public. They would indeed draw me out of that obscurity which I have enjoyed for many years, and expose me in public places to several salutes and civilities, which have been always very disagreeable to me; for the greatest pain I can suffer, is the being talked to, and being stared at. It is for this reason likewise, that I keep my complexion and dress as very great secrets; though it is not impossible but I may make discoveries of both, in the progress of the work I have undertaken.

After having been thus particular upon myself, I shall in to-morrow's Paper give an account of those gentlemen who are concerned with me in this work. For, as I have before intimated, a plan of it is laid and concerted (as all other matters of importance are) in a Club. However, as my friends have engaged me to stand in the front, those who have a mind to correspond with me, may direct their letters *To the Spectator,* at Mr. *Buckley*'s in *Little Britain.* For I must further acquaint the reader, that though our Club meets only on *Tuesdays* and *Thursdays,* we have appointed a committee to sit every night, for the inspection of all such Papers as may contribute to the advancement of the public weal.

1 March 1711

No. 26. [On Westminster Abbey]

Pallida mors aequo pulsat pede pauperum tabernas
Regumque turres. O beate Sexti,
Vitae summa brevis spem nos vetat inchoare longam.
Jam te premet nox, fabulaeque manes,
*Et domus exilis Plutonia———*Hor.[35]

35. "Pale death with foot impartial knocks at the poor man's cottage and at princes' palaces. Despite thy fortune, Sestius, life's brief span forbids thy entering on far-reaching hopes. Soon shall the night of Death enshroud thee, and the phantom shades and Pluto's cheerless hall"; Horace, *Odes,* I.4.13–17. This *Spectator* paper appeared on Good Friday.

When I am in a serious humour, I very often walk by myself in *Westminster* Abbey; where the gloominess of the place, and the use to which it is applied, with the solemnity of the building, and the condition of the people who lie in it, are apt to fill the mind with a kind of melancholy, or rather thoughtfulness, that is not disagreeable. I yesterday passed a whole afternoon in the church-yard, the cloisters, and the church, amusing myself with the tomb-stones and inscriptions that I met with in those several regions of the dead. Most of them recorded nothing else of the buried person, but that he was born upon one day and died upon another: the whole history of his life being comprehended in those two circumstances, that are common to all mankind. I could not but look upon these registers of existence, whether of brass or marble, as a kind of satire upon the departed persons; who had left no other memorial of them, but that they were born and that they died. They put me in mind of several persons mentioned in the battles of heroic poems, who have sounding names given them, for no other reason but that they may be killed, and are celebrated for nothing but being knocked on the head.

Γλαῦκόν τε Μέδοντά τε Θερσίλοχόν τε. Hom.

Glaucumque, Medontaque, Thersilochumque. Vir.[36]

The life of these men is finely described in Holy Writ by *the path of an arrow,* which is immediately closed up and lost.[37]

Upon my going into the church, I entertained myself with the digging of a grave; and saw in every shovel-full of it that was thrown up, the fragment of a bone or skull intermixed with a kind of fresh mouldering earth that some time or other had a place in the composition of an human body. Upon this, I began to consider with myself what innumerable multitudes of people lay confused together under the pavement of that ancient cathedral; how men and women, friends and enemies, priests and sol-

36. Glaucus, Medon, and Thersilochus were heroes of the Trojan War in Homer's *Iliad* (XVII.216) and Virgil's *Aeneid* (VI.483).
37. "Or like as when an arrow is shot at a mark, it parteth the air, which immediately cometh together again . . . so we in like manner, as soon as we were born, began to draw to our end"; see Apocrypha, Wisdom of Solomon, 5:12–13.

diers, monks and prebendaries, were crumbled amongst one another, and blended together in the same common mass; how beauty, strength, and youth, with old-age, weakness, and deformity, lay undistinguished in the same promiscuous heap of matter.

After having thus surveyed this great magazine of mortality, as it were, in the lump; I examined it more particularly by the accounts which I found on several of the monuments which are raised in every quarter of that ancient fabric. Some of them were covered with such extravagant epitaphs, that, if it were possible for the dead person to be acquainted with them, he would blush at the praises which his friends have bestowed upon him. There are others so excessively modest, that they deliver the character of the person departed in *Greek* or *Hebrew,* and by that means are not understood once in a twelve-month. In the Poetical Quarter, I found there were poets who had no monuments, and monuments which had no poets. I observed indeed that the present war had filled the church with many of these unin-habited monuments, which had been erected to the memory of persons whose bodies were perhaps buried in the plains of *Blenheim,* or in the bo-som of the ocean.[38]

I could not but be very much delighted with several modern epitaphs, which are written with great elegance of expression and justness of thought, and therefore do honour to the living as well as to the dead. As a foreigner is very apt to conceive an idea of the ignorance or politeness of a nation from the turn of their public monuments and inscriptions, they should be submitted to the perusal of men of learning and genius before they are put in execution. Sir *Cloudesly Shovel's* monument has very often given me great offence: instead of the brave rough *English* Admiral, which was the distinguishing character of that plain gallant man, he is represented on his tomb by the figure of a beau, dressed in a long perriwig, and reposing him-self upon velvet cushions under a canopy of state.[39] The inscription is an-swerable to the monument; for instead of celebrating the many remarkable actions he had performed in the service of his country, it acquaints us only

38. The Battle of Blenheim (13 August 1704), in which 52,000 English and Austrian troops led by the Duke of Marlborough confronted 60,000 French and Bavarian troops, marked the English victory in the War of the Spanish Succession.
39. The British admiral Sir Cloudesly Shovel (1650–1707), known for his hot temper and cruel discipline, was drowned in the wreck of his ship off the Scilly Isles.

with the manner of his death, in which it was impossible for him to reap any honour. The *Dutch,* whom we are apt to despise for want of genius, show an infinitely greater taste of antiquity and politeness in their buildings and works of this nature, than what we meet with in those of our own country. The monuments of their admirals, which have been erected at the public expence, represent them like themselves; and are adorned with rostral crowns and naval ornaments, with beautiful festoons of sea-weed, shells, and coral.

But to return to our subject. I have left the repository of our *English* kings for the contemplation of another day,[40] when I shall find my mind disposed for so serious an amusement. I know that entertainments of this nature are apt to raise dark and dismal thoughts in timorous minds, and gloomy imaginations; but for my own part, though I am always serious, I do not know what it is to be melancholy; and can therefore take a view of Nature in her deep and solemn scenes, with the same pleasure as in her most gay and delightful ones. By this means I can improve myself with those objects, which others consider with terror. When I look upon the tombs of the great, every emotion of envy dies in me; when I read the epitaphs of the beautiful, every inordinate desire goes out; when I meet with the grief of parents upon a tomb-stone, my heart melts with compassion; when I see the tomb of the parents themselves, I consider the vanity of grieving for those whom we must quickly follow: when I see kings lying by those who deposed them, when I consider rival wits placed side by side, or the holy men that divided the world with their contests and disputes, I reflect with sorrow and astonishment on the little competitions, factions, and debates of mankind. When I read the several dates of the tombs, of some that died yesterday, and some six hundred years ago, I consider that great day when we shall all of us be contemporaries, and make our appearance together.

30 March 1711

40. See *Spectator* no. 329 in which the Spectator visits the tombs of the Abbey with Sir Roger de Coverly.

No. 46. [The Spectator's Notes]

Non bene junctarum discordia semina rerum. Ovid.[41]

When I want materials for this Paper, it is my custom to go abroad in quest of game; and when I meet any proper subject, I take the first opportunity of setting down an hint of it upon paper. At the same time I look into the letters of my correspondents, and if I find any thing suggested in them that may afford matter of speculation, I likewise enter a minute of it in my collection of materials. By this means I frequently carry about me a whole sheet-full of hints, that would look like a rhapsody of nonsense to any body but myself: there is nothing in them but obscurity and confusion, raving and inconsistency. In short, they are my speculations in the first principles, that (like the world in its chaos) are void of all light, distinction and order.

About a week since there happened to me a very odd accident, by reason of one of these my papers of minutes which I had accidentally dropped at *Lloyd's* Coffee-house, where the auctions are usually kept. Before I missed it, there were a cluster of people who had found it, and were diverting themselves with it at one end of the coffee-house: it had raised so much laughter among them, before I had observed what they were about, that I had not the courage to own it. The boy of the coffee-house, when they had done with it, carried it about in his hand, asking every body if they had dropped a written paper; but no body challenging it, he was ordered by those merry gentlemen who had before perused it, to get up into the auction-pulpit, and read it to the whole room, that if any one would own it they might. The boy accordingly mounted the pulpit, and with a very audible voice read as follows.

MINUTES

Sir Roger de Coverly's Country-Seat————Yes, for I hate long Speeches————Query, if a good Christian may be a Conjurer————*Childermas-day,* Saltseller, House-Dog, Screech-Owl, Cricket,————Mr. *Thomas Inkle* of *London,* in the good

41. "Warring seeds of ill-matched elements"; Ovid, *Metamorphoses,* I.9.

Ship called the *Achilles. Yarico*———*Ægrescitque medendo*[42]—
———Ghosts———The Lady's Library———Lion by Trade a
Tailor———Dromedary called *Bucephalus*———Equipage
the Lady's *summum bonum*———*Charles Lillie* to be taken
Notice of———Short Face a Relief to Envy———Redundan-
cies in the three Professions———King *Latinus* a Recruit—
—Jew devouring an Ham of Bacon———*Westminster-
Abbey*———*Grand Cairo*———Procrastination———*April
Fools*———Blue Boars, Red Lions, Hogs in Armour———
Enter a King and two Fidlers *solus*———Admission into the
Ugly Club———Beauty, how improveable———Families of
true and false Humour———The Parrot's School-Mistress—
———Face half *Pict* half *British*———No Man to be an Hero of
a Tragedy under six Foot———Club of Sighers———Letters
from Flower-Pots, Elbow-Chairs, Tapestry-Figures, Lion,
Thunder———The Bell rings to the Puppet-Show———Old
Woman with a Beard Married to a Smock-faced Boy———My
next Coat to be turn'd up with Blue———Fable of Tongs and
Gridiron———Flower Dyers———The Soldier's Prayer—
—Thank ye for nothing, says the Gally-Pot———*Pactolus* in
Stockings, with golden Clocks to them———Bamboos, Cud-
gels, Drum-sticks———Slip of my Land-lady's eldest Daugh-
ter———The black Mare with a Star in her Forehead———
The Barber's Pole———Will. Honeycomb's Coat-Pocket——
—*Caesar's* Behaviour and my own in Parallel Circumstances—
———Poem in Patch-work———*Nulli gravis est percussus
Achilles*[43]———The Female Conventicler———The Ogle-
Master.

42. The Latin phrase means, "it gets worse in trying to heal it"; see Virgil, *Aeneid*, XII.46. Addison alludes to the story of Thomas Inkle, an English mer- chant, and Yarico, a woman from the West Indies, that was first introduced in *Spec- tator* no. 11. Yarico pleaded with Inkle, upon their return to England, that he not sell her, telling him that she was pregnant with his child. But he only made use of the in- formation to raise her price.

43. "It will hurt no one's feelings to hear how Achilles was slain"; Juvenal, *Satires,* I.163.

The reading of this paper made the whole coffee-house very merry; some of them concluded it was written by a madman, and others by some body that had been taking notes out of the Spectator. One who had the appearance of a very substantial citizen, told us, with several politic winks and nods, that he wished there was no more in the paper than what was expressed in it: that for his part, he looked upon the dromedary, the gridiron, and the barber's pole, to signify something more than what is usually meant by those words; and that he thought the coffee-man could not do better, than to carry the paper to one of the Secretaries of State. He further added, that he did not like the name of the outlandish man with the golden clock in his stockings. A young *Oxford* scholar, who chanced to be with his uncle at the coffee-house, discovered to us who this *Pactolus* was; and by that means turned the whole scheme of this worthy citizen into ridicule.[44] While they were making their several conjectures upon this innocent paper, I reached out my arm to the boy, as he was coming out of the pulpit, to give it me; which he did accordingly. This drew the eyes of the whole company upon me; but after having cast a cursory glance over it, and shook my head twice or thrice at the reading of it, I twisted it into a kind of match, and lit my pipe with it. My profound silence, together with the steadiness of my countenance, and the gravity of my behaviour during this whole transaction, raised a very loud laugh on all sides of me; but as I had escaped all suspicion of being the author, I was very well satisfied; and applying myself to my pipe and the *Post-Man,* took no further notice of any thing that passed about me.

My reader will find, that I have already made use of above half the contents of the foregoing paper; and will easily suppose, that those subjects which are yet untouched, were such provision as I had made for his future entertainment. But as I have been unluckily prevented by this accident, I shall only give him the letters which relate to the two last hints. The first of them I should not have published, were I not informed that there is many an husband who suffers very much in his private affairs by the indiscreet

44. Here the personification of Pactolus, a Lydian river legendary for its golden sands, wears stockings with ornamental designs on the sides (known as "clocks")—clearly a farcical, foppish character, who might have made a good subject for an essay. Unlike other of the Spectator's "notes," though, he never did.

zeal of such a partner as is hereafter mentioned; to whom I may apply the barbarous inscription quoted by the Bishop of *Salisbury* in his travels; *Dum nimia pia est, facta est impia.*[45]

> *Sir,*
>
> I am one of those unhappy men that are plagued with a gospel-gossip, so common among dissenters (especially Friends).[46] Lectures in the morning, church-meetings at noon, and preparation-sermons at night, take up so much of her time, 'tis very rare she knows what we have for dinner, unless when the preacher is to be at it. With him come a tribe, all brothers and sisters it seems; while others, really such, are deemed no relations. If at any time I have her company alone, she is a mere sermon pop-gun, repeating and discharging texts, proofs, and applications so perpetually, that however weary I may go to bed, the noise in my head will not let me sleep till towards morning. The misery of my case, and great numbers of such sufferers, plead your pity and speedy relief; otherwise [I] must expect, in a little time, to be lectured, preached, and prayed into want, unless the happiness of being sooner talked to death prevent it.
>
> *I am, &c.*
> R. G.

The second letter, relating to the Ogling Master, runs thus.

> *Mr.* Spectator,
>
> I am an *Irish* gentleman, that have travelled many years for my improvement; during which time I have accomplished myself in the whole Art of Ogling, as it is at present practised in all the polite nations of *Europe*. Being thus qualified, I intend,

45. "Through too much piety she becomes impious"; quoted in Bishop Gilbert Burnet's *Travels; or, Letters Containing What Seemed Most Remarkable in Switzerland, Italy, France and Germany* (Amsterdam, 1687), 3.

46. "Friends" are Quakers, one of a number of dissenting Protestant sects based on scruples with particular points of the doctrine of the Church of England that emerged in the seventeenth century in Britain.

by the advice of my friends, to set up for an Ogling-Master. I
teach the Church Ogle in the morning, and the Play-house
Ogle by candle-light. I have also brought over with me a new
flying Ogle fit for the Ring; which I teach in the dusk of the
evening, or in any hour of the day by darkening one of my windows. I have a manuscript by me called *The compleat Ogler*,[47]
which I shall be ready to show you upon any occasion: in the
mean time, I beg you will publish the substance of this letter in
an advertisement, and you will very much oblige,

Your, &c.

23 April 1711

No. 58. [On True and False Wit]

Ut pictura poesis erit———Hor.[48]

Nothing is so much admired, and so little understood, as wit. No Author
that I know of has written professedly upon it; and as for those who make
any mention of it, they only treat on the subject as it has accidentally fallen
in their way, and that too in little short reflections, or in general declama-
tory flourishes, without entering into the bottom of the matter. I hope
therefore I shall perform an acceptable work to my countrymen, if I treat at
large upon this subject; which I shall endeavour to do in a manner suitable
to it, that I may not incur the censure which a famous critic bestows upon
one who had written a treatise upon *the Sublime* in a low groveling style.[49]
I intend to lay aside a whole week for this undertaking, that the scheme of
my thoughts may not be broken and interrupted; and I dare promise myself, if my readers will give me a week's attention, that this great city will be
very much changed for the better by next *Saturday* night. I shall endeavour
to make what I say intelligible to ordinary capacities; but if my readers meet
with any Paper that in some parts of it may be a little out of their reach, I

47. After Izaak Walton's *The Compleat Angler* (1653).
48. "A poem is like a picture"; Horace, *Ars poetica*, 361.
49. Longinus begins his treatise *Peri hupsous* (On the Sublime) by criticizing
Caecilius, a Sicilian rhetorician, for his overly cluttered style.

would not have them discouraged, for they may assure themselves the next shall be much clearer.

As the great and only end of these my speculations is to banish vice and ignorance out of the territories of *Great Britain,* I shall endeavour as much as possible to establish among us a taste of polite writing. It is with this view that I have endeavoured to set my readers right in several points relating to operas and tragedies; and shall from time to time impart my notions of comedy, as I think they may tend to its refinement and perfection. I find by my bookseller that these Papers of criticism, with that upon humour, have met with a more kind reception than indeed I could have hoped for from such subjects; for which reason I shall enter upon my present undertaking with greater cheerfulness.

In this, and one or two following Papers, I shall trace out the history of false wit, and distinguish the several kinds of it as they have prevailed in different ages of the world. This I think the more necessary at present, because I observed there were attempts on foot last winter to revive some of those antiquated modes of wit that have been long exploded out of the Commonwealth of Letters. There were several satires and panegyrics handed about in acrostic, by which means some of the most arrant undisputed blockheads about the Town began to entertain ambitious thoughts, and to set up for polite authors. I shall therefore describe at length those many arts of false wit, in which a writer does not show himself a man of a beautiful genius, but of great industry.

The first species of false wit which I have met with is very venerable for its antiquity, and has produced several pieces which have lived very near as long as the *Iliad* itself: I mean those short poems printed among the minor *Greek* poets, which resemble the figure of an Egg, a Pair of Wings, an Ax, a Shepherd's Pipe, and an Altar.[50]

As for the first, it is a little oval poem, and may not improperly be called a Scholar's Egg. I would endeavour to hatch it, or, in more intelligible language, to translate it into *English,* did not I find the interpretation of it very difficult; for the author seems to have been more intent upon the figure of his poem, than upon the sense of it.

---

50. Cf. Ralph Winterton's *Poetæ Minores Græci* (1677), which illustrates the same examples in the same order.

The Pair of Wings consist of twelve verses, or rather feathers, every verse decreasing gradually in its measure according to its situation in the wing. The subject of it (as in the rest of the poems which follow) bears some remote affinity with the figure, for it describes a god of love, who is always painted with wings.

The Ax methinks would have been a good figure for a lampoon, had the edge of it consisted of the most satirical parts of the work; but as it is in the original, I take it to have been nothing else but the posy of an ax which was consecrated to *Minerva,* and was thought to have been the same that *Epeus* made use of in the building of the *Trojan* Horse; which is a hint I shall leave to the consideration of the critics.[51] I am apt to think that the posie was written originally upon the ax, like those which our modern cutlers inscribe upon their knives; and that therefore the posie still remains in its ancient shape, though the ax itself is lost.

The Shepherd's Pipe may be said to be full of music, for it is composed of nine different kinds of verses, which by their several lengths resemble the nine stops of the old musical instrument, that is likewise the subject of the poem.

The Altar is inscribed with the epitaph of *Troilus* the son of *Hecuba;* which, by the way, makes me believe, that these false pieces of wit are much more ancient than the authors to whom they are generally ascribed; at least I will never be persuaded, that so fine a writer as *Theocritus* could have been the author of any such simple works.[52]

It was impossible for a man to succeed in these performances who was not a kind of painter, or at least a designer: he was first of all to draw the outline of the subject which he intended to write upon, and afterwards conform the description to the figure of his subject. The poetry was to contract or dilate itself according to the mould in which it was cast. In a word, the verses were to be cramped or extended to the dimensions of the frame that

51. A posy is a motto. Minerva was the Roman goddess of wisdom and Epeus the chief craftsman of the Trojan Horse; see Virgil, *Aeneid,* II.264.

52. The Trojan prince Troilus, son of Priam and Hecuba, was killed by Achilles; his love for the faithless Cressida was familiar through both Chaucer's *Troilus and Criseyde* and Shakespeare's *Troilus and Cressida.* Theocritus was an ancient Greek poet famous for his bucolic idylls.

was prepared for them; and to undergo the fate of those persons whom the tyrant *Procrustes* used to lodge in his iron bed; if they were too short he stretched them on a rack, and if they were too long chopped off a part of their legs, till they fitted the couch which he had prepared for them.

Mr. *Dryden* hints at this obsolete kind of wit in one of the following verses, in his *Mac Fleckno;* which an *English* reader cannot understand, who does not know that there are those little poems abovementioned in the shape of wings and altars.

> ————*Chuse for thy Command*
> *Some peaceful Province in Acrostick Land;*
> *There may'st thou Wings display, and Altars raise,*
> *And torture one poor Word a thousand Ways.*[53]

This fashion of false wit was revived by several poets of the last age, and in particular may be met with among Mr. *Herbert's* poems; and, if I am not mistaken, in the translation of *Du Bartas.*[54] I do not remember any other kind of work among the moderns which more resembles the performances I have mentioned, than that famous picture of King *Charles* I which has the whole book of *Psalms* written in the lines of the face and the hair of the head. When I was last at *Oxford* I perused one of the whiskers; and was reading the other, but could not go so far in it as I would have done, by reason of the impatience of my friends and fellow-travellers, who all of them pressed to see such a piece of curiosity. I have since heard, that there is now an eminent writing-master in town, who has transcribed all the *Old Testament* in a full-bottomed perriwig; and if the fashion should introduce the thick kind of wigs which were in vogue some few years ago, he promises to add two or three supernumerary locks that shall contain all the *Apocrypha*. He designed this wig originally for King *William*, having disposed of the

53. John Dryden's *Mac Flecknoe* (1682) was a satire on the playwright and poet laureate Thomas Shadwell (1642–92); Addison quotes lines 205–8 here.

54. George Herbert's *The Temple* (1633) contains the picture poems "The Altar" and "Easter Wings." Joshua Silvester's 1605 edition of Guillaume Du Bartas's *Divine Weeks and Works* contains anagrams and concrete poems in its editorial apparatus.

two books of *Kings* in the two forks of the fore top; but that glorious monarch dying before the wig was finished, there is a space left in it for the face of any one who has a mind to purchase it.

But to return to our ancient poems in picture, I would humbly propose, for the benefit of our modern smatterers in poetry, that they would imitate their brethren among the Ancients in those ingenious devices. I have communicated this thought to a young poetical lover of my acquaintance, who intends to present his mistress with a copy of verses made in the shape of her fan; and, if he tells me true, has already finished the three first sticks of it. He has likewise promised me to get the measure of his mistress's marriage-finger, with a design to make a posy in the fashion of a ring which shall exactly fit it. It is so very easy to enlarge upon a good hint, that I do not question but my ingenious readers will apply what I have said to many other particulars; and that we shall see the Town filled in a very little time with poetical tippets, handkerchiefs, snuff-boxes, and the like female-ornaments. I shall therefore conclude with a word of advice to those admirable *English* authors who call themselves Pindaric writers,[55] that they would apply themselves to this kind of wit without loss of time, as being provided better than any other poets with verses of all sizes and dimensions.

7 May 1711

No. 81. [Party Patches]

Qualis ubi audito venantum murmure Tigris
Horruit in maculas————Statius.[56]

About the middle of last winter I went to see an *Opera* at the theatre in the *Hay-Market*, where I could not but take notice of two parties of very fine women, that had placed themselves in the opposite side-boxes, and seemed drawn up in a kind of battle-array one against another. After a short survey of them, I found they were *Patched* differently; the faces, on one hand, being spotted on the right side of the forehead, and those upon the other on

55. The Greek poet Pindar was known for the ornate verse structure of his odes.

56. "Just as when a tigress hearing the noise of hunters is terrified at the meshes"; Statius, *Thebaid*, II.128–29.

the left.[57] I quickly perceived that they cast hostile glances upon one another; and that their patches were placed in those different situations, as party-signals to distinguish friends from foes. In the middle-boxes, between these two opposite bodies, were several ladies who patched indifferently on both sides of their faces, and seemed to sit there with no other intention but to see the *Opera*. Upon enquiry I found, that the body of *Amazons* on my right hand, were Whigs; and those on my left, Tories; and that those who had placed themselves in the middle-boxes were a neutral party, whose faces had not yet declared themselves. These last, however, as I afterwards found, diminished daily, and took their party with one side or the other; insomuch that I observed in several of them, the patches which were before dispersed equally, are now all gone over to the Whig or Tory side of the face. The censorious say, That the men whose hearts are aimed at are very often the occasions that one part of the face is thus dishonoured, and lies under a kind of disgrace, while the other is so much set off and adorned by the owner; and that the patches turn to the right or to the left, according to the principles of the man who is most in favour. But whatever may be the motives of a few fantastical coquets, who do not patch for the public good, so much as for their own private advantage; it is certain, that there are several women of honour who patch out of principle, and with an eye to the interest of their country. Nay, I am informed, that some of them adhere so steadfastly to their party, and are so far from sacrificing their zeal for the public to their passion for any particular person, that in a late draft of marriage-articles a lady has stipulated with her husband, that, whatever his opinions are, she shall be at liberty to patch on which side she pleases.

I must here take notice, that *Rosalinda,* a famous Whig partizan, has most unfortunately a very beautiful mole on the Tory part of her forehead; which, being very conspicuous, has occasioned many mistakes, and given an handle to her enemies to misrepresent her face, as though it had revolted from the Whig interest. But whatever this natural patch may seem to intimate, it is well known that her notions of government are still the same. This unlucky mole however has misled several coxcombs; and, like the

---

57. Face patches were pieces of silk used to cover blemishes, particularly those caused by smallpox. By the Restoration, they had become a fashion accessory among the elite.

hanging out of false colours,[58] made some of them converse with *Rosa-linda* in what they thought the spirit of her party, when on a sudden she has given them an unexpected fire, that has sunk them all at once. If *Rosalinda* is unfortunate in her mole, *Nigranilla* is as unhappy in a pimple, which forces her, against her inclinations, to patch on the Whig side.

I am told that many virtuous matrons, who formerly have been taught to believe that this artificial spotting of the face was unlawful, are now reconciled by a zeal for their cause, to what they could not be prompted by a concern for their beauty. This way of declaring war upon one another, puts me in mind of what is reported of the tigress, that several spots rise in her skin when she is angry; or as Mr. *Cowley* has imitated the verses that stand as the motto of this Paper,

> ———*She Swells with angry Pride,*
> *And calls forth all her Spots on ev'ry side.*[59]

When I was in the theatre the time abovementioned, I had the cu-riosity to count the patches on both sides, and found the Tory patches to be about twenty stronger than the Whig; but to make amends for this small in-equality, I the next morning found the whole puppet-show filled with faces spotted after the Whiggish manner. Whether or no the ladies had retreated hither in order to rally their forces I cannot tell; but the next night they came in so great a body to the opera, that they outnumbered the enemy.

This account of party-patches will, I am afraid, appear improbable to those who live at a distance from the fashionable world; but as it is a dis-tinction of a very singular nature, and what perhaps may never meet with a parallel, I think I should not have discharged the office of a faithful Specta-tor had I not recorded it.

I have, in former Papers, endeavoured to expose this party-rage in women,[60] as it only serves to aggravate the hatreds and animosities that

58. A warship would sometimes hoist the flag of its enemy (false colors) in order to pass safely through lines of enemy ships.

59. Abraham Cowley, *Davideis* (1656), III.403–4.

60. See, e.g., *Spectator* no. 57, in which the Spectator lectures women about the unsuitability of "party rage" to the fair sex and the havoc it plays upon beauty.

reign among men, and in a great measure deprives the fair sex of those peculiar charms with which Nature has endowed them.

When the *Romans* and *Sabines* were at war, and just upon the point of
giving battle, the women, who were allied to both of them, interposed with
so many tears and entreaties, that they prevented the mutual slaughter
which threatened both parties, and united them together in a firm and lasting peace.

I would recommend this noble example to our *British* ladies, at a time
when their country is torn with so many unnatural divisions, that if they
continue, it will be a misfortune to be born in it. The *Greeks* thought it so
improper for women to interest themselves in competitions and contentions, that for this reason, among others, they forbade them, under pain
of death, to be present at the *Olympic* Games, notwithstanding these were
the public diversions of all *Greece*.

As our *English* women excel those of all nations in beauty, they should
endeavour to outshine them in all other accomplishments proper to the
sex, and to distinguish themselves as tender mothers and faithful wives,
rather than as furious partizans. Female virtues are of a domestic turn. The
family is the proper province for private women to shine in. If they must be
showing their zeal for the public, let it not be against those who are perhaps
of the same family, or at least of the same religion or nation, but against
those who are the open, professed, undoubted enemies of their faith, liberty, and country. When the *Romans* were pressed with a foreign enemy,
the ladies voluntarily contributed all their rings and jewels to assist the government under a public exigence; which appeared so laudable an action in
the eyes of their countrymen, that from thenceforth it was permitted by a
law to pronounce public orations at the funeral of a woman in praise of the
deceased person, which till that time was peculiar to men.[61] Would our *English* ladies, instead of sticking on a patch against those of their own country, show themselves so truly public-spirited as to sacrifice every one her
necklace against the common enemy, what decrees ought not to be made in
favour of them?

Since I am recollecting upon this subject such passages as occur to my

61. During of the Second Punic War (218–201 B.C.), Roman women responded to the suggestion of Marcus Lavinus to do as Addison describes.

memory out of ancient authors, I cannot omit a sentence in the celebrated funeral oration of *Pericles,* which he made in honour of those brave *Athenians* that were slain in a fight with the *Lacedemonians.* After having addressed himself to the several ranks and orders of his countrymen, and shown them how they should behave themselves in the public cause, he turns to the female part of his audience; "And as for you (says he) I shall advise you in very few words: aspire only to those virtues that are peculiar to your sex; follow your natural modesty, and think it your greatest commendation not to be talked of one way or other."[62]

2 June 1711.

No. 106. [A Visit to Sir Roger's]

——*Hic tibi Copia*
Manabit ad plenum benigno
Ruris honorum opulenta cornu. Hor.[63]

Having often received an invitation from my friend Sir Roger de Coverly to pass away a month with him in the Country, I last week accompanied him thither, and am settled with him for some time at his country-house, where I intend to form several of my ensuing Speculations. Sir Roger, who is very well acquainted with my humour, lets me rise and go to bed when I please, dine at his own table or in my chamber as I think fit, sit still and say nothing without bidding me be merry. When the gentlemen of the Country come to see him, he only shows me at a distance: as I have been walking in his fields I have observed them stealing a sight of me over an hedge, and have heard the Knight desiring them not to let me see them, for that I hated to be stared at.

I am the more at ease in Sir Roger's family, because it consists of sober and staid persons; for as the Knight is the best master in the world, he seldom changes his servants; and as he is beloved by all about him, his servants never care for leaving him: by this means his domestics are all in years, and

62. See Thucydides, *The History of the Peloponnesian War,* trans. Rex Warner (Harmondsworth, England: Penguin, 1954), 151.

63. "In this spot shall rich abundance of the glories of the field flow to the full for thee from bounteous horn"; Horace, *Odes,* I.17.14–16.

grown old with their master. You would take his valet de chambre for his brother, his butler is grey-headed, his groom is one of the gravest men that I have ever seen, and his coachman has the looks of a privy-counsellor. You see the goodness of the master even in the old housedog, and in a grey pad that is kept in the stable with great care and tenderness out of regard to his past services, though he has been useless for several years.[64]

I could not but observe with a great deal of pleasure the joy that appeared in the countenances of these ancient domestics upon my friend's arrival at his country-seat. Some of them could not refrain from tears at the sight of their old master; every one of them pressed forward to do something for him, and seemed discouraged if they were not employed. At the same time the good old Knight, with a mixture of the father and the master of the family, tempered the enquiries after his own affairs with several kind questions relating to themselves. This humanity and good-nature engages every body to him, so that when he is pleasant upon any of them, all his family are in good humour, and none so much as the person whom he diverts himself with: on the contrary, if he coughs, or betrays any infirmity of old age, it is easy for a stander-by to observe a secret concern in the looks of all his servants.

My worthy friend has put me under the particular care of his butler, who is a very prudent man, and, as well as the rest of his fellow-servants, wonderfully desirous of pleasing me, because they have often heard their master talk of me as of his particular friend.

My chief companion, when Sir Roger is diverting himself in the woods or the fields, is a very venerable man, who is ever with Sir Roger, and has lived at his house in the nature of a chaplain above thirty years. This gentleman is a person of good sense and some learning, of a very regular life and obliging conversation: he heartily loves Sir Roger, and knows that he is very much in the old Knight's esteem; so that he lives in the family rather as a relation than a dependant.

I have observed in several of my Papers, that my friend Sir Roger, amidst all his good qualities, is something of an humourist; and that his virtues, as well as imperfections, are as it were tinged by a certain extrava-

64. The grey pad is an easy-paced riding horse, so-called for his padded saddle.

gance, which makes them particularly *his,* and distinguishes them from those of other men. This cast of mind, as it is generally very innocent in itself, so it renders his conversation highly agreeable, and more delightful than the same degree of sense and virtue would appear in their common and ordinary colours. As I was walking with him last night, he asked me how I liked the good man whom I have just now mentioned? and without staying for my answer, told me, That he was afraid of being insulted with Latin and Greek at his own table; for which reason, he desired a particular friend of his at the university to find him out a clergyman rather of plain sense than much learning, of a good aspect, a clear voice, a sociable temper, and, if possible, a man that understood a little of back-gammon. My friend, says Sir Roger, found me out this gentleman, who, besides the endowments required of him, is, they tell me, a good scholar though he does not show it. I have given him the parsonage of the parish; and because I know his value, have settled upon him a good annuity for life. If he out-lives me, he shall find that he was higher in my esteem than perhaps he thinks he is. He has now been with me thirty years; and though he does not know I have taken notice of it, has never in all that time asked any thing of me for himself, though he is every day soliciting me for something in behalf of one or other of my tenants his parishioners. There has not been a law-suit in the parish since he has lived among them: if any dispute arises, they apply themselves to him for the decision; if they do not acquiesce in his judgment, which I think never happened above once, or twice at most, they appeal to me. At his first settling with me, I made him a present of all the good sermons which have been printed in *English,* and only begged of him that every *Sunday* he would pronounce one of them in the pulpit. Accordingly, he has digested them into such a series, that they follow one another naturally, and make a continued system of practical divinity.

As Sir Roger was going on in his story, the gentleman we were talking of came up to us; and upon the Knight's asking him who preached tomorrow (for it was *Saturday* night) told us, the Bishop of St. *Asaph* in the morning, and Doctor *South* in the afternoon. He then showed us his list of preachers for the whole year, where I saw with a great deal of pleasure Archbishop *Tillotson;* Bishop *Saunderson,* Doctor *Barrow,* Doctor *Calamy,* with several living authors who have published Discourses of Practical Divinity.[65] I no sooner saw this venerable man in the pulpit, but I very much approved of my friend's insisting upon the qualifications of a good aspect and a clear voice; for I was so charmed with the gracefulness of his figure and delivery, as well as with the discourses he pronounced, that I think I never passed any time more to my satisfaction. A sermon repeated after this manner, is like the composition of a poet in the mouth of a graceful actor.

I could heartily wish that more of our country-clergy would follow this example; and instead of wasting their spirits in laborious compositions of their own, would endeavour after a handsome elocution, and all those other talents that are proper to enforce what has been penned by greater masters. This would not only be more easy to themselves, but more edifying to the people.

2 July 1711

No. 112. [Sir Roger at Church]

Ἀθανάτους μὲν πρῶτα θεούς, νόμῳ ὡς
διάκεινται τιμᾶ———Pyth.[66]

I am always very well pleased with a Country *Sunday;* and think, if keeping holy the seventh day were only a human institution, it would be the best method that could have been thought of for the polishing and civilizing of mankind. It is certain the country-people would soon degenerate into a kind of savages and barbarians, were there not such frequent returns of a stated time, in which the whole village meet together with their best faces, and in their cleanliest habits, to converse with one another upon indifferent subjects, hear their duties explained to them, and join together in adoration

65. Popular preachers during the reign of Charles II: Doctor Robert South (1634–1716) is praised in *Tatler* no. 61 and quoted in nos. 205 and 211. Steele quotes John Tillotson (1630–94), archbishop of Canterbury, in *Spectator* no. 103. Robert Saunderson (1587–1663), chaplain to Charles I and later Bishop of Lincoln, held strong Tory views that would have pleased Sir Roger. Isaac Barrow (1630–77) was a distinguished mathematician as well as preacher; Edmund Calamy (1600–1666) was an eminent Presbyterian.

66. "Indeed, first revere the immortal gods, as it is set down by law"; attributed to Pythagoras, *Golden Verses,* 1–2.

of the supreme being. *Sunday* clears away the rust of the whole week, not only as it refreshes in their minds the notions of religion, but as it puts both the sexes upon appearing in their most agreeable forms, and exerting all such qualities as are apt to give them a figure in the eye of the village. A country-fellow distinguishes himself as much in the *Church-yard*, as a citizen does upon the *Change;* the whole parish-politics being generally discussed in that place either after sermon or before the bell rings.

My friend Sir Roger being a good church-man, has beautified the inside of his church with several texts of his own choosing: he has likewise given a handsome pulpit-cloth, and railed in the communion-table at his own expence. He has often told me, that at his coming to his estate he found his parishioners very irregular; and that in order to make them kneel and join in the responses, he gave every one of them a hassock and a Common-prayer Book; and at the same time employed an itinerant singing-master, who goes about the country for that purpose, to instruct them rightly in the tunes of the Psalms; upon which they now very much value themselves, and indeed out-do most of the country churches that I have ever heard.

As Sir Roger is landlord to the whole congregation, he keeps them in very good order, and will suffer no body to sleep in it besides himself; for if by chance he has been surprized into a short nap at sermon, upon recovering out of it he stands up and looks about him, and if he sees any body else nodding, either wakes them himself, or sends his servant to them. Several other of the old Knight's particularities break out upon these occasions: sometimes he will be lengthening out a verse in the singing-psalms, half a minute after the rest of the congregation have done with it; sometimes, when he is pleased with the matter of his devotion, he pronounces *Amen* three or four times to the same prayer; and sometimes stands up when every body else is upon their knees, to count the congregation, or see if any of his tenants are missing.

I was yesterday very much surprized to hear my old friend, in the midst of the service, calling out to one *John Matthews* to mind what he was about, and not disturb the congregation. This *John Matthews* it seems is remarkable for being an idle fellow, and at that time was kicking his heels for his diversion. This authority of the Knight, though exerted in that odd manner which accompanies him in all circumstances of life, has a very good effect upon the parish, who are not polite enough to see any thing ridiculous in his behaviour; besides that, the general good sense and worthiness of his character, make his friends observe these little singularities as foils that rather set off than blemish his good qualities.

As soon as the sermon is finished, no body presumes to stir till Sir Roger is gone out of the church. The Knight walks down from his seat in the chancel between a double row of his tenants, that stand bowing to him on each side; and every now and then enquires how such an one's wife, or mother, or son, or father do whom he does not see at church; which is understood as a secret reprimand to the person that is absent.

The Chaplain has often told me, that upon a Catechizing-day, when Sir Roger has been pleased with a boy that answers well, he has ordered a Bible to be given him next day for his encouragement; and sometimes accompanies it with a flitch of bacon to his mother. Sir Roger has likewise added five pounds a year to the Clerk's place; and that he may encourage the young fellows to make themselves perfect in the church-service, has promised upon the death of the present Incumbent, who is very old, to bestow it according to merit.

The fair understanding between Sir Roger and his Chaplain, and their mutual concurrence in doing good, is the more remarkable, because the very next village is famous for the differences and contentions that rise between the Parson and the 'Squire, who live in a perpetual state of war. The Parson is always preaching at the 'Squire, and the 'Squire to be revenged on the Parson never comes to church. The 'Squire has made all his tenants atheists and tithe-stealers;[67] while the Parson instructs them every *Sunday* in the dignity of his order, and insinuates to them in almost every sermon, that he is a better man than his patron. In short, matters are come to such an extremity, that the 'Squire has not said his prayers either in public or private this half year; and that the Parson threatens him, if he does not mend his manners, to pray for him in the face of the whole congregation.

Feuds of this nature, though too frequent in the Country, are very fatal to the ordinary people; who are so used to be dazzled with riches, that they pay as much deference to the understanding of a man of an estate, as of

67. Tenants who did not attend church services avoided paying the 10 percent tax, or tithe, on their earnings.

a man of learning; and are very hardly brought to regard any truth, how important soever it may be, that is preached to them, when they know there are several men of five hundred a year who do not believe it.

9 July 1711

No. 130. [Sir Roger and the Gypsies]

————*Semperque recentes*
Convectare juvat praedas, & vivere rapto. Virg.[68]

As I was yesterday riding out in the fields with my friend Sir Roger, we saw at a little distance from us a troop of Gypsies. Upon the first discovery of them, my friend was in some doubt whether he should not exert the *Justice of the Peace* upon such a band of lawless vagrants; but not having his Clerk with him, who is a necessary counsellour on these occasions, and fearing that his poultry might fare the worse for it, he let the thought drop: but at the same time gave me a particular account of the mischiefs they do in the Country, in stealing people's goods and spoiling their servants.[69] If a stray piece of linnen hangs upon an hedge, says Sir Roger, they are sure to have it; if a hog loses his way in the fields, it is ten to one but he becomes their prey; our geese cannot live in peace for them; if a man prosecutes them with severity, his hen-roost is sure to pay for it: they generally straggle into these parts about this time of the year; and set the heads of our servant-maids so agog for husbands, that we do not expect to have any business done, as it should be, whilst they are in the Country. I have an honest dairy-maid who crosses their hands with a piece of silver every summer; and never fails being promised the handsomest young fellow in the parish for her pains. Your friend the butler has been fool enough to be seduced by them; and though he is sure to lose a knife, a fork, or a spoon every time his fortune is told him, generally shuts himself up in the pantry with an old Gypsy for above half an hour once in a twelve-month. Sweet-hearts are the things they live upon, which they bestow very plentifully upon all those that apply them-

68. "It is ever their joy to bear away fresh booty, and to live on plunder"; Virgil, *Aeneid*, VII.748–49.
69. To exercise his powers as justice of the peace would be to make an arrest. His clerk, trained in law, would give advice on such occasions.

selves to them. You see now and then some handsome young jades among them: the sluts have often very white teeth and black eyes.

Sir Roger observing that I listened with great attention to his account of a people who were so entirely new to me, told me, That if I would they should tell us our fortunes. As I was very well pleased with the Knight's proposal, we rode up and communicated our hands to them. A *Cassandra* of the crew,[70] after having examined my lines very diligently, told me, That I loved a pretty maid in a corner, that I was a good woman's man, with some other particulars which I do not think proper to relate. My friend Sir Roger alighted from his horse, and exposing his palm to two or three that stood by him, they crumpled it into all shapes, and diligently scanned every wrinkle that could be made in it; when one of them who was older and more sun-burnt than the rest, told him, That he had a widow in his line of life: upon which the Knight cried, Go, go, you are an idle baggage; and at the same time smiled upon me. The Gypsy finding he was not displeased in his heart, told him, after a further enquiry into his hand, that his true-love was constant, and that she should dream of him tonight. My old friend cried pish, and bid her go on. The Gypsy told him that he was a bachelor, but would not be so long; and that he was dearer to some body than he thought: the Knight still repeated, She was an idle baggage, and bid her go on. Ah Master says the Gypsy, that roguish leer of yours makes a pretty woman's heart ache; you ha'n't that simper about the mouth for nothing— The uncouth gibberish with which all this was uttered, like the darkness of an oracle, made us the more attentive to it. To be short, the Knight left the money with her that he had crossed her hand with, and got up again on his horse.

As we were riding away, Sir Roger told me, that he knew several sensible people who believed these Gypsies now and then foretold very strange things; and for half an hour together appeared more jocund than ordinary. In the height of his good humour, meeting a common beggar upon the road who was no conjuror, as he went to relieve him he found his pocket was picked: that being a kind of palmistry at which this race of vermin are very dexterous.

70. The Trojan princess Cassandra, a daughter of Priam and Hecuba, possessed the gift of prophecy, though it was her peculiar curse never to be believed.

I might here entertain my reader with historical remarks on this idle profligate people, who infest all the countries of *Europe,* and live in the midst of governments in a kind of commonwealth by themselves. But instead of entering into observations of this nature, I shall fill the remaining part of my Paper with a story which is still fresh in *Holland,* and was printed in one of our monthly accounts about twenty years ago.

"As the *Trekschuyt,* or Hackney-boat, which carries passengers from *Leiden* to *Amsterdam,* was putting off, a boy running along the side of the canal, desired to be taken in; which the Master of the Boat refused, because the lad had not quite money enough to pay the usual fare. An eminent merchant being pleased with the looks of the boy, and secretly touched with compassion towards him, paid the money for him, and ordered him to be taken on board. Upon talking with him afterwards, he found that he could speak readily in three or four languages, and learned upon further examination that he had been stolen away when he was a child by a Gypsy, and had rambled ever since with a gang of those strollers up and down several parts of *Europe.* It happened that the merchant, whose heart seems to have inclined towards the boy by a secret kind of instinct, had himself lost a child some years before. The parents, after a long search for him, gave him for drowned in one of the canals with which that country abounds; and the mother was so afflicted at the loss of a fine boy, who was her only son, that she died for grief of it. Upon laying together all particulars, and examining the several moles and marks by which the mother used to describe the child when he was first missing, the boy proved to be the son of the merchant, whose heart had so unaccountably melted at the sight of him. The lad was very well pleased to find a father, who was so rich, and likely to leave him a good estate; the father, on the other hand, was not a little delighted to see a son return to him, whom he had given for lost, with such a strength of constitution, sharpness of understanding, and skill in languages."

Here the printed story leaves off; but if I may give credit to reports, our linguist having received such extraordinary rudiments towards a good education, was afterwards trained up in every thing that becomes a gentleman; wearing off by little and little all the vicious habits and practices that he had been used to in the course of his peregrinations: nay, it is said, that he has since been employed in foreign courts upon national business, with great reputation to himself and honour to those who sent him, and that he has visited several countries as a public minister, in which he formerly wandered as a Gypsy.

30 July 1711

No. 235. [The Trunk-Maker as Drama Critic]

——*Populares*
Vincentem strepitus——Hor.[71]

There is nothing which lies more within the province of a Spectator than public shows and diversions; and as among these there are none which can pretend to vie with those elegant entertainments that are exhibited in our theatres, I think it particularly incumbent on me to take notice of every thing that is remarkable in such numerous and refined assemblies.

It is observed, that of late years, there has been a certain person in the Upper Gallery of the play-house, who when he is pleased with any thing that is acted upon the stage, expresses his approbation by a loud knock upon the benches, or the wainscot, which may be heard over the whole theatre. This person is commonly known by the name of the *Trunk-maker in the Upper-Gallery.*[72] Whether it be, that the blow he gives on these occasions resembles that which is often heard in the shops of such artizans, or that he was supposed to have been a real trunk-maker, who after the finishing of his day's work, used to unbend his mind at these public diversions with his hammer in his hand, I cannot certainly tell. There are some, I

71. "Able to drown the clamours of the pit"; Horace, *Ars poetica*, ll. 81–82.
72. Trunk makers were associated with the demolition of literary works because they lined trunks with paper from books that did not sell. Cf. Henry Fielding's "Uses to Which Learning Is Put" in chap. 5 of this volume.

know, who have been foolish enough to imagine it is a spirit which haunts the Upper-Gallery, and from time to time makes those strange noises; and the rather, because he is observed to be louder than ordinary every time the ghost of *Hamlet* appears. Others have reported, that it is a dumb man, who has chosen this way of uttering himself, when he is transported with any thing he sees or hears. Others will have it to be the play-house thunderer,[73] that exerts himself after this manner in the Upper-Gallery, when he has nothing to do upon the roof.

But having made it my business to get the best information I could in a matter of this moment, I find that the Trunk-maker, as he is commonly called, is a large black man, whom no body knows. He generally leans forward on a huge oaken plant with great attention to every thing that passes upon the stage. He is never seen to smile; but upon hearing anything that pleases him, he takes up his staff with both hands, and lays it upon the next piece of timber that stands in his way with exceeding vehemence: after which he composes himself in his former posture, till such time as something new sets him again at work.

It has been observed his blow is so well timed, that the most judicious critic could never except against it. As soon as any shining thought is expressed in the poet, or any uncommon grace appears in the actor, he smites the bench or wainscot. If the audience does not concur with him, he smites a second time; and if the audience is not yet awaked, looks round him with great wrath, and repeats the blow a third time, which never fails to produce the clap. He sometimes lets the audience begin the clap of themselves, and at the conclusion of their applause ratifies it with a single thwack.

He is of so great use to the play-house, that it is said a former Director of it, upon his not being able to pay his attendance by reason of sickness, kept one in pay to officiate for him till such time as he recovered; but the person so employed, though he laid about him with incredible violence, did it in such wrong places, that the audience soon found out it was not their old friend the Trunk-maker.

It has been remarked, that he has not yet exerted himself with vigour this season. He sometimes plies at the Opera; and upon *Nicolini*'s first ap-

73. Whose job was to produce the sound of thunder for theatrical performances.

pearance, was said to have demolished three benches in the fury of his applause.[74] He has broken half a dozen oaken plants upon *Dogget,* and seldom goes away from a tragedy of *Shakespeare,* without leaving the wainscot extremely shattered.[75]

The players do not only connive at this his obstreperous approbation, but very cheerfully repair at their own cost whatever damages he makes. They had once a thought of erecting a kind of wooden anvil for his use, that should be made of a very sounding plank, in order to render his strokes more deep and mellow; but as this might not have been distinguished from the music of a kettle drum, the project was laid aside.

In the mean while I cannot but take notice of the great use it is to an audience, that a person should thus preside over their heads, like the Director of a Concert, in order to awaken their attention, and beat time to their applauses. Or to raise my simile, I have sometimes fancied the Trunk-maker in the Upper Gallery to be like *Virgil*'s Ruler of the Winds, seated upon the top of a mountain, who, when he struck his sceptre upon the side of it, roused an hurricane, and set the whole cavern in an uproar.[76] It is certain the Trunk-maker has saved many a good play, and brought many a graceful actor into reputation, who would not otherwise have been taken notice of. It is very visible, as the audience is not a little abashed, if they find themselves betrayed into a clap, when their friend in the Upper-Gallery does not come into it; so the actors do not value themselves upon the clap, but regard it as a mere *Brutum fulmen,* or empty noise,[77] when it has not the sound of the oaken plant in it. I know it has been given out by those who are enemies to the Trunk-maker, that he has sometimes been bribed to be in the interest of a bad poet, or a vicious player; but this is a surmise, which has no foundation; his strokes are always just, and his admonitions seasonable; he does not deal about his blows at random, but always hits the right

74. Nicolini was the stage name of the opera singer Nicola Grimaldi (1673–1732).

75. The oaken plant is an allusion to Edmund Spenser, *The Faerie Queene:* "Himselfe vnto his weapon he betooke, / That was an oaken plant, which lately hee / Rent by the root" (VI.vii.24). Thomas Doggett (d. 1721) was a comic actor.

76. See Virgil, *Aeneid,* I.81–83.

77. Literally, "bolt of lightning"; there is a pun on *clap* (venereal disease), associated with the licentiousness of the theaters.

nail upon the head. The inexpressible force wherewith he lays them on, sufficiently shows the evidence and strength of his conviction. His zeal for a good author is indeed outrageous, and breaks down every force and partition, every board and plank, that stands within the expression of his applause.

As I do not care for terminating my thoughts in barren speculations, or in reports of pure matter of fact, without drawing something from them for the advantage of my countrymen, I shall take the liberty to make an humble proposal, that whenever the Trunk-maker shall depart this life, or whenever he shall have lost the spring of his arm by sickness, old age, infirmity, or the like, some able-bodied Critic should be advanced to this post, and have a competent salary settled on him for life, to be furnished with bamboos for operas, crabtree-cudgels for comedies, and oaken plants for tragedy, at the public expence.[78] And to the end that this place should always be disposed of, according to merit, I would have none preferred to it, who has not given convincing proofs, both of a sound judgment and a strong arm, and who could not, upon occasion, either knock down an ox or write a comment upon *Horace*'s Art of Poetry. In short, I would have him a due composition of *Hercules* and *Apollo,* and so rightly qualified for this important office, that the *Trunk-maker* may not be missed by our posterity.

20 November 1711

No. 409. [On Taste]

———*Musaeo contingere cuncta lepore.* Lucr.[79]

Gratian very often recommends *the fine taste,* as the utmost perfection of an accomplished man.[80] As this word arises very often in conversation, I

78. Bamboo wood, which is hollow, suits the airy nature of opera; crab-tree cudgels, producing a sharp snap, suit the liveliness of comedy; and solid oak is heavy enough for tragedy.

79. "To grace each subject with wit"; Lucretius, *De rerum natura* (On the Nature of Things), I.934. Addison alters the quotation from "musaeo contingens cuncta lepore."

80. The Spanish Baroque writer Baltasar Gracián y Morales (1601–58), whose *Agudeza y arte de ingenio* (Wit and the Art of Invention, 1642) outlines the literary style known as "Conceptismo," which is characterized by directness (as op-

shall endeavour to give some account of it, and to lay down rules how we may know whether we are possessed of it, and how we may acquire that fine taste of writing, which is so much talked of among the Polite World.

Most languages make use of this metaphor, to express that faculty of the mind, which distinguishes all the most concealed faults and nicest perfections in writing. We may be sure this metaphor would not have been so general in all tongues, had there not been a very great conformity between that mental taste, which is the subject of this Paper, and that sensitive taste which gives us a relish of every different flavour that affects the palate. Accordingly we find, there are as many degrees of refinement in the intellectual faculty, as in the sense, which is marked out by this common denomination.

I knew a person who possessed the one in so great a perfection, that after having tasted ten different kinds of tea, he would distinguish, without seeing the colour of it, the particular sort which was offered him; and not only so, but any two sorts of them that were mixed together in an equal proportion; nay, he has carried the experiment so far, as upon tasting the composition of three different sorts, to name the parcels from whence the three several ingredients were taken. A man of a fine taste in writing will discern after the same manner, not only the general beauties and imperfections of an author, but discover the several ways of thinking and expressing himself, which diversify him from all other authors, with the several foreign infusions of thought and language, and the particular authors from whom they were borrowed.

After having thus far explained what is generally meant by a fine taste in writing, and shown the propriety of the metaphor which is used on this occasion, I think I may define it to be *that faculty of the soul, which discerns the beauties of an author with pleasure, and the imperfections with dislike*. If a man would know whether he is possessed of this faculty, I would have him read over the celebrated works of Antiquity, which have stood the test of so many different ages and countries; or those works among the Moderns, which have the sanction of the politer part of our contemporaries. If upon the perusal of such writings he does not find himself delighted in an ex-

---

posed to ornate diction and syntactic ostentation) and creative thought (as opposed to conventional, uninspired content).

traordinary manner, or if, upon reading the admired passages in such authors, he finds a coldness and indifference in his thoughts, he ought to conclude, not (as is too usual among tasteless readers) that the author wants those perfections which have been admired in him, but that he himself wants the faculty of discovering them.

He should, in the second place, be very careful to observe, whether he tastes the distinguishing perfections, or, if I may be allowed to call them so, the specific qualities of the author whom he peruses; whether he is particularly pleased with *Livy* for his manner of telling a story, with *Sallust* for his entering into those internal principles of action which arise from the characters and manners of the persons he describes, or with *Tacitus* for his displaying those outward motives of safety and interest, which give birth to the whole series of transactions which he relates.[81]

He may likewise consider, how differently he is affected by the same thought, which presents itself in a great writer, from what he is when he finds it delivered by a person of an ordinary genius. For there is as much difference in apprehending a thought clothed in *Cicero's* language, and that of a common author, as in seeing an object by the light of a taper, or by the light of the sun.

It is very difficult to lay down rules for the acquirement of such a taste as that I am here speaking of. The faculty must in some degree be born with us, and it very often happens, that those who have other qualities in perfection are wholly void of this. One of the most eminent mathematicians of the age has assured me, that the greatest pleasure he took in reading *Virgil,* was in examining *Aeneas* his voyage by the map; as I question not but many a modern compiler of history would be delighted with little more in that divine author, than in the bare matters of fact.

But notwithstanding this faculty must in some measure be born with us, there are several methods for cultivating and improving it, and without which it will be very uncertain, and of little use to the person that possesses it. The most natural method for this purpose is to be conversant among the writings of the most polite authors. A man who has any relish for fine writing, either discovers new beauties, or receives stronger impressions from the

81. Livy (59 B.C.–A.D. 17), Sallust (86–35 B.C.), and Tacitus (A.D. 56–after 117) were historians of Roman antiquity.

masterly strokes of a great author every time he peruses him: besides that he naturally wears himself into the same manner of speaking and thinking.

Conversation with men of a polite genius is another method for improving our natural taste. It is impossible for a man of the greatest parts to consider any thing in its whole extent, and in all its variety of lights. Every man, besides those general observations which are to be made upon an author, forms several reflections that are peculiar to his own manner of thinking; so that conversation will naturally furnish us with hints which we did not attend to, and make us enjoy other men's parts and reflections as well as our own. This is the best reason I can give for the observation which several have made, that men of great genius in the same way of writing seldom rise up singly, but at certain periods of time appear together, and in a body; as they did at *Rome* in the reign of *Augustus,* and in *Greece* about the age of *Socrates.* I cannot think that *Corneille, Racine, Moliere, Boileau, la Fontaine, Bruyere, Bossu,* or the *Daciers,* would have written so well as they have done, had they not been friends and contemporaries.[82]

It is likewise necessary for a man who would form to himself a finished taste of good writing, to be well versed in the works of the best *critics* both ancient and modern. I must confess that I could wish there were authors of this kind, who, beside the mechanical rules which a man of very little taste may discourse upon, would enter into the very spirit and soul of fine writing, and show us the several sources of that pleasure which rises in the mind upon the perusal of a noble work. Thus although in poetry it be absolutely necessary that the unities of time, place and action, with other points of the same nature, should be thoroughly explained and understood; there is still something more essential to the art, something that elevates and astonishes the fancy, and gives a greatness of mind to the reader, which few of the critics besides *Longinus* have considered.[83]

82. The French playwrights Pierre Corneille (1606–84), Jean Racine (1639–99), and Molière (Jean-Baptiste Poquelin, 1622–73); the poets Jean de La Fontaine (1621–80) and Nicolas Boileau-Despréaux (1636–1711); the critic René Le Bossu (1631–80); the moral essayist Jean de La Bruyère (1645–96); and the classical scholars André Dacier (1651–1722) and his wife Anne Lefèvre Dacier (1654–1720).

83. Boileau produced the first French translation of Longinus's *Peri hupsous* in 1674. The Aristotelian unities of time, place, and action governed classical drama; Samuel Johnson later championed Shakespeare's digression from these rules.

Our general taste in *England* is for epigram, turns of wit, and forced conceits, which have no manner of influence, either for the bettering or enlarging the mind of him who reads them, and have been carefully avoided by the greatest writers, both among the Ancients and Moderns. I have endeavoured in several of my Speculations to banish this *Gothic* taste, which has taken possession among us. I entertained the Town for a week together with an essay upon wit, in which I endeavoured to detect several of those false kinds which have been admired in the different ages of the world; and at the same time to show wherein the nature of true wit consists. I afterwards gave an instance of the great force which lies in a natural simplicity of thought to affect the mind of the reader, from such vulgar pieces as have little else besides this single qualification to recommend them. I have likewise examined the works of the greatest poet which our nation or perhaps any other has produced, and particularized most of those rational and manly beauties which give a value to that divine work.[84] I shall next *Saturday* enter upon an essay *on the Pleasures of the Imagination,* which, though it shall consider that subject at large, will perhaps suggest to the reader what it is that gives a beauty to many passages of the finest writers both in prose and verse. As an undertaking of this nature is entirely new, I question not but it will be received with candour.

19 June 1712

No. 411. [The Pleasures of the Imagination]

Avia Pieridum peragro loca, nullius ante
Trita solo; juvat integros accedere fontis;
Atque haurire:————Lucr.[85]

Our sight is the most perfect and most delightful of all our senses. It fills the mind with the largest variety of ideas, converses with its objects at the great-

84. The poet is John Milton, the work *Paradise Lost.* Addison recalls his essays on wit (*Spectator* nos. 58, in this volume, and 59–63), on ballads (nos. 70, 74, 85), and on Milton (no. 267). His series on "The Pleasures of the Imagination" includes nos. 411–21.

85. "I traverse pathless tracts of the Pierides never yet trodden by foot. I love to approach virgin springs and there to drink"; Lucretius, *De rerum natura,* I.926–28.

est distance, and continues the longest in action without being tired or satiated with its proper enjoyments. The sense of feeling can indeed give us a notion of extention, shape, and all other ideas that enter at the eye, except colours; but at the same time it is very much straitened and confined in its operations, to the number, bulk, and distance of its particular objects. Our sight seems designed to supply all these defects, and may be considered as a more delicate and diffusive kind of touch, that spreads itself over an infinite multitude of bodies, comprehends the largest figures, and brings into our reach some of the most remote parts of the universe.

It is this sense which furnishes the imagination with its ideas; so that by the pleasures of the imagination or fancy (which I shall use promiscuously) I here mean such as arise from visible objects, either when we have them actually in our view, or when we call up their ideas into our minds by paintings, statues, descriptions, or any the like occasion. We cannot indeed have a single image in the fancy that did not make its first entrance through the sight; but we have the power of retaining, altering and compounding those images, which we have once received, into all the varieties of picture and vision that are most agreeable to the imagination; for by this faculty a man in a dungeon is capable of entertaining himself with scenes and landscapes more beautiful than any that can be found in the whole compass of Nature.

There are few words in the *English* language which are employed in a more loose and uncircumscribed sense than those of the *Fancy* and the *Imagination*. I therefore thought it necessary to fix and determine the notion of these two words, as I intend to make use of them in the thread of my following Speculations, that the reader may conceive rightly what is the subject which I proceed upon. I must therefore desire him to remember, that by the Pleasures of the Imagination, I mean only such pleasures as arise originally from sight, and that I divide these pleasures in two kinds: my design being first of all to discourse of those Primary Pleasures of the Imagination, which entirely proceed from such objects as are before our eyes; and in the next place to speak of those Secondary Pleasures of the Imagination which flow from the ideas of visible objects, when the objects are not actually before the eye, but are called up into our memories, or formed into agreeable visions of things that are either absent or fictitious.

The Pleasures of the Imagination, taken in their full extent, are not so gross as those of sense, nor so refined as those of the understanding. The last are, indeed, more preferable, because they are founded on some new knowledge or improvement in the mind of man; yet it must be confessed, that those of the imagination are as great and as transporting as the other. A beautiful prospect delights the soul, as much as a demonstration; and a description in *Homer* has charmed more readers than a chapter in *Aristotle*. Besides, the pleasures of the imagination have this advantage, above those of the understanding, that they are more obvious, and more easy to be acquired. It is but opening the eye, and the scene enters. The colours paint themselves on the fancy, with very little attention of thought or application of mind in the beholder. We are struck, we know not how, with the symmetry of any thing we see, and immediately assent to the beauty of an object, without enquiring into the particular causes and occasions of it.

A man of a polite imagination is let into a great many pleasures, that the vulgar are not capable of receiving. He can converse with a picture, and find an agreeable companion in a statue. He meets with a secret refreshment in a description, and often feels a greater satisfaction in the prospect of fields and meadows, than another does in the possession. It gives him, indeed, a kind of property in every thing he sees, and makes the most rude uncultivated parts of Nature administer to his pleasures: so that he looks upon the world, as it were, in another light, and discovers in it a multitude of charms, that conceal themselves from the generality of mankind.

There are indeed, but very few who know how to be idle and innocent, or have a relish of any pleasures that are not criminal; every diversion they take is at the expence of some one virtue or another, and their very first step out of business is into vice or folly. A man should endeavour, therefore, to make the sphere of his innocent pleasures as wide as possible, that he may retire into them with safety, and find in them such a satisfaction as a wise man would not blush to take. Of this nature are those of the imagination, which do not require such a bent of thought as is necessary to our more serious employments, nor at the same time, suffer the mind to sink into that negligence and remissness, which are apt to accompany our more sensual delights, but, like a gentle exercise to the faculties, awaken them from sloth and idleness, without putting them upon any labour or difficulty.

We might here add, that the pleasures of the fancy are more conducive to health than those of the understanding, which are worked out by

dint of thinking, and attended with too violent a labour of the brain. Delightful scenes, whether in Nature, painting, or poetry, have a kindly influence on the body, as well as the mind, and not only serve to clear and
brighten the imagination, but are able to disperse grief and melancholy, and
to set the animal spirits in pleasing and agreeable motions. For this reason
Sir *Francis Bacon,* in his Essay upon Health, has not thought it improper to
prescribe to his reader a poem or a prospect, where he particularly dissuades
him from knotty and subtle disquisitions, and advises him to pursue studies, that fill the mind with splendid and illustrious objects, as histories, fables, and contemplations of Nature.[86]

I have in this Paper, by way of introduction, settled the notion of
those pleasures of the imagination which are the subject of my present undertaking, and endeavoured, by several considerations, to recommend to
my reader the pursuit of those pleasures. I shall, in my next Paper, examine
the several sources from whence these pleasures are derived.[87]

21 June 1712

No. 529. [On Rank and Precedence]

Singula quaeque locum teneant sortita decenter. Hor.[88]

Upon the hearing of several late disputes concerning rank and precedence,
I could not forbear amusing myself with some observations, which I have
made upon the Learned World, as to this great particular. By the Learned
World I here mean at large, all those who are any way concerned in works of
literature, whether in the writing, printing or repeating part. To begin with
the Writers; I have observed that the author of a *Folio,* in all companies and
conversations, sets himself above the author of a *Quarto;* the author of a
Quarto above the author of an *Octavo;* and so on, by a gradual descent and
subordination, to an author in *Twenty-Fours.*[89] This distinction is so well

86. See Bacon's "Of Regiment of Health" (1625).

87. Addison's Spectator no. 412 examines the pleasures derived from the
sight of things that are great (large), uncommon, or beautiful.

88. "Let each style keep the becoming place allotted it"; Horace, *Ars poetica,*
l. 92.

89. Addison ranks authors according to the physical size of their book. A fo-

observed, that in an assembly of the learned, I have seen a *Folio* writer place himself in an elbow-chair, when the author of a *Duodecimo* has, out of a just deference to his superior quality, seated himself upon a squabb. In a word, authors are usually ranged in company after the same manner as their works are upon a shelf.

The most minute pocket-author hath beneath him the writers of all pamphlets, or works that are only stitched. As for the pamphleteer, he takes place of none but of the authors of single sheets, and of that fraternity who publish their labours on certain days, or on every day of the week.[90] I do not find that the precedency among the individuals, in this latter class of writers, is yet settled.

For my own part, I have had so strict a regard to the ceremonial which prevails in the Learned World, that I never presumed to take place of a pamphleteer till my daily Papers were gathered into those two first volumes, which have already appeared.[91] After which, I naturally jumped over the heads not only of all pamphleteers, but of every *Octavo* writer in *Great-Britain,* that had written but one book. I am also informed by my bookseller, that six *Octavos* have at all times been looked upon as an equivalent to a *Folio,* which I take notice of the rather, because I would not have the Learned World surprized, if after the publication of half a dozen volumes I take my place accordingly. When my scattered forces are thus rallied, and reduced into regular bodies, I flatter myself that I shall make no despicable figure at the head of them.

Whether these rules, which have been received time out of mind in the Common-Wealth of Letters, were not originally established with an eye to our paper manufacture, I shall leave to the discussion of others, and shall only remark further in this place, that all printers and booksellers take the

---

lio is the largest size in which books were printed (from a full-sized printer's sheet folded once, like a newspaper); a quarto is half the size of a folio; an octavo a quarter of the size; a duodecimo a sixth of the size, and a twenty-four a twelfth.

90. Even the pamphleteer, whose works were stitched together but not bound in boards, took priority over the periodical essayist, whose numbers appeared on single folio-sized sheets, also called broadsides or broadsheets.

91. Volumes 1 and 2 of *The Spectator* had been published in January 1712 in octavo.

wall of one another, according to the abovementioned merits of the authors to whom they respectively belong.[92]

I come now to that point of precedency which is settled among the three Learned Professions, by the wisdom of our laws. I need not here take notice of the rank which is allotted to every doctor in each of these professions, who are all of them, though not so high as Knights, yet a degree above 'Squires; this last order of men being the illiterate body of the nation, are consequently thrown together into a class below the three Learned Professions.[93] I mention this for the sake of several rural 'Squires, whose reading does not rise so high as to *the present State of England*,[94] and who are often apt to usurp that precedency which by the laws of their country is not due to them. Their want of learning, which has planted them in this station, may in some measure extenuate their misdemeanour, and our professors ought to pardon them when they offend in this particular, considering that they are in a state of ignorance, or as we usually say, do not know their right hand from their left.

There is another tribe of persons who are retainers to the Learned World, and who regulate themselves upon all occasions by several laws peculiar to their body. I mean the Players or Actors of both sexes. Among these it is a standing and uncontroverted principle, that a tragedian always takes place of a comedian; and 'tis very well known the merry drolls who make us laugh are always placed at the lower end of the table, and in every entertainment give way to the dignity of the buskin.[95] It is a stage maxim, Once a king and always a king. For this reason it would be thought very absurd in Mr. *Bullock*, notwithstanding the height and gracefulness of his person, to sit at the right hand of an hero, though he were but five foot high.[96] The same distinction is observed among the ladies of the theatre. Queens

92. To take the wall is to take precedence, as a lady or social superior, by walking on the inside of the sidewalk (though these did not exist as such) so as to avoid being splashed by mud from the road.

93. Namely, lawyers, physicians, and clergymen.

94. The subtitle of *Angliae Notitia,* an annual listing of knights, peers, members of Parliament, and other titled citizens.

95. A boot reaching to the calf worn by ancient Greek tragedians; in the hierarchy of the arts, tragedy ranks over comedy.

96. William Bullock (1657–c. 1740) regularly played low comic roles.

and heroines preserve their rank in private conversation, while those who are waiting-women and maids of honour upon the stage, keep their distance also behind the scenes.

I shall only add, that by a parity of reason, all writers of tragedy look upon it as their due to be seated, served, or saluted before comic writers: those who deal in tragi-comedy usually taking their seats between the authors of either side. There has been a long dispute for precedency between the tragic and heroic poets. *Aristotle* would have the latter yield the *Pas* to the former, but Mr. *Dryden* and many others would never submit to this decision.[97] Burlesque writers pay the same deference to the heroic, as comic writers to their serious brothers in the drama.

By this short table of laws, order is kept up, and distinction preserved in the whole Republic of Letters.

6 November 1712

97. To "yield the Pas" is to give precedence. According to Aristotle (*Poetics*), tragedy has all of the advantages of epic verse without being confined to a single event and therefore presents broader possibilities. John Dryden, in "The Authors Apology for Heroique Poetry; and Poetique Licence" in *The State of Innocence, and Fall of Man: An Opera* (1677), is more concerned with defending the serious arts (tragedy and epic, which he does not always distinguish) against critics. In his translation of Virgil he argues specifically against Aristotle with such statements as "A Heroick Poem, truly such, is undoubtedly the greatest Work which the Soul of Man is capable to perform" and "Tragedy is the miniature of Humane Life; an Epick Poem is the draught at length"; "And besides, what Virtue is there in a Tragedy, which is not contain'd in an Epick Poem?"; *The Works of Virgil: Containing His Pastorals, Georgics, and Æneis,* trans. John Dryden (London, 1697), 203–5.

THREE

Eliza Haywood
(c. 1693–1756)

ACTRESS, PLAYWRIGHT, POET, translator, and novelist, Eliza Haywood (née Fowler) navigated the troubled waters of London literary life, supporting herself and her two children through her professional talents. In the persona of the "Female Spectator," she claimed to have received an education "more liberal than is ordinarily allowed to Persons of my Sex," and indeed she became an important voice in the English periodical essay tradition. "An unfortunate marriage has reduc'd me to the melancholly necessity of depending on my Pen for the support of my self and two children," she wrote. Alexander Pope parodied her in *The Dunciad* (1728) as a voluptuary with "Two babes of love close clinging to her waste," recalling her own erotic novels, including *Love in Excess* (1719–20). While little is known of Haywood's early life, we do know that she was active in the London theatrical scene, performing in Henry Fielding's Little Haymarket Theatre company and conducting her own literary warfare against Robert Walpole, who was no friend to the arts. As Lord High Treasurer and de facto prime minister, he was responsible for the notorious Licensing Act of 1737, which imposed government censorship on the British stage, requiring the Lord Chamberlain to approve all plays before they were mounted. Fielding, Haywood, and their friends parodied Walpole, but Fielding did not spare Haywood, parodying her as "Mrs. Novel" in *The Author's Farce* (1730). This prompted her riposte, *The Opera of Operas* (1733), playing on Fielding's *The Tragedy of Tragedies; or, The Life and Death of Tom Thumb the Great* (1731).

In the 1740s Haywood gained a reputation as a periodical essayist with *The Female Spectator,* published in twenty-four monthly installments from April 1744 through May 1746, and *The Parrot,* published in nine numbers from 2 August through 4 October 1746. Dubbed "an Addison in petticoats" by later critics, she continued the early essayists' didactic mission of reforming the minds and manners of the times. Her periodical papers tended to run long, adapting narrative techniques from the novel and offering moralistic precepts upon graphic stories of adultery, gambling, and parental tyranny, among other things. Her *Parrot* reported on explicitly political material, which did not find favor without the scandalous content of *The Female Spectator.* Haywood continued to publish into the 1750s, including a novel, *Betsy Thoughtless* (1751), and another weekly periodical, *The Young Lady* (1756), shortly after the commencement of which she became ill and died.

Selections are excerpted from Eliza Haywood, *The Female Spectator* (London, 1745), and Haywood, *The Parrot: With a Compendium of the Times* (London, 1746).

The Female Spectator
No. 1. [Martesia and Clitander]

. . . Could fourteen have the power of judging of itself, or for itself, who that knew the beautiful *Martesia* at that age, but would have depended on her conduct!—*Martesia,* descended of the most illustrious race, possessed of all that dignity of sentiment befitting her high birth, endued by Nature with a surprizing wit, judgment, and penetration, and improved by every aid of education.—*Martesia,* the wonder and delight of all who saw or heard her, gave the admiring world the greatest expectations that she would one day be no less celebrated for all those virtues which render amiable the conjugal state, than she at that time was for every other perfection that do honour to the sex.

Yet how, alas, did all these charming hopes vanish into air! Many noble youths, her equals in birth and fortune, watched her increase of years for declaring a passion, which they feared as yet would be rejected by those who had the disposal of her; but what their respect and timidity forbade them to attempt, a more daring and unsuspected rival ventured at, and succeeded in. Her unexperienced heart approved his person, and was pleased with the protestations he made her of it. In fine, the novelty of being addressed in that manner, gave a double grace to all he said, and she never thought herself so happy as in his conversation. His frequent visits at length were taken notice of; he was denied the privilege of seeing her, and she was no longer permitted to go out without being accompanied by some person who was to be a spy upon her actions. She had a great spirit, impatient of controul, and this restraint served only to heighten the inclination she before had to favour him:—she indulged the most romantic ideas of his merit and his love:—her own flowing fancy invented a thousand melancholy and tender soliloquies, and set them down as made by him in this separation: it is not, indeed, to be doubted, but that he was very much mortified at the impediment he found in the prosecution of his courtship; but whether he took this method of disburdening his affliction, neither she nor any body else could be assured. It cannot, however, be denied, but that he pursued means much more efficacious for the attainment of his wishes. By bribes, promises, and entreaties, he prevailed on a person who came frequently to the house to convey his letters to her, and bring back her answers. This correspondence was, perhaps, of greater service to him, than had the freedom of their interviews not been prevented: she consented to be his, and to make good her word, ventured her life, by descending from a two pair of stairs window,[1] by the help of quilt, blankets, and other things fastened to it, at the dead of night. His coach and six waited to receive her at the end of the street, and conveyed her to his country seat, which reaching soon after break of day, his chaplain made them too fast for any authority to separate.

As he was of an ancient honourable family, and his estate very considerable, her friends in a short time were reconciled to what was now irremediable, and they were looked upon as an extreme happy pair. But soon, too soon the fleeting pleasures fled, and in their room anguish and bitterness of heart succeeded.

Martesia, in a visit she made to a lady of her intimate acquaintance, unfortunately happened to meet the young *Clitander;* he was just returned from his travels, had a handsome person, an infinity of gaiety, and a certain something in his air and deportment which had been destructive to the peace and reputation of many of our sex. He was naturally of an amorous disposition, and being so, felt all the force of charms, which had some effect

---

1. A window at the front or back of a house located in the small compartment on the landing between two sets of stairs.

even on the most cold and temperate. Emboldened by former successes, the knowledge *Martesia* was another's did not hinder him from declaring to her the passion she had inspired him with. She found a secret satisfaction in hearing him, which she was yet too young to consider the dangers of, and therefore endeavoured not to suppress till it became too powerful for her to have done so, even had she attempted it with all her might; but the truth is, she now experienced in *reality* a flame she had but *imagined* herself possessed of for him who was now her husband, and was too much averse to the giving herself pain to combat with an inclination which seemed to her fraught only with delights.

The house where their acquaintance first began, was now the scene of their future meetings: the mistress of it was too great a friend to gallantry herself to be any interruption to the happiness they enjoyed in entertaining each other without witnesses. How weak is virtue when love and opportunity combine! Though no woman could have more refined and delicate notions than *Martesia*, yet all were ineffectual against the solicitations of her adored *Clitander*. One fatal moment destroyed at once all her own exalted ideas of honour and reputation, and the principles early instilled into her mind by her virtuous preceptors.

The consequence of this amour was a total neglect of husband, house, and family. Herself abandoned, all other duties were so too. So manifest a change was visible to all that knew her, but most to her husband, as most interested in it. He truly loved, and had believed himself truly beloved by her. Loth he was to think his misfortune real, and endeavoured to find some other motive for the aversion she now expressed for staying at home, or going to any of those places where they had been accustomed to visit together; but she either knew not how to dissemble, or took so little pains to do it, that he was, in spite of himself, convinced all that affection she so lately had professed, and given him testimonies of, was now no more. He examined all his actions, and could find nothing in any of them that could give occasion for so sad a reverse. He complained to her one day, in the tenderest terms, of the small portion she had of late allowed him of her conversation:—entreated, that if by any inadvertency he had offended her, she would acquaint him with his fault, which he assured her he would take care never to repeat.—Asked if there was any thing in her settlement or jointure[2] she could wish to have altered, and assured her she need but let him know her commands to be instantly obeyed.

To all this she replied with the most stabbing indifference.—That she knew not what he meant.—That as she had accused him with nothing, he had no reason to think she was dissatisfied.—But that people could not be always in the same humour, and desired he would not give himself nor her the trouble of making any farther interrogatories.

He must have been as insensible, as he is known to be the contrary, had such a behaviour not opened his eyes; he no longer doubted of his fate, and resolving, if possible, to find out the author of it, he caused her chair[3] to be watched wherever she went, and took such effectual methods, as soon informed him of the truth.

In his first emotions of his rage he was for sending a challenge to this destroyer of his happiness; but in his cooler moments he rejected that design as too injurious to the reputation of *Martesia*, who was still dear to him, and whom he flattered himself with being able one day to reclaim.

It is certain he put in practice every tender stratagem that love and wit could furnish him with for that purpose; but she appearing so far from being moved at any thing he either said or did, that, on the contrary, her behaviour was every day more cold; he at last began to expostulate with her, gave some hints that her late conduct was not unknown to him, and that though he was willing to forgive what was past, yet as a husband, it was not consistent with his character to bear any future insults of that nature. This put her beyond all patience. She reproached him in the bitterest terms for daring to harbour the least suspicion of her virtue, and censuring her innocent amusements as crimes; and perhaps was glad of this opportunity of testifying her remorse for having ever listened to his vows, and cursing before his face the hour that joined their hands.

2. Because a married woman had no legal property rights at this time, financial arrangements were settled prior to marriage; the jointure stipulated financial conditions upon the event of the husband's decease.

3. Sedan chairs were enclosed chairs with windows or curtains borne on poles by carriers. They were cheaper than hackney coaches and available for hire in London starting in the seventeenth century as an early form of the taxi, with the advantage that they could take the passenger right up to the door.

They now lived so ill a life together, that not having sufficient proofs for a divorce,[4] he parted beds, and though they continued in one house, behaved to each other as strangers: never ate at the same table but when company was there, and then only to avoid the questions that would naturally have been asked had it been otherwise; neither of them being desirous the world should know any thing of their disagreement.

But while they continued to treat each other in a manner so little conformable to their first hopes, or their vows pledged at the holy altar, *Martesia* became pregnant: this gave the first alarm to that indolence of nature she hitherto had testified; her husband would now have it in his power to sue out a divorce; and though she would have rejoiced to have been separated from him on any other terms, yet she could not support the thoughts of being totally deprived of all reputation in the world. She was not ignorant of the censures she incurred, but had pride and spirit enough to enable her to despise whatever was said of her, while it was not backed by proof; but the glaring one she was now about to give struck shame and confusion to her soul. She left no means untried to procure an abortion; but failing in that, she had no other recourse than to that friend who was the sole confidante of her unhappy passion, who comforted her as well as she could, and assured her, that when the hour approached she need have no more to do than to come directly to her house, where every thing should be prepared for the reception of a woman in her condition.

To conceal the alteration in her shape, she pretended indisposition, saw little company, and wore only loose gowns. At length the so much dreaded moment came upon her at the dead of night; and in the midst of all that rack of nature, made yet more horrible by the agonies of her mind, she rose, rung for her woman, and telling her she had a frightful dream concerning that lady, whom she knew she had the greatest value for of any person upon earth, ordered her to get a chair, for she could not be easy unless she went and saw her herself. The woman was strangely surprized, but her lady was always absolute in her commands. A chair was brought, and without any other company or attendance than her own distracted thoughts,

4. According to English law, a man could petition the House of Lords for a divorce if he had convincing proof of his wife's adultery. (Until the twentieth century, a woman had to prove desertion or cruelty in addition to adultery.)

she was conveyed to the only asylum where she thought her shame might find a shelter.

A midwife being prepared before, she was safely delivered of a daughter, who expired almost as soon as born; and to prevent as much as possible all suspicion of the truth, she made herself be carried home the next morning, where she went to bed, and lay several days under pretence of having sprained her ankle.

But not all the precautions she had taken were effectual enough to prevent some people from guessing and whispering what had happened. Those whose nearness in blood gave them a privilege of speaking their minds, spared not to tell her all that was said of her; and those who dared not take that liberty, showed by their distant looks and reserved behaviour, whenever she came in presence, how little they approved her conduct. She was too discerning not to see into their thoughts, nor was her innate pride of any service to keep up her spirits on this occasion. To add to her discontents, *Clitander* grew every day more cool in his respects, and she soon after learned he was on the point of marriage with one far inferior to herself in every charm both of mind and person. In fine, finding herself deserted by her relations, and the greatest part of her acquaintance, without love, without respect, and reduced to the pity of those, who, perhaps, had nothing but a greater share of circumspection to boast of, she took a resolution to quit *England* for ever, and having settled her affairs with her husband, who by this time had entered into other amusements, and, it is probable, was very well satisfied to be eased of the constraint her presence gave him, readily agreed to remit her the sum agreed between them, to be paid yearly to whatever part of the world she chose to reside in, she then took leave of a country of which she had been the idol, and which now seemed to her as too unjust in not being blind to what she desired should be concealed.

Behold her now in a voluntary banishment from friends and country, and roaming round the world in fruitless search of that tranquility she could not have failed enjoying at home in the bosom of a consort equally beloved as loving. Unhappy charming lady, born and endued with every quality to attract universal love and admiration, yet by one inadvertent step undone and lost to every thing the world holds dear, and only more conspicuously wretched by having been conspicuously amiable.

But methinks it would be hard to charge the blame of indiscreet marriages on the young ladies themselves: parents are sometimes, by an over caution, guilty of forcing them into things, which otherwise would be far distant from their thoughts. I am very certain it is not because the *Italian,* *Spanish,* or *Portuguese* women are so much warmer in their constitutions than those of other nations, but because they are so cruelly debarred from all conversation with the men, that makes them so readily accept the first offer that presents itself. Where opportunities are scarce, they are glad to speak their minds at once, and fear to *deny* lest it should not be in their power afterward to *grant.* Even in *Turkey,* where our travellers boast of having had such success among the women, I have known several that were married to *English* gentlemen, and permitted to live after the custom of our country, who have made very excellent wives. In *France,* the people are, questionless, the gayest and most alert in the world, and allow the greatest liberties to their women; yet to hear of a clandestine marriage among them is a kind of prodigy, and though no place affords scenes of gallantry equal to it in any degree of proportion, yet I believe there is none where fewer false steps are made, or husbands have less reason to complain of the want of chastity in their wives. Nature in all ages is abhorrent of restraint, but in youth especially, as more headstrong and impetuous, it will hazard every thing to break through laws it had no hand in making. It therefore betrays a want of policy, as well as an unjust austerity, to seclude a young lady, and shut her up from all intercourse with the men, for fear she should find one among them who might happen to please her too well. Chance may in a moment destroy all that the utmost care can do; and I say a woman is in far less danger of losing her heart, when every day surrounded with a variety of gay objects, than when by some accident she falls into the conversation of a single one. A girl, who is continually hearing fine things said to her, regards them but as words of course; they may be flattering to her vanity for the present, but will leave no impression behind them on her mind: but she, who is a stranger to the gallant manner with which polite persons treat our sex, greedily swallows the first civil thing said to her, takes what perhaps is meant as a mere compliment for a declaration of love, and replies to it in terms which either expose her to the designs of him who speaks, if he happens to have any in reality, or if he has not, to his ridicule in all company he comes into.

For this reason the Country-bred ladies, who are never suffered to come to Town for fear their faces should be spoiled by the small-pox, or their reputations ruined by the beaux, become an easier prey to the artifices of mankind, than those who have had an education more at large: as they rarely stir beyond their father's pales, except to church, the parson, if he be a forward man, and has courage to throw a love song, or copy of verses to Miss over the wall, or slip it into her hand in a visit he pays the family, has a rare opportunity of making his fortune; and it is well when it happens no worse; many a 'Squire's daughter has clambered over hedge and stile, to give a rampant jump into the arms of a young jolly haymaker or plough-man.

Our *London* ladies are indeed very rarely laid under such restrictions; but whenever it happens to be the case, as Nature is the same in all, the consequence will be so too. Would Miss *Eagaretta* have ever condescended to marry the greasy footman that run before her chair, had he not been the only man her over-careful father permitted her to speak to? Or would *Armonia* have found any charms in a *Mousetrap* or *Leathern Apron*, had she been indulged the conversation of a *white Staff*?[5] . . .

April 1744

The Parrot
No. 1. [Introduces Herself and Anticipates Critics]

Well, I am got upon my swing,—the Town are gathering thick about me, and I have liberty to prate (as my publisher flatters himself) to a very crowded audience; but as vain as he, and some others would make me, I am sensible that the greatest part come only to divert themselves. Be it so, I shall make it my endeavour that they may not be disappointed, and at the same time also to answer the expectations of those who have a better opinion of my abilities: I say *abilities*, for most people who know me, will allow me to be *a Bird of Parts;* and, indeed, I cannot well be otherwise, considering the various scenes of life I have gone through, the many different nations I have lived among, the conversation I have had with all degrees of people, the opportunities Fortune has thrown in my way of improving my-

5. A mousetrap man is a person who makes, sells, or sets mousetraps; an apron man is a mechanic; a White Staff is a high-ranking officer of the crown.

self, under the most learned and witty persons of their times, and the wonderful events that have fallen within the compass of my observation.

But in order to give a more perfect idea of what I am, it will not, I think, be amiss to make a brief recital of my travels, and the company I have kept during the course of a long series of years.

I drew my first breath in *Java*, a large island in the *East-Indies*, but was taken so very young from my parents, that I have nothing to say in regard to my family: all my remembrance furnishes me with, of those early years of life, is, that I was carried to *Batavia*, a *Dutch* settlement, and was a great favourite with the Governor of that place; but his lady, happening to take a disgust to me, obliged him to give me away to a *French* merchant, who came there on some affairs of commerce, and on his return home, was again presented to a widow of quality at *Versailles*.

I believe I should not wrong this lady if I said she had gained the better side of fifty, but in *France* there are no old women. Her house was a scene of perpetual gaiety, and as I then began to have some distinguishing notion of the world, and the manners of mankind, was highly diverted with the gallantries of those who visited her. But my mirth lasted not long; she happened one day to strike me, on which I grew sullen, would not speak either to herself or any of her friends, and was at last turned out of doors.

I then fell to the lot of an *Abbeé*, eminent for his wit and learning: with him I improved myself very much; he took great delight in me, and I believe we should never have parted, if the wife of a certain great officer, with whom he had an amour, had not begged me from him.

For a time this lady was extremely fond of me, but unluckily breaking off with her lover, she grew out of humour with me for his sake, used me very ill, and gave me to one who was indeed a great philosopher, but withal quite whimsical, insomuch as I may truly say my life was a burden to me.

A few months, however, released me from that uneasy situation, and I became the property of a gentleman who was going to make the tour of *Germany:* he took me with him, we called at all the different courts which compose that huge Empire, and I had the opportunity of observing in some of them such cabals and intrigues, as might have amazed a creature of much more experience than I had then to boast of.

We afterwards passed through *Flanders*, saw *Brussels*, *Antwerp*, and several other fine cities, then fell down into *Holland,* from thence took shipping for *England,* and so home again by the way of *Calais.*

The curiosity of this benevolent patron not being yet sufficiently gratified, we set out again, crossed some part of the *Pyrenoean* Mountains and proceeded to *Madrid,* where, in spite of the *Spanish* formality and stiffness, I had the honour of being taken notice of by most of the grandees, and even by the infants *Don Carlos,* and *Don Philip,* who were at that time too young to have entertained any of those ambitious views their Mother-Queen has since instilled into them.[6]

Here we stayed several months, and there was no talk of our removing, when all at once I was disposed of to a nobleman who was going to *Holland* in a public capacity; but soon after our arrival, I fell into disgrace with him, was confined in a dark room for eight days, then sent to the house of a Burgo-Master, whose daughter, for he had no wife, was sole manager of the family. She had little, or rather no taste at all of my qualifications, and exchanged me for a bird, I must say, of much less value than myself, and [I] was brought a second time to *England;* where, happening into various families successively, I had the pleasure of seeing several parts of this beautiful island, to which before I had been a stranger.

After many changes, I was at length recommended to a young nobleman, who being just come to his estate, was impatient to make a figure in foreign parts; with him I revisited *France,* stayed there a considerable time, thence passed the *Alps* into *Italy,* a country, which, with great justice, is styled the Garden of the World: at one of those polite courts I had the satisfaction of pleasing the most lovely and accomplished person, that Nature ever framed, or Education polished; it was at his own request that I was taken into his retinue, and there it was that I had all could flatter my ambition: whoever had any favour to solicit of him, were sure to make their court first to me: I was complimented, admired, and caressed infinitely beyond what one of my species could expect; and to crown the blessings I enjoyed, was (what very few in elevated stations can boast of) perfectly con-

6. The two sons (*infantes*) of Queen Isabella, second wife of the recently deceased Philip V, were half-brothers to the new King Ferdinand VI. Don Carlos later became Charles III and his younger brother Philip the Duke of Parma.

tented. But the felicity was too great to be permanent;—an *English* lady, who had too many charms to be refused any thing, would needs have me from my master, and with her I returned once more into this country, where I have experienced almost as frequent vicissitudes of Fortune as there are to be found in the climate, having been, in the space of three years, in no less than fifty-five families of vastly different ranks and dispositions.

You will wonder, and with reason, that being in such high estimation as I pretend to have been, I was so readily and so often parted with by those who had me in possession; it appearing that my so frequent change of place was not at my own option, but that of those to whom I belonged. In answer, therefore, to any query may be made on this point, I shall as freely lay open my errors, as I am willing to publish my perfections; for you will always find I scorn the mean subterfuges of equivocation and evasion, and, above all things, detest a lie, how much soever practised and brought into fashion by my superiors.

My great facility in learning the languages, joined with a happy memory, and a voluble delivery, doubtless it was that rendered me so acceptable among strangers, and my conversation so agreeable on a first acquaintance: certain it is, that could I have been as secret as I was accounted learned and eloquent, I might have been entrusted in the quality of an interpreter to a first minister, (as some I have known who understood no other than their mother-tongue;) but, to my very great misfortune, I never was blest with the retentive faculty; I was sure to report whatever I heard, and not seldom to those in whose presence I ought to have been most cautious; so that I was soon looked upon as a dangerous bird, and I must indeed confess, that very great disappointments, dissensions, and mischiefs of various kinds have sometimes been occasioned merely by my blabbing. This unlucky quality it was, and only this, which brought me into disgrace, where, otherwise, I should have been most beloved, and obliged those who had any thing to conceal, to get rid of me as soon as possible.

You see, good people, what you are to expect: I deal ingenuously with you; therefore, if any one among you communicates to me what he would not have a matter of universal *Chit-Chat,* let him blame himself when he finds it is so.

Philosophers may argue as they please, but there is no such thing as totally changing Nature: what is born with us will sometimes peep out, in spite of precept or education; unless, as some have endeavoured to prove, the *humours* and *will of action* is lodged in the *blood*, which, by being drained out and exchanged for that of another creature, the system of the *mind* would be reversed, and different *propensities* arise with the different *animalculæ;* but should I, in order to get rid of this tale-telling inclination, submit to such an experiment, which (by the bye) not the whole Royal Society, nor all the virtuosos in the world should prevail on me to do, pray who can answer that I might not imbibe some other as *bad,* or perhaps *worse* property than that which had been expunged?

Besides, I am apt to think, that in mature examination I shall not be found to deserve half the blame that has been charged upon me; for, if by *chance,* (for I never do mischief by design) some unhappy consequences may have attended my talkativeness, it has rarely happened, but where persons' *actions* justly incur punishment of some kind or other; and being out of the letter of the law, can only suffer through the shame of discovery. The truly *wise* and *virtuous* have nothing to apprehend from me, and I will venture to maintain, even to the teeth of my most virulent accusers, that what they would represent as so unpardonable a transgression, is in reality productive of more *Good* than *Evil.*

For example; if a laudable enterprize miscarries through my inadvertent discovery of it, may not a pernicious one also be prevented from taking effect by the same means? And which of these two sorts most abound in the world, I appeal to your own observation, and am pretty confident you need go no farther to answer, whether I have not more frequent opportunities of *preserving* than *prejudicing* mankind by my communicative faculty. The midnight whisper through the bars of a window, or the key-hole of a door, by me repeated the next morning, has saved many a husband's honour, a virgin's chastity, and a whole family's disgrace.

In fine, it is certain, and must be owned by every one who consults his reason, and is willing to judge without partiality, that I am capable of conferring very great obligations on those in *public* as well as *private* life, if listened to with due attention.

Mark me then, and suppose me not a mere *Parrot,* which without distinction utters all he hears, and is the echo of every foolish rumour; but a thing,—a thing to which I cannot give a name, but I mean a thing sent by the gods, and by them inspired to utter only sacred truths. I must not say an

Oracle, because it would savour too much of *Paganism.* I would wish you, however, to imagine me somewhat extraordinary, because what I say will have the greater weight with you.

I dare answer that you will all acknowledge, none are above the benefit of information. A *Courtier* then may learn from me whether the preferment he is about to receive, is granted as the reward of his merit, or as the bait to ensnare his *honesty.* A *Statesman,* who sacrifices all to his *ambitious views,* may be told by me, on what a dangerous precipice he stands, and even a sovereign prince be apprized of that which perhaps none else about him have courage or integrity enough to acquaint him with: I mean, what is generally said of his government, and by that useful knowledge be enabled to pursue such measures as will make his *People happy,* and consequently *himself truly great.*

But what is all this to us, you will say; those at the head of *our* affairs stand in no need of such a monitor. Every *Courtier* here desires *grandeur* only to have more opportunities of doing *good to the public;* all our *Statesmen* are perfect *patriots.* We have a *Sovereign,* who centers all his wishes in the peace, opulence, and glory of his *Subjects;* who loves us as his *Children,* and is so far from encroaching on our rights, that he is himself the best guardian of our laws and liberties; and we, in return *revere* him as a *Father* and almost *adore* him as a *God.* What can be added to the felicity of our present condition? We know the blessings we enjoy, and want not to be told any thing would diminish our content. Far be it from the *Parrot* to attempt it.

You may be assured I shall never report grievances till they are generally complained of, and that is not likely to be the case, while his present Majesty, or any of his truly royal and magnanimous issue remain; yet as what *has been, may again be,* and it is impossible that the most sanguine should answer for futurity, it is good to have a remedy at hand in all events; and it cannot, therefore, be thought too presuming in me to say, that the disturbances I may sometimes create, are more than atoned for by my power of doing service, if ever an occasion should demand it.

Much with justice might be alleged in vindication of my character, but time and your own experience will best speak for me; and I shall add no more, for fear of appearing too tedious on a matter, which, to some people, will seem of so little importance.

As I take upon me, however, to harangue you in this public manner, it is highly expedient I should give you the motives which induce me to do so; and as I never will forfeit my sincerity for the sake of compliment, I will declare, though it may be thought a little unpolite, that the *principal* one is to gratify my own insatiable itch of talking.

The *others,* no less genuine, and a great deal more obliging, stand in the following rank.

First, because I have gathered from the many different characters, circumstances, and behaviour of the persons I have been among, a number of various occurrences equally instructive and entertaining in the relation.

Secondly, because I have treasured up in my mind a very choice collection of curious pieces, both ancient and modern, which cannot fail of being an agreeable amusement to the learned part of mankind, while they improve and enlarge, at the same time, the understanding of the less knowing.

Thirdly, because, if I were silent, the Town would, in all probability, be deprived of the pleasure and emolument these elegant pieces will afford, some of which I brought with me from very distant realms, and others that I am sure have been imparted only to me.

Fourthly, and as a consequence of the other, to draw *modest Merit* from the obscurity it often lies under, and to humble the pride of those who assume too much on the indulgence of the Town.

Fifthly, as since my being in this country, some of my kindred, who live in very great repute, have done me the favour to own me, and have promised me their assistance, I would not neglect the favours they offer, and through their means the opportunity of obliging the public.

And lastly, to rectify several errors and mistakes which Prejudice has introduced, to the disgrace of Reason, whether it be either in serious or trifling matters; whether in your mode of dress and behaviour to each other, or in the higher concerns of religion and morality.

If I succeed in any one of these propositions, I hope to be allowed not to prate insignificantly; but if in all of them, you cannot without ingratitude refuse me the praise of having spoke to very great purpose.

I am no stranger to the difficulties of the task I undertake; I hear from all hands, that one ought to be endued with extraordinary talents, indeed, to please in a nation where there are many very great judges, and infinitely more who imagine themselves so; it is not the former I am so much afraid of; good sense is for the most part, accompanied with good nature, but the

Would-be-Wits, are of all animals, that I know of, the most troublesome and dangerous.

A whole *posse* of these, whom I think you call *Critics*, will likely fall upon me; they will cavil at my style, my manner, perhaps hunt out a verb misplaced, and then triumph in my want of grammar; they will quote rules on rules against me, quarrel with my figures in speech, find fault with this *contrast*, and that *antithesis*, and cry shame on my ill *rhetoric*. But let them look to themselves; every thing, when attacked, has a right to make use of what weapons of defence are in their power: if they rail against the *diction* of the *Parrot*, the *Parrot* will cry out against the *vices* and *follies* of *humanity*: if they bring down their *Horace*, their *Cicero*, and their *Virgil*, I shall be obliged to have recourse to *Socrates, Seneca, Epictetus, Juvenal*, and some other old gentlemen, who, perhaps, they will like as little to be told of. I can set *maxim* against *mode*, and am able to produce undeniable proofs, that the *Parrot* cannot be more unskilled in *oratory*, than some *men* are in *morality*, or the precepts of right reason. A very strong, and withal mortifying contrast (which, however disagreeable to the *ear*, could not be disputed by the *understanding*,) might be made between the customs and manners practiced by the *former* and the *present* race of *Britons;* but I am sensible, that it is not by cutting strokes any error is to be reformed, and shall therefore sacrifice to the general good, whatever resentments some few particular persons may happen to excite in me.

But whither am I running? It is more than probable all this might have been spared: twenty to one but you'll say, I am a creature beneath envy, and consequently detraction, and that I only affect to imagine myself in danger of abuse, in order to provoke it. Well, if this should be the case, I have the example of some of your greatest Wits to keep me in countenance. It is well known, that many a fine genius owes its *eclat* to the anonymous railing of a bosom friend and confidante; or for want of such a one, to the being turned against itself; and I can see no reason why I should be debarred from making use of this innocent stratagem to raise my reputation, if I had a mind to it, any more than any other of my fellow labourers, for the entertainment of the public.

I might, however, give you assurances, on assurances, that I am wholly free from all vanity of this sort; that I would not attempt to impose on the understanding of any of my hearers, and no way aim at popular ap-

plause, farther than as I may be found to deserve it; but after all, few, perhaps, will give credit to what I say upon this score; so upon the whole, believe it will be the best way to drop the matter, and leave every one to judge
as he thinks proper, both in regard to myself and the discourses I shall hereafter present the public with.

2 August 1746

No. 2. [Oram]

. . . I happened once to live in a family, where a very famous *Courtezan* had
lodgings; *Oram,* the admired, the universally beloved *Oram,* came one day
to visit her, but she being at that time not in order to receive him, he was
conducted into a parlour where I was; but he took not the least notice of
me, nor would I presume to begin a conversation: the sun shining very hot,
a great number of flies were buzzing about the room, some of whom had
the *insolence* to come upon the face and hands of *Oram;* to punish this want
of respect, and, at the same time, to amuse himself, he frequently attempted
to seize them; but soon perceiving their extreme agility constantly eluded
his grasp, and also that they had little stings, which, if provoked, would annoy him more, he had recourse to a stratagem. He went to the tea-table,
took a lump of sugar, which having wetted, he laid on the frame of the window; the poor insects immediately settled about it, and, tempted with the
sweetness, fell into the power of him who stood ready to catch them, as
they indulged themselves in sucking the dangerous bait. The manner in
which he treated them, when in his hands, was various, pulling off the legs
of some, the wings of others, and the heads of the largest; with this he
seemed highly diverted, and laughed very heartily to see the severed limbs
and mangled carcasses lie spread upon the field of action; for my part, I said
nothing all the while, for fear of incurring a displeasure, which might have
been no less fatal to me, but rejoiced when a summons from the lady called
him up stairs, and I was eased of the presence of so formidable a guest.

One who has been a stranger to the character of *Oram,* would, from
this, have been apt to compare him with that *Roman* emperor, who, it is
said, delighted himself with plucking out the eyes of these insects;[7] and I

7. A reference to Titus Flavius Domitian (51–96), who had a reputation

must acknowledge that his behaviour appeared to me at first to have somewhat in it of cruelty; but when I considered how much he is extolled for
compassion, generosity, and every humane virtue, I presently accused my
premature supposition, and concluded that these wretches did not only deserve their fate, but also that *Oram,* in his great wisdom, knew it was better
even for themselves to be divested of those limbs, which while they were
masters of, enabled them to be vexatious to those of a superior species, and
so be exposed to continual hazards of the death they now sustained, and,
when once past, they could have no more to apprehend.

The only objection that remained was, wherefore, since they were to
die, he did not kill them at one blow, and not prolong their misery, by destroying first one part of them, and then another; but when I remembered
how numerous a race they were, and that the sun was continually raising
them fresh recruits, I judged he did this by way of *Terrorem* to the rest,
who, seeing the fate of their brothers, would bend their flight another way,
and no more molest a place sacred to Love and *Oram.*

These reasons, which undoubtedly are such as the friends of *Oram*
would give, may, perhaps, be looked upon by his enemies, as somewhat far-
fetched; but if people consider how difficult it is to find arguments to *excuse,* much less to *excite applause* for actions of this kind, mine will be the
better relished.

I could, however, with all my endeavours, find none more plausible,
nor indeed any other at all; and as I was willing to reconcile, if possible, the
character of *Oram* with his behaviour, did not give myself much trouble to
examine how far the sentiments were just, but took them upon trust, a privilege which I thought I might allow to my own, as well as to those of other
people's.

I flatter myself, this will serve as a great proof of the deference I pay to
your profound penetration, and entirely clear me from all suspicion of any
intention to depreciate it to the rest of the world. I am not certain, notwithstanding, but this dissertation on a foreign foible, may not be looked upon
as impertinent, by those who, by my own confession, are not tainted with
it. In answer to this cavil, that is, if any such should be made, I beg leave to

---

for cruelty. His head is portrayed in the Cathedral of Orvieto, hence the allusion to
the "Orvietan" as an antidote below.

remind you, that as *antidotes,* in case of any danger from *poison,* are absolutely necessary, so showing the absurdity of *judging* without *thinking,* may serve as an *Orvietan* against the contagion of ill example, and help to prevent you from ever adopting a meanness so unworthy of you.

It is the great respect I bear you, makes me take this liberty; for, as I have already hinted; that impetuosity which is so natural to you, would, in all probability, hurry you to extravagancies, not altogether allowable in a *good* cause, but monstrous in a *bad* one. You, therefore, I say, above all other nations, should be more than ordinarily cautious how you attach yourself to any one principle, and very sure you have made choice of that which is right, before you venture to defend it, or pretend to impose it on others; which nothing is more plain than that you would attempt, when you had once taken it for granted in your own minds; and as your opinions would be various, and each man equally tenacious, hence would arise continual jars, quarrels, and every kind of mischief to yourselves, besides exposing you to the ridicule of all your laughing neighbours. A melancholy proof of this fell under my observation, which, because it may serve as a warning to others not to fall into the same ungovernable rashness, I think it will be kind to relate.

On my first coming into *England,* I was acquainted with two young gentlemen, who, though they were not at all of kin, loved each other as brothers: they were not only inseparable companions, but such friends as one shall seldom hear of since the days of *Castor* and *Pollux,* or the famed *Pylades* and *Orestes.*[8] Whatever the world calls pleasure, would have been no pleasure to either, had the other not partook of it; their comforts, their disappointments were mutual, and the only difference between them, was, that the person to whom either of these happened, seemed less affected with it than his friend; in fine, none that knew them, but believed that, had such an exigence made trial of their sincerity, neither would have refused any danger, or even death itself, for the safety of the other's life.

8. Castor and Pollux from Roman mythology were twin brothers (the Gemini) descended from Zeus and their mortal mother, Leda; they were the brothers of Helen of Troy. The young Greek heroes Pylades and Orestes (the son of Agamemnon, who murdered his mother, Clytemnestra, to avenge her murder of his father) were legendary for their intimate friendship.

But see how little dependence is to be placed on human resolutions, or even inclinations! how one unhappy moment may cancel the work of many years, and utterly erase what seemed most indelible! These two, whose friendship no adverse turns of Fortune, no considerations of self-interest, nor any new engagements could have broken off; these two, I say, did, for a very trifle, an idle whim, in which neither had concern, suffer themselves to be so far provoked, as to point the murdering sword against each other's breast.

A passage in the *Roman* history, differently related by *Justin* and *Tacitus*,[9] occasioned a warm dispute between them, each strenuously maintaining the credit of his favourite author, and tenacious of his own opinion; at length it came to that unpardonable expression of *You-lie,* which being given by one, was that instant returned by the other; the swords of both were immediately drawn,—they made but one pass, but it was a fatal one, and reached the heart of the younger of the two: he fell immediately, and the house being alarmed at the noise, several of the family came into the room, and found one of these dear companions breathing his last, and the other in agonies not to be described, about to give himself that fate, his tumultuous passion had inflicted on his friend; they prevented this act of desperation, but were obliged to yield him to that confinement and examination, the law exacts from those who are guilty of the crime he was. He took his trial, pleaded guilty, as to the fact, but it being easily seen to be unpremeditated, his life was spared; though both in public and private, he declared he desired nothing so much as death. How terrible an effect was here of that impatience of opposition I have been speaking of! What, alas! as the Poet says,

Was *Justin* to the one, or *Tacitus* to the other?[10]

Yet, for the reputation of authors, long since dead, and of whose veracity in reciting facts, neither of these gentlemen could be certain, were

9. The Roman historians Marcus Junianus Justinus, known for his redaction of Pompeius Trogus's *Historiarum philippicarum* (Philippic Histories), and Publius Cornelius Tacitus, author of several Roman histories.

10. An adaptation of Hamlet's "What's Hecuba to him or he to Hecuba, / That he should weep for her?"; Shakespeare, *Hamlet,* II.ii.560–61.

they rendered wholly forgetful of all considerations of their former amity, and each happened, by his wild fury, to attempt the destruction of that life, which, not an hour before, he would have risked, more than his own, for the preservation of.

It is a true characteristic of the people of *England,* that they are easily *led,* but impossible to be *drove* to anything; they *yield* on *soothing,* but are *obstinate* on *controul:* how careful ought they to be, therefore, that they imbibe no notions, which to persevere in, would be either shameful or prejudicial.

Perhaps you will call this a nobleness of mind, a stability of resolution: I grant it is so, and highly praise-worthy in the defence of just and laudable principles, such as it must be acknowledged, yours are at present. But if ever a change should happen in your way of thinking, and you should be as virulent in asserting a quite contrary opinion, how dreadful would it be! And I must put you in remembrance, however you may take it, that I have not complimented you so far as to say, you have ever been famous for continuing long in the same mind.

Neither were this so much to be lamented impetuosity of nature, ever attended with any of those dismal consequences we often see it is; nothing is more strange than that every one who finds it in himself will not, for the sake of the very thing he espouses, endeavour to suppress, or at least to restrain it as much as possible from breaking out, either in words or actions. None ever yet got the better in an argument, by seeming to enforce it: disdain will then shut up the heart of his antagonist against all conviction, and he will think it a meanness of spirit to give his assent even to the best reasons, when delivered in an authoritative way.

Moderation, therefore, good manners, and gentleness of behaviour to those of different principles, of what kind soever, is certainly not only the best and the wisest way, but also the most likely to bring them over; and as there are some shining examples of this virtue among you, it is a great misfortune they are not more generally *admired,* and then they could not fail of being more generally *imitated.*

9 August 1746

Samuel Johnson
(1709–84)

THE SON OF A PROVINCIAL bookseller from Litchfield, Samuel Johnson rose to London literary fame as a poet, an essayist, a biographer, the first lexicographer of the English language, and a critical canonizer of English literary history. In addition to his periodical papers for *The Rambler* (1750–52) and *The Adventurer* (1752–54), and "The Idler" series in *The Universal Chronicle* (1758–60), he published poems, including "London" (1738) and "The Vanity of Human Wishes" (1749), a satirical novel (*Rasselas,* 1759), a critical edition of Shakespeare (1765), a travel narrative (*A Journey to the Western Islands of Scotland,* 1775), and a series of biographical essays (*Lives of the English Poets,* 1779–81). In his own day, Johnson was known for his personality as much as his writing, and many of his trenchant insights into human nature and society were recorded by his biographer James Boswell, who made it his mission to transcribe the witticisms, aphorisms, maxims, and epigrams that readily dropped from the lips of this master prose stylist.

At mid-century Johnson ventured into the English essay tradition with his periodical *The Rambler,* published as a twopenny sheet from 20 March 1750 to 14 March 1752. During that time, he was compiling his monumental *Dictionary of the English Language* (1755), a literary work in its own right. Like his definition of the lexicographer as "a harmless drudge," his definition of the essay as "a loose sally of the mind; an irregular undigested piece" may be self-consciously tongue in cheek, for it is hardly borne out in his own papers. Discarding the apparatus of the coffeehouse culture that shaped *The Tatler* and *The Spectator,* Johnson turned instead to the meditative space of his own "closet," or study. In adopting the persona of the Rambler, he invoked his Addisonian precursor, who begins *Spectator* no. 3 recalling "one of my late Rambles, or rather Speculations." Johnson rambles through a wide range of human concerns in his essays, and, as Boswell wrote of the periodical, "in no writings whatever can be found more bark and steel for the mind."[1] (Perhaps a little Steele, too.) A decade later, in "The Idler," Johnson displayed his gift for humor in a persona intended both as a self-parody and a poignant critique of the nature of readerly (and writerly) "idleness." The series, published weekly from April 1758 through April 1760, coincided with his marriage to Elizabeth ("Tetty") Porter, a widow twenty-one years his senior, and the happiness of their union probably contributed to Johnson's encomiums on marriage in his periodical essays.

Selections are from Samuel Johnson, *The Rambler,* 4th ed. (London, 1756), and Johnson, *The Idler* (Dublin, 1762); "Idler" no. 22 is from *The Universal Chronicle* (1758), where it first appeared.

The Rambler
No. 4. [On Modern Romances, or Novels]

Simul et jucunda et idonea dicere Vitae. Hor.

And join both profit and delight in one. Creech.[2]

The works of fiction, with which the present generation seems more particularly delighted, are such as exhibit life in its true state, diversified only by accidents that daily happen in the world, and influenced by passions and qualities which are really to be found in conversing with mankind.[3]

This kind of writing may be termed not improperly the comedy of romance, and is to be conducted nearly by the rules of comic poetry. Its province is to bring about natural events by easy means, and to keep up curiosity without the help of wonder: it is therefore precluded from the machines and expedients of the heroic romance, and can neither employ giants to snatch away a lady from the nuptial rites, nor knights to bring her back

---

1. James Boswell, *Life of Johnson* (1791; London: Campbell, 1992), 132.

2. "To utter words at once both pleasing and helpful to life"; Horace, *Ars poetica* (Art of Poetry), l. 334, which was translated in 1684 by Thomas Creech.

3. Johnson is referring to the developing genre of the novel, which had grown to encompass works like Tobias Smollett's *Roderick Random* (1748) and Henry Fielding's *Tom Jones* (1749).

from captivity; it can neither bewilder its personages in deserts, nor lodge them in imaginary castles.

I remember a remark made by Scaliger upon Pontanus,[4] that all his writings are filled with the same images; and that if you take from him his lillies and his roses, his satyrs and his dryads, he will have nothing left that can be called poetry. In like manner, almost all the fictions of the last age will vanish, if you deprive them of a hermit and a wood, a battle and a shipwreck.

Why this wild strain of imagination found reception so long, in polite and learned ages, it is not easy to conceive; but we cannot wonder that, while readers could be procured, the authors were willing to continue it: for when a man had by practice gained some fluency of language, he had no further care than to retire to his closet, let loose his invention, and heat his mind with incredibilities; a book was thus produced without fear of criticism, without the toil of study, without knowledge of nature, or acquaintance of life.

The task of our present writers is very different; it requires, together with that learning which is to be gained from books, that experience which can never be attained by solitary diligence, but must arise from general converse, and accurate observation of the living world. Their performances have, as Horace expresses it, *plus oneris quantum veniae minus*, little indulgence, and therefore more difficulty.[5] They are engaged in portraits of which every one knows the original, and can detect any deviation from exactness of resemblance. Other writings are safe, except from the malice of learning, but these are in danger from every common reader; as the slipper ill executed was censured by a shoemaker who happened to stop in his way at the Venus of Appelles.[6]

But the fear of not being approved as just copiers of human manners, is not the most important concern that an author of this sort ought to have

4. The Italian humanist scholar Julius Caesar Scaliger (1484–1588) discusses the poet Giovanni Pontano (in Latin, Jovianus Pontanus, 1426–1503) in his *Poetices libri septem* (Poetics, Book 7), VI.4.

5. Horace, *Epistles,* II.i.170.

6. Pliny, in *Natural History,* XXXV.xxxvi.85, notes that the fourth-century B.C. painter Apelles of Kos was willing to redraw a sandal on the advice of a cobbler but not to alter the human form, remarking, "ne supra crepidam sutor" (a shoemaker in his criticism must not go beyond the sandal).

before him. These books are written chiefly to the young, the ignorant, and the idle, to whom they serve as lectures of conduct, and introductions into life. They are entertainment of minds unfurnished with ideas, and therefore easily susceptible of impressions; not fixed by principles, and therefore easily following the current of fancy; not informed by experience, and consequently open to very false suggestion and partial account.

That the highest degree of reverence should be paid to youth, and that nothing indecent should be suffered to approach their eyes and ears; are precepts extorted by sense and virtue from an ancient writer, by no means eminent for chastity of thought.[7] The same kind, though not the same degree of caution, is required to every thing which is laid before them, to secure them from unjust prejudices, perverse opinions, and incongruous combinations of images.

In the romances formerly written, every transaction and sentiment was so remote from all that passes among men, that the reader was in very little danger of making any applications to himself; the virtues and crimes were equally beyond his sphere of activity; and he amused himself with heroes and with traitors, deliverers and persecutors, as with beings of another species, whose actions were regulated upon motives of their own, and who had neither faults nor excellencies in common with himself.

But when an adventurer is leveled with the rest of the world, and acts in such scenes of the universal drama, as may be the lot of any other man; young spectators fix their eyes upon him with closer attention, and hope by observing his behavior and success to regulate their own practices, when they shall be engaged in the like part.

For this reason these familiar histories may perhaps be made of greater use than the solemnities of professed morality and convey the knowledge of vice and virtue with more efficacy than axioms and definitions. But if the power of example is so great, as to take possession of the memory by a kind of violence, and produce effects almost without the intervention of the will, care ought to be taken that, when the choice is unrestrained, the best examples only should be exhibited; and that which is likely to operate so strongly, should not be mischievous or uncertain in its effects.

7. Juvenal, *Satires,* XIV.

The chief advantage which these fictions have over real life is, that their authors are at liberty, though not to invent, yet to select objects, and to cull from the mass of mankind, those individuals upon which the attention ought most to be employed; as a diamond, though it cannot be made, may be polished by art, and placed in such a situation, as to display that luster which before was buried among common stones.

It is justly considered as the greatest excellency of art, to imitate nature; but it is necessary to distinguish those parts of nature, which are most proper for imitation: greater care is still required in representing life, which is so often discoloured by passion, or deformed by wickedness. If the world be promiscuously described, I cannot see of what use it can be to read the account; or why it may not be as safe to turn the eye immediately upon mankind, as upon a mirror which shows all that presents itself without discrimination.

It is therefore not a sufficient vindication of character, that it is drawn as it appears, for many characters ought never to be drawn; nor a narrative, that the train of events is agreeable to observation and experience, for that observation which is called knowledge of the world, will be found much more frequently to make men cunning than good. The purpose of these writings is surely not only to show mankind, but to provide that they may be seen hereafter with less hazard; to teach the means of avoiding the snares which are laid by TREACHERY for INNOCENCE, without infusing any wish for that superiority with which the betrayer flatters his vanity; to give the power of counteracting fraud, without the temptation to practise it; to initiate youth by mock encounters in the art of necessary defence, and to increase prudence without impairing virtue.

Many writers, for the sake of following nature, so mingle good and bad qualities in their principal personages, that they are both equally conspicuous; and as we accompany them through their adventures with delight, and are led by degrees to interest ourselves in their favour, we lose the abhorrence of their faults, because they do not hinder our pleasure, or, perhaps, regard them with some kindness for being united with so much merit.

There have been men indeed splendidly wicked, whose endowments threw a brightness on their crimes, and whom scarce any villainy made perfectly detestable, because they never could be wholly divested of their excellencies; but such have been in all ages the great corrupters of the world, and their resemblance ought no more to be preserved, than the art of murdering without pain.

Some have advanced, without due attention to the consequences of this notion, that certain virtues have their correspondent faults, and therefore that to exhibit either apart is to deviate from probability. Thus men are observed by Swift to be "Grateful in the same degree as they are Resentful."[8] This principle, with others of the same kind, supposes man to act from a brute impulse, and pursue a certain degree of inclination, without any choice of the object; for, otherwise, though it should be allowed that gratitude and resentment arise from the same constitution of the passions, it follows not that they will be equally indulged when reason is consulted; yet unless that consequence be admitted, this sagacious maxim becomes an empty sound, without any relation to practice or to life.

Nor is it evident, that even the first motions to these effects are always in the same proportion. For pride, which produces quickness of resentment, will obstruct gratitude, by unwillingness to admit that inferiority which obligation implies; and it is very unlikely, that he who cannot think he receives a favour will acknowledge or repay it.

It is of the most importance to mankind, that positions of this tendency should be laid open and confuted; for while men consider good and evil as springing from the same root, they will spare the one for the sake of the other, and in judging, if not of others at least of themselves, will be apt to estimate their virtues by their vices. To this fatal error all those will contribute, who confounded the colours of right and wrong, and instead of helping to settle their boundaries, mix them with so much art, that no common mind is able to disunite them.

In narratives, where historical veracity has no place, I cannot discover why there should not be exhibited the most perfect idea of virtue; of virtue not angelical, nor above probability, for what we cannot credit we shall never imitate, but the highest and purest that humanity can reach, which, exercised in such trials as the various revolutions of things shall bring upon it, may, by conquering some calamities, and enduring others, teach us what we may hope, and what we can perform. Vice, for vice is necessary to be shown, should always disgust; nor should the graces of gaiety, or the dig-

8. Jonathan Swift, *Miscellanies* (1727), 2:354.

nity of courage, be so united with it, as to reconcile it to the mind. Wherever it appears, it should raise hatred by the malignity of its practices, and contempt by the meanness of its stratagems; for while it is supported by either parts or spirit, it will be seldom heartily abhorred. The Roman tyrant was content to be hated, if he was but feared; and there are thousands of readers of romances willing to be thought wicked, if they may be allowed to be wits.[9] It is therefore to be steadily inculcated, that virtue is the highest proof of understanding, and the only solid basis of greatness; and that vice is the natural consequence of narrow thoughts, that it begins in mistake, and ends in ignominy.

31 March 1750

No. 14. [On the Life of an Author vs. His Writing]

————————*Nil fuit unquam*
Sic dispar sibi————————Hor.

Sure such a various creature ne'er was known. Francis.[10]

Among the many inconsistencies which folly produces, or infirmity suffers in the human mind, there has often been observed a manifest and striking contrariety between the life of an author and his writings; and Milton, in a letter to a learned stranger, by whom he had been visited, with great reason congratulates himself upon the consciousness of being found equal to his own character, and having preserved in a private and familiar interview that reputation which his works had procured him.[11]

Those whom the appearance of virtue, or the evidence of genius, have tempted to a nearer knowledge of the writer in whose performances they

9. The emperor Caligula, according to Suetonius, held as his maxim: "Oderint dum metuant" (Let them hate me, so they but fear me).

10. "Never was a creature so inconsistent"; Horace, *Satires,* I.iii.18–19. While Johnson believed that "the lyrical part of Horace can never be perfectly translated," he thought that "Francis has done it the best." Here he quotes from Philip Francis's 1746 edition of Horace's *Satires.*

11. See Milton's letter to Emeric Bigot of 24 March 1656/57 in *The Works of John Milton,* 18 vols., ed. Frank Allen Patterson et al. (New York: Columbia University Press 1936), 12:85.

may be found, have indeed had frequent reason to repent their curiosity; the bubble that sparkled before them has become common water at the touch; the phantom of perfection has vanished when they wished to press it to their bosom. They have lost the pleasure of imagining how far humanity may be exalted, and, perhaps, felt themselves less inclined to toil up the steeps of virtue, when they observe those who seem best able to point the way, loitering below, as either afraid of the labour, or doubtful of the reward.

It has been long the custom of the oriental monarchs to hide themselves in gardens and palaces, to avoid the conversation of mankind, and to be known to their subjects only by their edicts. The same policy is no less necessary to him that writes, than to him that governs; for men would not more patiently submit to be taught, than commanded, by one known to have the same follies and weaknesses with themselves. A sudden intruder into the closet of an author would perhaps feel equal indignation with the officer, who having long solicited admission into the presence of Sardanapalus, saw him not consulting upon laws, enquiring into grievances, or modelling armies, but employed in feminine amusements, and directing the ladies in their work.[12]

It is not difficult to conceive, however, that for many reasons a man writes much better than he lives. For, without entering into refined speculations, it may be shown much easier to design than to perform. A man proposes his schemes of life in a state of abstraction and disengagement, exempt from the enticements of hope, the solicitations of affection, the importunities of appetite, or the depressions of fear, and is in the same state with him that teaches upon land the art of navigation, to whom the sea is always smooth, and the wind always prosperous.

The mathematicians are well acquainted with the difference between pure science, which has to do only with ideas, and the application of its laws to the use of life, in which they are constrained to submit to the imperfection of matter and the influence of accidents. Thus, in moral discussions it is to be remembered that many impediments obstruct our practice, which

12. The story is recounted by Diodorus of Sicily in the Loeb Classical Library of History, 1:428–31; Sardanapalus was a legendary Assyrian king noted for his luxurious lifestyle.

very easily give way to theory. The speculatist is only in danger of erroneous reasoning, but the man involved in life has his own passions, and those of others, to encounter, and is embarrassed with a thousand inconveniences, which confound him with variety of impulse, and either perplex or obstruct his way. He is forced to act without deliberation, and obliged to choose before he can examine; he is surprised by sudden alterations of the state of things, and changes his measures according to superficial appearances; he is led by others, either because he is indolent, or because he is timorous; he is sometimes afraid to know what is right, and sometimes finds friends or enemies diligent to deceive him.

We are, therefore, not to wonder that most fail, amidst tumult, and snares, and danger, in the observance of those precepts, which they laid down in solitude, safety, and tranquility, with a mind unbiased, and with liberty unobstructed. It is the condition of our present state to see more than we can attain, the exactest vigilance and caution can never maintain a single day of unmingled innocence, much less can the utmost efforts of incorporated mind reach the summits of speculative virtue.

It is, however, necessary for the idea of perfection to be proposed, that we may have some object to which our endeavours are to be directed; and he that is most deficient in the duties of life, makes some atonement for his faults, if he warns others against his own failings, and hinders, by the salubrity of his admonitions, the contagion of his example.

Nothing is more unjust, however common, than to charge with hypocrisy him that expresses zeal for those virtues, which he neglects to practise; since he may be sincerely convinced of the advantages of conquering his passions, without having yet obtained the victory, as a man may be confident of the advantages of a voyage, or a journey, without having courage or industry to undertake it, and may honestly recommend to others, those attempts which he neglects himself.

The interest which the corrupt part of mankind have in hardening themselves against every motive to amendment, has disposed them to give to these contradictions, when they can be produced against the cause of virtue, that weight which they will not allow them in any other case. They see men act in opposition to their interest, without supposing, that they do not know it; those who give way to the sudden violence of passion, and forsake the most important pursuits for petty pleasures, are not supposed to have changed their opinions, or to approve their own conduct. In moral or religious questions alone, they determine the sentiments by the actions, and charge every man with endeavouring to impose upon the world, whose writings are not confirmed by his life. They never consider that they themselves neglect, or practise something every day, inconsistently with their own settled judgment, nor discover that the conduct of the advocates for virtue can little increase, or lessen, the obligations of their dictates; argument is to be invalidated only by argument, and is in itself of the same force, whether or not it convinces him by whom it is proposed.

Yet since this prejudice, however unreasonable, is always likely to have some prevalence, it is the duty of every man to take care lest he should hinder the efficacy of his own instructions. When he desires to gain the belief of others, he should show that he believes himself; and when he teaches the fitness of virtue by his reasonings, he should, by his example, prove its possibility: thus much at least may be required of him, that he shall not act worse than others because he writes better, nor imagine that, by the merit of his genius, he may claim indulgence beyond mortals of the lower classes, and be excused for want of prudence, or neglect of virtue. BACON, in his History of the winds, after having offered something to the imagination as desirable, often proposes lower advantages in its place to the reason as attainable.[13] The same method may be sometimes pursued in moral endeavours, which this philosopher has observed in natural enquiries; having first set positive and absolute excellence before us, we may be pardoned though we sink down to humbler virtue, trying, however, to keep our point always in view, and struggling not to lose ground, though we cannot gain it.

It is recorded of Sir Matthew Hale, that he, for a long time, concealed the consecration of himself to the stricter duties of religion, lest, by some flagitious and shameful action, he should bring piety into disgrace.[14] For

13. See Bacon's "Historia Ventorum" (History of the Winds, 1622), in *Works*, ed. James Spedding, Robert Leslie Ellis, and Douglas Denton Heath (London, 1887), 2:73.
14. See Gilbert Burnet, *Life and Death of Sir Matthew Hale, Kt.* (London, 1681), 141–42. Hale (1609–76) was Lord Chief Justice of England under the reign of Charles II.

the same reason, it may be prudent for a writer, who apprehends that he shall not enforce his own maxims by his domestic character, to conceal his name that he may not injure them.

There are, indeed, a greater number whose curiosity to gain a more familiar knowledge of successful writers, is not so much prompted by an opinion of their power to improve as to delight, and who expect from them not arguments against vice, or dissertations on temperance or justice, but flights of wit, and sallies of pleasantry, or, at least, acute remarks, nice distinctions, justness of sentiment, and elegance of diction.

This expectation is, indeed, specious and probable, and yet, such is the fate of all human hopes, that it is very often frustrated, and those who raise admiration by their books, disgust by their company. A man of letters for the most part spends, in the privacies of study, that season of life in which the manners are to be softened into ease, and polished into elegance, and, when he has gained knowledge enough to be respected, has neglected the minuter acts by which he might have pleased. When he enters life, if his temper be soft and timorous, he is diffident and bashful, from the knowledge of his defects; or if he was born with spirit and resolution, he is ferocious and arrogant from the consciousness of his merit: he is either dissipated by the awe of company, and unable to recollect his reading, and arrange his arguments; or he is hot, and dogmatical, quick in opposition, and tenacious in defence, disabled by his own violence, and confused by his haste to triumph.

The graces of writing and conversation are of different kinds, and though he who excels in one might have been with opportunities and application equally successful in the other, yet as many please by extemporary talk, though utterly unacquainted with the more accurate method, and more laboured beauties, which composition requires; so it is very possible that men, wholly accustomed to works of study, may be without that readiness of conception, and affluence of language, always necessary to colloquial entertainment. They may want address to watch the hints which conversation offers for the display of their particular attainments, or they may be so much unfurnished with matter on common subjects, that discourse not professedly literary glides over them as heterogeneous bodies, without admitting their conceptions to mix in the circulation.

A transition from an author's books to his conversation, is too often like an entrance into a large city, after a distant prospect. Remotely, we see nothing but spires of temples, and turrets of palaces, and imagine it the residence of splendor, grandeur, and magnificence; but, when we have passed the gates, we find it perplexed with narrow passages, disgraced with despicable cottages, embarrassed with obstructions, and clouded with smoke.

5 May 1750

No. 82. [On a Virtuoso]

Omnia Castor emis, sic fiet ut omnia vendas. Martial, VII.98.

Who buys without discretion, buys to sell.[15]

To the Rambler.
Sir,
It will not be necessary to solicit your good will by any formal preface, when I have informed you, that I have long been known as the most laborious and zealous virtuoso that the present age has had the honour of producing, and that inconveniencies have been brought upon me by an unextinguishable ardour of curiosity, and an unshaken perseverance in the acquisition of the productions of art and nature.

It was observed, from my entrance into the world, that I had something uncommon in my disposition, and that there appeared in me very early tokens of superior genius. I was always an enemy to trifles; the playthings which my mother bestowed upon me I immediately broke that I might discover the method of their structure, and the causes of their motions; of all the toys with which children are delighted I valued only coral, and as soon as I could speak, asked, like Peiresc, innumerable questions which the maids about me could not resolve.[16] As I grew older I was more thoughtful and serious, and instead of amusing myself with puerile diver-

15. "You buy up everything, Castor; so it will come to pass that you sell up everything"; Martial, *Epigrams,* VII.98. Johnson gives his own translation of the Roman poet.

16. A coral is a teething ring. Nicolas-Claude Fabri de Peiresc (1580–1637) was a scientist and antiquarian collector, or virtuoso.

sions, made collections of natural rarities, and never walked into the fields without bringing home stones of remarkable forms, or insects of some uncommon species. I never entered an old house, from which I did not take away the painted glass, and often lamented that I was not one of that happy generation who demolished the convents and monasteries, and broke windows by law.[17]

Being thus early possessed by a taste for solid knowledge, I passed my youth with very little disturbance from passions and appetites, and having no pleasure in the company of boys and girls, who talked of plays, politics, fashions, or love, I carried on my enquiries with incessant diligence, and had amassed more stones, mosses, and shells, than are to be found in many celebrated collections, at an age in which the greatest part of young men are studying under tutors, or endeavouring to recommend themselves to notice by their dress, their air, and their levities.

When I was two and twenty years old, I became, by the death of my father, possessed of a small estate in land, with a very large sum of money in the public funds, and must confess that I did not much lament him, for he was a man of mean parts, bent rather upon growing rich than wise. He once fretted at the expence of only ten shillings, which he happened to overhear me offering for the sting of a hornet, though it was a cold moist summer, in which very few hornets had been seen. He often recommended to me the study of physic, in which, said he, you may at once gratify your curiosity after natural history, and increase your fortune by benefiting mankind. I heard him, Mr. Rambler, with pity, and as there was no prospect of elevating a mind formed to grovel, suffered him to please himself with hoping that I should sometime follow his advice. For you know that there are men, with whom, when they have once settled a notion in their heads, it is to very little purpose to dispute.

Being now left wholly to my own inclinations, I very soon enlarged the bounds of my curiosity, and contented myself no longer with such rarities as required only judgment and industry, and when once found, might be had for nothing. I now turned my thoughts to *Exotics* and *Antiques,* and

17. In 1538 Henry VIII took steps against the authority of the pope when he began the dissolution of the monasteries in England and Wales, confiscating church buildings and property.

became so well known for my generous patronage of ingenious men, that my levee was crowded with visitants, some to see my museum, and others to increase its treasures, by selling me whatever they had brought from other countries.

I had always a contempt of that narrowness of conception, which contents itself with cultivating some single corner of the field of science; I took the whole region into my view, and wished it of yet greater extent. But no man's power can be equal to his will. I was forced to proceed by slow degrees, and to purchase what chance or kindness happened to present. I did not, however, proceed without some design, or imitate the indiscretion of those, who begin a thousand collections, and finish none. Having been always a lover of geography, I determined to collect the maps drawn in the rude and barbarous times, before any regular surveys, or just observations; and have, at a great expence, brought together a volume, in which, perhaps, not a single country is laid down according to its true situation, and by which, he that desires to know the errors of the ancient geographers may be amply informed.

But my ruling passion is patriotism: my chief care has been to procure the products of our own country; and as Alfred received the tribute of the Welch in wolves' heads,[18] I allowed my tenants to pay their rents in butterflies, till I had exhausted the papilionaceous tribe. I then directed them to the pursuit of other animals, and obtained, by this easy method, most of the grubs and insects, which land, air, or water can supply. I have three species of earthworms not known to the naturalists, have discovered a new ephemera, and can show four wasps that were taken torpid in their winter quarters. I have, from my own ground, the longest blade of grass upon record, and once accepted, as a half year's rent for a field of wheat, an ear containing more grains than had been seen before upon a single stem.

One of my tenants so much neglected his own interest, as to supply me, in a whole summer, with only two horse-flies, and those of little more than the common size; and I was upon the brink of seizing for arrears,

18. A reference to the English king Eadgar (r. 957–75) who converted the tax of gold and silver in Wales into an annual tribute of 300 wolves' heads in an effort to reduce the number of wolves on the British mainland. The anecdote somehow became attached to the more famous Anglo-Saxon king Alfred (or Aelfred) the Great (c. 849–99).

when his good fortune threw a white mole in his way, for which he was not only forgiven, but rewarded.

These, however, were petty acquisitions, and made at small expence; nor should I have ventured to rank myself among the virtuosi without better claims. I have suffered nothing worthy the regard of a wise man to escape my notice: I have ransacked the old and the new world, and been equally attentive to past ages and the present. For the illustration of ancient history, I can show a marble, of which the inscription, though it is not now legible, appears from some broken remains of the letters, to have been *Tuscan*, and therefore probably engraved before the foundation of *Rome*. I have two pieces of porphyry found among the ruins of *Ephesus*, and three letters broken off by a learned traveller from the monuments at *Persepolis;* a piece of stone which paved the *Areopagus* of *Athens*, and a plate without figures or characters which was found at *Corinth*, and which I therefore believe to be that metal which was once valued before gold. I have sand gathered out of the *Granicus;* a fragment of *Trajan's* bridge over the *Danube;* some of the mortar which cemented the water-course of *Tarquin;* a horse shoe broken on the *Flaminian* way; and a turf with five daisies dug from the field of *Pharsalia*.[19]

I do not wish to raise the envy of unsuccessful collectors, by too pompous a display of my scientific wealth, but cannot forbear to observe, that there are few regions of the globe which are not honoured with some memorial in my cabinets. The Persian monarchs are said to have boasted the greatness of their empire, by being served at their tables with drink from the Ganges and the Danube: I can show one vial, of which the water was formerly an icicle on the crags of Caucasus, and another that contains what once was snow on the top of Atlas; in a third is dew brushed from a banana in the gardens of Ispahan; and, in another, brine that has rolled in the

19. All classical souvenirs: the Areopagus is a hill in Athens dedicated to Ares that in classical times it held the homicide court; the Granicus is a river in Asia Minor where Alexander the Great triumphed over the Persians; Trajan's bridge on the lower Danube provided supplies to the Roman legions; L. Tarquinius Pricius built a water drainage system in Rome to empty the Tiber; the Flaminian Way was an ancient Roman road leading to Gaul built by Gaius Flaminius; Pharsalia refers to the Battle of Pharsalus in 48 B.C. between Julius Caesar and Pompey the Great; the "metal" is Corinthian bronze.

Pacific Ocean. I flatter myself that I am writing to a man who will rejoice at the honour which my labours have procured to my country, and therefore, I shall tell you that Britain can by my care boast of a snail that has crawled upon the wall of China; a humming bird which an American princess wore in her ear; the tooth of an elephant who carried the queen of Siam; the skin of an ape that was kept in the palace of the great mogul; a ribbon that adorned one of the maids of a Turkish sultana; and a scimitar once wielded by a soldier of Abas the Great.[20]

In collecting antiquities of every country, I have been careful to choose only by intrinsic worth, and real usefulness, without regard to party or opinions. I have therefore a lock of Cromwell's hair in a box turned from a piece of the royal oak; and keep, in the same drawers, sand scraped from the coffin of King Richard, and a commission signed by Henry the Seventh. I have equal veneration for the ruff of Elizabeth and the shoe of Mary of Scotland; and should lose, with like regret, a tobacco-pipe of Raleigh, and a stirrup of King James. I have paid the same price for a glove of Lewis, and a thimble of Queen Mary; for a fur cap of the Czar, and a boot of Charles of Sweden.[21]

You will easily imagine that these accumulations were not made without some diminution of my fortune, for I was so well known to spare no cost, that at every sale some bid against me for hire, some for sport, and some for malice; and if I asked the price of any thing it was sufficient to double the demand. For curiosity, trafficking thus with avarice, the wealth of India had not been enough; and I, by little and little, transferred all my money from the funds to my closet: here I was inclined to stop, and live upon my estate in literary leisure, but the sale of the Harleian collection shook my resolution: I mortgaged my land, and purchased thirty medals, which I could never find before.[22] I have at length bought till I can buy no

20. Abbas I of Persia (1557–1629).

21. All monarchs of the early modern period (except for Sir Walter Raleigh, statesman and poet under Elizabeth I who was imprisoned in the Tower of London by James I), whose relics the virtuoso collected. Lewis is Louis VII of France.

22. A colorful figure of eighteenth-century political life, Robert Harley, first Earl of Oxford and Mortimer (1661–1724), was an avid book collector who owned more than six thousand volumes of books and manuscripts, mainly focused on sixteenth- and seventeenth-century English history, at the time of his death. The collection is now owned by the British Museum.

longer, and the cruelty of my creditors has seized my repository; I am therefore condemned to disperse what the labour of an age will not re-assemble. I submit to that which cannot be opposed, and shall, in a short time, declare a sale. I have, while it is yet in my power, sent you a pebble, picked up by Tavernier on the banks of the Ganges;[23] for which I desire no other recompence than that you will recommend my catalogue to the public.

QUISQUILIUS[24]

29 December 1750

No. 113. [On the Trials of Courtship]

————*Uxorem, Posthume, ducis?*
Dic, quâ Tisiphone, quibus exagitare colubris? Juvenal.

A sober man like thee to change his life!
What fury wou'd possess thee with a wife? Dryden.[25]

To the Rambler.

Sir,

I know not whether it is always a proof of innocence to treat censure with contempt. We owe so much reverence to the wisdom of mankind, as justly to wish, that our own opinion of our merit may be ratified by the concurrence of other suffrages; and since guilt and infamy must have the same effect upon intelligences unable to pierce beyond external appearance, and influenced often rather by example than precept, we are obliged to refute a false charge, lest we should countenance the crime which we have never committed. To turn away from an accusation with supercilious silence, is equally in the power of him that is hardened by villainy, and inspirited by innocence. The wall of brass which Horace erects upon a clear conscience,

23. The cartographer Melchior Tavernier (1564–1644), who published maps and atlases.

24. From the Latin word meaning rubbish, or refuse.

25. "Posthumus, are you, you who once had your wits, taking to yourself a wife? Tell me what Tisiphone, what snakes are driving you mad?"; Juvenal, *Satires,* VI.28–29. John Dryden's translation is from 1697.

may be sometimes raised by impudence or power;[26] and we should always wish to preserve the dignity of virtue by adorning her with graces which wickedness cannot assume.

For this reason I have determined no longer to endure, with either patient or sullen resignation, a reproach, which is, at least in my opinion, unjust; but will lay my case honestly before you, that you or your readers may at length decide it.

Whether you will be able to preserve your boasted impartiality, when you hear, that I am considered as an adversary by half the female world, you may surely pardon me for doubting, notwithstanding the veneration to which you may imagine yourself entitled by your age, your learning, your abstraction, or your virtue. Beauty, Mr. Rambler, has often overpowered the resolutions of the firm, and the reasonings of the wise, roused the old to sensibility, and subdued the rigorous to softness.

I am one of those unhappy beings, who have been marked out as husbands for many different women, and deliberated a hundred times on the brink of matrimony. I have discussed all the nuptial preliminaries so often, that I can repeat the forms in which jointures are settled, pin-money[27] secured, and provisions for younger children ascertained; but am at last doomed by general consent to everlasting solitude, and excluded by an irreversible decree from all hopes of connubial felicity. I am pointed out by every mother, as a man whose visits cannot be admitted without reproach; who raises hopes only to embitter disappointment, and makes offers only to seduce girls into a waste of that part of life, in which they might gain advantageous matches, and become mistresses[28] and mothers.

I hope you will think, that some part of this penal severity may justly be remitted, when I inform you, that I never yet professed love to a woman without sincere intentions of marriage; that I have never continued an appearance of intimacy from the hour that my inclination changed, but to preserve her whom I was leaving from the shock of abruptness, or the ig-

---

26. "Be this our wall of bronze, to have no guilt at heart, no wrongdoing to turn us pale"; Horace, *Epistles,* I.i.60–61.

27. An allowance given by a husband to his wife for personal expenses.

28. Meaning mistresses of their own homes.

nominy of contempt; that I always endeavoured to give the ladies an opportunity of seeming to discard me; and that I never forsook a mistress for larger fortune, or brighter beauty, but because I discovered some irregularity in her conduct, or some depravity in her mind; not because I was charmed by another, but because I was offended by herself.

I was very early tired of that succession of amusements by which the thoughts of most young men are dissipated, and had not long glittered in the splendour of an ample patrimony before I wished for the calm of domestic happiness. Youth is naturally delighted with sprightliness and ardour, and therefore I breathed out the sighs of my first affection at the feet of the gay, the sparkling, the vivacious Ferocula.[29] I fancied to myself a perpetual source of happiness in wit never exhausted, and spirit never depressed; looked with veneration on her readiness of expedients, contempt of difficulty, assurance of address, and promptitude of reply; considered her as exempt by some prerogative of nature from the weakness and timidity of female minds; and congratulated myself upon a companion superior to all common troubles and embarrassments. I was, indeed, somewhat disturbed by the unshaken perseverance with which she enforced her demands of an unreasonable settlement; yet I should have consented to pass my life in union with her, had not my curiosity led me to a crowd gathered in the street, where I found Ferocula, in presence of hundreds, disputing for sixpence with a chairman. I saw her in so little need of assistance, that it was no breach of the laws of chivalry to forbear interposition, and I spared myself the shame of owning her acquaintance. I forgot some point of ceremony at our next interview, and soon provoked her to forbid me her presence.

My next attempt was upon a lady of great eminence for learning and philosophy. I had frequently observed the barrenness and uniformity of connubial conversation, and therefore thought highly of my own prudence and discernment when I selected from a multitude of wealthy beauties, the deep-read Misothea,[30] who declared herself the inexorable enemy of ignorant pertness, and puerile levity; and scarcely condescended to make tea, but for the linguist, the geometrician, the astronomer, or the poet. The queen of the Amazons was only to be gained by the hero who could conquer her in single combat; and Misothea's heart was only to bless the

29. Derived from the Latin *ferox*, fierce.
30. Etymologically, god-hater.

scholar who could overpower her by disputation. Amidst the fondest trans-
ports of courtship she could call for a definition of terms, and treated every
argument with contempt that could not be reduced to regular syllogism.
You may easily imagine, that I wished this courtship at an end; but when I
desired her to shorten my torments, and fix the day of my felicity, we were
led into a long conversation, in which Misothea endeavoured to demon-
strate the folly of attributing choice and self-direction to any human being.
It was not difficult to discover the danger of committing myself for ever to
the arms of one who might at any time mistake the dictates of passion, or
the calls of appetite, for the decree of fate; or consider cuckoldom as necessary to the general system, as a link in the everlasting chain of successive
causes. I therefore told her, that destiny had ordained us to part; and that
nothing should have torn me from her but the talons of necessity.

I then solicited the regard of the calm, the prudent, the economical
Sophronia,[31] a lady who considered wit as dangerous, and learning as su-
perfluous; and thought that the woman who kept her house clean, and her
accounts exact, took receipts for every payment, and could find them at a
sudden call, enquired nicely after the condition of the tenants, read the
price of stocks once a week, and purchased every thing at the best market,
could want no accomplishments necessary to the happiness of a wise man.
She discoursed with great solemnity on the care and vigilance which the su-
perintendence of a family demands; observed how many were ruined by
confidence in servants; and told me, that she never expected honesty but
from a strong chest, and that the best storekeeper was the mistress's eye.
Many such oracles of generosity she uttered, and made every day new improvements in her schemes for the regulation of her servants, and the distribution of her time. I was convinced, that whatever I might suffer from
Sophronia, I should escape poverty; and we therefore proceeded to adjust
the settlements according to her own rule, "fair and softly." But one morning her maid came to me in tears to entreat my interest for a reconciliation
to her mistress, who had turned her out at night for breaking six teeth in a
tortoise-shell comb: she had attended her lady from a distant province, and
having not lived long enough to save much money, was destitute among
strangers, and though of a good family, in danger of perishing in the streets,
or of being compelled by hunger to prostitution. I made no scruple of

31. Derived from *sophia*, the Greek word for wisdom.

promising to restore her; but upon my first application to Sophronia was answered with an air which called for approbation, that if she neglected her own affairs, I might suspect her of neglecting mine; that the comb stood her in three half-crowns; that no servant should wrong her twice; and that indeed, she took the first opportunity of parting with Phyllida, because, though she was honest, her constitution was bad, and she thought her very likely to fall sick. Of our conference I need not tell you the effect; it surely may be forgiven me, if on this occasion I forgot the decency of common forms.

From two more ladies I was disengaged by finding, that they entertained my rivals at the same time, and determined their choice by the liberality of our settlements. Another I thought myself justified in forsaking, because she gave my attorney a bribe to favour her in the bargain; another, because I could never soften her to tenderness, till she heard that most of my family had died young; and another, because to increase her fortune by expectations, she represented her sister as languishing and consumptive.

I shall in another letter give the remaining part of my history of courtship.[32] I presume that I should hitherto have injured the majesty of female virtue, had I not hoped to transfer my affection to higher merit.

I am, &c.

HYMENAEUS[33]

16 April 1751

No. 161. [On the Previous Inhabitants of His Garret]

Οἵη περ φύλλων γενεή, τοίη δὲ καὶ ἀνδρῶν. Hom.[34]

Frail as the leaves that quiver on the sprays,
Like them man flourishes, like them decays.

Mr. Rambler,

Sir,

You have formerly observed that curiosity often terminates in barren knowledge, and that the mind is prompted to study and enquiry rather by

32. See *Rambler* no. 115.

33. Derived from Hymen, the Greek god of marriage.

34. "But if thou art of men, who eat the fruit of the field, draw nigh, that thou mayest the sooner enter the toils of destruction"; Homer, *Iliad,* VI.146. Unless otherwise identified, the translations in the text are Johnson's.

the uneasiness of ignorance, than the hope of profit. Nothing can be of less importance to any present interest than the fortune of those who have been long lost in the grave, and from whom nothing now can be hoped or feared. Yet to rouse the zeal of a true antiquary little more is necessary than to mention a name which mankind have conspired to forget; he will make his way to remote scenes of action through obscurity and contradiction, as *Tully* sought amidst bushes and brambles the tomb of *Archimedes*.[35]

It is not easy to discover how it concerns him that gathers the produce or receives the rent of an estate, to know through what families the land has passed, who is registered in the Conqueror's survey as its possessor,[36] how often it has been forfeited by treason, or how often sold by prodigality. The power or wealth of the present inhabitants of a country cannot be much increased by an enquiry after the names of those barbarians, who destroyed one another twenty centuries ago, in contests for the shelter of woods or convenience of pasturage. Yet we see that no man can be at rest in the enjoyment of a new purchase till he has learned the history of his grounds from the ancient inhabitants of the parish, and that no nation omits to record the actions of their ancestors, however bloody, savage and rapacious.

The same disposition, as different opportunities call it forth, discovers itself in great or little things. I have always thought it unworthy of a wise man to slumber in total inactivity only because he happens to have no employment equal to his ambition or genius; it is therefore my custom to apply my attention to the objects before me, and as I cannot think any place wholly unworthy of notice that affords a habitation to a man of letters, I have collected the history and antiquities of the several garrets in which I have resided.

Quantulacunque estis, vos ego magna voco.[37]

How small to others, but how great to me!

Many of these narratives my industry has been able to extend to a considerable length; but the woman with whom I now lodge has lived only

35. See Marcus Tullius Cicero, *Tusculan Disputations*, V.xxiii.64.

36. A reference to the Domesday Book, a register of property compiled on the order of William the Conqueror.

37. "However small thou art, I name thee mighty!"; Ovid, *Amores*, III.xv.14.

eighteen months in the house, and can give no account of its ancient revolutions; the plaisterer, having, at her entrance, obliterated by his white-wash, all the smoky memorials which former tenants had left upon the ceiling, and perhaps drawn the veil of oblivion over politicians, philosophers, and poets.

When I first cheapened my lodgings, the landlady told me, that she hoped I was not an author, for the lodgers on the first floor had stipulated that the upper rooms should not be occupied by a noisy trade. I very readily promised to give no disturbance to her family, and soon dispatched a bargain on the usual terms.

I had not slept many nights in my new apartment before I began to enquire after my predecessors, and found my landlady, whose imagination is filled chiefly with her own affairs, very ready to give me information.

Curiosity, like all other desires, produces pain as well as pleasure. Before she began her narrative, I had heated my head with expectations of adventures and discoveries, of elegance in disguise, and learning in distress; and was somewhat mortified when I heard, that the first tenant was a tailor, of whom nothing was remembered but that he complained of his room for want of light; and, after having lodged in it a month, and paid only a week's rent, pawned a piece of cloth which he was trusted to cut out, and was forced to make a precipitate retreat from this quarter of the town.

The next was a young woman newly arrived from the country, who lived for five weeks with great regularity, and became by frequent treats very much the favourite of the family, but at last received visits so frequently from a cousin in *Cheapside,* that she brought the reputation of the house into danger, and was therefore dismissed with good advice.

The room then stood empty for a fortnight; my landlady began to think that she had judged hardly, and often wished for such another lodger. At last an elderly man of a grave aspect, read the bill, and bargained for the room, at the very first price that was asked. He lived in close retirement, seldom went out till evening, and then returned early, sometimes cheerful, and at other times dejected. It was remarkable, that whatever he purchased, he never had small money in his pocket, and though cool and temperate on other occasions, was always vehement and stormy till he received his change. He paid his rent with great exactness, and seldom failed once a week to requite my landlady's civility with a supper. At last, such is the fate of human felicity, the house was alarmed at midnight by the constable, who demanded to search the garrets. My landlady assuring him that he had mistaken the door, conducted him up stairs, where he found the tools of a coiner; but the tenant had crawled along the roof to an empty house, and escaped; much to the joy of my landlady, who declares him a very honest man, and wonders why any body should be hanged for making money when such numbers are in want of it. She however confesses that she shall for the future always question the character of those who take her garret without beating down the price.

The bill was then placed again in the window, and the poor woman was teazed for seven weeks by innumerable passengers, who obliged her to climb with them every hour up five stories, and then disliked the prospect, hated the noise of a public street, thought the stairs narrow, objected to a low ceiling, required the walls to be hung with fresher paper, asked questions about the neighbourhood, could not think of living so far from their acquaintance, wished the window had looked to the south rather than the west, told how the door and chimney might have been better disposed, bid her half the price that she asked, or promised to give her earnest the next day, and came no more.

At last, a short meagre man, in a tarnished waistcoat, desired to see the garret, and when he had stipulated for two long shelves and a larger table, hired it at a low rate. When the affair was completed, he looked round him with great satisfaction, and repeated some words which the woman did not understand. In two days he brought a great box of books, took possession of his room, and lived very inoffensively, except that he frequently disturbed the inhabitants of the next floor by unseasonable noises. He was generally in bed at noon, but from evening to midnight he sometimes talked aloud with great vehemence, sometimes stamped as in rage, sometimes threw down his poker, then clattered his chairs, then sat down in deep thought, and again burst out into loud vociferations; sometimes he would sigh as oppressed with misery, and sometimes shake with convulsive laughter. When he encountered any of the family he gave way or bowed, but rarely spoke, except that as he went up stairs he often repeated,

————Ὅς ὑπέρτατα δώματα ναίει.[38]

This habitant th' aerial regions boast.

hard words, to which his neighbours listened so often, that they learned them without understanding them. What was his employment she did not venture to ask him, but at last heard a printer's boy enquire for the author.

My landlady was very often advised to beware of this strange man, who, though he was quiet for the present, might perhaps become outrageous in the hot months; but as she was punctually paid, she could not find any sufficient reason for dismissing him, till one night he convinced her by setting fire to his curtains, that it was not safe to have an author for her inmate.

She had then for six weeks a succession of tenants, who left the house on Saturday, and instead of paying their rent, stormed at their landlady. At last she took in two sisters, one of whom had spent her little fortune in procuring remedies for a lingering disease, and was now supported and attended by the other: she climbed with difficulty to the apartment, where she languished eight weeks, without impatience or lamentation, except for the expence and fatigue which her sister suffered, and then calmly and contentedly expired. The sister followed her to the grave, paid the few debts which they had contracted, wiped away the tears of useless sorrow, and returning to the business of common life, resigned to me the vacant habitation.

Such, Mr. *Rambler,* are the changes which have happened in the narrow space where my present fortune has fixed my residence. So true is it that amusement and instruction are always at hand for those who have skill and willingness to find them; and so just is the observation of *Juvenal,* that a single house will show whatever is done or suffered in the world.[39]

I am, Sir, &c.
1 October 1751

38. "And has his dwelling most high"; Hesiod, *Works and Days,* l. 8.
39. "If you would know what mankind is like . . . one court-house will suffice; spend a few days in it, and when you come out, dare to call yourself unfortunate"; Juvenal, *Satires,* XIII.159–61.

No. 188. [On Being Liked vs. Being Respected]

————*Si te colo,* Sexte, *non amabo.* Mart.

The more I honour thee, the less I love.[40]

None of the desires dictated by vanity is more general, or less blameable than that of being distinguished for the arts of conversation. Other accomplishments may be possessed without opportunity of exerting them, or wanted without danger that the defect can often be remarked; but as no man can live otherwise than in an hermitage, without hourly pleasure or vexation, from the fondness or neglect of those about him, the faculty of giving pleasure is of continual use. Few are more frequently envied than those who have the power of forcing attention wherever they come, whose entrance is considered as a promise of felicity, and whose departure is lamented, like the recess of the sun from northern climates, as a privation of all that enlivens fancy, or inspirits gaiety.

It is apparent, that to excellence in this valuable art, some peculiar qualifications are necessary; for every one's experience will inform him, that the pleasure which men are able to give in conversation, holds no stated proportion to their knowledge or their virtue. Many find their way to the tables and the parties of those who never consider them as of the least importance in any other place; we have all, at one time or other, been content to love those whom we could not esteem, and been persuaded to try the dangerous experiment of admitting him for a companion whom we knew to be too ignorant for a counsellor, and too treacherous for a friend.

I question whether some abatement of character is not necessary to general acceptance. Few spend their time with much satisfaction under the eye of uncontestable superiority; and therefore, among those whose presence is courted at assemblies of jollity, there are seldom found men eminently distinguished for powers or acquisitions. The wit whose vivacity condemns slower tongues to silence, the scholar whose knowledge allows no man to fancy that he instructs him, the critic who suffers no fallacy to pass undetected, and the reasoner who condemns the idle to thought, and the negligent to attention, are generally praised and feared, reverenced and avoided.

40. "But if I cultivate you, Sextus, I shall not love you"; Martial, *Epigrams,* II.lv.3.

He that would please must rarely aim at such excellence as depresses his hearers in their own opinion, or debars them from the hope of contributing reciprocally to the entertainment of the company. Merriment, extorted by sallies of imagination, sprightliness of remark, or quickness of reply, is too often what the *Latins* call, the *Sardinian Laughter,*[41] a distortion of the face, without gladness of heart.

For this reason, no style of conversation is more extensively acceptable than the narrative. He who has stored his memory with slight anecdotes, private incidents, and personal particularities, seldom fails to find his audience favourable. Almost every man listens with eagerness to contemporary history; for almost every man has some real or imaginary connection with a celebrated character, some desire to advance, or oppose a rising name. Vanity often co-operates with curiosity. He that is a hearer in one place qualifies himself to become a speaker in another; for though he cannot comprehend a series of argument, or transport the volatile spirit of wit without evaporation, he yet thinks himself able to treasure up the various incidents of a story, and pleases his hopes with the information which he shall give to some inferior society.

Narratives are for the most part heard without envy, because they are not supposed to imply any intellectual qualities above the common rate. To be acquainted with facts not yet echoed by plebeian mouths, may happen to one man as well as to another, and to relate them when they are known, has in appearance so little difficulty, that every one concludes himself equal to the task.

But it is not easy, and in some situations of life not possible, to accumulate such a stock of materials as may support the expence of continual narration; and it frequently happens, that they who attempt this method of ingratiating themselves, please only at the first interview; and, for want of new supplies of intelligence, wear out their stories by continual repetition.

There would be, therefore, little hope of obtaining the praise of a good companion, were it not to be gained by more compendious methods; but such is the kindness of mankind to all, except those who aspire to real merit and rational dignity, that every understanding may find some way to

41. A sardonic grin or sneer, supposedly derived from a Sardinian herb so bitter that it caused the face to contort.

excite benevolence; and whoever is not envied, may learn the art of procuring love. We are willing to be pleased, but are not willing to admire; we favour the mirth or officiousness that solicits our regard, but oppose the worth or spirit that enforces it.

The first place among those that please, because they desire only to please, is due to the *merry fellow,* whose laugh is loud, and whose voice is strong; who is ready to echo every jest with obstreperous approbation, and countenance every frolic with vociferations of applause. It is not necessary to a merry fellow to have in himself any fund of jocularity, or force of conception; it is sufficient that he always appears in the highest exaltation of gladness, for the greater part of mankind are gay or serious by infection, and follow without resistance the attraction of example.

Next to the merry fellow is the *good-natured man,* a being generally without benevolence, or any other virtue, than such as indolence and insensibility confer. The characteristic of a good-natured man is to bear a joke; to sit unmoved and unaffected amidst noise and turbulence, profaneness and obscenity; to hear every tale without contradiction; to endure insult without reply; and to follow the stream of folly, whatever course it shall happen to take. The good-natured man is commonly the darling of the petty wits, with whom they exercise themselves in the rudiments of raillery; for he never takes advantage of failings, nor disconcerts a puny satirist with unexpected sarcasms; but while the glass continues to circulate, contentedly bears the expence of uninterrupted laughter, and retires rejoicing at his own importance.

The *modest man* is a companion of a yet lower rank, whose only power of giving pleasure is not to interrupt it. The modest man satisfies himself with peaceful silence, which all his companions are candid enough to consider as proceeding not from inability to speak, but willingness to hear.

Many, without being able to attain any general character of excellence, have some single art of entertainment which serves them as a passport through the world. One I have known for fifteen years the darling of a weekly club, because every night, precisely at eleven, he begins his favourite song, and during the vocal performance by correspondent motions of his hand, chalks out a giant upon the wall. Another has endeared himself to a long succession of acquaintances by sitting among them with his wig reversed; another by contriving to smut the nose of any stranger who was to be initiated in the club; another by purring like a cat, and then pretending to be frighted; and another by yelping like a hound, and calling to the drawers to drive out the dog.

Such are the arts by which cheerfulness is promoted, and sometimes friendship established; arts, which those who despise them should not rigorously blame, except when they are practised at the expence of innocence; for it is always necessary to be loved, but not always necessary to be reverenced.[42]

4 January 1752

No. 191. [A Young Belle's Complaint]

Cereus in Vitium flecti, Monitoribus asper. Hor.

The youth————
Yielding like wax, th' impressive folly bears;
Rough to reproof, and slow to future cares. Francis.[43]

To the Rambler.
Dear Mr. Rambler,

I have been four days confined to my chamber by a cold, which has already kept me from three plays, nine sales, five shows, and six card-tables, and put me seventeen visits behind-hand; and the doctor tells my mamma, that if I fret and cry, it will settle in my head, and I shall not be fit to be seen these six weeks. But, dear Mr. *Rambler,* how can I help it? at this very time *Melissa* is dancing with the prettiest gentleman;—she will breakfast with him to-morrow, and then run to two auctions, and hear compliments, and have presents; then she will be drest, and visit, and get a ticket to the play; then go to cards, and win, and come home with two flambeaus before her chair. Dear Mr. *Rambler,* who can bear it?

My aunt has just brought me a bundle of your papers for my amuse-

42. Johnson defies Niccolò Machiavelli's claim that "it is far better to be feared than loved if you cannot be both"; *The Prince,* trans. George Bull (London: Penguin, 1999), 54.

43. "Soft as wax for moulding to evil"; Horace, *Ars poetica,* l. 163, with Philip Francis's 1743 translation.

ment. She says, you are a philosopher, and will teach me to moderate my desires, and look upon the world with indifference. But, dear sir, I do not wish, nor intend to moderate my desires, nor can I think it proper to look upon the world with indifference, till the world looks with indifference on me. I have been forced, however, to sit this morning a whole quarter of an hour with your paper before my face; but just as my aunt came in, *Phyllida* had brought me a letter from Mr. *Trip,* which I put within the leaves, and read about *absence* and *inconsolableness,* and *ardour,* and *irresistible passion,* and *eternal constancy,* while my aunt imagined, that I was puzzling myself with your philosophy, and often cried out, when she saw me look confused, "If there is any word that you do not understand, child, I will explain it."

Dear soul! how old people that think themselves wise may be imposed upon! But it is fit that they should take their turn, for I am sure, while they can keep poor girls close in the nursery, they tyrannize over us in a very shameful manner, and fill our imaginations with tales of terror, only to make us live in quiet subjection, and fancy that we can never be safe but by their protection.

I have a mamma and two aunts, who have all been formerly celebrated for wit and beauty, and are still generally admired by those that value themselves upon their understanding, and love to talk of vice and virtue, nature and simplicity, and beauty, and propriety; but if there was not some hope of meeting me, scarcely a creature would come near them that wears a fashionable coat. These ladies, Mr. *Rambler,* have had me under their government fifteen years and a half, and have all that time been endeavouring to deceive me by such representations of life as I now find not to be true; but I knew not whether I ought to impute them to ignorance or malice, as it is possible the world may be much changed since they mingled in general conversation.

Being desirous that I should love books, they told me, that nothing but knowledge could make me an agreeable companion to men of sense, or qualify me to distinguish the superficial glitter of vanity from the solid merit of understanding; and that a habit of reading would enable me to fill up the vacuities of life without the help of silly or dangerous amusements, and preserve me from the snares of idleness and the inroads of temptation.

But their principal intention was to make me afraid of men, in which they succeeded so well for a time, that I durst not look in their faces, or be left alone with them in a parlour; for they made me fancy, that no man ever spoke but to deceive, or looked but to allure; that the girl who suffered him that had once squeezed her hand, to approach her a second time was on the brink of ruin; and that she who answered a billet,[44] without consulting her relations, gave love such power over her, that she would certainly become either poor or infamous.

From the time that my leading-strings were taken off, I scarce heard any mention of my beauty but from the milliner, the mantua-maker, and my own maid;[45] for my mamma never said more, when she heard me commended, but "The girl is very well," and then endeavoured to divert my attention by some enquiry after my needle, or my book.

It is now three months since I have been suffered to pay and receive visits, to dance at public assemblies, to have a place kept for me in the boxes, and to play at Lady *Racket's* rout; and you may easily imagine what I think of those who have so long cheated me with false expectations, disturbed me with fictitious terrors, and concealed from me all that I have found to make the happiness of woman.

I am so far from perceiving the usefulness or necessity of books, that if I had not dropped all pretensions to learning, I should have lost Mr. *Trip*, whom I once frighted into another box, by retailing some of *Dryden's* remarks upon a tragedy; for Mr. *Trip* declares, that he hates nothing like hard words, and I am sure, there is not a better partner to be found; his very walk is a dance. I have talked once or twice among ladies about principles and ideas, but they put their fans before their faces, and told me, I was too wise for them, who for their part, never pretended to read any thing but the play-bill, and then asked me the price of my best head.[46]

Those vacancies of time which are to be filled up with books, I have never yet obtained; for, consider, Mr. *Rambler*, I go to bed late, and therefore cannot rise early; as soon as I am up, I dress for the gardens; then walk in the park; then always go to some sale or show, or entertainment at the little theatre; then must be dressed for dinner; then must pay my visits; then

44. A billet-doux, or love letter.
45. Leading strings were thin straps of fabric attached to children's clothing and used as a leash to keep them from straying and to guide them as they learned to walk. A mantua was a type of loose-fitting gown.
46. Headdress.

walk in the park; then hurry to the play; and from thence to the card-table. This is the general course of the day, when there happens nothing extraordinary; but sometimes I ramble into the country and come again to a ball; sometimes I am engaged for a whole day and part of the night. If, at any time, I can gain an hour by not being at home, I have so many things to do, so many orders to give to the milliner, so many alterations to make in my clothes, so many visitants' names to read over, so many invitations to accept or refuse, so many cards to write, and so many fashions to consider, that I am lost in confusion, forced at last to let in company or step into my chair, and leave half my affairs to the direction of my maid.

This is the round of my day; and when shall I either stop my course, or so change it as to want a book? I suppose it cannot be imagined, that any of these diversions will be soon at an end. There will always be gardens, and a park, and auctions, and shows, and play-houses, and cards; visits will always be paid, and clothes always be worn; and how can I have time unemployed upon my hands?

But I am most at a loss to guess for what purpose they related such tragic stories of the cruelty, perfidy, and artifices of men, who, if they ever were so malicious and destructive, have certainly now reformed their manners. I have not, since my entrance into the world, found one who does not profess himself devoted to my service, and ready to live or die, as I shall command him. They are so far from intending to hurt me, that their only contention is, who shall be allowed most closely to attend, and most frequently to treat me; when different places of entertainment, or schemes of pleasure are mentioned, I can see the eye sparkle and the cheeks glow of him whose proposals obtain my approbation; he then leads me off in triumph, adores my condescension, and congratulates himself that he has lived to the hour of felicity. Are these, Mr. *Rambler,* creatures to be feared? Is it likely that any injury will be done me by those who can enjoy life only while I favour them with my presence?

As little reason can I yet find to suspect them of stratagems and fraud. When I play at cards, they never take advantage of my mistakes, nor exact from me a rigorous observation of the game. Even Mr. *Shuffle,* a grave gentleman, who has daughters older than myself, plays with me so negligently, that I am sometimes inclined to believe he loses his money by design, and yet he is so fond of play, that he says, he will one day take me to his house in the country; that we may try by ourselves who can conquer. I have not yet promised him; but when the town grows a little empty, I shall think upon it, for I want some trinkets, like *Letitia's*, to my watch. I do not doubt my luck, but must study some means of amusing my relations.

For all these distinctions I find myself indebted to that beauty which I was never suffered to hear praised, and of which, therefore, I did not before know the full value. This concealment was certainly an intentional fraud, for my aunts have eyes like other people, and I am every day told, that nothing but blindness can escape the influence of my charms. Their whole account of that world which they pretend to know so well, has been only one fiction entangled with another; and though the modes of life oblige me to continue some appearances of respect, I cannot think that they, who have been so clearly detected in ignorance or imposture, have any right to the esteem, veneration, or obedience of,

Sir, Yours,
Bellaria.
14 January 1752.

The Idler
No. 1. [Introducing the Idler]

Vacui sub umbra
Lusimus. Hor.[47]

Those who attempt periodical essays seem to be often stopped in the beginning, by the difficulty of finding a proper title. Two writers, since the time of the Spectator, have assumed his name, without any pretensions to lawful inheritance; an effort was once made to revive the Tatler;[48] and the strange appellations, by which other Papers have been called, show that the authours were distressed, like the natives of *America,* who come to the *Europeans* to beg a name.

It will be easily believed of the *Idler,* that if his title had required any

47. "If ever in idle hour beneath the shade I have sung"; Horace, *Odes,* I.xxxii.1–2. The poet is referring to a trivial song that shall yet live on.

48. References to *The Universal Spectator* (1728–46), *The Female Spectator* (1744–46), *The Spectator* (1753–54), and *The Tatler Revived* (1750).

search, he never would have found it. Every mode of life has its conveniencies. The *Idler,* who habituates himself to be satisfied with what he can most easily obtain, not only escapes labours which are often fruitless, but sometimes succeeds better than those who despise all that is within their reach, and think every thing more valuable as it is harder to be acquired.

If similitude of manners be a motive to kindness, the *Idler* may flatter himself with universal patronage. There is no single character under which such numbers are comprised. Every man is, or hopes to be, an *Idler.* Even those who seem to differ most from us are hastening to encrease our fraternity; as peace is the end of war, so to be idle is the ultimate purpose of the busy.

There is perhaps no appellation by which a writer can better denote his kindred to the human species. It has been found hard to describe Man by an adequate definition. Some philosophers have called him a reasonable animal, but others have considered reason as a quality of which many creatures partake. He has been termed likewise a laughing animal; but it is said that some men have never laughed. Perhaps Man may be more properly distinguished as an Idle Animal; for there is no man who is not sometimes idle. It is at least a definition from which none that shall find it in this Paper can be excepted; for who can be more idle than the reader of the *Idler?*

That the definition may be complete, idleness must be not only the general, but the peculiar characteristic of Man; and perhaps man is the only being that can properly be called idle, that does by others what he might do himself, or sacrifices duty or pleasure to the love of ease.

Scarcely any name can be imagined from which less envy or competition is to be dreaded. The *Idler* has no rivals or enemies. The Man of Business forgets him; the Man of Enterprize despises him; and though such as tread the same track of life, fall commonly into jealousy and discord, *Idlers* are always found to associate in peace, and he who is most famed for doing nothing, is glad to meet another as idle as himself.

What is to be expected from this Paper, whether it will be uniform or various, learned or familiar, serious or gay, political or moral, continued or interrupted, it is hoped that no reader will enquire. That the *Idler* has some scheme, cannot be doubted; for to form schemes is the *Idler's* privilege. But though he has many projects in his head, he is now grown sparing of communication, having observed, that his hearers are apt to remember what he forgets himself; that his tardiness of execution exposes him to the encroachments of those who catch a hint and fall to work; and that very specious plans, after long contrivance and pompous displays, have subsided in weariness without a trial, and without miscarriage have been blasted by derision.

Something the *Idler*'s character may be supposed to promise. Those that are curious after diminutive history, who watch the revolutions of families, and the rise and fall of characters either male or female, will hope to be gratified by this Paper; for the *Idler* is always inquisitive and seldom retentive. He that delights in obloquy and satire, and wishes to see clouds gathering over any reputation that dazzles him with its brightness, will snatch up the *Idler*'s essays with a beating heart. The *Idler* is naturally censorious; those who attempt nothing themselves think every thing easily performed, and consider the unsuccessful always as criminal.

I think it necessary to give notice, that I make no contract, nor incur any obligation. If those who depend on the *Idler* for intelligence and entertainment, should suffer the disappointment which commonly follows ill-placed expectations, they are to lay the blame only on themselves.

Yet hope is not wholly to be cast away. The *Idler*, though sluggish, is yet alive, and may sometimes be stimulated to vigour and activity. He may descend into profoundness, or tower into sublimity; for the diligence of an *Idler* is rapid and impetuous, as ponderous bodies forced into velocity move with violence proportionate to their weight.

But these vehement exertions of intellect cannot be frequent, and he will therefore gladly receive help from any correspondent, who shall enable him to please without his own labour. He excludes no style, he prohibits no subject; only let him that writes to the *Idler* remember, that his letters must not be long; no words are to be squandered in declarations of esteem, or confessions of inability; conscious dulness has little right to be prolix, and praise is not so welcome to the *Idler* as quiet.

15 April 1758

No. 17. [On Scientists and Cruelty to Animals]

The rainy weather which has continued the last month, is said to have given great disturbance to the inspectors of barometers. The oraculous glasses have deceived their votaries; shower has succeeded shower, though they predicted sunshine and dry skies; and by fatal confidence in these fallacious promises, many coats have lost their gloss, and many curls been moistened to flaccidity.

This is one of the distresses to which mortals subject themselves by the pride of speculation. I had no part in this learned disappointment, who am content to credit my senses, and to believe that rain will fall when the air blackens, and that the weather will be dry when the sun is bright. My caution indeed does not always preserve me from a shower. To be wet may happen to the genuine *Idler,* but to be wet in opposition to theory, can befall only the *Idler* that pretends to be busy. Of those that spin out life in trifles, and die without a memorial, many flatter themselves with high opinions of their own importance, and imagine that they are every day adding some improvement to human life. To be idle and to be poor have always been reproaches, and therefore every man endeavours with his utmost care, to hide his poverty from others, and his *Idleness* from himself.

Among those whom I never could persuade to rank themselves with *Idlers,* and who speak with indignation of my morning sleeps and nocturnal rambles; one passes the day in catching spiders that he may count their eyes with a microscope; another erects his head, and exhibits the dust of a marigold separated from the flower with dexterity worthy of *Leeuwenhoeck* himself.[49] Some turn the wheel of electricity, some suspend rings to a loadstone, and find that what they did yesterday they can do again to-day. Some register the changes of the wind, and die fully convinced that the wind is changeable. There are men yet more profound, who have heard that two colourless liquors may produce a colour by union, and that two cold bodies will grow hot if they are mingled: they mingle them, and produce the effect expected, say it is strange, and mingle them again.

The *Idlers* that sport only with inanimate nature may claim some indulgence; if they are useless they are still innocent: but there are others, whom I know not how to mention without more emotion than my love of quiet willingly admits. Among the inferiour professors of medical knowledge, is a race of wretches, whose lives are only varied by varieties of cruelty;

---

49. Antoni van Leeuwenhoek (1632–1723), Dutch naturalist and microscopist.

whose favourite amusement is to nail dogs to tables and open them alive; to try how long life may be continued in various degrees of mutilation, or with the excision or laceration of the vital parts; to examine whether burning irons are felt more acutely by the bone or tendon; and whether the more lasting agonies are produced by poison forced into the mouth or injected into the veins.

It is not without reluctance that I offend the sensibility of the tender mind with images like these. If such cruelties were not practised it were to be desired that they should not be conceived, but since they are published every day with ostentation, let me be allowed once to mention them, since I mention them with abhorrence.

Mead has invidiously remarked of *Woodward* that he gathered shells and stones, and would pass for a Philosopher.[50] With pretensions much less reasonable, the anatomical novice tears out the living bowels of an animal, and styles himself Physician, prepares himself by familiar cruelty for that profession which he is to exercise upon the tender and the helpless, upon feeble bodies and broken minds, and by which he has opportunities to extend his arts of torture, and continue those experiments upon infancy and age, which he has hitherto tried upon cats and dogs.

What is alleged in defence of these hateful practices, every one knows; but the truth is, that by knives, fire, and poison, knowledge is not always sought, and is very seldom attained. The experiments that have been tried, are tried again; he that burned an animal with irons yesterday, will be willing to amuse himself with burning another to-morrow. I know not, that by living dissections any discovery has been made by which a single malady is more easily cured. And if the knowledge of physiology has been somewhat increased, he surely buys knowledge dear, who learns the use of the lacteals at the expence of his humanity.[51] It is time that universal resentment should

50. The British physician Richard Mead refers to "one *Woodward*, professor of physick at *Gresham-College:* who, having served an apprenticeship to a linnen-draper, after that, scraped together a parcel of cockle-shells, pebbles, minerals, and the lord knows what trumpery of the like fossile tribe . . . took it into his head, forsooth, to set up for a philosopher"; *A Discourse of the Small-Pox and Measles* (London, 1747), vii.

51. An allusion to the anatomical demonstration of July 1622 in which the

arise against these horrid operations, which tend to harden the heart, extinguish those sensations which give man confidence in man, and make the physician more dreadful than the gout or stone.

5 August 1758

No. [22].[52] [The Vulture's Speech on War]

Many naturalists are of opinion, that the animals which we commonly consider as mute, have the power of imparting their thoughts to one another. That they can express general sensations is very certain; every being that can utter sounds, has a different voice for pleasure and for pain. The hound informs his fellows when he scents his game; the hen calls her chickens to their food by her cluck, and drives them from danger by her scream.

Birds have the greatest variety of notes; they have indeed a variety, which seems almost sufficient to make a speech adequate to the purposes of a life, which is regulated by instinct, and can admit little change or improvement. To the cries of birds, curiosity or superstition has been always attentive; many have studied the language of the feathered tribes, and some have boasted that they understood it.

The most skilful or most confident interpreters of the Silvan Dialogues have been commonly found among the philosophers of the East,[53] in a country where the calmness of the air, and the mildness of the seasons, allow the student to pass a great part of the year in groves and bowers. But what may be done in one place by peculiar opportunities, may be performed in another by peculiar diligence. A shepherd of Bohemia has, by long abode in the forests, enabled himself to understand the voice of birds;

Italian surgeon Gaspare Aselli, while displaying the abdominal viscera of a dog, discovered her lacteal vessels.

52. Johnson cut this essay, the original "Idler" no. 22, which appeared in *The Universal Chronicle,* from the first collected edition (1761) because of its incendiary material, renumbering all subsequent essays.

53. Probably a reference to the Platonic dialogues, themselves derived from an early literary form used by the Greeks and Indians for rhetorical instruction and entertainment.

at least he relates with great confidence a story of which the credibility may be considered by the learned.

"As I was sitting, (said he) within a hollow rock, and watching my sheep that fed in the valley, I heard two vultures interchangeably crying on the summit of the cliff. Both voices were earnest and deliberate. My curiosity prevailed over my care of the flock; I climbed slowly and silently from crag to crag, concealed among the shrubs, till I found a cavity where I might sit and listen without suffering, or giving disturbance.

"I soon perceived, that my labour would be well repaid; for an old vulture was sitting on a naked prominence, with her young about her, whom she was instructing in the arts of a vulture's life, and preparing, by the last lecture, for their final dismission to the mountains and the skies.

"My children, said the old Vulture, you will the less want my instructions because you have had my practice before your eyes; you have seen me snatch from the farm the household fowl, you have seen me seize the leveret in the bush, and the kid in the pasture, you know how to fix your talons, and how to balance your flight when you are laden with your prey. But you remember the taste of more delicious food; I have often regaled you with the flesh of man. Tell us, said the young vultures, where man may be found, and how he may be known; his flesh is surely the natural food of a vulture. Why have you never brought a man in your talons to the nest? He is too bulky, said the mother; when we find a man, we can only tear away his flesh and leave his bones upon the ground. Since man is so big, said the young ones, how do you kill him. You are afraid of the wolf and of the bear, by what power are vultures superior to man, is man more defenseless than a sheep? We have not the strength of man, returned the mother, and I am sometimes in doubt whether we have the subtilty; and the vultures would seldom feast upon his flesh, had not nature, that devoted him to our uses, infused into him a strange ferocity, which I have never observed in any other being that feeds upon the Earth. Two herds of men will often meet and shake the Earth with noise, and fill the air with fire. When you hear noise and see fire which flashes along the ground, hasten to the place with your swiftest wing, for men are surely destroying one another; you will then find the ground smoking with blood and covered with carcasses, of which many are dismembered and mangled for the convenience of the vulture. But when men have killed their prey, said the pupil, why do they not eat it?

When the wolf has killed a sheep he suffers not the vulture to touch it till he has satisfied himself. Is not man another kind of wolf? Man, said the mother, is the only beast who kills that which he does not devour, and this quality makes him so much a benefactor to our species. If men kill our prey and lay it in our way, said the young one, what need shall we have of labouring for ourselves? Because man will, sometimes, replied the mother, remain for a long time quiet in his den. The old vultures will tell you when you are to watch his motions. When you see men in great numbers moving close together, like a flight of storks, you may conclude that they are hunting, and that you will soon revel in human blood. But still, said the young one, I would gladly know the reason of this mutual slaughter. I could never kill what I could not eat. My Child, said the mother, this is a question which I cannot answer, though I am reckoned the most subtle bird of the mountain. When I was young I used frequently to visit the aerie of an old vulture who dwelt upon the Carpathian rocks; he had made many observations; he knew the places that afforded prey round his habitation, as far in every direction as the strongest wing can fly between the rising and setting of the summer sun; he had fed year after year on the entrails of men. His opinion was, that men had only the appearance of animal life, being really vegetables with a power of motion; and that as the boughs of an oak are dashed together by the storm, that swine may fatten upon the falling acorns, so men are by some unaccountable power driven one against another, till they lose their motion, that vultures may be fed. Others think they have observed something of contrivance and policy among these mischievous beings, and those that hover more closely round them, pretend, that there is, in every herd, one that gives directions to the rest, and seems to be more eminently delighted with a wide carnage. What it is that entitles him to such pre-eminence we know not; he is seldom the biggest or the swiftest, but he shows by his eagerness and diligence that he is, more than any of the others, a friend to vultures."

9 September 1758

No. 36. [On the Bugbear Style]

The great differences that disturb the peace of mankind, are not about ends but means. We have all the same general desires, but how those desires shall be accomplished will for ever be disputed. The ultimate purpose of government is temporal, and that of religion is eternal happiness. Hitherto we agree; but here we must part, to try, according to the endless varieties of passion and understanding combined with one another, every possible form of government, and every imaginable tenet of religion.

We are told by *Cumberland,* that *Rectitude,* applied to action or contemplation, is merely metaphorical; and that as a *right* line describes the shortest passage from point to point, so a *right* action effects a good design by the fewest means; and so likewise a *right* opinion is that which connects distant truths by the shortest train of intermediate propositions.[54]

To find the nearest way from truth to truth, or from purpose to effect, not to use more instruments where fewer will be sufficient, not to move by wheels and levers what will give way to the naked hand, is the great proof of a healthful and vigorous mind, neither feeble with helpless ignorance, nor overburdened with unwieldy knowledge.

But there are men who seem to think nothing so much the characteristic of a genius, as to do common things in an uncommon manner; like *Hudibras* to *tell the clock by Algebra,* or like the Lady in Dr. *Young*'s Satires, *to drink Tea by stratagem.*[55] To quit the beaten track only because it is known, and take a new path, however crooked or rough, because the straight was found out before.

Every man speaks and writes with intent to be understood, and it can seldom happen but he that understands himself might convey his notions to another, if, content to be understood, he did not seek to be admired; but when once he begins to contrive how his sentiments may be received, not with most ease to his reader, but with most advantage to himself, he then transfers his consideration from words to sounds, from sentences to periods, and as he grows more elegant becomes less intelligible.

It is difficult to enumerate every species of authors whose labours counteract themselves. The man of exuberance and copiousness, who dif-

54. See Richard Cumberland, *A Philosophical Enquiry into the Laws of Nature,* originally published in Latin in 1672 and translated by John Towers in 1750.

55. "And wisely tell what hour o'th'day / The Clock does strike, by *Algebra*"; Samuel Butler, *Hudibras,* I.i.125–26. "For her *own* breakfast she'll project a scheme / Nor *take* her *Tea* without a *stratagem*"; Edward Young, "Love of Fame, the Universal Passion," in *Seven Characteristical Satires,* VI.187–88.

fuses every thought through so many diversities of expression, that it is lost like water in a mist. The ponderous dictator of sentences, whose notions are delivered in the lump, and are, like uncoined bullion, of more weight than use. The liberal illustrator, who shows by examples and comparisons what was clearly seen when it was first proposed; and the stately son of demonstration, who proves with mathematical formality what no man has yet pretended to doubt.

There is a mode of style for which I know not that the Masters of Oratory have yet found a name, a style by which the most evident truths are so obscured that they can no longer be perceived, and the most familiar propositions so disguised that they cannot be known. Every other kind of eloquence is the dress of sense, but this is the mask, by which a true master of his art will so effectually conceal it, that a man will as easily mistake his own positions if he meets them thus transformed, as he may pass in a masquerade his nearest acquaintance.

This style may be called the *terrific,* for its chief intention is to terrify and amaze; it may be termed the *repulsive,* for its natural effect is to drive away the reader; or it may be distinguished, in plain *English,* by the denomination of the *bugbear style,*[56] for it has more terror than danger, and will appear less formidable, as it is more nearly approached.

A mother tells her infant, that *two and two make four,* the child remembers the proposition, and is able to count four to all the purposes of life, till the course of his education brings him among philosophers, who fright him from his former knowledge, by telling him that four is a certain aggregate of units; that all numbers being only the repetition of an unit, which, though not a number itself, is the parent, root, or original of all number, *four* is the denomination assigned to a certain number of such repetitions. The only danger is, lest, when he first hears these dreadful sounds, the pupil should run away; if he has but the courage to stay till the conclusion, he will find that, when speculation has done its worst, two and two still make four.

An illustrious example of this species of eloquence, may be found in *Letters concerning Mind.* The author begins by declaring, that *the sorts of things are things that now are, have been, and shall be, and the things that*

56. A bugbear is a source or dread or irritation.

strictly ARE. In this position, except the last clause, in which he uses something of the scholastic language, there is nothing but what every man has heard and imagines himself to know. But who would not believe that some wonderful novelty is presented to his intellect, when he is afterwards told, in the true *bugbear* style, that *the* Ares, *in the former sense, are things that lie between the* Have-beens *and* Shall-bes. *The* Have-beens *are things that are past; the* Shall-bes *are things that are to come; and the things that* ARE, in the latter sense, *are things that have not been, nor shall be, nor stand in the midst of such as are before them or shall be after them. The things that have been, and shall be, have respect to present, past, and future. Those likewise that now* ARE *have moreover place; that, for instance, which is here, that which is to the East, that which is to the West.*[57]

All this, my dear reader, is very strange; but though it be strange, it is not new; survey these wonderful sentences again, and they will be found to contain nothing more than very plain truths, which till this Author arose had always been delivered in plain language.

23 December 1758

No. 44. [The Burden of Memory]

Memory is, among the faculties of the human mind, that of which we make the most frequent use, or rather that of which the agency is incessant or perpetual. Memory is the primary and fundamental power, without which there could be no other intellectual operation. Judgment and Ratiocination suppose something already known, and draw their decisions only from experience. Imagination selects ideas from the treasures of Remembrance, and produces novelty only by varied combinations. We do not even form conjectures of distant, or anticipations of future events, but by concluding what is possible from what is past.

The two offices of Memory are Collection and Distribution; by one images are accumulated, and by the other produced for use. Collection is always the employment of our first years, and Distribution commonly that of our advanced age.

To collect and reposite the various forms of things, is far the most

57. See John Petvin, *Letters Concerning Mind* (London, 1750), 40–41.

pleasing part of mental occupation. We are naturally delighted with novelty, and there is a time when all that we see is new. When first we enter into the world, whithersoever we turn our eyes, they meet Knowledge with Pleasure at her side; every diversity of Nature pours ideas in upon the soul; neither search nor labour are necessary; we have nothing more to do than to open our eyes, and curiosity is gratified.

Much of the pleasure which the first survey of the world affords, is exhausted before we are conscious of our own felicity, or able to compare our condition with some other possible state. We have therefore few traces of the joy of our earliest discoveries; yet we all remember a time when Nature had so many untasted gratifications, that every excursion gave delight which can now be found no longer, when the noise of a torrent, the rustle of a wood, the song of birds, or the play of lambs, had power to fill the attention, and suspend all perception of the course of time.

But these easy pleasures are soon at an end; we have seen in a very little time so much, that we call out for new objects of observation, and endeavour to find variety in books and life. But study is laborious, and not always satisfactory; and conversation has its pains as well as pleasures; we are willing to learn, but not willing to be taught; we are pained by ignorance, but pained yet more by another's knowledge.

From the vexation of pupillage men commonly set themselves free about the middle of life, by shutting up the avenues of intelligence, and resolving to rest in their present state; and they, whose ardour of enquiry continues longer, find themselves insensibly forsaken by their instructors. As every man advances in life, the proportion between those that are younger, and that are older than himself, is continually changing; and he that has lived half a century, finds few that do not require from him that information which he once expected from those that went before him.

Then it is that the magazines of memory are opened, and the stores of accumulated knowledge are displayed by vanity or benevolence, or in honest commerce of mutual interest. Every man wants others, and is therefore glad when he is wanted by them. And as few men will endure the labour of intense meditation without necessity, he that has learned enough for his profit or his honour, seldom endeavours after further acquisitions.

The pleasure of recollecting speculative notions would not be much less than that of gaining them, if they could be kept pure and unmingled with the passages of life; but such is the necessary concatenation of our thoughts, that good and evil are linked together, and no pleasure recurs but associated with pain. Every revived idea reminds us of a time when something was enjoyed that is now lost, when some hope was yet not blasted, when some purpose had yet not languished into sluggishness or indifference.

Whether it be that life has more vexations than comforts, or, what is in the event just the same, that evil makes deeper impression than good, it is certain that few can review the time past without heaviness of heart. He remembers many calamities incurred by folly, many opportunities lost by negligence. The shades of the dead rise up before him, and he laments the companions of his youth, the partners of his amusements, the assistants of his labours, whom the hand of death has snatched away.

When an offer was made to *Themistocles* of teaching him the art of memory, he answered, that he would rather wish for the art of forgetfulness.[58] He felt his imagination haunted by phantoms of misery which he was unable to suppress, and would gladly have calmed his thoughts with some *oblivious antidote*. In this we all resemble one another; the hero and the sage are, like vulgar mortals, overburdened by the weight of life, all shrink from recollection, and all wish for an art of forgetfulness.

17 February 1759

No. 60. [Dick Minim, the Critic]

Criticism is a study by which men grow important and formidable at very small expence. The power of invention has been conferred by Nature upon few, and the labour of learning those sciences which may, by mere labour, be obtained, is too great to be willingly endured; but every man can exert such judgment as he has upon the works of others; and he whom Nature has made weak, and Idleness keeps ignorant, may yet support his vanity by the name of a critic.

58. Cicero reports this of the Athenian statesman Themistocles (c. 524–c. 460 B.C.) in *De finibus bonorum et malorum* (About the Ends of Goods and Evils), II.xxxii.104.

I hope it will give comfort to great numbers who are passing thro' the world in obscurity, when I inform them how easily distinction may be obtained. All the other powers of literature are coy and haughty, they must be long courted, and at last are not always gained; but criticism is a goddess easy of access and forward of advance, who will meet the slow and encourage the timorous; the want of meaning she supplies with words, and the want of spirit she recompenses with malignity.

This profession has one recommendation peculiar to itself, that it gives vent to malignity without real mischief. No genius was ever blasted by the breath of critics. The poison which, if confined, would have burst the heart, fumes away empty hisses, and malice is set at ease with very little danger to merit. The critic is the only man whose triumph is without another's pain, and whose greatness does not rise upon another's ruin.

To a study at once so easy and so reputable, so malicious and so harmless, it cannot be necessary to invite my readers by a long or laboured exhortation; it is sufficient, since all would be critics if they could, to show by one eminent example that all can be critics if they will.

Dick Minim, after the common course of puerile studies, in which he was no great proficient, was put apprentice to a Brewer, with whom he had lived two years, when his uncle died in the city, and left him a large fortune in the stocks. Dick had for six months before used the company of the lower players, of whom he had learned to scorn a trade, and being now at liberty to follow his genius, he resolved to be a man of wit and humour. That he might be properly initiated in his new character, he frequented the coffeehouses near the theatres, where he listened very diligently, day after day, to those who talked of language and sentiments, and unities and catastrophes, till by slow degrees he began to think that he understood something of the Stage, and hoped in time to talk himself.

But he did not trust so much to natural sagacity, as wholly to neglect the help of books. When the theatres were shut,[59] he retired to *Richmond* with a few select writers, whose opinions he impressed upon his memory by unwearied diligence; and when he returned with other wits to town, was able to tell, in very proper phrases, that the chief business of art is to copy

59. That is, during the summer.

nature; that a perfect writer is not to be expected, because genius decays as judgment increases; that the great art is the art of blotting, and that according to the rule of *Horace* every piece should be kept nine years.[60]

Of the great authors he now began to display the characters, laying down as an universal position that all had beauties and defects. His opinion was, that *Shakespeare,* committing himself wholly to the impulse of Nature, wanted that correctness which learning would have given him; and that *Johnson,* trusting to learning, did not sufficiently cast his eye on Nature.[61] He blamed the *stanza* of *Spencer,* and could not bear *hexameters* of *Sidney. Denham* and *Waller* he held the first reformers of *English* Numbers, and thought that if *Waller* could have obtained the strength of *Denham,* or *Denham* the sweetness of *Waller,* there had been nothing wanting to complete a Poet. He often expressed his commiseration of *Dryden's* poverty, and his indignation at the age which suffered him to write for bread; he repeated with rapture the first lines of *All for Love,* but wondered at the corruption of taste which could bear any thing so unnatural as rhyming Tragedies. In *Otway* he found uncommon powers of moving the passions, but was disgusted by his general negligence, and blamed him for making a Conspirator his Hero; and never concluded his disquisition, without remarking how happily the sound of the clock is made to alarm the audience. *Southern* would have been his favourite, but that he mixes comic with tragic

60. "Nonumque premature in annum, membranis intus positis: delere licebit quod non edideris; nescit vox missa reverti" (Then put your parchment in the closet and keep it back till the ninth year. What you have not published you can destroy; the word once sent forth can never come back"; Horace, *Ars poetica,* l. 388.

61. He means Ben Jonson; this opinion, like the ones that follow, were critical commonplaces of the time. References below are to the Spenserian stanza used in *The Faerie Queene* (1596); the six-beat line as used in the first sonnet of Sir Philip Sidney's *Astrophel and Stella* (1591); the Cavalier poets Edmund Waller (1606–87) and John Denham (1615–69); John Dryden's heroic drama *All for Love* (1678); the Restoration playwrights Thomas Otway (specifically, *Venice Preserved,* 1682), Thomas Southerne (1660–1746), Nicholas Rowe (1674–1718), and William Congreve (1670–1729); Addison's tragedy *Cato* (1713); Matthew Prior (1624–1721), author of the long poem "Solomon on the Vanity of World" (1718); the neoclassical poets Jonathan Swift (1667–1745) and Alexander Pope (1688–1744); and Edmund Smith's 1707 drama *Phaedra and Hippolitus.*

scenes, intercepts the natural course of the passions, and fills the mind with a wild confusion of mirth and melancholy. The versification of *Rowe* he thought too melodious for the stage, and too little varied in different passions. He made it the great fault of *Congreve*, that all his persons were wits, and that he always wrote with more art than nature. He considered *Cato* rather as a poem than a play, and allowed *Addison* to be the complete master of allegory and grave humour, but paid no great deference to him as a critic. He thought the chief merit of *Prior* was in his easy tales and lighter poems, though he allowed that his *Solomon* had many noble sentiments elegantly expressed. In *Swift* he discovered an inimitable vein of irony, and an easiness which all would hope and few would attain. *Pope* he was inclined to degrade from Poet to Versifier, and thought his Numbers rather luscious than sweet. He often lamented the neglect of *Phaedra and Hippolitus*, and wished to see the stage under better regulations.

These assertions passed commonly uncontradicted; and if now and then an opponent started up, he was quickly repressed by the suffrages of the company, and *Minim* went away from every dispute with elation of heart and increase of confidence.

He now grew conscious of his abilities, and began to talk of the present state of dramatic poetry; wondered what was become of the comic genius which supplied our ancestors with wit and pleasantry, and why no writer could be found that durst now venture beyond a Farce. He saw no reason for thinking that the vein of humour was exhausted, since we live in a country where liberty suffers every character to spread itself to its utmost bulk, and which therefore produces more originals than all the rest of the world together. Of tragedy he concluded business to be the soul, and yet often hinted that love predominates too much upon the modern stage.

He was now an acknowledged critic, and had his own seat in the coffee-house, and headed a party in the pit. *Minim* has more vanity than ill-nature, and seldom desires to do much mischief; he will perhaps murmur a little in the ear of him that sits next him, but endeavours to influence the audience to favour, by clapping when an actor exclaims *ye Gods,* or laments the misery of his country.

By degrees he was admitted to rehearsals, and many of his friends are of opinion, that our present Poets are indebted to him for their happiest thoughts; by his contrivance the bell was rung twice in *Barbarossa,* and by his persuasion the author of *Cleone* concluded his play without a couplet;[62] for what can be more absurd, said *Minim*, than that part of a play should be rhymed, and part written in blank verse? and by what acquisition of faculties is the speaker who never could find rhymes before, enabled to rhyme at the conclusion of an act!

He is the great investigator of hidden beauties, and is particularly delighted when he finds *the Sound an Echo to the Sense*.[63] He has read all our poets with particular attention to this delicacy of versification, and wonders at the supineness with which their Works have been hitherto perused, so that no man has found the sound of a drum in this distich,

> When Pulpit, Drum Ecclesiastick,
> Was beat with fist instead of a stick;

And that the wonderful lines upon honour and a bubble have hitherto passed without notice.

> Honour is like the glassy Bubble,
> Which costs Philosophers such trouble,
> Where one part crack'd, the whole does fly,
> And Wits are crack'd to find out why.[64]

In these verses, says *Minim*, we have two striking accommodations of the sound to the sense. It is impossible to utter the two lines emphatically without an act like that which they describe; *Bubble* and *Trouble* causing a momentary inflation of the cheeks by the retention of the breath, which is afterwards forcibly emitted, as in the practice of *blowing bubbles*. But the greatest excellence is in the third line, which is *cracked* in the middle to express a crack, and then shivers into monosyllables. Yet has this diamond lain neglected with common stones, and among the innumerable admirers of

62. Plays by John Brown and Robert Dodsley, produced in 1754 and 1758, respectively.

63. Pope, *Essay on Criticism*, I.365.

64. See Samuel Butler, *Hudibras*, I.i.11–12 and II.ii.385–88.

Hudibras the observation of this superlative passage has been reserved for the sagacity of *Minim*.

9 June 1759

No. 84. [On Biography vs. Autobiography]

Biography is, of the various kinds of narrative writing, that which is most eagerly read, and most easily applied to the purposes of life.

In romances, when the wild field of possibility lies open to invention, the incidents may easily be made more numerous, the vicissitudes more sudden, and the events more wonderful; but from the time of life when Fancy begins to be over-ruled by Reason and corrected by Experience, the most artful tale raises little curiosity when it is known to be false; though it may, perhaps, be sometimes read as a model of a neat or elegant style, not for the sake of knowing what it contains, but how it is written; or those that are weary of themselves, may have recourse to it as a pleasing dream, of which, when they awake, they voluntarily dismiss the images from their minds.

The examples and events of history press, indeed, upon the mind with the weight of truth; but when they are reposited in the memory, they are oftener employed for show than use, and rather diversify conversation than regulate life. Few are engaged in such scenes as give them opportunities of growing wiser by the downfall of statesmen or the defeat of generals. The stratagems of war, and the intrigues of courts, are read by far the greater part of mankind with the same indifference as the adventures of fabled heroes, or the revolutions of a fairy region. Between falsehood and useless truth there is little difference. As gold which he cannot spend will make no man rich, so knowledge which he cannot apply will make no man wise.

The mischievous consequences of vice and folly, of irregular desires and predominant passions, are best discovered by those relations which are levelled with the general surface of life, which tell not how any man became great, but how he was made happy; not how he lost the favour of his prince, but how he became discontented with himself.

Those relations are therefore commonly of most value in which the writer tells his own story. He that recounts the life of another, commonly dwells most upon conspicuous events, lessens the familiarity of his tale to increase its dignity, shows his favourite at a distance decorated and magnified like the ancient actors in their tragic dress, and endeavours to hide the man that he may produce a hero.

But if it be true which was said by a *French* Prince, *That no man was a Hero to the servants of his chamber,*[65] it is equally true that every man is yet less a hero to himself. He that is most elevated above the crowd by the importance of his employments or the reputation of his genius, feels himself affected by fame or business but as they influence his domestic life. The high and low, as they have the same faculties and the same senses, have no less similitude in their pains and pleasures. The sensations are the same in all, though produced by very different occasions. The prince feels the same pain when an invader seizes a province, as the farmer when a thief drives away his cow. Men thus equal in themselves will appear equal in honest and impartial biography; and those whom Fortune or Nature place at the greatest distance may afford instruction to each other.

The writer of his own life has at least the first qualification of an historian, the knowledge of the truth; and though it may be plausibly objected that his temptations to disguise it are equal to his opportunities of knowing it, yet I cannot but think that impartiality may be expected with equal confidence from him that relates the passages of his own life, as from him that delivers the transactions of another.

Certainty of knowledge not only excludes mistake but fortifies veracity. What we collect by conjecture, and by conjecture only can one man judge of another's motives or sentiments, is easily modified by fancy or by desire; as objects imperfectly discerned, take forms from the hope or fear of the beholder. But that which is fully known cannot be falsified but with reluctance of understanding, and alarm of conscience; of understanding, the lover of truth; of conscience, the sentinel of virtue.

65. Attributed to Louis II de Bourbon, Prince de Condé (1621–86), and memorialized by Montaigne in his *Essays* (III.ii). Thomas Carlyle records that the epigram has also been "attributed to a variety of authors from Antigonus I, King of Sparta, to Montaigne and Goethe, and to two witty Frenchwomen, Mme. Cornuel and Mme. de Sévingé"; *On Heroes, Hero-Worship, and the Heroic in History,* ed. Michael K. Goldberg (Berkeley: University of California Press, 1993), 350.

He that writes the Life of another is either his friend or his enemy, and wishes either to exalt his praise or aggravate his infamy; many temptations to falsehood will occur in the disguise of passions, too specious to fear much resistance. Love of virtue will animate panegyric, and hatred of wickedness embitter censure. The zeal of gratitude, the ardour of patriotism, fondness for an opinion, or fidelity to a party, may easily overpower the vigilance of a mind habitually well disposed, and prevail over unassisted and unfriended veracity.

But he that speaks of himself has no motive to falsehood or partiality except self-love, by which all have so often been betrayed, that all are on the watch against its artifices. He that writes an apology for a single action, to confute an accusation, or recommend himself to favour, is indeed always to be suspected of favouring his own cause; but he that sits down calmly and voluntarily to review his life for the admonition of posterity, or to amuse himself, and leaves this account unpublished, may be commonly presumed to tell truth, since falsehood cannot appease his own mind, and fame will not be heard beneath the tomb.

24 November 1759

No. 94. [On the Abatement of Learning and Bad Writing]

It is common to find young men ardent and diligent in the pursuit of knowledge, but the progress of life very often produces laxity and indifference; and not only those who are at liberty to choose their business and amusements, but those likewise whose professions engage them in literary enquiries pass the latter part of their time without improvement, and spend the day rather in any other entertainment than that which they might find among their books.

This abatement of the vigour of curiosity is sometimes imputed to the insufficiency of learning. Men are supposed to remit their labours, because they find their labours to have been vain; and to search no longer after truth and wisdom, because they at last despair of finding them.

But this reason is for the most part very falsely assigned. Of learning, as of virtue, it may be affirmed, that it is at once honoured and neglected. Whoever forsakes it will for ever look after it with longing, lament the loss which he does not endeavour to repair, and desire the good which he wants resolution to seize and keep. The Idler never applauds his own idleness, nor does any man repent of the diligence of his youth.

So many hindrances may obstruct the acquisition of knowledge, that there is little reason for wondering that it is in a few hands. To the greater part of mankind the duties of life are inconsistent with much study, and the hours which they would spend upon letters must be stolen from their occupations and their families. Many suffer themselves to be lured by more spritely and luxurious pleasures from the shades of Contemplation, where they find seldom more than a calm delight, such as, though greater than all others, if its certainty and its duration be reckoned with its power of gratification, is yet easily quitted for some extemporary joy, which the present moment offers, and another perhaps will put out of reach.

It is the great excellence of Learning that it borrows very little from time or place; it is not confined to season or to climate, to cities or to the country, but may be cultivated and enjoyed where no other pleasure can be obtained. But this quality, which constitutes much of its value, is one occasion of neglect; what may be done at all times with equal propriety, is deferred from day to day, till the mind is gradually reconciled to the omission, and the attention is turned to other objects. Thus habitual idleness gains too much power to be conquered, and the soul shrinks from the idea of intellectual labour and intenseness of meditation.

That those who profess to advance Learning sometimes obstruct it, cannot be denied; the continual multiplication of books not only distracts choice but disappoints enquiry. To him that has moderately stored his mind with images, few writers afford any novelty; or what little they have to add to the common stock of learning is so buried in the mass of general notions, that, like silver mingled with the ore of lead, it is too little to pay for the labour of separation; and he that has often been deceived by the promise of a title, at last grows weary of examining, and is tempted to consider all as equally fallacious.

There are indeed some repetitions always lawful, because they never deceive. He that writes the history of past times, undertakes only to decorate known facts by new beauties of method or of style, or at most to illustrate them by his own reflections. The Author of a system, whether moral or physical, is obliged to nothing beyond care of selection and regularity of disposition. But there are others who claim the name of Authors merely to disgrace it, and fill the world with volumes only to bury letters in their own rubbish. The Traveller who tells, in a pompous folio, that he saw the *Pantheon* at *Rome*, and the *Medicean Venus* at *Florence;* the Natural Historian who, describing the productions of a narrow island, recounts all that it has in common with every other part of the world; the Collector of Antiquities, that accounts every thing a curiosity which the ruins of *Herculaneum* happen to emit, though an instrument already shown in a thousand repositories, or a cup common to the ancients, the moderns, and all mankind, may be justly censured as the persecutors of students, and the thieves of that time which never can be restored.

2 February 1760

No. 103. [On Last Things]

Respicere ad longæ jussit spatia ultima vitæ. Juv.[66]

Much of the pain and pleasure of mankind arises from the conjectures which every one makes of the thoughts of others; we all enjoy praise which we do not hear, and resent contempt which we do not see. The *Idler* may therefore be forgiven, if he suffers his imagination to represent to him what his readers will say or think when they are informed that they have now his last paper in their hands.

Value is more frequently raised by scarcity than by use. That which lay neglected when it was common, rises in estimation as its quantity becomes less. We seldom learn the true want of what we have till it is discovered that we can have no more.

This essay will, perhaps, be read with care even by those who have not yet attended to any other; and he that finds this late attention recompensed, will not forbear to wish that he had bestowed it sooner.

Though the *Idler* and his readers have contracted no close friendship they are perhaps both unwilling to part. There are few things not purely evil, of which we can say, without some emotion of uneasiness, *this is the last.* Those who never could agree together, shed tears when mutual discontent has determined them to final separation; of a place which has been frequently visited, though without pleasure, the last look is taken with

66. "Look to the last lap of a long life"; Juvenal, *Satires,* X.275.

heaviness of heart; and the *Idler,* with all his chillness of tranquillity, is not wholly unaffected by the thought that his last essay is now before him.

This secret horrour of the last is inseparable from a thinking being whose life is limited, and to whom death is dreadful. We always make a secret comparison between a part and the whole; the termination of any period of life reminds us that life itself has likewise its termination; when we have done any thing for the last time, we involuntarily reflect that a part of the days allotted us is past, and that as more is past there is less remaining.

It is very happily and kindly provided, that in every life there are certain pauses and interruptions, which force consideration upon the careless, and seriousness upon the light; points of time where one course of action ends and another begins; and by vicissitude of fortune, or alteration of employment, by change of place, or loss of friendship, we are forced to say of something, *this is the last.*

An even and unvaried tenour of life always hides from our apprehension the approach of its end. Succession is not perceived but by variation; he that lives to-day as he lived yesterday, and expects that, as the present day is, such will be the morrow, easily conceives time as running in a circle and returning to itself. The uncertainty of our duration is impressed commonly by dissimilitude of condition; it is only by finding life changeable that we are reminded of its shortness.

This conviction, however forcible at every new impression, is every moment fading from the mind; and partly by the inevitable incursion of new images, and partly by voluntary exclusion of unwelcome thoughts, we are again exposed to the universal fallacy; and we must do another thing for the last time, before we consider that the time is nigh when we shall do no more.

As the last *Idler* is published in that solemn week which the Christian world has always set apart for the examination of the conscience, the review of life, the extinction of earthly desires and the renovation of holy purposes[67] I hope that my readers are already disposed to view every incident with seriousness, and improve it by meditation; and that when they see this series of trifles brought to a conclusion, they will consider that by outliving

67. The last issue of "The Idler" was published during Holy Week (the week before Easter).

the *Idler*, they have passed weeks, months, and years which are now no longer in their power; that an end must in time be put to every thing great as to every thing little; that to life must come its last hour, and to this system of being its last day, the hour at which probation ceases, and repentance will be vain; the day in which every work of the hand, and imagination of the heart shall be brought to judgment, and an everlasting futurity shall be determined by the past.

    5 April 1760

FIVE
Henry Fielding
(1707–54)

HENRY FIELDING, BEST REMEMBERED as a novelist and dramatist, entered the periodical essay tradition at the peak of his career with *The Covent Garden Journal* (1752). Unlike his earlier journalistic ventures (*The Champion, The Patriot, The Jacobite Journal*), his *Covent Garden Journal* was intended as a cultural rather than a political forum. It carried on the effort to reform the manners and morals of the age, if with more satiric bite than had been seen previously in periodical essays. The Covent Garden section of London was a rough-and-tumble medley of entertainment spots, which in addition to Covent Garden Theatre included Turkish baths, gin shops, taverns, brothels, and coffeehouses where the "rabble" could mix with society members and artists. Will's Coffee House was located on the north side of Bow Street, the district's principal strip, otherwise known as "Thieving Lane," and Button's on the south side, just two doors from Covent Garden Theatre. Fielding, a former justice of the peace in Westminster, founded the first metropolitan police force, known as the Bow Street Runners, in 1749 to clear the area of its criminals and cheats.

With more than two dozen plays performed at Drury Lane Theatre, Fielding ended his successful career as a dramatist when Robert Walpole instituted the theater Licensing Act, severely restricting artistic freedom through censorship. In *The Champion,* under the name of Captain Hercules Vinegar, Fielding had "tried" the playwright Colley Cibber for "the Murder of the *English* language," and twelve years later, on 4 January 1752, he began "the Grub-Street Paper War" in the persona of Sir Alexander Drawcansir, judge or "Censor of Great Britain." The name derives from a character in the Restoration comedy *The Rehearsal* (1671) by the rakish George Villiers, second Duke of Buckingham. There, Drawcansir parodies the heroes of John Dryden's dramas: "I drink, I huff, I strut, look big and stare; / And all this I can do, because I dare" (IV.i). Fielding's Drawcansir likewise descends from high drama to comedy, taking aim at the "mere Mechanics" of the Republic of Letters.

Selections are from Henry Fielding, *The Covent Garden Journal,* ed. Gerard E. Jensen (New Haven: Yale University Press, 1915).

The Covent Garden Journal
By Sir Alexander Drawcansir, Knt., Censor of Great Britain

No. 1. Introduction to a Journal of the Present Paper War Between the Forces Under Sir Alexander Drawcansir, and the Army of Grubstreet

Before I had fully resolved to draw my pen, and to take the field in the warfare of Writing, I duly considered not only my own strength, but the force of the enemy. I am therefore well apprized of the difficulties I have to encounter: I well know the present dreadful condition of the great Empire of Letters; the state of anarchy that prevails among Writers; and the great revolution which hath lately happened in the Kingdom of Criticism; that the constitutions of Aristotle, Horace, Longinus, and Bossu,[1] under which the State of Criticism so long flourished, have been entirely neglected, and the government usurped by a set of fellows, entirely ignorant of all those laws. The consequence of which hath been the dissolution of that ancient friendship and amity which subsisted between the Author and the Critic, so much to the mutual advantage of both people, and that the latter hath long declared war against the former. I know how cruelly this war hath been carried on, and the great devastation which hath been made in the literary world, chiefly by means of a large body of irregulars, composed of Beaux, Rakes, Templars, Cits, Lawyers, Mechanics, School-boys, and fine Ladies, who have been admitted to the *Jus Civitatis,*[2] by the usurpers in the realms of Criticism, without knowing one word of the ancient laws, and original

1. References to Aristotle's *Poetics,* Horace's *Ars poetica* (Art of Poetry), Longinus's *Peri hupsous* (On the Sublime), and René Le Bossu's *Traité du poème épique* (Treatise on Epic Poetry).
    2. The legal order of the state or city; the right of citizenship. A Cit was a city dweller, generally a middle-class person aspiring to higher status.

constitution of that body of which they have professed themselves to be members. I am, farther, sensible of the revolt which hath been of the Authors to the Critics; many of the meanest among the former, having become very considerable and principal *leaders* among the latter.

All these circumstances put together do most certainly afford a most gloomy prospect, and are sufficient to dismay a very enterprizing genius; but I have often reflected with approbation on the advice given to Caius Piso, in Tacitus, *to appear in open arms in defence of a just and glorious cause, rather than to await the event of a tame and abject submission.*[3] How much more noble is it in a great Author to fall with his pen in his hand, than quietly to sit down, and see the Press in the possession of an army of Scribblers, who, at present, seem to threaten the Republic of Letters with no less devastation than that which their ancestors the Goths, Huns, Vandals, &c. formerly poured in on the Roman Empire!

When I had taken a firm resolution of opposing this swarm of Vandals, I concerted my measures in the best manner I was able.

In the first place I reviewed my veterans which were all drawn up in their ranks before me. The Greeks led by Homer, Aristotle, Thucydides, Demosthenes, Lucian, and Longinus. The Romans under the command of Virgil, Horace, Cicero, Tacitus, Terence and Quinctilian. A most formidable body, all in gilt armour, and on whom I can rely with great assurance, as I am convinced the enemy hold not the least correspondence with them; a circumstance which gives me some little suspicion of my French forces, of which I have a considerable body, with Moliere and Bossu at their head; but though some of the enemy have been taken dabbling with these, I am well assured they are not likely to come to a perfect good understanding with them.

Besides these, I have a large body of English veterans, under Bacon and Locke, sent me in by Major-General A. Millar, who is a faithful ally of the Republic of Letters, and who hath himself raised this body, all staunch friends to the cause.[4]

3. Probably an indirect reference to Tacitus's discussion of Caius Piso's role in the conspiracy against Nero in Book XV of the *Annales*.

4. Andrew Millar (1707–68), a bookseller and publisher located on the Strand, assembled a formidable staff of literary advisers and paid high prices for literary works.

In the next place, I have taken sufficient care to strengthen myself by alliances with all the Moderns of any considerable force; but as this hath been carried on by secret treaties, I cannot, as yet, publish the names of my allies.

4 January 1752

No. 4. [On the Meaning of Common Words]

———Nanum cujusdam Atlanta vocamus:
Æthiopem Cygnum: parvam extortamque puellam
Europen. Canibus pigris Scabieque vetusta
Lævibus, et siccæ lambentibus Ora lucernæ
Nomen erit Pardus, Tigris, Leo; si quid ad-huc est
*Quod fremat in Terris violentius.———*Juv. Sat. 8.[5]

"One may observe," says Mr. Locke, "in all languages, certain words, that, if they be examined, will be found, in their first original, and their appropriated use, not to stand for any clear and distinct ideas." Mr. Locke gives us the instances "of wisdom, glory, grace. Words which are frequent enough (says he) in every man's mouth; but if a great many of those who use them, should be asked what they mean by them, they would be at a stand, and not know what to answer: a plain proof, that though they have learned those sounds, and have them ready at their tongue's end; yet there are no determined ideas laid up in their minds, which are to be expressed to others by them."[6]

Besides the several causes by him assigned of the abuse of words, there is one, which, though the great philosopher hath omitted it, seems to have contributed not a little to the introduction of this enormous evil. This is that privilege which divines and moral writers have assumed to themselves of doing violence to certain words, in favour of their own hypotheses,

5. "We call some one's dwarf an 'Atlas,' his blackamoor 'a swan'; an ill-favoured, misshapen girl we call 'Europa'; lazy hounds that are bald with chronic mange, and who lick the edges of a dry lamp, will bear the names of 'Pard,' 'Tiger,' 'Lion,' or of any other animal in the world that roars more fiercely"; Juvenal, *Satires,* VIII.32–37.

6. John Locke, *An Essay Concerning Human Understanding,* III.x.2–3.

and of using them in a sense often directly contrary to that which custom (the absolute Lord and Master, according to Horace, of all the modes of speech) hath allotted them.[7]

Perhaps, indeed, this fault may be seen in somewhat a milder light, (and I would always see the blemishes of such writers in the mildest). It may not, perhaps, be so justly owing to any designed opposition to custom as a total ignorance of it. An ignorance which is almost inseparably annexed to a collegiate life, and which any man, indeed, may venture to own without blushing.

But whatever may be the cause of this abuse of words, the consequence is certainly very bad: for whilst the author and the world receive different ideas from the same words, it will be pretty difficult for them to comprehend each other's meaning; and hence, perhaps, it is that so many gentlemen and ladies have contracted a general odium to all works of religion or morality; and that many others have been readers in this way all their lives without understanding what they read, consequently without drawing from it any practical use.

It would, perhaps, be an office very worthy the labour of a good commentator to explain certain hard words which frequently occur in the works of Barrow, Tillotson, Clark, and others of this kind.[8] Such are heaven, hell, judgment, righteousness, sin, &c. All which, it is reasonable to believe, are at present very little understood.

Instead, however, of undertaking this task myself, at least, at present, I shall apply the residue of this Paper to the use of such writers only. I shall here give a short glossary of such terms as are at present greatly in use, and shall endeavour to fix to each those exact ideas which are annexed to every [one] of them in the world; for while the learned in colleges do, as I apprehend, consider them all in a very different light, their labours are not likely to do much service to the polite part of mankind.

7. See Horace, *Ars poetica*, 71–72.
8. The theologians John Tillotson (1630–94), Isaac Barrow (1630–77), and Gilbert Clerke (1626–97).

A Modern Glossary.

ANGEL. The name of a woman, commonly of a very bad one.

AUTHOR. A laughing stock. It means likewise a poor fellow, and in general an object of contempt.

BEAR. A country gentleman; or, indeed, any animal upon two legs that doth not make a handsome bow.

BEAUTY. The qualification with which women generally go into keeping.[9]

BEAU. With the article A before it, means a great favourite of all women.

BRUTE. A word implying plain-dealing and sincerity, but more especially applied to a philosopher.

CAPTAIN. ⎫
⎬ Any stick of wood with a head to it, and a piece of black ribband upon that head.
COLONEL. ⎭

CREATURE. A quality expression of low contempt, properly confined only to the mouths of ladies who are Right Honourable.

CRITIC. Like *Homo,* a name common to all [the] human race.

COXCOMB. A word of reproach, and yet, at the same time, signifying all that is most commendable.

DAMNATION. A term appropriated to the theatre; though sometimes more largely applied to all works of invention.

DEATH. The final end of man; as well of the *thinking part of the body,* as of all the other parts.

DRESS. The principal accomplishment of men and women.

DULNESS. A word applied by all writers to the wit and humour of others.

EATING. A science.

FINE. An adjective of a very peculiar kind, destroying, or, at least, lessening the force of the substantive to which it is joined: as *fine* gentlemen, *fine* lady, *fine* house, *fine* clothes, *fine* taste;— in all which *fine* is to be understood in a sense somewhat synonymous with useless.

9. That is, become kept mistresses.

FOOL. A complex idea, compounded of poverty, honesty, piety, and simplicity.

GALLANTRY. Fornication and adultery.

GREAT. Applied to a thing, signifies bigness; when to a man, often littleness, or meanness.

GOOD. A word of as many different senses as the Greek word Ἔχω, or as the Latin *Ago*:[10] for which reason it is but little used by the polite.

HAPPINESS. Grandeur.

HONOUR. Duelling.

HUMOUR. Scandalous lies, tumbling and dancing on the rope.

JUDGE. ⎫
⎬ An old woman.
JUSTICE. ⎭

KNAVE. The name of four cards in every pack.

KNOWLEDGE. In general, means knowledge of the Town; as this is, indeed, the only kind of knowledge ever spoken of in the polite world.

LEARNING. Pedantry.

LOVE. A word properly applied to our delight in particular kinds of food; sometimes metaphorically spoken of the favourite objects of all our *appetites*.

MARRIAGE. A kind of traffic carried on between the two sexes, in which both are constantly endeavouring to cheat each other, and both are commonly losers in the end.

MISCHIEF. Fun, sport, or pastime.

MODESTY. Awkwardness, rusticity.

NO BODY. All the people in Great Britain, except about 1200.

NONSENSE. Philosophy, especially the philosophical writings of the Ancients, and more especially of Aristotle.

OPPORTUNITY. The season of cuckoldom.

PATRIOT. A candidate for a place at court.

POLITICS. The art of getting such a place.

PROMISE. Nothing.

10. The Greek *echo* means "to own, possess"; the Latin *ago*, "to act."

RELIGION. A word of no meaning; but which serves as a bug-bear to frighten children with.

RICHES. The only thing upon earth that is really valuable, or desirable.

ROGUE.
RASCAL. } A man of a different party from yourself.

SERMON. A sleeping-dose.

SUNDAY. The best time for playing at cards.

SHOCKING. An epithet which fine ladies apply to almost every thing. It is, indeed, an interjection (if I may so call it) of delicacy.

TEMPERANCE. Want of spirit.

TASTE. The present whim of the Town, whatever it be.

TEASING. Advice; chiefly that of a husband.

VIRTUE.
VICE. } Subjects of discourse.

WIT. Prophaneness, indecency, immorality, scurrility, mimicry, buffoonery. Abuse of all good men, and especially of the clergy.

WORTH. Power. Rank. Wealth.

WISDOM. The art of acquiring all three.

WORLD. Your own acquaintance.

14 January 1752

No. 6. [Uses to Which Learning Is Put]

Quam multi tineas pascunt, blattasque diserti!
Et redimunt soli carmina docta coci!
Nescio quid plus est quod donat secula chartis,
Victurus genium debet habere liber. Mart. lib. 6.[11]

How many fear the Moth's and Bookworm's Rage,
And Pastry-Cooks, sole Buyers in this Age?

11. "How many good poets are food for moths and bookworms, and only cooks buy their accomplished verses! There is something more that gives centuries to paper. A book that is to live must have a Genius"; Martial, *Epigrams*, VI.lxi.7–10.

What can these Murtherers of Wit controul?
To be immortal, Books must have a soul.

There are no human productions to which Time seems so bitter and malicious an enemy, as to the works of the learned: for though all the pride and boast of art must sooner, or later, yield to this great destroyer; though all the labours of the architect, the statuary, and the painter, must share the same mortality with their authors; yet, with these, Time acts in a gentler and milder manner, allows them generally a reasonable period of existence, and brings them to an end by a gradual and imperceptible decay: so that they may seem rather cut off by the fatal laws of necessity, than to be destroyed by any such act of violence, as this cruel tyrant daily executes on us writers.

It is true, indeed, there are some exceptions to this rule; some few works of learning have not only equalled, but far exceeded, all other human labours in their duration; but alas! how very few are these, compared to that vast number which have been swallowed up by this great destroyer. Many of them cut off in their very prime; others in their early youth; and others, again, at their very birth; so that they can scarce be said ever to have been.

And, as to the few that remain to us, is not their long existence to be attributed to their own unconquerable spirit, and rather to the weakness, than to the mercy of Time? Have not many of their authors foreseen, and foretold, the endeavours which would be exerted to destroy them, and have boldly asserted their just claim to immortality, in defiance of all the malice, all the cunning, and all the power of Time?

Indeed, when we consider the many various engines which have been employed for this destructive purpose, it will be matter of wonder, that any of the writings of Antiquity have been able to make their escape. This might almost lead us into a belief, that the writers were really possessed of that divinity, to which some of them pretended, especially as those which seem to have had the best pretensions to this divinity, have been almost the only ones which have escaped into our hands.

And here, not to mention those great engines of destruction which Ovid so boldly defies, such as swords, and fire, and the devouring moths of Antiquity,[12] how many cunning methods hath the malice of Time in-

12. Swords and fire are frequently defied in Ovid's *Metamorphoses*, which itself has defied bookworms, moths of antiquity, and other ravagers.

vented, of later days, to extirpate the works of the learned, and to convert the invention of paper, and even of printing, to the total abolition of those very works which they were so ingeniously calculated to perpetuate.

The first of these, decency will permit me barely to hint to the reader. It is the application of it to a use for which parchment and vellum, the ancient repositories of learning, would have been utterly unfit. To this cunning invention of Time, therefore, printing and paper have chiefly betrayed the Learned; nor can I see, without indignation, the booksellers, those great enemies of authors, endeavouring by all their sinister arts to propagate so destructive a method: for what is commoner than to see books advertised to be printed *on a superfine, delicate, soft Paper,* and again, *very proper to be had in all families,* a plain insinuation to what use they are adapted, according to these lines.

> *Lintott's for gen'ral Use are fit,*
> *For some Folks read, but all Folks———*.[13]

By this abominable method, the whole works of several modern authors have been so obliterated, that the most curious searcher into Antiquity, hereafter, will never be able to wipe off the injuries of Time.

And, yet, so truly do the booksellers verify that old observation, *dulcis odor lucri ex re qualibet,* that they are daily publishing several works, manifestly calculated for this use only; nay, I am told, that one of them is, by means of a proper translator, preparing the whole works of Plato for the B———.[14]

Next to the booksellers are the trunk-makers, a set of men who have of late years made the most intolerable depredations on modern learning.

13. Alexander Pope, "Verses to Be Prefix'd Before Bernard Lintot's *New Miscellany,*" ll. 29–30. Barnaby Bernard Lintott (1675–1736) was a publisher (of Pope, Steele, and John Gay, among others) and a bookseller.

14. The Latin phrase means "Wherever money comes from, it smells sweet"; an apothegm quoted in John Davies's 1659 legal and economic treatise *Jus imponendi vectigalia; or, The Learning touching Customs, Tonnage, Poundage, and Impositions on Merchandizes Asserted as Well from the Rules of Common and Civil Law as of Generall Reason and Policy of State.* "B———" stands for "bum." Fielding is referring to the use of waste paper (in this case, book pages) as toilet paper.

The ingenious Hogarth hath very finely satirized this, by representing several of the most valuable productions of these times on the way to the trunk-maker.[15] If these persons would line a trunk with a whole pamphlet, they might possibly do more good than harm; for then, perhaps, the works of last year might be found in our trunks, when they were possibly to be found no where else; but so far from this, they seem to take a delight in dismembering authors; and in placing their several limbs together in the most absurd manner. Thus while the bottom of a trunk contains a piece of poetry, the top presents us with a sheet of romance, and the sides and ends are adorned with mangled libels of various kinds.

The third species of these depredators, are the pastry cooks.[16] What indignation must it raise in a lover of the Moderns, to see some of their best performances stained with the juice of gooseberries, currants, and damascenes! But what concern must the author himself feel on such an occasion; when he beholds those writings, which were calculated to support the glorious cause of disaffection or infidelity, humbled to the ignoble purpose of supporting a tart or a custard! So, according to the poet,

> *Great Alexander dead, and turn'd to Clay,*
> *May stop a Hole to keep the Wind away.*[17]

But, besides the injuries done to learning by this method, there is another mischief which these pastry cooks may thus propagate in the society: for many of these wondrous performances are calculated only for the use and inspection of the few, and are by no means proper food for the mouths of babes and sucklings. For instance, that the Christian religion is a mere cheat and imposition on the public, nay, that the very being of a God is a matter of great doubt and incertainty, are discoveries of too deep a nature to perplex the minds of children with; and it is better, perhaps, till they come to a certain age, that they should believe quite the opposite doctrines. Again, as children are taught to obey and honour their superiors, and to

15. In William Hogarth's 1751 engraving "Beer Street," a large container of books is headed to "Mr. Pastem the Trunk maker" in Saint Paul's Churchyard. Trunks were commonly lined with old newspapers, pamphlets, or pages from books.

16. Shopkeepers used to wrap their baked goods and produce in old paper.

17. See Shakespeare, *Hamlet*, V.i.208 – 9.

keep their tongues from evil-speaking, lying, and slandering, to what good purposes can it tend to show them that the very contrary is daily practiced and suffered and supported in the world? Is not this to confound their understandings, and almost sufficient to make them neglect their learning? Lastly, there are certain Arcana Naturae,[18] in disclosing which the Moderns have made great progress: now whatever merit there may be in such denudations of Nature, if I may so express myself, and however exquisite a relish they may afford to *very* adult persons of both sexes in their closets, they are surely too speculative and mysterious for the contemplation of the young and tender, into whose hands tarts and pies are most likely to fall.

Now as these three subjects, namely, infidelity, scurrility, and indecency, have principally exercised the pens of the Moderns, I hope for the future, pastry cooks will be more cautious than they have lately been. In short, if they have no regard to learning, they will have some, I hope, to morality.

The same caution may be given to grocers and chandlers; both of whom are too apt to sell their figs, raisins, and sugar to children, without enough considering the poisonous vehicle in which they are conveyed. At the waste paper market, the cheapness of the commodity is only considered; and it is easy to see with what goods that market is likely to abound; since though the Press hath lately swarmed with libels against our religion and government, there is not a single writer of any reputation in this kingdom, who hath attempted to draw his pen against either.

But to return to that subject from which I seem to have a little digressed. How melancholy a consideration must it be to a modern author, that the labours, I might call them the offspring of his brain, are liable to so many various kinds of destruction, that what Tibullus says of the numerous avenues to death may be here applied.

———*Leti mille repente viæ.*[19]

To Death there are a thousand sudden Ways.

18. "Secrets of nature."
19. "Now the sea slays, and there are a thousand ways of sudden death"; Tibullus, *Delia*, iii.50.

For my own part, I never walk into Mrs. Dodd's shop, and survey all that vast and formidable host of Papers and Pamphlets arranged on her shelves, but the noble lamentation of Xerxes occurs to my mind; who, when he reviewed his army, on the banks of the Hellespont, is said to have grieved, for that not one of all those hundreds of thousands would be living an hundred years from that time. In the same manner, have I said to myself, "How dreadful a thought is it, that of all these numerous and learned works, none will survive to the next year?" But, within that time,

————*All will become,*
Martyrs to Pyes, and Relicts of the B————.[20]

I was led into these reflections by an accident which happened to me the other day, and which all lovers of Antiquity will esteem a very fortunate one. Having had the curiosity to examine a written paper, in which my baker enclosed me two hot rolls, I have rescued from oblivion one of the most valuable fragments, that I believe is now to be found in the world. I have ordered it to be fairly transcribed, and shall very soon present it to my readers, with my best endeavours, by a short comment, to illustrate a piece which appears to have remained to us from the most distant and obscure ages.

21 January 1752.

No. 27. [On Betters and the Mob]

————*Pudet hæc opprobria nobis,*
Et dici potuisse, Et non potuisse refelli. Ovid.[21]

'Tis true 'tis Pity, and Pity 'tis, 'tis true.[22]

Of all the oppressions which the rich are guilty of, there seems to be none more impudent and unjust than their endeavour to rob the poor of a

20. See John Dryden *Mac Flecknoe* (1682), ll. 100–101.
21. "Ashamed am I that such an insult could have been uttered and yet could not be answered"; Ovid, *Metamorphoses,* I.758–59.
22. Shakespeare, *Hamlet,* II.ii.98–99.

title, which is most clearly the property of the latter. Not contented with all the Honorables, Worshipfuls, Reverends, and a thousand other proud epithets which they exact of the poor, and for which they give in return nothing but Dirt, Scrub, Mob, and such like, they have laid violent hands on a word, to which they have not the least pretence or shadow of any title.

The word I mean is the comparative of the adjective Good, namely BETTER, or as it is usually expressed in the plural number BETTERS. An appellative which all the rich usurp to themselves, and most shamefully use when they speak of, or to the poor: for do we not every day hear such phrases as these. *Do not be saucy to your* BETTERS. *Learn to behave yourself before your* BETTERS. *Pray know your* BETTERS, &c.

It is possible that *the Rich* have been so long in possession of this, that they may now lay a kind of prescriptive claim to the property; but however that be, I doubt not but to make it appear, that if the word Better is to be understood as the comparative of *Good,* and is meant to convey an idea of superior goodness, it is with the highest impropriety applied to the rich, in comparison with the poor.

And this I the rather undertake, as the usurpation which I would obviate, hath produced a very great mischief in society; for the poor having been deceived into an opinion (for monstrous as it is, such an opinion hath prevailed) that the rich are their Betters, have been taught to honour, and of consequence to imitate the examples of those, whom they ought to have despised; while the rich on the contrary are misled into a false contempt of what they ought to respect, and by this means lose all the advantage which they might draw from contemplating *the exemplary Lives* of these their *real Betters.*

First then let us imagine to ourselves, a person wallowing in wealth, and lolling in his chariot, his mind torn with ambition, avarice, envy, and every other bad passion, and his brain distracted with schemes to deceive and supplant some other man, to cheat his neighbour or perhaps the public, what a glorious use might such a person derive to himself, as he is rolled through the outskirts of the Town by due meditations, on the lives of those who dwell in stalls and cellars! What a noble lesson of true Christian patience and contentment may such a person learn from his Betters, who enjoy the highest cheerfulness in their poor condition; their minds being disturbed by no unruly passion, nor their heads by any racking cares!

Where again shall we look for an example of temperance? In the stinking kitchens of the rich, or under the humble roofs of the poor? Where for prudence but among those who have the fewest desires? Where for fortitude, but among those who have every natural evil to struggle with?

In modesty, I think, there will be little difficulty in knowing where we are to find our Betters: for to this virtue there can be nothing more diametrically opposite than pride. Whenever therefore we observe persons stretching up their heads and looking with an air of contempt on all around them, we may be well assured there is no modesty there. Indeed I never yet heard it enumerated among all the bad qualities of an oyster-woman or a cinder-wench, that *she had a great deal of Pride,* and consequently there is at least a possibility that such may have a great deal of modesty, whereas it is absolutely impossible that those to whom much pride belongs, should have any tincture of its opposite virtue.

Nor are the pretensions of these same Betters less strongly supported in that most exalted virtue of justice, witness the daily examples which they give of it in their own persons. When a man was punished for his crimes the Greeks said that he *gave Justice.* Now this is a gift almost totally confined to the poor, and it is a gift, which they very seldom fail of making as often as there is any very pressing occasion. Who can remember to have seen a rich man whipped at the cart's tail! And how seldom (I am sorry to say it) are such exalted to the pillory, or sentenced to transportation! And as for the more reputable, namely the capital punishments, how rarely do we see them executed on the rich! Whereas their Betters, to their great honour be it spoken, do very constantly make all these gifts of justice to the society, which the other part have it much more in their power to serve by showing the same regard to this virtue.

As for chastity, it is a matter which I shall handle with great delicacy and tenderness, as it principally concerns that lovely part of the creation, for whom I have the sincerest regard. On this head therefore, I shall only whisper, that if our ladies of fashion were sometimes for variety only to take a ride through St. Giles's, they might find *Something* in the air there as wholesome as in that of Hanover or Grosvenor-Square.[23]

23. Saint Giles was a crowded, working-class section of eighteenth-century London.

It may perhaps, be objected to what I have hitherto advanced, that I have ONLY mentioned the Cardinal Virtues,[24] which, (possibly from the popish epithet assigned to them) are at present held in so little repute, that no man is conceived to be the better for possessing them, or the worse for wanting them. I will now therefore proceed to a matter so necessary to the genteel character; that a superior degree of excellence in it hath been universally allowed by all gentlemen, in the most essential manner, to constitute *our Betters.*

My sagacious reader, I make no doubt, already perceives I am going to mention decency, the characteristic, as it is commonly thought, of a gentleman; and perhaps it formerly was so; but at present it is so far otherwise, that, if our People of Fashion will examine the matter fairly and without prejudice, they cannot have the least decency left, if they refuse to allow, that, in this instance, the Mob are most manifestly their Betters.

Who that hath observed the behaviour of an audience at the playhouse, can doubt a moment to what part he should give the preference in decency! Here indeed I must be forced, however against my inclination, to prefer the upper ladies (I mean those who sit in the upper regions of the House) to the lower. Some, perhaps, may think the pit an exception to this rule; but I am sorry to say, that I have received information by some of my spies, that the example of the boxes hath of late corrupted the manners of their Betters in the pit; and that several shopkeepers' wives and daughters have begun to interrupt the performance, by laughing, tittering, giggling, chattering, and such like behaviour, highly unbecoming all persons who have any regard to decency: whereas nothing of this kind hath been imputed, as I have yet heard, to the ladies in either gallery, who may be truly said to be ABOVE all these irregularities.

I readily allow, that on certain occasions the gentlemen at the top of the House are rather more vociferous than those at the bottom: but to this I shall give three answers; first, that the voice of men is stronger and louder than that of beaus. Secondly, that on these occasions, as at the first night of a new play, the entertainment is to be considered as among the audience, all of whom are actors in such scenes. Lastly, as these entertainments all begin

24. The four Cardinal Virtues were justice, fortitude, prudence, and temperance.

below-stairs, the concurrence of the galleries is to be attributed to the politeness of our Betters who sit there, and to that decent condescension which they show in concurring with the manners of their inferiors.

Nor do these, our Betters, give us examples of decency in their own persons only; they take the utmost care to preserve decency in their inferiors, and are a kind of Deputies to the Censor in all public places. Who is it that prevents the stage being crowded with grotesque figures, a mixture of the human with the baboon species? Who (I say) but the Mob? The gentlemen in the boxes observe always the profoundest tranquility on all such occasions; but no sooner doth one of these apparitions present its frightful figure before the scenes, than the Mob, *from their profound Regard to Decency,* are sure to command him OFF.

And should any Persons of Fashion in the boxes, expose themselves to public notice by any indecent particularities of behaviour; from whom would they receive immediate correction and admonishment, but from the Mob who are (for this purpose perhaps) placed over them?

Was it not for this tender care of decency in the Mob, who knows what spectacles the desire of novelty and distinction would often exhibit in our streets? For let persons be guilty of the highest Enormities of this kind, they may meet a hundred People of Fashion without receiving a single rebuke. But the Mob never fail to express their indignation on all indecencies of this kind: and it is, perhaps, the awe of the Mob alone which prevents People of Condition, as they call themselves, from becoming more egregious apes than they are, of all the extravagant modes and follies of Europe.

Thus, I think, I have fully proved what I undertook to prove. I do not pretend to say, that the Mob have no faults; perhaps they have many. I assert *no more* than this, that they are in all laudable qualities very greatly superior to those who have hitherto, with much injustice, pretended to look down upon them.

In this attempt I may perhaps have given offence to some of the inferior sort, but I am contented with the assurance of having espoused the cause of truth; and in so doing, I am well convinced *I shall please all who are* REALLY MY BETTERS.

4 April 1752

SIX

William Cowper

(1731–1800)

THE SON OF A RECTOR FROM Hertfordshire, William Cowper attended Westminster School from 1742 to 1749 with the satirists George
Colman and Bonnell Thornton and the poets Charles Churchill and
Robert Lloyd. Later he became a barrister, but, bored by the tediousness of
his profession, he preferred lounging in coffeehouses with his former
schoolfellows and discussing literary and cultural affairs. Together they
formed the "Nonsense Club," whose weekly periodical, *The Connoisseur,*
ran for 140 numbers from 1754 to 1756 as a sprightly offspring of *The Spectator.* The year it ended, Cowper fell in love with his cousin, but their parents refused to let them marry. He suffered a nervous breakdown six years
later, when he tried drowning, stabbing, poisoning, and hanging himself,
though none of these suicide methods worked. He was subsequently sent
to an insane asylum at Saint Alban's, where he was seized with a religious
passion. Upon his release, he moved in with an evangelical family in Hunt-
ington whose materfamilias, Mary Unwin, nursed him, playing the role of
the mother he had lost when he was five. In 1773 he experienced a further
mental breakdown and tried to kill himself according to what he believed
was God's command. That effort too failed, and he gave up religious worship, convinced, until the end of his life, that he was eternally damned.

As a religious poet who struggled with insanity, Cowper might seem
an unlikely exponent of the urbane essay. But he participated in the shift of
the essay tradition in the second half of the eighteenth century toward a literary concern with "the natural." This had its parallel in the poetry of sensibility, distinguished by Cowper's own long poem *The Task* (1785). In his
essays for *The Connoisseur,* Cowper adopted the serial's first-person persona, "Mr. Town, Critic and Censor-General." Although he published only
a handful of essays, these were memorable for their good-natured satire of
men and manners. Their targets ranged from scandalmongers and conver-

sational misfits to awkward old bachelors. Leigh Hunt, in his literary autobiography, later looked back and recalled that the "lively papers of the *Connoisseur* gave me an entirely fresh and delightful sense of the merits of essay-writing."

Selections are from George Colman and Bonnell Thornton, eds., *The Connoisseur* (London, 1756).

The Connoisseur

No. III. [On Mothers' Sons]

Tandem desine matrem. Hor.[1]

> With dear mamma O make not such a pother!
> But strive to be a man before your mother.

The generality of the young unmarried ladies of the present age dislike no company so much as the elderly persons of their own sex, whether married or unmarried. Going with an old maiden aunt, a mamma, or grandmamma to the play, or to *Ranelagh,*[2] is so insipid an amusement, that it robs their entertainment of the very name of a party of pleasure. To be handed into a box, walk in the public gardens, or make one at a card-table at a rout, with a sprightly young nobleman, or gallant colonel of the guards, has some life in it; but to be kept perpetually under the wing of an old lady, can have no charms for a woman of spirit. The presence of these antiquated females imposes a constraint on their behaviour: they are, indeed, like the *Duennas* in *Spain,*[3] spies on the conduct of the gay and young; and a good old gentle-woman, with a blooming beauty by her side, watches her every motion, and is as much frighted, if the pretty creature makes any advances to a man, as an hen, who has been foster-mother to a brood of ducklings, is alarmed at their taking to the water.

This loose coquet behaviour so much in vogue, and consequently so

1. "Cease at length to follow thy mother"; Horace, Ode I.xxiii.11.
2. London pleasure gardens, containing a rotunda for such entertainments as dancing, fireworks, masquerades, and concerts.
3. Duennas were older women who acted as governesses and companions for girls in Spanish families.

genteel, has, I must own, no charms in my eye, as a modest deportment appears to me most natural and becoming in the fair sex; and I am always glad to see a young lady of sufficient sense and discretion, to behave with an innocent cheerfulness, instead of apparent uneasiness and constraint, before her more aged female relations. But though a daughter should prefer no company to her mother, a son, who always dangled at the side of his mamma, would appear as ridiculous, as if he wore his sister's petticoats: and however amiable this maidenly demeanor might seem in a young girl, I cannot view it with equal approbation in the character of a Male-Virgin;—a character, with which I shall here present the reader, as drawn by one of my correspondents.

To Mr. *TOWN*.
    SIR,
    You have already given us several instances of those ambiguous creatures among the men, who are both male and female: permit me to add to them an account of those lady-like gentlemen, whom we may distinguish by the title of *their mother's own sons;* who have in vain changed the bib and leading-strings for the breeches, and stick as close to their mammas, as a great calf to the side of an old cow. I am intimately acquainted with one of these overgrown babies; who is indeed too big to be dandled in lap, or fed with a pap-spoon, though he is no more weaned from his mother, than if he had not yet quitted the nursery.
    The delicate BILLY SUCKLING is the contempt of the men, the jest of the women, and the darling of his mamma. She dotes on him to distraction; and is in perpetual admiration of his wit, and anxiety for his health. The good young gentleman, for his part, is neither undutiful nor ungrateful: she is the only woman, that he does not look on with indifference; and she is his tutoress, his physician, and his nurse. She provides his broth every evening; will not suffer him to look into a book by candle-light, lest he should hurt his eyes; and takes care to have his bed warmed: nay, I have known him sit with his mamma's white handkerchief round his neck through a whole visit, to guard him from the wind of that *ugly door,* or that *terrible chink in the wainscot.*
    But however familiarly he may behave in his addresses to his mother, and whatever little acts of gallantry may pass between them, no encouragement can prevail on him to treat other women with the same freedom. Be-

ing once desired at a ball to dance a minuet, instead of taking out any of the young ladies, he could pitch upon no partner so agreeable, to whom he might offer the compliment of his hand, as his mother; and I remember, when he was once called upon in a large company at a tavern to give a lady in his turn, he plainly showed who was the sole mistress of his affections, by toasting his mother. The gallant custom of challenging a lady to drink a bumper, by leaving it to her option whether she will have *hob* or *nob,* frequently gives a delicious flavour to the liquor, especially when, as I have known it happen, joining the lips of the glasses has made a prelude to a meeting between the lips of the parties: but he could not be prevailed on to accept a glass of claret from the fairest hand, though a kiss were sure to follow it. I have known him so very nice, as to refuse a glass of sack filled with walnuts, which had been peeled by the snowy fingers of a beautiful young lady; though I have seen him smack his lips after a glass of raisin wine, in which his prudent mother had been dabbling with her snuffy finger, in order to fish out the small particles of cork, which might possibly have choked him. If a lady drops her fan, he sits without any emotion, and suffers her to stoop for it herself; or if she strikes her tea-cup against the saucer to give notice that it is empty, he pays no regard to the signal, but sees her walk up to the tea-table, without stirring from his chair. He would rather leave the most celebrated beauty, in crossing the street, to the mercy of a drayman, than trust her with his little finger: though at the same time should his mother be so distressed, he would not scruple to bear as much of her weight as he could stand under, and to redeem her silk stockings from jeopardy, would even expose his own.

One would imagine, that this extreme coyness and reserve, in which he so remarkably differs from the generality of his own sex, would in another respect as effectually distinguish him from the generality of women: I mean, that being less polite in his address than a footman, we should hardly expect to find him more loquacious than a chambermaid. But this is really the case: suffer him to take the lead in conversation, and there are certain topics, in which the most prating gossip at a christening would find it difficult to cope with him. The strength of his constitution is his favourite theme: he is constantly attempting to prove, that he is not susceptible of the least injury from cold; though a hoarseness in his voice, and the continual interruptions of a consumptive cough, give him the lie in his throat at the end of every sentence. The instances, indeed, by which he endeavours to prove his hardiness, unluckily rather tend to convince us of the delicacy of his frame, as they seldom amount to more than his having kicked off the bed-clothes in his sleep, laid aside one of his flannel waistcoats in a hot day, or tried on a new pair of pumps, before they had been sufficiently aired. For the truth of these facts he always appeals to his mamma, who vouches for him with a sigh, and protests that his carelessness would ruin the constitution of an horse.

I am now coming to the most extraordinary part of his character. This pusillanimous creature thinks himself, and would be thought, a Buck. The noble fraternity of that order find, that their reputation can be no otherwise maintained, than by prevailing on an *Irish* chairman now and then to favour them with a broken head, or by conferring the same token of their esteem on the unarmed and defenceless waiters at a tavern. But these feats are by no means suited to the disposition of our hero: and yet he always looks upon his harmless exploits as the bold frolics of a Buck. If he escapes a nervous fever a month, he is quite a Buck: if he walks home after it is dark, without his mamma's maid to attend him, he is quite a Buck: if he sits up an hour later than his usual time, or drinks a glass or two of wine without water, he calls it a debauch; and because his head does not ache the next morning, he is quite a Buck. In short, a woman of the least spirit within the precincts of St. *James's* would demolish him in a week, should he pretend to keep pace with her in her irregularities; and yet he is ever dignifying himself with the appellation of a Buck.

Now might it not be giving this gentleman an useful hint, Mr. Town, to assure him, that while milk and water is his darling liquor, a Bamboo cane his Club, and his mother the sole object of his affections, the World will never join in denominating him a Buck: that if he fails in this attempt, he is absolutely excluded from every order in society; for whatever his deserts may be, no assembly of antiquated virgins can ever acknowledge him for a sister, nature having as deplorably disqualified him for that rank in the community, as he has disqualified himself for every other: and that, though he never can arrive at the dignity of leading apes in hell,[4] he may

4. The phrase is used for "old maids" in Shakespeare's *Much Ado About Nothing,* where Beatrice says, "Therefore I will even take sixpence in earnest of the bearherd and lead his apes into hell" (II.i.34–36).

possibly be condemned to dangle in that capacity, at the apron-string of an old maid in the next world, for having so abominably resembled one in this.

I am, Sir, your humble servant,

W. C.

11 March 1756.

No. 115. [On Being a Bachelor]

*—Cœlebs quid agam?—*Hor.[5]

With an Old Bachelor how things miscarry!
What shall I do? go, hang myself? or marry?

To Mr. *Town.*

SIR,   *April 5, 1756.*

No man is a sincerer friend to innocent pleasantry, or more desirous of promoting it, than myself. Raillery of every kind, provided it be confined within due bounds, is, in my opinion, an excellent ingredient in conversation; and I am never displeased, if I can contribute to the harmless mirth of the company, by being myself the subject of it: but, in good truth, I have neither a fortune, a constitution, nor a temper, that will enable me to chuckle and shake my sides, while I suffer more from the festivity of my friends, than the spleen or malice of my enemies could possibly inflict upon me; nor do I see any reason, why I should so far move the mirthful indignation of the ladies, as to be teazed and worried to death in mere sport, for no earthly reason, but that I am what the world calls an Old Bachelor.

The female part of my acquaintance entertain an odd opinion, that a Bachelor is not in fact a rational creature; at least, that he has not the sense of feeling in common with the rest of mankind; that a Bachelor may be beaten like a flock-fish; that you may thrust pins into his legs, and wring him by the nose; in short, that you cannot take too many liberties with a Bachelor. I am at a loss to conceive on what foundation these romping philosophers have grounded their hypothesis, though at the same time I am a melancholy proof of its existence, as well as of its absurdity.

5. "What I, a bachelor, am doing . . ."; Horace, *Odes,* III.viii.1. Cowper rightly translates this as a question.

A friend of mine, whom I frequently visit, has a wife and three daughters, the youngest of which has persecuted me these ten years. These ingenious young ladies have not only found out the sole end and purpose of my being themselves, but have likewise communicated their discovery to all the girls in the neighbourhood: so that, if they happen at any time to be apprized of my coming, (which I take all possible care to prevent) they immediately dispatch half a dozen cards to their faithful allies, to beg the favour of their company to drink coffee, and *help teaze* Mr. *Ironside*. Upon these occasions, my entry into the room is sometimes obstructed by a cord, fastened across the bottom of the door-case; which, as I am a little near-sighted, I seldom discover, till it has brought me upon my knees before them. While I am employed in brushing the dust from my black rollers, or chafing my broken shins, my wig is suddenly conveyed away, and either stuffed behind the looking-glass, or tossed from one to the other so dextrously and with such velocity, that, after many a fruitless attempt to recover it, I am obliged to sit down bare-headed, to the great diversion of the spectators. The last time I found myself in these distressful circumstances, the eldest girl, a sprightly mischievous jade, stepped briskly up to me, and promised to restore my wig, if I would play her a tune on a small flute she held in her hand. I instantly applied it to my lips, and blowing lustily into it, to my inconceivable surprise, was immediately choked and blinded with a cloud of soot, that issued from every hole in the instrument. The younger part of the company declared I had not executed the conditions, and refused to surrender my wig; but the father, who had a rough kind of facetiousness about him, insisted on its being delivered up, and protested that he never knew the *Black Joke* better performed in his life.

I am naturally a quiet inoffensive animal, and not easily ruffled; yet I shall never submit to these indignities with patience, till I am satisfied I deserve them. Even the old maids of my acquaintance, who, one would think, might have a fellow-feeling for a brother in distress, conspire with their nieces to harass and torment me: and it is not many nights, since Miss *Diana Grizzle* utterly spoiled the only superfine suit I have in the world, by pinning the skirts of it together with a red-hot poker. I own, my resentment of this injury was so strong, that I determined to punish it by kissing the offender, which in cool blood I should never have attempted. The satisfaction, however, which I obtained by this imprudent revenge, was much like what a man of honour feels on finding himself run through the body by the scoundrel who had offended him. My upper lip was transfixed with a large corkin pin,[6] which in the scuffle she had conveyed into her mouth; and I doubt not, that I shall carry the *memorem labris notam* (the Mark of this *Judas*-kiss) from an old maid to the grave with me.[7]

These misfortunes, or others of the same kind, I encounter daily: but at these seasons of the year, which give a sanction to this kind of practical wit, and when every man thinks he has a right to entertain himself at his friend's expence, I live in hourly apprehensions of more mortifying adventures. No miserable dunghill-cock, devoted a victim to the wanton cruelty of the mob, would be more terrified at the approach of a *Shrove-Tuesday*, were he endued with human reason and forecast, then I am at the approach of a merry *Christmas* or the First of *April*. No longer ago than last *Thursday*, which was the latter of these festivals, I was pestered with mortifying presents from the ladies; obliged to pay the carriage of half a dozen oyster-barrels stuffed with brick-bats, and ten packets by the post containing nothing but old news-papers. But what vexed me the most, was the being sent fifty miles out of town, on that day, by a counterfeit express from a dying relation.

I could not help reflecting, with a sigh, on the resemblance between the imaginary grievance of poor *Tom* in the tragedy of *Lear*, and those which I really experienced. I, like him, was led through ford and whirlpool, o'er bog and quagmire; and though knives were not laid under my pillow, minced horse-hair was strewed upon my sheets: like him, I was made to ride on an hard-trotting horse through the most dangerous ways, and found, at the end of my journey, that I had only been coursing my own shadow.[8]

As much a sufferer as I am by the behaviour of the women in general, I must not forget to remark, that the pertness and sauciness of an old maid is particularly offensive to me. I cannot help thinking, that the virginity of these ancient misses is at least as ridiculous, as my own celibacy. If I am to

6. Corking pin, a pin of the largest size.

7. "Memorem dente labris notam" (the frenzied lad has with his teeth imprinted a lasting mark upon the lips); Horace, *Odes*, I.xiii.12.

8. Shakespeare's Edgar, disguised as Tom o' Bedlam (a madman), laments that he is made "to ride on a bay trotting-horse over four-inched bridges, to course his own shadow for a traitor"; *King Lear*, III.iv.48–54.

be condemned for having never made an offer, they are as much to blame for having never accepted one: if I am to be derided for having never married, who never attempted to make a conquest; they are more properly the objects of derision, who are still unmarried, after having made so many. Numberless are the proposals they have rejected, according to their own account: and they are eternally boasting of the havoc they have formerly made among the knights, baronets, and 'squires, at *Bath, Tunbridge,* and *Epsom,*[9] while a tattered madrigal perhaps, a snip of hair, or the portrait of a cherry-cheeked gentleman in a milk-white periwig, are the only remaining proofs of those beauties, which are now withered like the short-lived rose, and have only left the virgin thorn remaining.

Believe me, Mr. Town, I am almost afraid to trust you with the publication of this epistle: the ladies, whom I last mentioned, will be so exasperated on reading it, that I must expect no quarter at their hands for the future; since they are generally as little inclined to forgiveness in their old-age, as they were to pity and compassion in their youth. One expedient, however, is left me, which, if put in execution, will effectually screen me from their resentment.

I shall be happy, therefore, if by your means I may be permitted to inform the ladies, that as fusty an animal as they think me, it is not impossible but by a little gentler treatment, than I have hitherto met with, I may be humanized into an husband. As an inducement to them to relieve me from my present uneasy circumstances, you may assure them, that I am rendered so exceeding tractable by the very severe discipline I have undergone, that they may mould and fashion me to their minds with ease; and, consequently, that by marrying me a woman will save herself all that trouble, which a wife of any spirit is obliged to take with an unruly husband, who is absurd enough to expect from her a strict performance of the marriage vow, even in the very minute article of obedience: that, so far from contradicting a lady, I shall be mighty well satisfied, if she contents herself with contradicting me: that, if I happen at any time inadvertently to thwart her inclinations, I shall think myself rightly served, if she boxes my ears, spits in my face, or treads upon my corns: that, if I approach her lips, when she is not in

9. Fashionable eighteenth-century spa towns in England, where guests could "take the waters."

a kissing humour, I shall expect she will bite me by the nose; or, if I take her by the hand at an improper season, that she will instantly begin to pinch, scratch, and claw, and apply her fingers to those purposes, which they were certainly intended by nature to fulfil. Add to these accomplishments, so requisite to make the married state happy, that I am not much turned of fifty, can tie on my cravat, fasten a button, or mend an hole in my stocking without any assistance.

I am, Sir, your humble servant,
Christopher Ironside
8 April 1756

No. 119. [On Keeping a Secret]

Plenus rimarum sum, huc et illuc perfluo. Ter.[10]

Leaky at bottom; if those chinks you stop,
In vain;—the Secret will run o'er at top.

There is no mark of our confidence taken more kindly by a friend, than the entrusting him with a Secret; nor any which he is so likely to abuse. Confidantes in general are like crazy fire-locks, which are no sooner charged and cocked, than the spring gives way, and the report immediately follows. Happy to have been thought worthy the confidence of one friend, they are impatient to manifest their importance to another; till between them and their friend, and their friend's friend, the whole matter is presently known to *all our friends round the Wrekin*.[11] The secret catches as it were by contact, and like electrical matter breaks forth from every link in the chain, almost at the same instant. Thus the whole Exchange may be thrown into a buzz tomorrow, by what was whispered in the middle of *Marlborough Downs* this morning;[12] and in a week's time the streets may ring with the

10. "I'm full of cracks, I leak all over. So if you wish the secret kept speak the truth"; Terence, *Eunuchus* (The Eunuch), I.ii.105.
11. A phrase common in Shropshire—site of the Wrekin, a landmark hill with an Iron Age fort at the summit—to mean the long way around.
12. A rural area in Wiltshire between London and South Wales.

intrigue of a woman of fashion, bellowed out from the foul mouths of the hawkers, though at present it is known to no creature living, but her gallant and her waiting-maid.

As the talent of Secrecy is of so great importance to society, and the necessary commerce between individuals cannot be securely carried on without it, that this deplorable weakness should be so general is much to be lamented. You may as well pour water into a funnel, or a sieve, and expect it to be retained there, as commit your concerns to so slippery a companion. It is remarkable, that in those men who have thus lost the faculty of reten-tion, the desire of being communicative is always most prevalent, where it is least to be justified. If they are intruded with a matter of no great mo-ment, affairs of more consequence will perhaps in a few hours shuffle it en-tirely out of their thoughts: but if any thing be delivered to them with an air of earnestness, a low voice, and the gesture of a man in terror for the conse-quence of its being known; if the door is bolted, and every precaution taken to prevent a surprise; however they may promise secrecy, and however they may intend it, the weight upon their minds will be so extremely oppressive, that it will certainly put their tongues in motion.

This breach of trust, so universal amongst us, is perhaps in great mea-sure owing to our education. The first lesson our little masters and misses are taught, is to become blabs and tell-tales: they are bribed to divulge the petty intrigues of the family below stairs to papa and mamma in the parlour, and a doll or an hobby-horse is generally the encouragement of a propen-sity, which could scarcely be atoned for by a whipping. As soon as children can lisp out the little intelligence they have picked up in the hall or the kitchen, they are admired for their wit: if the butler has been caught kissing the housekeeper in his pantry, or the footman detected in romping with the chambermaid, away flies little *Tommy* or *Betsy* with the news; the parents are lost in admiration of the pretty rogue's understanding, and reward such un-common ingenuity with a kiss and a sugar-plum.

Nor does an inclination to Secrecy meet with less encouragement at school. The governantes at the boarding-school teach miss to be a good girl, and tell them every thing she knows: thus, if any young lady is unfor-tunately discovered eating a green apple in a corner, if she is heard to pro-nounce a naughty word, or is caught picking the letters out of another miss's sampler, away runs the chit,[13] who is so happy as to get the start of the rest, screams out her information as she goes; and the prudent matron chucks her under the chin, and tells her that she is a good girl, and every body will love her.

The management of our young gentlemen is equally absurd: in most of our schools, if a lad is discovered in a scrape, the impeachment of an accomplice, as at the *Old Bailey,* is made the condition of a pardon. I remember a boy, engaged in robbing an orchard, who was unfortunately taken prisoner in an apple-tree, and conducted, under a strong guard of the farmer and his dairy-maid, to the master's house. Upon his absolute refusal to discover his associates, the pedagogue undertook to lash him out of his fidelity, but finding it impossible to scourge the secret out of him, he at last gave him up for an obstinate villain, and sent him to his father, who told him he was ruined, and was going to disinherit him for not betraying his school-fellows. I must own I am not fond of thus drubbing our youth into treachery; and am much more pleased with the request of *Ulysses,* when he went to *Troy,* who begged of those who were to have the charge of *Telemachus,* that they would, above all things, teach him to be just, sincere, faithful, and *to keep a Secret.*[14]

Every man's experience must have furnished him with instances of confidantes who are not to be relied on, and friends who are not to be trusted; but few perhaps have thought it a character so well worth their attention, as to have marked out the different degrees into which it may be divided, and the different methods by which Secrets are communicated.

Ned Trusty is a tell-tale of a very singular kind. Having some sense of his duty, he hesitates a little at the breach of it. If he engages never to utter a syllable, he most punctually performs his promise; but then he has the knack of insinuating by a nod and a shrug well-timed, or a seasonable leer, as much as others can convey in express terms. It is difficult, in short, to determine, whether he is more to be admired for his resolution in not mentioning, or his ingenuity in disclosing a Secret. He is also excellent at a

13. A derogatory term for an immature or disrespectful girl.

14. The plot of Homer's *Odyssey* hinged on the ability of Odysseus's son Telemachus to keep Odysseus's identity secret from the suitors of Penelope when Odysseus (Ulysses) returns home.

"doubtful phrase," as *Hamlet* calls it, or an "ambiguous giving out"; and
his conversation consists chiefly of such broken innuendoes, as

> *Well, I know—or, I could—an if I would—*
> *Or, if I list to speak—or, there be, an if there might, &c.*[15]

Here he generally stops; and leaves it to his hearers to draw proper infer-
ences from these piece-meal premises. With due encouragement, however,
he may be prevailed on to slip the padlock from his lips, and immediately
overwhelms you with a torrent of secret history, which rushes forth with
more violence for having been so long confined.

Poor *Meanwell,* though he never fails to transgress, is rather to be
pitied than condemned. To trust him with a Secret, is to spoil his appetite,
to break his rest, and to deprive him for a time of every earthly enjoyment.
Like a man who travels with his whole fortune in his pocket, he is terrified if
you approach him, and immediately suspects, that you come with a felonious intent to rob him of his charge. If he ventures abroad, it is to walk in
some unfrequented place, where he is least in danger of an attack. At home,
he shuts himself up from his family, paces to and fro in his chamber, and has
no relief but from muttering over to himself, what he longs to publish to
the world; and would gladly submit to the office of town-cryer, for the liberty of proclaiming it in the market-place. At length, however, weary of his
burden, and resolved to bear it no longer, he consigns it to the custody of
the first friend he meets, and returns to his wife with a cheerful aspect, and
wonderfully altered for the better.

Careless is perhaps equally undesigning, though not equally excusable. Entrust him with an affair of the utmost importance, on the concealment of which your fortune and happiness depend: he hears you with a
kind of half-attention, whistles a favourite air, and accompanies it with the
drumming of his fingers upon the table. As soon as your narration is ended,
or perhaps in the middle of it, he asks your opinion of his sword-knot,
damns his tailor for having dressed him in a snuff-coloured coat, instead of
a *pompadour,*[16] and leaves you in haste to attend an auction; where, as if he

15. See Shakespeare, *Hamlet*, I.v.176–80.
16. A shade of crimson or pink.

meant to dispose of his intelligence to the best bidder, he divulges it, with a voice as loud as the auctioneer's; and when you tax him with having played you false, he is heartily sorry for it, but never knew that it was to be a Secret.

To these I might add the character of the open and unreserved, who thinks it a breach of friendship to conceal any thing from his intimates; and the impertinent, who having by dint of observation made himself master of your Secret, imagines he may lawfully publish the knowledge it has cost him so much labour to obtain, and considers that privilege, as the reward due to his industry. But I shall leave these, with many other characters, which my reader's own experience may suggest to him, and conclude with prescribing, as a short remedy for this evil,—That no man may betray the counsel of his friend, let every man keep his own.

6 May 1756

No. 138. [On Conversation]

Servatâ semper lege et ratione loquendi. Juv.[17]

Your talk to decency and reason suit,
Nor prate like fools, or gabble like a brute.

In the comedy of the *Frenchman in London,* which we are told was acted at *Paris* with universal applause for several nights together, there is a character of a rough *Englishman,* who is represented as quite unskilled in the graces of conversation; and his dialogue consists almost entirely of a repetition of the common salutation of *how do you do, how do you do?*[18] Our nation has, indeed, been generally supposed to be of a sullen and uncommunicative disposition; while, on the other hand, the loquacious *French* have been allowed to possess the art of conversing beyond all other people. The *Englishman* requires to be wound up frequently, and stops as soon as he is down; but the *Frenchman* runs on in a continued alarum. Yet it must be acknowledged, that, as the *English* consist of very different humours, their

17. "Who observes all the rules and laws of language"; Juvenal, *Satires,* VI.453.
18. A translation of Monsieur de Boissy's *The Frenchman in London* was published in London in 1755.

manner of discourse admits of great variety: but the whole *French* nation converse alike; and there is no difference in their address between a *Marquis* and a *Valet de Chambre*. We may frequently see a couple of *French* barbers accosting each other in the street, and paying their compliments with the same volubility of speech, the same grimace, and action, as two courtiers on the *Thuilleries*.

I shall not attempt to lay down any particular rules for conversation, but rather point out such faults in discourse and behaviour, as render the company of half mankind rather tedious than amusing. It is in vain, indeed, to look for conversation, where we might expect to find it in the greatest perfection, among persons of fashion: there it is almost annihilated by universal card-playing: insomuch that I have heard it given as a reason, why it is impossible for our present writers to succeed in the dialogue of genteel comedy, that our people of quality scarce ever meet but to game. All their discourse turns upon the odd trick and the four honours: and it is no less a maxim with the votaries of Whist than with those of *Bacchus,* that talking spoils company.

Every one endeavours to make himself as agreeable to society as he can: but it often happens, that those, who most aim at shining in conversation, over-shoot their mark. Though a man succeeds, he should not (as is frequently the case) engross the whole talk to himself; for that destroys the very essence of conversation, which is talking together. We should try to keep up conversation like a ball bandied to and fro from one to the other, rather than seize it all to ourselves, and drive it before us like a foot-ball. We should likewise be cautious to adapt the matter of our discourse to our company; and not talk *Greek* before ladies, or of the last new furbelow to a meeting of country justices.

But nothing throws a more ridiculous air over our whole conversation, than certain peculiarities, easily acquired, but very difficultly conquered and discarded. In order to display these absurdities in a truer light, it is my present purpose to enumerate such of them, as are most commonly to be met with; and first to take notice of those buffoons in society, the Attitudinarians and Face-makers. These accompany every word with a peculiar grimace or gesture: they assent with a shrug, and contradict with a twisting of the neck; are angry by a wry mouth, and pleased in a caper or a minuet step. They may be considered as speaking Harlequins; and their rules of eloquence are taken from the posture-master. These should be condemned to converse only in dumb show with their own persons in the looking-glass: as well as the Smirkers and Smilers, who so prettily set off their faces, together with their words, by a *je-ne-sçai-quoi* between a grin and a dimple. With these we may likewise rank the affected tribe of Mimics, who are constantly taking off the peculiar tone of voice or gesture of their acquaintance: though they are such wretched imitators, that (like bad painters) they are frequently forced to write the name under the picture, before we can discover any likeness.

Next to these, whose elocution is absorbed in action, and who converse chiefly with their arms and legs, we may consider the professed speakers. And first, the Emphatical; who squeeze, and press, and ram down every syllable with excessive vehemence and energy. These orators are remarkable for their distinct elocution and force of expression: they dwell on the important particles *of* and *the,* and the significant conjunctive *and;* which they seem to hawk up, with much difficulty, out of their own throats, and to cram them, with no less pain, into the ears of their auditors. These should be suffered only to syringe (as it were) the ears of a deaf man, through an hearing-trumpet: though I must confess, that I am equally offended with the Whisperers or Low Speakers, who seem to fancy all their acquaintance deaf, and come up so close to you, that they may be said to measure noses with you, and frequently overcome you with the full exhalations of a stinking breath. I would have these oracular gentry obliged to talk at a distance through a speaking-trumpet, or apply their lips to the walls of a whispering-gallery. The Wits, who will not condescend to utter any thing but a *bon mot,* and the Whistlers or Tune-hummers, who never articulate at all, may be joined very agreeably together in concert: and to these tinkling cymbals I would also add the sounding brass; the Bawler, who inquires after your health with the bellowing of a town-crier.

The Tatlers, whose pliable pipes are admirably adapted to the "soft parts of conversation," and sweetly "prattling out of fashion," make very pretty music from a beautiful face and a female tongue;[19] but from a rough manly voice and coarse features, mere nonsense is as harsh and dissonant as a jig from an Hurdy-Gurdy. The Swearers I have spoken of in a former pa-

19. See Shakespeare, *Othello,* III.iii.268 and II.i.207.

per; but the Half-Swearers, who split, and mince, and fritter their oaths into *gad's bud, ad's fish,* and *demmee,* the *Gothic* Humbuggers, and those who "nick-name God's creatures,"[20] and call a man a cabbage, a crab, a queer cub, an odd fish, and an unaccountable *muskin,* should never come into company without an interpreter. But I will not tire my reader's patience by pointing out all the pests of conversation; nor dwell particularly on the Sensibles, who pronounce dogmatically on the most trivial points, and speak in sentences; the Wonderers, who are always *wondering* what o'clock it is, or *wondering* whether it will rain or no, or *wondering* when the moon changes; the Phraseologists, who explain a thing by *all that,* or enter into particulars with *this and that and t'other;* and, lastly, the Silent Men, who seem afraid of opening their mouths, lest they should catch cold, and literally observe the precept of the gospel, by letting their conversation be only *yea yea,* and *nay nay.*[21]

The rational intercourse kept up by conversation, is one of our principal distinctions from brutes. We should therefore endeavour to turn this peculiar talent to our advantage, and consider the organs of speech as the instruments of understanding: we should be very careful not to use them as the weapons of vice, or tools of folly, and do our utmost to unlearn any trivial or ridiculous habits, which tend to lessen the value of such an inestimable prerogative. It is, indeed, imagined by some philosophers, that even birds and beasts (though without the power of articulation) perfectly understand one another by the sounds they utter; and that dogs, cats, &c. have each a particular language to themselves, like different nations. Thus it may be supposed, that the nightingales of *Italy* have as fine an ear for their own native wood-notes, as any *Signor* or *Signora* for an *Italian* Air; that the boars of *Westphalia* gruntle as expressively through the nose, as the inhabitants in *High-German;* and that the frogs in the dykes of *Holland* croak as intelligibly, as the natives jabber their *Low Dutch.* However this may be, we may consider those, whose tongues hardly seem to be under the influence of reason, and do not keep up the proper convention of human creatures, as imitating the language of different animals. Thus, for instance, the

20. Shakespeare, *Hamlet,* III.i.148. For the essay on swearers, see *The Connoisseur* no. 108 (19 February 1756).

21. "But let your communication be, Yea, yea; Nay, nay: for whatsoever is more than these cometh of evil"; Matthew 5:37.

affinity between Chatterers and Monkeys, and Praters and Parrots, is too obvious not to occur at once: Grunters and Growlers may be justly compared to Hogs: Snarlers are Curs, that continually show their teeth, but never bite; and the Spitfire Passionate are a sort of wild Cats, that will not bear stroking, but will purr when they are pleased. Complainers are Scriech-Owls; and Story-tellers, always repeating the same dull note, are Cuckows. Poets, that prick up their ears at their own hideous braying, are no better than Asses: Critics in general are venomous Serpents, that delight in hissing; and some of them, who have got by heart a few technical terms without knowing their meaning, are no other than Magpies. I myself, who have crowed to the whole town for near three years past, may perhaps put my readers in mind of a Dunghill Cock: but as I must acquaint them, that they will hear the last of me on this day fortnight, I hope they will then consider me as a Swan, who is supposed to sing sweetly at his dying moments.[22]

16 September 1756

22. In fact, *The Connoisseur* (and Mr. Town as its mouthpiece) concluded two weeks later with no. 140.

SEVEN

Oliver Goldsmith

(c. 1730–74)

BORN INTO GENTEEL POVERTY in rural isolation, Oliver Gold-
smith led a reckless life in literary London, earning his living by his pen and
practicing the arts of good living and conversation. His path to the publishing world was circuitous, including detours to Edinburgh to study medicine; to Leyden to continue his studies; and to Flanders, France, Switzerland, and northern Italy, where he rambled on foot, earning his keep by
playing the flute. He returned penniless to London in 1756 and began
churning out translations, voluminous histories of England, Rome, and the
planet, children's literature, reviews, and other articles for the periodical
press. Three years later he commenced weekly publication of *The Bee* (ranging from three to eight articles per number), in which he dexterously
adapted the stylistic techniques of earlier periodical essayists, drawing on a
full verbal spectrum of apology, gentle wit, irony, and moral earnestness. In
1760–61 he published a column entitled "The Citizen of the World" in *The
Public Ledger,* a series of letters from "a Chinese Philosopher, Residing in
London, to his Friends in the East." His periodical essays gained him considerable popularity and the support of Dr. Johnson, whom he viewed as a
rival but who welcomed him into his Club of prominent cultural figures
including the celebrated actor David Garrick, the political writer Edmund
Burke, and the painter Joshua Reynolds. Johnson also rescued Goldsmith
from the bailiffs on one occasion by wresting the manuscript of *The Vicar of
Wakefield* from him and selling it on his behalf to John Newbery (the "phil-
anthropic bookseller") for sixty guineas.

While Goldsmith's reputation was made with his periodical work, he
later went on to produce two long poems, *The Traveller* (1764) and *The Deserted Village* (1770); two comic plays, *The Good Natured Man* (1768) and
She Stoops to Conquer (1773); and a well-loved sentimental novel, *The Vicar
of Wakefield* (1766), which appealed to the sensibilities of the dawning Ro-

mantic age. Worn down by hard living and intemperance, he died in his mid-forties and was buried in an unmarked grave.

Selections are excerpted from Oliver Goldsmith, *The Bee; Being Essays on the Most Interesting Subjects* (London, 1759).

The Bee
Introduction

There is not, perhaps, a more whimsically dismal figure in nature, than a man of real modesty, who assumes an air of impudence; who, while his heart beats with anxiety, studies ease, and affects good-humour. In this situation, however, a periodical writer often finds himself, upon his first attempt to address the public in form. All his power of pleasing is damped by solicitude, and his cheerfulness dashed with apprehension. Impressed with the terrors of the tribunal before which he is going to appear, his natural humour turns to pertness, and for real wit he is obliged to substitute vivacity. His first publication draws a crowd; they part dissatisfied; and the author, never more to be indulged a favourable hearing, is left to condemn the indelicacy of his own address, or their want of discernment.

For my part, as I was never distinguished for address, and have often even blundered in making my bow, such bodings as these had like to have totally repressed my ambition. I was at a loss whether to give the public specious promises, or give none; whether to be merry or sad on this solemn occasion. If I should modestly decline all merit, it was too probable the hasty reader might have taken me at my word. If, on the other hand, like labourers in the Magazine trade, I had, with modest impudence, humbly presumed to promise an epitome of all the good things that ever were said or written, this might have disgusted those readers I most desire to please. Had I been merry, I might have been censured as *vastly low;* and had I been sorrowful, I might have been left to mourn in solitude and silence: in short, whichever way I turned, nothing presented but prospects of terror, despair, chandlers' shops, and waste paper.

In this debate between fear and ambition, my publisher happening to arrive, interrupted for a while my anxiety. Perceiving my embarrassment about making my first appearance, he instantly offered his assistance and advice. "You must know, Sir," says he, "that the republic of letters is at present divided into three classes. One writer, for instance, excels at a plan, or a title-page, another works away at the body of the book, and a third is a dab at an index. Thus a Magazine is not the result of any single man's industry, but goes through as many hands as a new pin, before it is fit for the public. I fancy, Sir," continues he, "I can provide an eminent hand, and upon moderate terms, to draw up a promising plan to smooth up our readers a little, and pay them as Colonel Charteris paid his seraglio, at the rate of three half-pence in hand, and three shillings more in promises."[1]

He was proceeding in his advice, which, however, I thought proper to decline, by assuring him, that as I intended to pursue no fixed method, so it was impossible to form any regular plan; determined never to be tedious in order to be logical, wherever pleasure presented, I was resolved to follow. Like the Bee, which I had taken for the title of my paper, I would rove from flower to flower, with seeming inattention, but concealed choice, expatiate over all the beauties of the season, and make my industry my amusement.[2]

This reply may also serve as an apology to the reader, who expects, before he sits down, a bill of his future entertainment. It would be improper to pall his curiosity by lessening his surprise, or anticipate any pleasure I am able to procure him, by saying what shall come next. Thus much, however, he may be assured of, that neither war nor scandal shall make any part of it. Homer finely imagines his deity turning away with horror from the prospect of a field of battle, and seeking tranquility among a nation noted for peace and simplicity.[3] Happy, could any effort of mine, but for a moment, repress that savage pleasure some men find in the daily accounts of

---

1. Francis Charteris, a notorious rake nicknamed "The Rape-Master General of Britain," was satirized by Pope, William Hogarth, and John Arbuthnot, among others. A seraglio is a harem.

2. The motto of *The Bee,* "Floriferus ut Apes in saltibus omnia libant, / Omnia Nos itidem" (as bees in the flowery glades sip all the sweets, so we likewise feed on all your golden words) is from Lucretius, *De rerum natura* (On the Nature of Things), III.11–12.

3. It is unclear what Goldsmith is referring to here.

human misery! How gladly would I lead them from scenes of blood and altercation, to prospects of innocence and ease, where every breeze breathes health, and every sound is but the echo of tranquility. . . .

6 October 1759

Happiness, in a Great Measure, Dependent on Constitution

When I reflect on the unambitious retirement in which I passed the earlier part of my life in the country, I cannot avoid feeling some pain in thinking that those happy days are never to return. In that retreat all nature seemed capable of affording pleasure: I then made no refinements on happiness, but could be pleased with the most awkward efforts of rustic mirth; thought cross-purposes the highest stretch of human wit; and questions and commands the most rational amusement for spending the evening.[4] Happy could so charming an illusion still continue. I find that age and knowledge only contribute to sour our dispositions. My present enjoyments may be more refined, but they are infinitely less pleasing. The pleasure Garrick gives can no way compare to that I have received from a country wag who imitated a quaker's sermon. The music of the finest singer is dissonance to what I felt when our old dairymaid sung me into tears with Johnny Armstrong's Last Good Night or the cruelty of Barbara Allen.[5]

Writers of every age have endeavoured to show that pleasure is in us, and not in the objects offered for our amusement. If the soul be happily disposed, every thing becomes a subject of entertainment; and distress will almost want a name. Every occurrence passes in review like the figures of a procession: some may be awkward, others ill dressed; but none but a fool is for this enraged with the master of the ceremonies.

4. Cross-purposes was a game played in a circle, in which each player received in a whisper a question from one neighbor and the answer to another question from the other; when the player repeated question and answer together out loud, the result was frequently amusing. Questions-and-Commands was another word game played in a circle, in which a commander asked other players questions that they had to answer or pay a forfeit; see, e.g., *The Spectator* no. 354 and James Gillray's 1788 print of that title.

5. Traditional country ballads.

I remember to have once seen a slave in a fortification in Flanders, who appeared no way touched with his situation. He was maimed, deformed, and chained; obliged to toil from the appearance of day till nightfall, and condemned to this for life; yet with all these circumstances of apparent wretchedness, he sung, would have danced, but that he wanted a leg, and appeared the merriest, happiest man of all the garrison. What a practical philosopher was here; an happy constitution supplied philosophy, and though seemingly destitute of wisdom, he was really wise. No reading or study had contributed to disenchant the fairyland around him. Every thing furnished him with an opportunity of mirth; and though some thought him, from his insensibility, a fool, he was such an idiot as philosophers might wish in vain to imitate.

They who, like him, can place themselves on that side of the world in which everything appears in a pleasing light, will find something in every occurrence to excite their good humour. The most calamitous events, either to themselves or others, can bring no new affliction: the whole world is to them a theatre, on which comedies are only acted.[6] All the bustle of heroism, or the rants of ambition, serve only to heighten the absurdity of the scene, and make the humour more poignant. They feel, in short, as little anguish at their own distress, or the complaints of others, as the undertaker, though dressed in black, feels sorrow at a funeral.

Of all the men I ever read of, the famous Cardinal de Retz possessed this happiness of temper in the highest degree.[7] As he was a man of gallantry, and despised all that wore the pedantic appearance of philosophy, wherever pleasure was to be sold, he was generally foremost to raise the auction. Being an universal admirer of the fair sex, when he found one lady cruel, he generally fell in love with another, from whom he expected a more favourable reception: if she too rejected his addresses, he never thought of retiring into deserts, or pining in hopeless distress. He persuaded himself, that instead of loving the lady, he only fancied he had loved her, and so all was well again. When fortune wore her angriest look, when he at last fell into the power of his most deadly enemy, Cardinal Mazarine, and was

6. That is, only comedies are acted.

7. The memoirs of Jean-François-Paul de Gondi, Cardinal de Retz (1614–79) were published in 1717.

confined a close prisoner in the Castle of Valenciennes, he never attempted to support his distress by wisdom or philosophy, for he pretended to neither. He laughed at himself and his persecutor, and seemed infinitely pleased at his new situation. In this mansion of distress, though secluded from his friends, though denied all the amusements, and even the conveniences of life, teased every hour by the impertinence of wretches who were employed to guard him, he still retained his good humour; laughed at all the little spite, and carried the jest so far as to be revenged, by writing the life of his gaoler.

All that philosophy can teach, is to be stubborn or sullen under misfortunes. The Cardinal's example will instruct us to be merry in circumstances of the highest affliction. It matters not whether our good humour be construed by others into insensibility, or even idiotism; it is happiness to ourselves, and none but a fool would measure his satisfaction by what the world thinks of it. For my own part I never pass by one of our prisons for debt, that I do not envy that felicity which is still going forward among those people, who forget the cares of the world by being shut out from its ambition.

Dick Wildgoose was one of the happiest silly fellows I ever knew. He was of the number of those good-natured creatures that are said to do no harm to any but themselves. Whenever Dick fell into any misery, he usually called it seeing life. If his head was broke by a chairman, or his pocket picked by a sharper, he comforted himself by imitating the Hibernian dialect of the one, or the more fashionable cant of the other. Nothing came amiss to Dick. His inattention to money matters had incensed his father to such a degree, that all the intercession of friends in his favour was fruitless. The old gentleman was on his death-bed. The whole family, and Dick among the number, gathered around him. I leave my second son, Andrew, said the expiring miser, my whole estate, and desire him to be frugal. Andrew, in a sorrowful tone, as is usual on these occasions, prayed heaven to prolong his life and health to enjoy it himself. I recommend Simon, my third son, to the care of his elder brother, and leave him beside four thousand pounds. Ah, father! cried Simon, (in great affliction to be sure,) may heaven give you life and health to enjoy it yourself! At last, turning to poor Dick; as for you, you have always been a sad dog—you'll never come to good; you'll never be rich; I'll leave you a shilling to buy an halter.[8] Ah! father, cries Dick, without any emotion, may heaven give you life and health to enjoy it yourself! This was all the trouble the loss of fortune gave this thoughtless, imprudent creature. However, the tenderness of an uncle recompensed the neglect of a father; and Dick is now not only excessively good-humoured, but competently rich.

The world, in short, may cry out at a bankrupt who appears at a ball; at an author who laughs at the public which pronounces him a dunce; at a general who smiles at the reproach of the vulgar; or the lady who keeps her good humour in spite of scandal; but such is the wisest behaviour that any of us can possibly assume; it is certainly a better way to oppose calamity by dissipation, than to take up the arms of reason or resolution to oppose it: by the first method we forget our miseries; by the last we only conceal them from others. By struggling with misfortunes, we are sure to receive some wounds in the conflict. The only method to come off victorious, is by running away.

13 October 1759

The Sagacity of Some Insects

To the Author of the Bee

Sir,—Animals, in general, are sagacious, in proportion as they cultivate society. The elephant and the beaver show the greatest signs of this when united; but when men intrude into their communities, they lose all their spirit of industry, and testify but a very small share of that sagacity, for which, when they are in a social state, they are so remarkable.

Among insects, the labours of the bee and the ant have employed the attention and admiration of the naturalist; but their whole sagacity is lost upon separation, and a single bee or ant seems destitute of every degree of industry, is the most stupid insect imaginable, languishes for a time in solitude, and soon dies.

Of all the solitary insects I have ever remarked, the spider is the most sagacious; and its actions, to me, who have attentively considered them,

8. In other words, a noose to hang himself.

seem almost to exceed belief. This insect is formed by nature for a state of war, not only upon other insects, but upon each other. For this state nature seems perfectly well to have formed it. Its head and breast are covered with a strong natural coat of mail, which is impenetrable to the attempts of every other insect, and its belly is enveloped in a soft pliant skin, which eludes the sting even of a wasp. Its legs are terminated by strong claws, not unlike those of a lobster, and their vast length, like spears, serves to keep every assailant at a distance.

Not worse furnished for observation than for an attack or a defence, it has several eyes, large, transparent, and covered with a horny substance, which, however, does not impede its vision. Besides this, it is furnished with a forceps above the mouth, which serves to kill or secure the prey already caught in its claws or its net.

Such are the implements of war with which the body is immediately furnished; but its net to entangle the enemy seems what it chiefly trusts to, and what it takes most pains to render as complete as possible. Nature has furnished the body of this little creature with a glutinous liquid, which, proceeding from the anus, it spins into a thread, coarser or finer as it chooses to contract or dilate its sphincter. In order to fix its thread, when it begins to weave it emits a small drop of its liquid against the wall, which, hardening by degrees, serves to hold the thread very firmly. Then receding from the first point, as it recedes the thread lengthens; and, when the spider has come to the place where the other end of the thread should be fixed, gathering up with its claws the thread which would otherwise be too slack, it is stretched tightly, and fixed in the same manner to the wall as before.

In this manner, it spins and fixes several threads parallel to each other, which, so to speak, serve as the warp to the intended web. To form the woof, it spins in the same manner its thread, transversely fixing one end to the first thread that was spun, and which is always the strongest of the whole web, and the other to the wall. All these threads, being newly spun, are glutinous, and therefore stick to each other whenever they happen to touch; and, in those parts of the web most exposed to be torn, our natural artist strengthens them, by doubling the threads sometimes six-fold.

Thus far naturalists have gone in the description of this animal; what follows, is the result of my own observation upon that species of the insect called an house spider. I perceived, about four years ago, a large spider in one corner of my room, making its web; and, though the maid frequently levelled her fatal broom against the labours of the little animal, I had the good fortune then to prevent its destruction; and, I may say, it more than paid me by the entertainment it afforded.

In three days the web was, with incredible diligence, completed; nor could I avoid thinking, that the insect seemed to exult in its new abode. It frequently traversed it round, examined the strength of every part of it, retired into its hole, and came out very frequently. The first enemy, however, it had to encounter was another and a much larger spider, which, having no web of its own, and having probably exhausted all its stock in former labours of this kind, came to invade the property of its neighbour. Soon, then, a terrible encounter ensued, in which the invader seemed to have the victory, and the laborious spider was obliged to take refuge in its hole. Upon this I perceived the victor using every art to draw the enemy from his stronghold. He seemed to go off, but quickly returned; and when he found all arts vain, began to demolish the new web without mercy. This brought on another battle, and, contrary to my expectations, the laborious spider became conqueror, and fairly killed his antagonist.

Now, then, in peaceable possession of what was justly its own, it waited three days with the utmost patience, repairing the breaches of its web, and taking no sustenance that I could perceive. At last, however, a large blue fly fell into the snare, and struggled hard to get loose. The spider gave it leave to entangle itself as much as possible, but it seemed to be too strong for the cobweb. I must own I was greatly surprised when I saw the spider immediately sally out, and in less than a minute weave a new net round its captive, by which the motion of its wings was stopped; and when it was fairly hampered in this manner, it was seized, and dragged into the hole.

In this manner it lived, in a precarious state; and nature seemed to have fitted it for such a life, for upon a single fly it subsisted for more than a week. I once put a wasp into the net; but when the spider came out in order to seize it as usual, upon perceiving what kind of an enemy it had to deal with, it instantly broke all the bands that held it fast, and contributed all that lay in its power to disengage so formidable an antagonist. When the wasp was at liberty, I expected the spider would have set about repairing the breaches that were made in its net, but those it seems were irreparable;

wherefore the cobweb was now entirely forsaken, and a new one begun, which was completed in the usual time.

I had now a mind to try how many cobwebs a single spider could furnish; wherefore I destroyed this, and the insect set about another. When I destroyed the other also, its whole stock seemed entirely exhausted, and it could spin no more. The arts it made use of to support itself, now deprived of its great means of subsistence, were indeed surprising. I have seen it roll up its legs like a ball, and lie motionless for hours together, but cautiously watching all the time; when a fly happened to approach sufficiently near, it would dart out all at once, and often seize its prey.

Of this life, however, it soon began to grow weary, and resolved to invade the possession of some other spider, since it could not make a web of its own. It formed an attack upon a neighbouring fortification with great vigour, and at first was as vigorously repulsed. Not daunted, however, with one defeat, in this manner it continued to lay siege to another's web for three days, and at length, having killed the defendant, actually took possession. When smaller flies happen to fall into the snare, the spider does not sally out at once, but very patiently waits till it is sure of them; for, upon his immediately approaching, the terror of his appearance might give the captive strength sufficient to get loose: the manner then is to wait patiently, till, by ineffectual and impotent struggles, the captive has wasted all its strength, and then he becomes a certain and an easy conquest.

The insect I am now describing lived three years; every year it changed its skin, and got a new set of legs. I have sometimes plucked off a leg, which grew again in two or three days. At first it dreaded my approach to its web, but at last it became so familiar as to take a fly out of my hand, and, upon my touching any part of the web, would immediately leave its hole, prepared either for a defence or an attack.

To complete this description, it may be observed, that the male spiders are much less than the females, and that the latter are oviparous. When they come to lay, they spread a part of their web under the eggs, and then roll them up carefully, as we roll up things in a cloth, and thus hatch them in their hole. If disturbed in their holes, they never attempt to escape without carrying this young brood in their forceps away with them, and thus frequently are sacrificed to their parental affection.

As soon as ever the young ones leave their artificial covering they begin to spin, and almost sensibly seem to grow bigger. If they have the good fortune, when even but a day old, to catch a fly, they fall-to with good appetites; but they live sometimes three or four days without any sort of sustenance, and yet still continue to grow larger, so as every day to double their former size. As they grow old, however, they do not still continue to increase, but their legs only continue to grow longer; and when a spider becomes entirely stiff with age, and unable to seize its prey, it dies at length of hunger.

THE CHARACTERISTICS OF GREATNESS

In every duty, in every science in which we would wish to arrive at perfection, we should propose for the object of our pursuit some certain station even beyond our abilities—some imaginary excellence, which may amuse and serve to animate our inquiry. In deviating from others, in following an unbeaten road, though we perhaps may never arrive at the wished-for object, yet it is possible we may meet several discoveries by the way; and the certainty of small advantages, even while we travel with security, is not so amusing as the hopes of great rewards, which inspire the adventurer. *Evenit nonnunquam,* says Quintilian, *ut aliquid grande inveniat qui semper quærit quod nimium est.*[9]

This enterprising spirit is, however, by no means the character of the present age: every person who should now leave received opinions, who should attempt to be more than a commentator upon philosophy, or an imitator in polite learning, might be regarded as a chimerical projector. Hundreds would be ready not only to point out his errors, but to load him with reproach. Our probable opinions are now regarded as certainties; the difficulties hitherto undiscovered as utterly inscrutable; and the writers of the last age inimitable, and therefore the properest models of imitation.

One might be almost induced to deplore the philosophic spirit of the age, which, in proportion as it enlightens the mind, increases its timidity,

9. "It sometimes happens that [the speaker] who always seeks what is beyond measure may occasionally hit on something grand"; Quintilian, *Institutio oratoria* (The Institution of Oratory), II.xii.5.3. The quotation is part of a longer sentence, in which Quintilian says that the "orator ineruditus" who goes "over the top" in his speeches occasionally makes a momentous impression.

and represses the vigour of every undertaking. Men are now content with being prudently in the right; which, though not the way to make new acquisitions, it must be owned, is the best method of securing what we have. Yet this is certain, that the writer who never deviates, who never hazards a new thought, or a new expression, though his friends may compliment him upon his sagacity, though criticism lifts her feeble voice in his praise, will seldom arrive at any degree of perfection. The way to acquire lasting esteem, is not by the fewness of a writer's faults, but the greatness of his beauties; and our noblest works are generally most replete with both.

An author who would be sublime, often runs his thoughts into burlesque: yet I can readily pardon his mistaking ten times for once succeeding. True genius walks along a line: and perhaps our greatest pleasure is in seeing it so often near falling, without being ever actually down.

Every science has its hitherto undiscovered mysteries, after which men should travel, undiscouraged by the failure of former adventurers. Every new attempt serves, perhaps, to facilitate its future invention. We may not find the Philosopher's stone,[10] but we shall probably hit upon new inventions in pursuing it. We shall perhaps never be able to discover the longitude, yet perhaps we may arrive at new truths in the investigation.[11]

Were any of those sagacious minds among us (and surely no nation, or no period, could ever compare with us in this particular), were any of those minds, I say, who now sit down contented with exploring the intricacies of another's system, bravely to shake off admiration, and, undazzled with the splendour of another's reputation, to chalk out a path to fame for themselves, and boldly cultivate untried experiment, what might not be the result of their inquiries, should the same study that has made them wise make them enterprising also? What could not such qualities united produce? But such is not the character of the English; while our neighbours of the Continent launch out into the oceans of science, without proper stores for the voyage, we fear shipwreck in every breeze, and consume in port those powers which might probably have weathered every storm.

10. A mythic substance, sought by alchemists, that was thought to turn base metals into gold and to bring eternal youth.

11. The British Longitude Act (1714) offered a monetary prize to anyone who could devise a practical method of fixing longitude at sea; the clockmaker John Harrison finally won the prize in 1773.

Projectors in a state are generally rewarded above their deserts; projectors in the republic of letters, never. If wrong, every inferior dunce thinks himself entitled to laugh at their disappointment; if right, men of superior talents think their honour engaged to oppose, since every new discovery is a tacit diminution of their own pre-eminence.

To aim at excellence, our reputation, our friends, and our all must be ventured; by aiming only at mediocrity, we run no risk, and we do little service. Prudence and greatness are ever persuading us to contrary pursuits. The one instructs us to be content with our station, and to find happiness in bounding every wish; the other impels us to superiority, and calls nothing happiness but rapture. The one directs to follow mankind, and to act and think with the rest of the world: the other drives us from the crowd, and exposes us as a mark to all the shafts of envy or ignorance.

Nec minus periculum ex magna fama quam ex mala.—Tacit.[12]

The rewards of mediocrity are immediately paid, those attending excellence generally paid in reversion. In a word, the little mind who loves itself, will write and think with the vulgar, but the great mind will be bravely eccentric, and scorn the beaten road, from universal benevolence.

27 October 1759

12. "For [there was] no less danger from great fame as from ill fame"; Tacitus, *De vita et moribus Iulii Agricolae* (The Life and Death of Julius Agricola), chap. 5; in context Tacitus says that his father-in-law decided to pursue military glory during a period when a sinister interpretation was placed on such ambition.

EIGHT

James Boswell
(1740–95)

JAMES BOSWELL, BORN TO THE hereditary position of ninth Laird of Auchinleck in Scotland, spent his adult life struggling against a paternal mandate to practice law. Having been foiled in his teenage attempt to convert to Catholicism and become a monk, he escaped from the University of Glasgow to London, where he abandoned himself to libertinism. His father intervened, and he returned to Edinburgh, enrolling in the university and passing his law exams in 1762. Allowed at last to return to London, he met Samuel Johnson in May the following year and began a relationship that changed the tenor of his life by introducing him to the world of arts and letters. Boswell's monthly "The Hypochondriack," which ran in *The London Magazine* for seventy numbers from 1777 through 1783, shows the influence on him of the Rambler and the Idler. Undertaken to combat a constitutional melancholy its author shared with the older essayist, it finds its voice somewhere between the moralizing tone of *The Rambler* and the emotional introspection of Boswell's successor in the essay tradition, Henry Mackenzie. Perhaps his habit of self-fictionalizing as he caroused through London's nightspots in disguise contributed to Boswell's facility with authorial postures, from scholar to man about town. In addition to his work on "The Hypochondriack," Boswell is known for his monumental *Life of Samuel Johnson* (1791) and *Journal of a Tour to the Hebrides* (1786), based on a trip in company with that august personage. During his later years, his health declined, owing to venereal disease and excessive drinking. Although he was married for twenty years to his cousin Margaret Montgomery, with whom he fathered two surviving sons and three daughters, Boswell could not overcome his penchant for gambling and prostitutes, and he also fathered two known illegitimate children.

Selections are from James Boswell, "The Hypochondriack," in *The London Magazine* (London, 1777–83).

The Hypochondriack
No. 39. On Hypochondria

In the multitude of my thoughts within me,
thy comforts delight my soul.—Psalms 94:19

The Hypochondriack is himself at this moment in a state of very dismal depression, so that he cannot be supposed capable of instructing or entertaining his readers. But after keeping them company as a periodical essayist for three years, he considers them as his friends, and trusts that they will treat him with a kindly indulgence. He is encouraged by the compliments which an unknown reader at the London Coffee-house has been pleased to pay him in this Magazine for last month. He may hope that there are many such readers.

Instead of giving this month an essay published formerly, of which I have a few, that after a proper revision I intend to adopt into this series, I have a mind to try what I can write in so wretched a frame of mind; as there may perhaps be some of my unhappy brethren just as ill as myself, to whom it may be soothing to know that I now write at all.

While endeavouring to think of a subject, that passage in the Psalms, which I have prefixed as a motto to this paper, presented itself to my mind. "In the multitude of my thoughts within me, thy comforts delight my soul."

Language cannot better express uneasy perturbation of spirits than the Psalmist has here done. There is in the idea of multitude, disorder, fluctuation, and tumult; and whoever has experienced what I now suffer, must feel his situation justly and strongly described.

Let us select some of those thoughts, the multitude of which confounds and overwhelms the mind of a Hypochondriack.

His opinion of himself is low and desponding. His temporary dejection makes his faculties seem quite feeble. He imagines that every body thinks meanly of him. His fancy roves over the variety of characters whom he knows in the world, and except some very bad ones indeed, they seem all better than his own. He envies the condition of numbers, whom, when in a sound state of mind, he sees to be far inferior to him. He regrets his having ever attempted distinction and excellence in any way, because the effect of his former exertions now serves only to make his insignificance more vexing to him. Nor has he any prospect of more agreeable days when he looks forward. There is a cloud as far as he can perceive, and he supposes it will be charged with thicker vapour, the longer it continues.

He is distracted between indolence and shame. Every kind of labour is irksome to him. Yet he has not resolution to cease from his accustomed tasks. Though he reasons within himself that contempt is nothing, the habitual current of his feelings obliges him to shun being despised. He acts therefore like a slave, not animated by inclination but goaded by fear.

Every thing appears to him quite [in]different. He repeats from Hamlet,

How weary, stale, flat, and unprofitable,
To me seem all the uses of this world.[1]

He begins actually to believe the strange theory, that nothing exists without the mind, because he is sensible, as he imagines, of a total change in all the objects of his contemplation. What formerly had engaging qualities has them no more. The world is one undistinguished wild.

His distempered fancy darts sudden livid glaring views athwart time and space. He cannot fix his attention upon any one thing, but has transient ideas of a thousand things; as one sees objects in the short intervals when the wind blows aside flame and smoke.

An extreme degree of irritability makes him liable to be hurt by every thing that approaches him in any respect. He is perpetually upon the fret; and though he is sensible that this renders him unmanly and pitiful he cannot help shewing it; and his consciousness that it is observed, exasperates him so, that there is great danger of his being harsh in his behaviour to all around him. He is either so weakly timid as to be afraid of every thing in which there is a possibility of danger, or he starts into the extremes of rashness and desperation. He ruminates upon all the evils that can happen to man, and wonders that he has ever had a moment's tranquility, as he never was nor ever can be secure. The more he thinks the more miserable he grows, and he may adopt the troubled exclamation in one of Dr. Young's tragedies:

1. See Shakespeare, *Hamlet*, I.ii.133–34.

Auletes, seize me, force me to my chamber,
There chain me down, and guard me from my self.[2]

Though his reason be entire enough, and he knows that his mind is sick, his gloomy imagination is so powerful that he cannot disentangle himself from its influence, and he is in effect persuaded that its hideous representations of life are true. In all other distresses there is the relief of hope. But it is the peculiar woe of melancholy, that hope hides itself in the dark cloud.

Could the Hypochondriack see any thing great or good or agreeable in the situation of others, he might by sympathy partake of their enjoyment. But his corrosive imagination destroys to his own view all that he contemplates. All that is illustrious in public life, all that is amiable and endearing in society, all that is elegant in science and in arts, affect him just with the same indifference, and even contempt, as the pursuits of children affect rational men. His fancied elevation and extent of thought prove his bane; for he is deprived of the aid which his mind might have from sound and firm understandings, as he admits of none such. Even his humanity towards the distressed is apt to be made of no avail. For as he cannot even have the idea of happiness, it appears to him immaterial whether they be relieved or not. Finding that his reason is not able to cope with his gloomy imagination, he doubts that he may have been under a delusion when it was cheerful; so that he does not even wish to be happy as formerly, since he cannot wish for what he apprehends is fallacious.

In the multitude of such thoughts as these, when the Hypochondriack is sunk in helpless and hopeless wretchedness, if he has recourse only to his fellow creatures and to objects upon earth—How blessed is the relief which he may have from the divine comforts of religion! from the comforts of GOD, the Father of Spirits, the Creator and Governour of the Universe, whose mercy is over all his other works, and who graciously hears the prayers of the afflicted.

In order to have these comforts, which not only relieve but "delight the soul," the Hypochondriack must take care to have the principles of our holy religion firmly established in his mind, when it is sound and clear, and

2. Edward Young, *Busiris, King of Egypt* (1719), Act III.

by the habitual exercise of piety to strengthen it, so as that the flame may live even in the damp and foul vapour of melancholy. Dreadful beyond description is the state of the Hypochondriack who is bewildered in universal scepticism. But when the mind is sick and distressed, and has need of religion, that is not the time to acquire it. The understanding is then wavering, and the temper capricious; and the best arguments may be ineffectual against prejudice.

By religion the Hypochondriack will have his mind fixed upon one invariable object of veneration, will have his troubled thoughts calmed by the consideration that he is here in a state of trial, that to contribute his part in carrying on the plan of providence in this state of being his duty, and that his sufferings however severe will be found beneficial to him in the other world, as having prepared him for the felicity of the saints above, which by some mysterious constitution, to be afterwards explained, requires in human beings a course of tribulation. And in the mean time he will have celestial emanations imparted to him.

While writing this paper, I have by some gracious influence been insensibly relieved from the distress under which I laboured when I began it. May the same happy change be experienced by any of my readers, in the like affliction, is my sincere prayer.

December 1780

No. 52. On Past and Present

Naturaliter audita visis laudamus libentius; et præsentia invidia, præterita veneratione prosequimur.—Velleius Paterculus.[3]

We are naturally more inclined to praise things of which
we have heard, than things which we ourselves see;
and we envy present merit, but venerate what is past.

The observation of *Pope* that "man never *is* but always *to be* blest" is not quite exact.[4] For, discontent casts a wishful eye backwards as well as forwards, and we have often sighed for a return of past scenes which when

3. Velleius, *Historia romana* (History of Rome), II.xcii.5.
4. Alexander Pope, *Essay on Man,* I.96.

present were dull or even disagreeable. As a great deal of man's happiness is in hope, a part of it is in recollection; and I have frequently experienced it as a kind circumstance in our constitution that agreeable circumstances are remembered with still more pleasure than they originally afforded; while disagreeable circumstances are softened in the memory.

There is something in distance, whether of time or of place, that affects the imagination with I know not what mysterious feelings of preference: and this I am persuaded is the chief cause of that strange propensity which may be traced in every recorded period of time, to lament "the degeneracy of the age," and gravely maintain that former times were much better in all respects than the present.

The Greeks and Romans delighted in fanciful representations of an early state of terrestrial felicity, to which they gave the name of the *Golden age,* when all was spontaneous fertility, serene temperature, amicable agreement, and gay delight. They supposed that there was at first a change considerably to the worse, and then came what they called the *Silver age.* But that at last the state of things grew as bad as what they themselves found them, and this was the *Iron age.*

In the Latin language, the word which signifies *older,* is also used to denote being more excellent—"*Antiquior, melior, potior, charior, quod quæ antiquiora sunt sint fere meliora*—because what are older are generally better," says *Ainsworth;*[5] and he quotes passages from *Cicero* and *Quintilian* where it carries that sense. Nay, in our own language, *old* is an epithet of respect. Witness that illustrious sound, which has made many a generous breast heave—OLD ENGLAND!

Since that iron age, it is truly curious, and if we are in good humour it must make us smile, to observe how not only the satirists, to whom some exaggeration is allowed, but the sober moralists of each succeeding age, have asserted, that it is worse than those which preceded it. They are not indeed very accurate in chronology. They by no means point out any definitive space of time between which and the sad period of depravation, a comparison may be made. It is enough to utter the general gloomy charge of being worse. But it should be considered, that this charge cannot possibly

5. Robert Ainsworth's *Thesaurus Linguae Latinae compendiarius* (1736) was the leading Latin-English dictionary of the time.

be true in all ages, for if it were, the world must have been at an end long before now.

Though I have assigned some unknown power in distance upon the human imagination as the chief cause of the preference given to former times over the present, I agree with *Velleius Paterculus* in the passage which I have taken as a motto to this paper, that there is also a mixture of envy which contributes to it. There is an acrimonious pride which secretly pervades most dispositions, and makes men unwilling to be sensible of the worth of their cotemporaries.

Of a similar nature with this, but more extensive in its influence, is that rigid false virtue which affects to despise and abhor human nature in general. A person of that character is thus strikingly addressed by *Fielding,* in one of his poems:

> O thou that dar'st thus proudly scorn thy kind,
> Search with impartial scrutiny thy mind.
> Disdaining outward flatterers to win,
> Dost thou not feed a flatterer within?
> While other passions temperance may guide,
> Feast not with too delicious meals thy pride.
> On vice triumphant while thy censures fall,
> Be sure no envy mixes with thy gall.

And afterwards,

> A peevish sour perverseness of the will
> Oft we miscall antipathy to ill.[6]

It is surely more agreeable to good notions of Providence, that the world should be in a progressive state of improvement; and I do sincerely think that this age is better than ancient times. *Shakespeare,* in his tragedy of *Macbeth,* admits that ancient times were worse in the most important concern of society:

6. Henry Fielding, *Of True Greatness: An Epistle to George Dodington, Esq.* (1740), ll. 41–48, 53–54.

I'th'olden time,
Ere human statute purg'd the general weal.[7]

And every candid thinking man must acknowledge with comfort the peace and security which we enjoy under the regular administration of justice.

War, of which I have testified my full disapprobation in a former paper,[8] though it still rages in spite of polished manners and Christian gentleness, is a much milder evil than in more rude ages. *Sir John Pringle,* in one of his excellent discourses from the chair of the Royal Society, has pointed out how much the modern improvements in gunnery have abated the horrours of human massacre in its very execution, and the tenderness with which prisoners, especially the sick and wounded, are treated, makes the temper of this age appear angelic, when compared with ancient ferocity.[9]

When we review the condition of our ancestors as authentically ascertained by public registers, and by histories, we find that the *old barons* lived in savage tyranny, and their vassals in servile dependence; that feuds between great families produced the most shocking scenes of rapine and murder; the successful perpetrators of which seem never to have felt remorse; and in short, that men very much resembled the wild beasts of the desert. Nor was there more honesty then than now, notwithstanding the expression "*prisca fides*—ancient fidelity,"[10] for, instances of the deepest cunning and most detestable treachery occur in the earliest annals.

We are insensibly deceived into an enthusiastic admiration of ancient characters, by having our fancies heated in our undistinguishing youthful days with the ballads in which violence is displayed with all the interesting appearances of heroism. This strengthens the natural disposition which mankind have to regard antiquity in general, which is so prevalent, that societies are formed for the express purpose of collecting and illustrating every thing that is old, no matter what it may have been in "its own day"; and perhaps there is no class of men more industrious and more zealous in

7. See Shakespeare, *Macbeth,* III.iv.74–75.
8. See "Hypochondriack" no. 3, "On War."
9. See John Pringle, *Six Discourses* (London, 1783), 279–81.
10. The phrase, meaning "old-world honour," is from Virgil, *Aeneid,* VI.878.

their pursuits than antiquaries. In *Leeds,* where one would not expect it, there is a very good public library, where strangers are treated with great civility, of which I for one retain a grateful sense. I there found a manuscript containing the coats of arms and descents of the families of the West Riding of Yorkshire, upon which there is this inscription which I copied as highly expressive of a true devotee to a museum: "Every ingenious fragment is venerable to the Virtuoso, and always pleasant to a curious inquisitive mind. But, a collector should have the industry of a Hercules; and the patience of a Socrates; an eye like Argus; and a purse like Crœsus."[11]

As rapine and murder were more frequent in former ages than this, and treachery as frequent, so, it cannot be denied that adultery was at least as frequent as it is now, and drunkenness a great deal more so. The two first crimes indeed decreased long before our time. But I will venture to say, that in other respects we have never had an age less criminal than this. The balance of morality is in our favour. And notwithstanding that of infidelity and irreligion which however is not louder than in former times, I have the satisfaction to think that good Christians have no reason to lament that either the number or the weight of believers is diminished. We have a pious prince upon the throne. We have great lights in the church. We have many distinguished men amongst the laity who have stood forth in support of the truth of Revelation.

If there be not so much reverence for "the powers that be" in this age as in some former periods, which I have regretted in my paper upon government,[12] I trust that is a temporary evil. The subject is too delicate for *The Hypochondriack* to say more. If there be less learning amongst us, there is a much more general diffusion of knowledge. The circulation of newspapers and magazines alone conveys so great a variety of information, instruction, and embellishment, through all ranks of people in this country, that their minds are enriched infinitely beyond those of the men of other times;

11. The mythical Greek hero Hercules performed twelve great labors. Socrates calmly committed suicide when condemned by the state. The all-seeing, hundred-eyed giant Argus guarded Zeus's lover Io in Greek myth. The sixth-century B.C. Lydian king Croesus was renowned for his wealth.

12. See "Hypochondriack" no. 19, "On Subordination in Government." "The powers that be"; Romans 13:1.

and surely the women in general of the present age have an unquestioned superiority over their sex in any former period.

We have the advantage of all the modern discoveries in science and in art, and of the numerous conveniences and elegant aids to pleasure, unknown to our ancestors. So that we may have more happiness in one day in London, than they could have in a large portion of their lives. It is narrow thinking to maintain, that it is more desirable to have few wants, I hope I have established in a former paper, my opinion that the more innocent pleasures we can enjoy the better we are.[13]

But I feel with peculiar fondness the advantage of this age over ancient times in civility of manners; not the constrained affectation and deceit recommended by a celebrated nobleman;[14] but such an habitual complacency and politeness as is intended only for the mutual happiness of social intercourse. *Ovid,* to whose poetical merit sufficient justice has not yet been done, gives us this thought in most beautiful verses in his Art of Love:

> *Prisca juvent alios, ego me nunc denique natum*
> *Gratulor; hæc ætas moribus apta meis.*
> *Non quia nunc terræ lentum subducitur aurum,*
> *Lectaque diverso littore concha venit.*
> *Nec quia decrescunt effosso marmore montes,*
> *Nec quia cærulea mole fugantur aquæ.*
> *Sed quia cultus adest, nec nostros mansit in annos*
> *Rusticitas priscis illa superstes avis.*

> Let ancient manners other men delight;
> But me the modern please as more polite.
> Not that materials now in gold are wrought,
> And distant shores for orient pearls are sought;
> Nor for that hills exhaust their marble veins,
> And structures rise whose bulk the sea restrains.

13. See "Hypochondriack" no. 40, "On Pleasure."

14. Philip Dormer Stanhope, Earl of Chesterfield, wrote letters (not intended for publication) on etiquette and self-comportment to his illegitimate son Philip Stanhope. When they were published posthumously by his widow in 1774, they attracted criticism from Johnson, Cowper, and others.

But that the world is civilized of late,
And polish'd from the rust of former date. *Congreve*.[15]

I suppose there never was an instance where both the original author and translator spoke their own sentiments more sincerely, than *Ovid* and *Congreve* in this passage; and I hope my readers will be pleased that *The Hypochondriack* appears for the first time in a new year in such good humour with the age in which they and he live.

January 1782

No. 58. On Hospitality

Τὸν φιλέοντ' ἐπὶ δαῖτα καλεῖν.—Hesiod[16]

Invite your friend to dine or sup with you.

Hospitality is the virtue which is in the most eminent degree its own reward. A man may have a full consciousness of benevolence in many other ways. But in hospitality he finds his consciousness confirmed and brightened by reflection from the complacent looks of his guests, while they sit around his board partaking of his good cheer.

At first view, hospitality appears to be a savage virtue, a virtue which can be exercised only in a rude state of society, where habitations are thinly scattered, and provisions scantily procured. For how can there be room for hospitality where all have enough of lodging and food? No doubt there is much more need of hospitality in uncultivated wilds than in improved districts; and accordingly it prevails more in the former than in the latter. In the former, strangers are rare, and in hospitality there is a mutual advantage to them and to those who entertain them, for intellectual entertainment is there communicated by almost any stranger. Whereas in the latter, strangers are so numerous, that there arise a class of men to whom it is a gainful traffic to furnish them every convenience and even every luxury for money; and of those who are received into private houses as friends, a choice is made by connection, recommendation, or taste.

15. William Congreve's 1725 translation of Ovid's *Ars amatoria* (Art of Love), III.169–76.
16. Hesiod, *Works and Days*, l. 342.

It is pleasing to think how sacred hospitality has been held in all nations. To violate its faith has been even looked upon as a crime of the utmost abhorrence, even amongst bands of robbers. "*Non hospes ab hospite tutus*—a want of security between the master of a house and his guests," is pointed out by *Ovid* amongst the abominations of corrupted manners.[17] I imagine the edict *Nautæ coupones stabularii* of the Roman law, by which landlords and shipmasters were made answerable for all kinds of property brought into their houses or ships by lodgers or passengers, has taken its rise from that care of every thing belonging to them, which the mind, carrying on the original idea of an entertainer of strangers, has imputed to them as a duty, as an indispensable charge; though I recollect the reason assigned is restraining their shameful frauds.

Old *Hesiod*, in the motto to this paper, counsels us to invite our friends to feast with us. The passage from whence it is taken proceeds to bid us not ask an enemy, but to be chiefly desirous of having the company of a near neighbour. There is something primitive in all this, which may serve as very good doctrine even at this day. An indiscriminate invitation to share with us, what should be uniformly esteemed a pledge of cordiality, I cannot approve. There is to be sure no occasion for being leagued together in bands offensive and defensive, as in former times, for absolute preservation of our lives and properties; nor is it necessary now, as it was then, to be pledged, while we drink, by a trusty friend with a drawn sword, lest we should be murdered while off our guard. But I would have none to sit down as entertainer and guest who are not at least free from ill-will to each other.

The more attentively we compare man with other animals, the more points of difference shall we find between him and them. Other animals take a pleasure in sharing the food they like best with their young, or even preferring them. But I believe man alone treats others of his nature in that manner. The entertainment given in the fable by the City Mouse to the Country Mouse, is not more founded on truth than their carrying on a conversation in very smart dialogue.[18] I have therefore always thought it the mark of a brutish disposition to feed alone, or even to eat perpetually

17. "Guest was not safe from host"; Ovid, *Metamorphoses*, I.144.
18. From "City Mouse, Country Mouse" in Aesop's *Fables*.

with one's own family, which is comparatively unsocial, and makes one figure a group of beasts in the same den day after day.

An interchange of entertaining is one of the varieties of life. No two things are quite alike. The poorest beggars will taste each other's brown crumbs, or half-picked bones and be amused with the difference. So in better situations, we taste each other's milk, or fruit, or mutton, or any thing else that is brought to the table; and we know the varieties of cookery, confectionary, and wines are infinite. When there is a good-humoured competition who shall have the best things for his friends, or when the excellence is divided, as when one has the best fish, another the best fowl, a third the best garden stuff, and there is a pleasant rotation of acknowledged advantage, it is very agreeable. But there have been violent animosities owing to contested tables; and even petty rivalships in pastry, or in syllabubs, have rankled in gentle bosoms.

Where a man entertains from ostentation, where

All is more than hospitably good,

as at the table of the sumptuous man in Parnell's Hermit,[19] there is no virtue, and of consequence no praise; though numbers will resort to enjoy the luxury, and inwardly laugh at the vanity of the master who exhibits like a showman. But the difference is easily perceived between such vanity and that real hearty wish to make others happy, with which some men in all ranks are blessed; for I will not exclude that blessing from any rank though envy may strive to create such a belief. I have seen it with exultation at the tables of the first nobility; and it cannot be denied that what is a blessing in a cottage, is, if equally genuine, a superlative blessing in a palace. It is one of the scriptural characteristics of a bishop to be "given to Hospitality."[20] It would be hard if the magnificence of a prelate, whose see has been piously endowed with a princely revenue, should put an absolute bar on a heart as good as Hooker's, while he "eat his bread in peace and privacy," as a wor-

19. A quotation from the Irish poet Thomas Parnell's *The Hermit*, l. 56, a moral conte (medieval narrative tale) in heroic couplets.
20. I Timothy 3:2.

thy parish priest.[21]And who will deny that such a heart may be found in a bishop.

The hospitality of convents never comes into my mind but with a feeling of reverential fondness. To entertain those to whom entertainment is truly a relief and a consolation is the hospitality recommended in the Gospel. For this, every one who is able, may find opportunities of one kind or other, which will be gladly embraced by indigent relations, or people of modest merit, who can barely live, and to whom the daily fare of the rich is a regale. This sort of laudable hospitality is still kept up at stated times in some places of this island. I once dined at Durham on a Sunday with the prebendary in residence.[22] A number of the poor who were good decent old people ate at table, and were helped bountifully. After dinner, every man of them had a glass of ale, and every woman a glass of sweet wine; and then each of them had a paper of tobacco, and withdrew to a hall to smoke it. I witnessed this scene with uncommon satisfaction.

There is something still worse than ostentatious entertaining, which is bringing people to a feast in order to domineer over them like a bashaw, compel their eating and drinking with all the rigour of an Egyptian taskmaster, to crush their opinions, stifle their pleasantry, or make them the butt of ridicule. Less oppressive, but troublesome enough, are those entertainers who expect to be flattered in one or other of the modes which the united ingenuity of such men and their sycophants have contrived. *Prior,* in what he calls an *Imitation of Chaucer,* has given us one instance:

> Full oft doth Mat with Topaz dine,
> Eateth bak'd meats, drinketh Greek wine;
> But Topaz his own werkes rehearseth,
> And Mat mote praise, what Topaz verseth.
> Now sure as saint did e'er shrive sinner
> Full hardly earnest Mat his dinner.[23]

---

21. See Izaak Walton's *Life of Hooker,* ed. John Gauden (London, 1682), 17–18. Richard Hooker (1554–1600) was a founder of Anglican theology. A see is the seat of a bishop's or archbishop's authority, the site on which a cathedral stands.

22. That is, with the canon of Durham Cathedral in the north of England.

23. Matthew Prior, "Erle Robert's Mice," II.1–6.

The thought is borrowed from *Martial,* Lib. III. Epig. 50, which begins,

> *Hæc tibi non alia est ad coenam causa vocandi*
> *Versiculos recites ut Ligurine tuos.*

To supper Ligurinus you invite
For nothing but your verses to recite.

There is in this epigram an humourous account of the different courses being loaded with their several proportions of the entertainer's poetry, extending to no less than five books. One would not eat grouse and drink canary on such terms.

Some men have a peculiar genius for entertaining well. They take delight in it, and do it with ease and alacrity, so that their tables are never-failing scenes of jovial society. Such men ought to have handsome fortunes because they can turn them to the best account. We must all recollect the warm encomiums usually made upon the master of the house, where we have enjoyed a happy day. "There never was a worthier man than our friend," is echoed from one guest to another in their way from his house.

We are told that *Swift,* when invited to dine on some favourite dishes, would say, "I don't mind your bill of fare, let me have your bill of company."[24] The bill of fare is, however, of some consequence, as is effectually, though tacitly, acknowledged by the numbers who flock to a good table. Good company I allow is a higher feast; but they do best together. There is a nice knowledge of character as well as a benevolent disposition displayed in sorting a company, an art in which I have known fewer people excel than in any other. Painting and music are not so difficult for the principles, the component parts are each a study. But when there is a company of eminent merit of various kinds, finely adapted, and all in exertion, the effect is exquisite indeed!

Such enjoyment as this, such *"noctes coenæque deum*—evenings and suppers of gods,"[25] can rarely be had, unless in large cities, where there is a multiplicity of choice, and companies are arranged by invitation. But to

24. See Jonathan Swift's *Journal to Stella,* "London, July 1711."
25. Horace, *Satires,* II.vi.65.

have this in the general course of life would be too luxuriously selfish; and they, who from felicity of circumstances are more refined and accomplished, should consider it as a duty to communicate some of their advantages to less fortunate, but worthy and modest neighbours in the country. This is genuine, kindly hospitality, which ought by all means to be promoted, that good will may be more diffused amongst different ranks, and the elegancies of the metropolis may in some degree be known by those who live at a distance from it, while at the same time, the fragments of feasting gladden the hearts of the poor.

I know of no legislature that has enforced hospitality by statute, except the parliament of Scotland; and it does them honour. It seems that about two centuries ago, a strange and shameful custom prevailed there for noblemen and gentlemen to desert their country seats, and reside altogether in towns, or if they did live at their country seats, to board themselves with their own servants, that they might not be at the expence of entertaining their neighbours, or relieving the poor. To restrain this, there was an act passed in the reign of James VI of Scotland, afterwards also I of England, 1581, Cap. 116, entitled—"Against the abuse of sum landed gentil-men, and utheris forbearing to keep house at their awin dwelling places." It is a singular curiosity, and as the Scottish acts are very short, I shall insert it completely for the amusement of my readers, subjoining a glossary of the most difficult words.

> "*Forasmeikle, as of lait there is croppen in amangis sum noblemen, prelates, baronnes, and gentil-men, in certaine pairts of this realme, being of gude livings, great abuse contrair the honour of the realme, and different from the honest frugalitie of their forebeares, passing to burrows-towns, clauchannes, and aile-houses with their houshaldes, and sum abiding in their awin places, usis to buird themselves and others to their awin servands, as in hostillaries, quhairon skaithful[26] and schameful inconvenients daylie falles out, to the offence of God, defrauding of the pure of their almes, sclander of the cuntrie, and hurt of the authours. For remeid quhairof, our Soveraine Lord, with

26. "Wherein frightful": "qu" is used for "wh" in medieval northern dialects.

advise of his three estates of this present parliament, hes statute and ordained: That every prelate, lord, barronne, and landed gentil-man, sall make his ordinair dwelling and residence at his awin house with his familie, in all time cumming, after the publication of the acts of this present parliament. For setting fordward of policie and decoration of their saides dwelling places, supporting of the pure with almes, and intertaining of friendschip with their nichtboures be all gude and honest means. And that they forbeare the said unhonest forme of buirding of themselves, and their families, and housholdes, in burrowes, clauchannes, and ailehouses, or in their awin houses, under the pains following: That is to say: ilk lord and prelate, under the pain of 500 markes, ilk great barronne under the pain of 300 markes, and ilk landed gentil-man under the pain of 200 markes. And gif they failzie,[27] being called and ordourlie convict of transgressing this present act, the saidis paines to be uplifted to our Soveraine Lord's use."

*Forasmeikle, forasmuch–croppen in, crept in–amangis, amongst–forebears, forefathers–clauchannes, villages–skaithful, hurtful–pure, poor–sclander, scandal–ilk, each.

Were the British parliament to make a similar statute, obliging our modern nobility and gentry to reside upon their estates, and never to come to London but bonâ fide upon real business, without paying a proportional fine toties quoties,[28] not only would laudable hospitality be more general, but a considerable addition to the revenue might be raised under a different title, but the same in effect with the late exploded tax on public amusements.

July 1782

27. If they fail.
28. A legal phrase meaning "as often as"; bona fide is Latin for "in good faith," or without deceit.

No. 70. On Concluding

Ἴθι δὴ πέραινε.—Aristophanes.[29]

Come, now, conclude.

To retire in proper time from any state of exertion is one of the most nice and difficult trials of human prudence and resolution. Every man of any classical education recollects the well known allusion to a horse growing aged, who ought no longer to be pushed on to the race lest he should be left behind breathless and contemptible.[30] But the misfortune is, that self-love deceives us exceedingly in the estimation of our mental abilities, so that we cannot be easily persuaded that they are in any degree decayed. Le Sage in his Gil Blas has given a just and diverting instance of this, in the old canon who was implacably offended at having a delicate hint suggested to him that he did not write so well as he had done in the vigour of life.[31]

My readers are now to be informed that this is the last essay of *The Hypochondriack,* a periodical paper, which I have published monthly for almost six years, and I flatter myself that my labours under that title shall not cease without some kindly sentiments of approbation in the breasts of those to whom they have afforded occasional entertainment.

It has been generally observed that we are sorry to part with one whom we have long known, provided he is not absolutely disagreeable to us. Upon this observation I found my hopes of being for a moment regretted by my readers; for a writer, though unknown, is always personified with sufficient distinctness by the imagination, so as to be the object of affection of one kind or other. I doubt if a writer has any such feeling towards those by whom he has been long known, but of whom he has no knowledge. His imagination does not settle upon any individuals of the number: but he has merely an idea of many in the abstract, which, although it may expand his

---

29. Aristophanes, *The Frogs,* l. 1283.

30. Cicero quotes the Roman poet Ennius—"He, like the gallant steed that often won / Olympic trophy in the final lap, / Now takes his rest when weakened by old age"—in *De senectute* (On Old Age), 5.

31. In fact, it was the archbishop of Granada who was so offended at the start of Book VII of Alain-René Lesage's *The Adventures of Gil Blas of Santillane* (1715–35), translated by Tobias Smollett in 1748.

pride or his ambition, cannot touch his heart. I, however, am conscious of a certain tenderness, while I am closing the scene of a species of literary existence, in which I own I have experienced sometimes anxiety, and sometimes self-complacency. This tenderness, it is plain from what I have said, is referable simply to my own mind. Yet it is an interesting fancy that there may be some of my readers so habituated to sympathize with the soul of the HYPOCHONDRIACK, that the instant of our being personally known to each other there would be a cordial friendship between us.

But, there must not be too positive expectations entertained of finding a similarity between an author's conversation and his writings. An author may have exhausted his mind into his works, so that nothing of any value remains for him to communicate. He may be able to collect and quicken his ideas in his closet, and have them dissipated, and as it were annihilated for a time, when in company. He may be an impostor, so as to have been assuming the appearance of virtuous or amiable qualities, which he no more possesses, than a player does many of the characters which he represents upon the stage with a vivacity of deception. For mimicry is indeed profound and universal, extending not only to manner, but to sentiment, and every part of mind, as is proved by the works of good dramatic writers, and I am sorry to add by the harangues of orators in different departments who ought to be in earnest. Indeed, there is nothing more delusive than the supposed character of an author, from reading his compositions. There may be fine thoughts on the surface of a coarse mind, as beautiful flowers are found growing upon rocks, upon bogs, nay upon dunghills. Besides the connection between authors and their works is very different in different persons. Their works may be compared to their clothes. Some wear them tight and stiff, some quite easy; and to some their works are like robes, which they put on only upon solemn occasions, and never wear in their common course of life. Of these varieties I have seen many examples, and could name several now alive, were it proper so to do it.

For myself, I cannot perfectly judge of my manner, which I have no doubt must vary with the fluctuation of my spirits. Nor can I boast that my practice is uniformly what it should be. But I am absolutely certain that in these papers my principles are most sincerely expressed. I can truly say in the words of Pope,

I love to pour out all myself as plain,
As downright Shippen, or as old Montaigne.[32]

Perhaps, indeed, I have poured out myself with more freedom than prudence will approve, and I am aware of being too much an egotist. But I trust that my readers will be generous enough not to take advantage of my openness and confidence, but rather treat me with a liberal indulgence.

Yet let it not be understood that I supplicate favour with an abject timidity. For I am not afraid of a fair trial by impartial judges. This comfort I have, that my intentions have all along been good, and that I cannot be condemned for having failed in my undertaking; because I undertook nothing determinate, but only to give a series of essays, which I have accordingly done. I perceive they are not so lively as I expected they would be. But they are more learned. And I beg I may not be charged with excessive arrogance, when I venture to say that they contain a considerable portion of original thinking. Be what they may, I should not have written them had I not been urged on by the obligation of a monthly task which I imposed upon myself. For except the first number, and the four which I mention as written several years ago, all of them were composed while the hour of publication was so near, that I had just time enough to do them with rapid agitation. Sometimes I had a few notes for a subject; sometimes not; and often have I wondered when I found my pages filled. Hurry has been upon many occasions pleaded as an excuse for the imperfections of a writer. The Hypochondriack has, besides, to plead what is peculiar to his own cast of mind, a hurry of spirits.

There is a pleasure, when one is indolent, to think that a task, to the performance of which one has been again and again subjected, and had some difficulty to make it out, is no longer to be required. But this pleasure, or rather comfort, does not last. For we soon feel a degree of uneasy languor, not merely in being without a stated exercise, but in being void of the usual consciousness of its regular returns, by which the mind has been agreeably braced.

---

32. Pope, *First Satire of the Second Book of Horace, Imitated*, ll. 51–52. William Shippen, a Jacobite member of Parliament and opponent of Robert Walpole, was an occasional poet.

A conclusion, however, should be put to a periodical paper, before its numbers have increased so much as to make it heavy and disgusting were it even of excellent composition, and this consideration is more necessary when it is entirely the work of one person, which in my first number I declared the Hypochondriack should be. I have resolved to end with number seventieth, from perhaps a whimsical regard to a number by which several interesting particulars are marked, the most interesting of which is the solemn reflection that "the days of our years are threescore years and ten."[33] To choose one number rather than another, where all numbers are rationally indifferent, there must be a motive, however slight. Such is my motive for fixing on Number Seventieth. It may be said, I need not to have told it.

Let me then have done, and bid my readers farewell with a good grace, instead of lingering on the verge of my departure. I know there is sometimes a good deal of hesitation in leaving a room filled with company whom we respect, and a man often sits long, from irresolution to rise and make a handsome bow, while retreating, which is one of the most exquisite lessons of the Marseilles of every age.[34] But this need not disconcert us who are not of great consequence, and therefore not much the object of attention. But a certain degree of presence of mind is required to be convinced that one is not of great consequence, the idea of which produces that bashfulness which the French very well express by the phrase *mauvaise honte*.[35] Frequently has it happened that when a man has thought every body was gazing upon him, and has slyly stolen a look, he has perceived not an eye directed his way. The mode of publication in which *The Hypochondriack* hath as yet appeared prevents him from knowing what has been the opinion which his readers have formed of his essays. He has only to add with his last breath in this character, that he knows he shall view these papers with relish or dissatisfaction, in different states of his mind. But, at all times he shall rejoice, if he is assured that his writings have in any degree contributed to the relief of the unhappy.

August 1783

33. Psalms 90:10.
34. Boswell may have in mind the eighteenth-century dancing master François Marcel.
35. Bad shame, sheepishness.

NINE

Henry Mackenzie

(1745–1831)

KNOWN AS "THE SCOTTISH ADDISON," Henry Mackenzie derives his literary reputation from his brief sentimental novel *The Man of Feeling* (1771). Yet he was also a master and innovator of the periodical essay form. Educated at the University of Edinburgh, he became an attorney and founded the "Mirror Club," a group of belletristically inclined young men who met in an Edinburgh pub to drink claret and read *The Spectator* aloud. Members included the poet and dramatist John Home, the judges Alexander Abercromby and William Macleod Bannatyne, and the physician William Cullen. Their own periodical in *Spectator* style, *The Mirror,* ran weekly from 23 January 1779 through 27 May 1780. Of the 110 numbers, Mackenzie wrote 42, including pieces on indolence and spring, whose impassioned attitude toward nature and melancholy sense of loss are characteristic of much British Romantic writing. *The Lounger,* a periodical similar in tone, followed five years later and ran from 6 February 1785 to 6 January 1787; Mackenzie contributed 57 of its 101 essays. His poignant series of country portraits, based on the Lounger's visit to Colonel Caustic and his sister Peggy, suggest the degree to which increasing commercialization was perceived as a threat to the Romantic man of feeling. In addition to his periodical work, Mackenzie was the author of other biographies; novels, including *Julia de Roubigné* (1773); and (mainly unsuccessful) drama. He became a Tory comptroller of taxes in 1804, married two years later at the age of sixty-one, and published his collected works two years after that.

Selections are from the first collected London edition (following eleven Edinburgh editions) of *The Mirror: A Periodical Paper, Published at Edinburgh in the Years 1779 and 1780* (London, 1822) and *The Lounger: A Periodical Paper, Published at Edinburgh in the Years 1785 and 1786,* 6th ed. (London, 1794).

The Mirror
No. 14. On Indolence

——*Inertibus horis*
Ducere sollicitæ jucunda oblivia vitæ. Hor.[1]

There are some weaknesses, which, as they do not strike us with the malignity of crimes, and produce their effects by imperceptible progress, we are
apt to consider as venial, and make very little scruple of indulging. But the
habit which apologises for these is a mischief of their own creation, which it
behoves us early to resist. We give way to it at first, because it may be conquered at any time; and, at last, excuse ourselves from the contest, because
it has grown too strong to be overcome.

Of this nature is *indolence,* a failing, I had almost said a vice, of all others the least alarming, yet, perhaps, the most fatal. Dissipation and intemperance are often the transient effects of youthful heat, which time allays,
and experience overcomes; but indolence "grows with our growth, and
strengthens with our strength,"[2] till it has weakened every exertion of public and private duty; yet so seducing, that its evils are unfelt, and its errors
unrepented of.

It is a circumstance of peculiar regret, that this should often be the
propensity of delicate and amiable minds. Men unfeeling and unsuscepti-
ble, commonly beat the beaten track with activity and resolution; the occupations they pursue and the enjoyments they feel, seldom much disappoint
the expectations they have formed; but persons endowed with that nice
perception of pleasure and pain which is annexed to sensibility, feel so much
undescribable uneasiness in their pursuits, and frequently so little satisfaction in their attainments, that they are too often induced to sit still, without
attempting the one or desiring the other.

The complaints which such persons make of their want of that success
which attends men of inferior abilities, are as unjust as unavailing. It is from
the use, not the possession of talents, that we get on in life: the exertion of

1. "When shall I be able, now with books of the ancients, now with sleep
and idle hours, to quaff sweet forgetfulness of life's cares!"; Horace, *Satires,* II.vi.
61–62.
2. Alexander Pope, "An Essay on Man," II.136.

very moderate parts outweighs the indecision of the brightest. Men possessed of the first, do things tolerably, and are satisfied; of the last, forbear doing things well, because they have ideas beyond them.

When I first resolved to publish this paper, I applied to several literary friends for their aid in carrying it on. From one gentleman in London, I had, in particular, very sanguine expectations of assistance. His genius and abilities I had early opportunities of knowing, and he is now in a situation most favourable to such productions, as he lives amidst the great and the busy world, without being much occupied either by ambition or business. His compositions at college, when I first became acquainted with him, were remarkable for elegance and ingenuity; and, as I knew he still spent much of his time in reading the best writers, ancient and modern, I made no doubt of his having attained such farther improvement of style, and extension of knowledge, as would render him a very valuable contributor to the MIR-ROR.

A few days ago, more than four months after I had sent him my letter, I received the following answer to it.

London, 1st March, 1779.

My Dear Friend,

I am ashamed to look on the date of this letter, and to recollect that of yours. I will not, however, add the sin of hypocrisy to my other failings, by informing you, as is often done in such cases, that hurry of business, or want of health, has prevented me from answering your letter. I will frankly confess, that I have had abundance of leisure, and been perfectly well since I received it; I can add, though, perhaps, you may not so easily believe me, that I have had as much inclination as opportunity; but the truth is (you know my weakness that way), I have wished, resolved, and re-resolved to write, as I do by many other things, without the power of accomplishing it. That disease of indolence, which you and my other companions used to laugh at, grows stronger and stronger upon me; my symptoms, indeed, are mortal; for I begin now to lose the power of struggling against the malady, sometimes to shut my ears against self-admonition, and admit of it as a lawful indulgence.

Your letter, acquainting me of the design of publishing a periodical paper, and asking my assistance in carrying it on, found me in one of the paroxysms of my disorder. The fit seemed to give way to the call of friendship, I got up from my easy chair, walked two or three turns through the room, read your letter again, looked at the Spectators, which stood, neatly bound and gilt, in the front of my book-press, called for pen, ink, and paper, and sat down, in the fervour of imagination, ready to combat vice, to encourage virtue, to form the manners, and to regulate the taste of millions of my fellow-subjects. A field fruitful and unbounded lay before me; I began to speculate on the prevailing vices and reigning follies of the times, the thousand topics which might arise for declamation, satire, ridicule, and humour; the picture of manners, the shades of character, the delicacies of sentiment. I was bewildered amidst this multitude and variety of subjects, and sat dreaming over the redundancy of matter and the ease of writing, till the morning was spent, and my servant announced dinner.

I arose, satisfied with having thought much on subjects proper for your paper. I dined, if you will allow me the expression, in company with those thoughts, and drank half a bottle of wine after dinner to our better acquaintance. When my man took away, I returned to my study, sat down at my writing-table, folded my paper into proper margins, wrote the word *Mirror* a-top, and filling my pen again, drew up the curtain, and prepared to delineate the scene before me. But I found things not quite in the situation I had left them: the groups were more confused, the figures less striking, the colours less vivid, than I had seen them before dinner. I continued, however, to look on them—I know not how long; for I was waked from a very sound nap, at half an hour past six, by Peter asking me if I chose to drink coffee.

I was ashamed and vexed at the situation in which he found me. I drank my first dish rather out of humour with myself; but, during the second, I began to account for it from natural causes; and, before the third was finished, had resolved that study was improper after *repletion,* and concluded the evening with the adventures of one of the *three Calendars,* out of *the Arabian Nights' Entertainments.*

For all this arrear I drew resolutely on to-morrow, and after breakfast prepared myself accordingly. I had actually gone so far as to write three introductory sentences, all of which I burnt; and was just blacking the letter *T,* for the beginning of a fourth, when Peter opened the door, and announced a gentleman, an old acquaintance, whom I had not seen for a considerable time. After he had sat with me for more than an hour, he rose to go away; I pulled out my watch, and I will fairly own I was not sorry to find it within a few minutes of one; so I gave up the morning for lost, and invited myself to accompany my friend in some visits he proposed making. Our tour concluded in a dinner at a tavern, whence we repaired to the play, and did not part till midnight. I went to bed without much self-reproach, by considering that intercourse with the world fits a man for reforming it.

I need not go through every day of the subsequent month; during which I remained in town, though there seldom passed one that did not remind me of what I owed to your friendship. It is enough to tell you, that during the first fortnight, I always found some apology for delaying the execution of my purpose; and, during the last, contented myself with the prospect of the leisure I should soon enjoy in the country, to which I was invited by a relation to spend some time with him previous to his coming to town for the winter. I arrived at his house about the middle of December. I looked on his fields, his walks, and his woods, which the extreme mildness of the season had still left in the garb of Thomson's philosophic melancholy,[3] as scenes full of inspiration, in which Genius might try her wings, and Wisdom meditate without interruption. But I am obliged to own, that, though I have walked there many a time; though my fancy was warmed with the scene, and shot out into a thousand excursions over the regions of romance, of melancholy, of sentiment, of humour, of criticism, and of science, she returned, like the first messenger of Noah, without having found a resting-place;[4] and I have, at last, strolled back to the house, where I sat listless in my chamber, with the irksome consciousness of some unperformed resolution, from which I was glad to be relieved by a summons to billiards, or a call to dinner.

Thus have I returned to town, as unprofitable in the moments of solitude and retirement as in those of business or society. Do not smile at the word *business:* what would be idleness to you is to me very serious employment: besides you know very well, that to be idle is often to be least at leisure. I am now almost hardy enough to lay aside altogether my resolu-

3. As expressed in James Thomson's popular poem in four books, entitled "*The Seasons*" (1726–30).

4. See Genesis 8:6–12, in which Noah sends out a raven from the ark to find out whether the flood waters have receded.

tion of writing in your paper; but I find that resolution a sort of bond against me, till you are good enough to cancel it, by saying you do not expect me to write. I have made a more than ordinary effort to give you this sincere account of my attempts to assist you. I have at least the consolation of thinking that you will not need my assistance. Believe me, with all my failings,

Most sincerely and affectionately yours,

——————.

P. S. I have just now learned by accident, that my nephew, a lad of fifteen, who is come to town from Harrow school, and lives at present with me, having seen one of your numbers about a week ago, has already written, and intends transmitting you, a political essay, signed Aristides, a pastoral, subscribed X. Y., and an acrostic on Miss E. M., without a signature.

13 March 1779

No. 16. Of Spring—Effects of That Season on Some Minds

O prima vera gioventu de l'anno,
Bella madre di fiori,
D'erbe novelle, e di novelli amori;
Tu torni ben, ma tecco
No tornano i sereni
E fortunati di de le mie gioie. Guarini.[5]

The effects of the return of spring have been frequently remarked, as well in relation to the human mind, as to the animal and vegetable world. The reviving power of this season has been traced from the fields to the herds that inhabit them, and from the lower classes of beings up to man. Gladness and joy are described as prevailing through universal nature, animating the low of the cattle, the carol of the birds, and the pipe of the shepherd.

I know not if it be from a singular, or a censurable disposition, that I

5. "O first genuine youth of the year, / Beautiful mother of flowers, / Of new grass and new loves; / Well you return, but with you / Return not the serenities / And fortunes of my lost joy"; Giovanni Battista Guarini, *Il pastor fido* (The Faithful Shepherd), III.i.1–6.

have often felt in my own mind something very different from this gaiety, supposed to be the inseparable attendant of the vernal scene. Amidst the returning verdure of the earth, the mildness of the air, and the serenity of the sky, I have found a still and quiet melancholy take possession of my soul, which the beauty of the landscape, and the melody of the birds, rather soothed than overcame.

Perhaps some reason may be given why this sort of feeling should prevail over the mind, in those moments of deeper pensiveness to which every thinking mind is liable, more at this time of the year than at any other. Spring, as the renewal of verdure and of vegetation, becomes naturally the season of remembrance. We are surrounded with objects new only in their revival, but which we acknowledge as our acquaintance in the years that are past. Winter, which stopped the progression of nature, removed them from us for a while, and we meet, like friends long parted, with emotions rather of tenderness than of gaiety.

This train of ideas once awakened, memory follows over a very extensive field. And, in such a disposition of mind, objects of cheerfulness and delight are, from those very qualities, the most adapted to inspire that milder sort of sadness which, in the language of our native bard, is "pleasant and mournful to the soul."[6] They will inspire this, not only from the recollection of the past, but from the prospect of the future; as an anxious parent, amidst the sportive gaiety of the child, often thinks of the cares of manhood and the sorrows of age.

This effect will, at least, be commonly felt by persons who have lived long enough to see, and had reflection enough to observe, the vicissitudes of life. Even those who have never experienced severe calamities will find, in the review of their years, a thousand instances of fallacious promises and disappointed hopes. The dream of childhood, and the project of youth, have vanished to give place to sensations of a very different kind. In the peace and beauty of the rural scene which spring first unfolds to us, we are apt to recall the former state, with an exaggerated idea of its happiness, and to feel the present with increased dissatisfaction.

But the pencil of memory stops not with the representation of our-

6. From James MacPherson's "The Death of Cuchullin" in *Poems of Ossian*, which he published fraudulently as ancient Scottish lays by the bard Ossian.

selves; it traces also the companions and friends of our early days, and marks the changes which they have undergone. It is a dizzy sort of recollection to think over the names of our school-fellows, and to consider how very few of them the maze of accidents, and the sweep of time, have left within our reach. This, however, is less pointed than the reflection on the fate of those whom affinity or friendship linked to our side, whom distance of place, premature death, or (sometimes not a less painful consideration) estrangement of affection, has disjoined from us forever.

I am not sure if the disposition to reflections of this sort be altogether a safe or a proper one. I am aware, that, if too much indulged, or allowed to become habitual, it may disqualify the mind for the more active and bustling scenes of life, and unfit it for the enjoyments of ordinary society; but, in a certain degree, I am persuaded it may be found useful. We are all of us too little inclined to look into our own minds, all apt to put too high a value on the things of this life. But a man under the impressions I have described will be led to look into himself, and will see the vanity of setting his heart upon external enjoyment. He will feel nothing of that unsocial spirit which gloomy and ascetic severities inspire; but the gentle, and not unpleasing melancholy that will be diffused over his soul, will fill it with a calm and sweet benevolence, will elevate him much above any mean or selfish passion. It will teach him to look upon the rest of the world as his brethren, travelling the same road, and subject to the like calamities with himself; it will prompt his wish to alleviate and assuage the bitterness of their sufferings, and extinguish in his heart every sentiment of malevolence or of envy.

Amidst the tide of pleasure which flows on a mind of little sensibility, there may be much social joy without any social affection; but, in a heart of the mould I allude to above, though the joy may be less, there will, I believe, be more happiness and more virtue.

It is rarely from the precepts of the moralist, or the mere sense of duty, that we acquire the virtues of gentleness, disinterestedness, benevolence, and humanity. The feelings must be won, as well as the reason convinced, before men change their conduct. To them the world addresses itself, and is heard: it offers pleasure to the present hour; and the promise of satisfaction in the future is too often preached in vain. But he who can feel that luxury of pensive tenderness of which I have given some faint sketches in this paper will not easily be won from the pride of virtue, and the dignity of thought, to the inordinate gratifications of vice, or the intemperate amusements of folly.

20 March 1779

The Lounger
No. 4. The Author Becomes Acquainted with Col. *Caustic*, a Fine Gentleman of the Last Age, Somewhat Severe in His Remarks on the Present

Laudator temporis acti. Juvenal.[7]

"Get thee a place, for I must be idle," says *Hamlet* to *Horatio* at the play.[8] It is often so with me at public places: I am more employed in attending to the spectators than to the entertainment; a practice which, in the present state of some of our entertainments, I frequently find very convenient. In me, however, it is an indolent, quiet sort of indulgence, which, if it affords some amusement to myself, does not disturb that of any other body.

At an assembly at which I happened to be present a few nights ago, my notice was peculiarly attracted by a gentleman with what is called a fresh look for his age, dressed in a claret-coloured coat, with gold buttons, of a cut not altogether modern, an embroidered waistcoat with very large flaps, a major wig, long ruffles nicely plaited (that looked however as if the fashion had come to them rather than that they had been made for the fashion); his white silk stockings ornamented with figured clocks,[9] and his shoes with high insteps, buckled with small round gold buckles. His sword, with a silver hilt somewhat tarnished, I might have thought only an article of his dress, had not a cockade in his hat marked him for a military man. It was some time before I was able to find out who he was, till at last my friend Mr. S——— informed me he was a very worthy relation of his, who had not been in town above twice these forty years; that an accidental piece of business had lately brought him from his house in the country, and he had been

7. Actually from Horace, *Ars poetica* (Art of Poetry), l. 173: "praiser of time past."

8. See Shakespeare, *Hamlet*, III.ii.88–89.

9. Stocking clocks were embroidered designs, sometimes in gold or silver thread, on either side of the ankle.

prevailed on to look on the ladies of Edinburgh at two or three public places before he went home again, that he might see whether they were as handsome as their mothers and grandmothers, whom he had danced with at balls, and squired to plays and concerts, near half a century ago. "He was," continued my friend, "a professed admirer and votary of the sex; and when he was a young man fought three duels for the honour of the ladies, in one of which he was run through the body, but luckily escaped with his life. The lady, however, for whom he fought, did not reward her knight as she ought to have done, but soon after married another man with a larger fortune; upon which he foreswore society in a great measure, and though he continued for several years to do his duty in the army, and actually rose to the rank of Lieutenant Colonel, mixed but little in the world, and has for a long space of time resided at his estate a determined bachelor, with some-what of misanthropy, and a great deal of good nature about him. If you please I will introduce you to him—Colonel Caustic, this is a very particu-lar friend of mine, who solicits the honour of being known to you."—The Colonel kissed me on both cheeks; and seeming to take a liking to my face, we appeared mutually disposed to be very soon acquainted.

Our conversation naturally began on the assembly, which I observed to be a full one. "Why, yes," said the Colonel, "here is crowd enough, and to spare; and yet your ladies seem to have been at a loss for partners. I sup-pose the greatest part of the men, or rather boys, whom I now see standing up to dance, have been brought in to make up a set, as people in the coun-try sometimes fill up the places in a dance with chairs, to help them to go through the figure. But as I came too late for the minuets, I presume the dressed gentlemen walked up stairs after they were ended."—"Why, Sir, there are now-a-days no minuets."—"No minuets!—(looking for a while at the company on the floor)—I don't wonder at it."—"Why perhaps, Colonel," said I, "these young gentlemen have not quite an aspect serious enough for the *pas grave;*[10] and yet yonder is one standing with his back to the fire."—"Why, yes, there is something of gravity, of almost melancholy on his face."—"Yes, *melancholy and gentleman-like,*" said I, "as *Master*

10. French phrase meaning "no problem"; the pun in the sentence is on its literal translation as "not serious."

Stephen in the play has it."[11]—"Why, that young man, Sir,—now that I have observed him closer,—with that roll of handkerchief about his neck, his square-cut striped vest, his large metal buttons and nankeen breeches,—Why, Sir, 'tis a stable-boy out of place!"

"Pray, who are those gentlemen," said Colonel Caustic, "who have ranged themselves in a sort of phalanx at the other end of the room, and seem, like the devil in Milton, to carry stern defiance on their brow?"[12]— "I have not the honour of their acquaintance," I replied; "but some of them I presume from the cockades in their hats"—"You do not say so," interrupted the Colonel. "Is that the military air of the present day? But you must be mistaken; they cannot be real soldiers: militia, or train-band subalterns, believe me, who, having neither seen service nor good company, contrive to look fierce, in order to avoid looking sheepish. I remember indeed of old, some of our *boys* used to put on that fierce air in coffee-houses and taverns; but they could never dream of wearing it before the ladies."—"I think, however," said Mr. S.———, smiling, "the ladies don't seem much afraid of them."—"Why, your ladies," answered the Colonel, "to say truth, have learned to look people in the face. During the little while I have been in town, I have met with some in my walks, in great coats, riding hats, and rattans,[13] whom I could not show an eye to: but I am newly come from the country: I shall keep a better countenance by and by."

At that moment a lady and her party, for whose appearance the dancers were waiting, were just entering the room, and seemed in a great hurry to get forward. Their progress, however, was a good deal impeded by a tall stout young man, who had taken his station just at the threshold, and leaning his back against one of the door-posts, with his right foot placed firm on the end of a bench, was picking his teeth with a perfect *nonchalance* to every thing around him. I saw the Colonel fasten a very angry look on him, and move his hand with a sort of involuntary motion towards my cane. The ladies had now got through the defile, and we stood back to

11. In Ben Jonson's *Every Man in His Humour,* Master Stephen resolves to give up swearing and "be more proud, and melancholy, and gentlemanlike than I have been" (I.ii.110–11).

12. See the description of Satan in Milton, *Paradise Lost,* IV.873, 885, 924.

13. Walking sticks made from palm.

make way for them. "Was there ever such a brute?" said Colonel Caustic. The young gentleman stalked up to the place where we were standing, put up his glass to his eye,[14] looked hard at the Colonel, and then—put it down again. The Colonel took snuff.

"Our sex," said I, "Colonel, is not perhaps improved in its public appearance; but I think you will own the other is not less beautiful than it was." He cast his eye round for a few minutes before he answered me. "Why, yes," said he, "Sir, here are many pretty, very pretty girls. That young lady in blue is a very *pretty girl*. I remember her grandmother at the same age; she was a *fine woman*."—"But the one next her, with the fanciful cap, and the *panache* of red and white feathers, with that elegant form, that striking figure, is not she a fine woman?"—"Why, no, Sir, not quite a fine woman; not quite such a woman, as a *man* (raising his chest as he pronounced the word *man*, and pressing the points of his three unemployed fingers gently on his bosom), as a man would be proud to stake his life for."

"But in short, Sir," continued he,—"I speak to you because you look like one that can understand me.—There is nothing about a woman's person merely (were she formed like the *Venus de Medicis*), that can constitute a *fine woman*. There is something in the look, the manner, the voice, and still more the silence, of such a one as I mean, that has no connection with any thing material; at least no more than just to make one think such a soul is lodged as it deserves.—In short, Sir, a fine woman,—I could have shown you some examples formerly.—I mean, however, no disparagement to the young ladies here; none, upon my honour; they are as well made, and if not better dressed, at least more dressed, than their predecessors; and their complexions I think are better. But I am an old fellow, and apt to talk foolishly."

"I suspect, Caustic," said my friend Mr. S———, "you and I are not quite competent judges of this matter. Were the partners of our dancing days to make their appearance here, with their humble foretops and brown unpowdered ringlets"—"Why, what then, Mr. S———?"—"Why, I think those high heads would overtop them a little, that's all." "Why, as for the *panache*," replied the Colonel, "I have no objection to the ornament itself;

14. The quizzing glass, a fashionable accessory for dandies, was a monocle magnifying lens held to the eye with a long handle.

there is something in the waving movement of it that is graceful, and not undignified; but in every sort of dress there is a certain character, a certain relation which it holds to the wearer. Yonder now, you'll forgive me, Sir (turning to me), yonder is a set of girls, I suppose, from their looks and their giggling, but a few weeks from the nursery, whose feathers are in such agitation, whisked about, high and low, on this side and on that,"—"Why, Sir, 'tis like the Countess of *Cassowar*'s menagerie scared by the entrance of her lap-dog."

"As to dress, indeed, in general," continued the Colonel, "that of a man or woman of fashion should be such as to mark some attention to appearance, some deference to society. The young men I see here, look as if they had just had time to throw off their boots after a fox-chase. But yet dress is only an accessory that should seem to belong to the wearer, and not the wearer to it. Some of the young ladies opposite to us are so made up of ornaments, so stuck round with finery, that an ill-natured observer might say, their milliner had sent them hither, as she places her doll in her shop-window, to exhibit her wares to the company."

Mr. S——— was going to reply, when he was stopped by the noise of a hundred tongues, which approached like a gathering storm from the card-room. 'Twas my Lady *Rumpus,* with a crowd of women and a mob of men in her suite. They were people of too much consequence to have any of that deference for society which the Colonel talked of. My nerves, and those of my friend S———, though not remarkably weak, could barely stand their approach; but Colonel Caustic's were quite overpowered.—We accompanied him in his retreat out of the dancing-room; and after drinking a dish of tea, by way of sedative, as the physicians phrase it, he called for his chair, and went home.

While we were sitting in the tea-room, Mr. S——— undertook the apology of my Lady Rumpus and her followers. "We must make allowance," said he, "for the fashion of the times. In these days, precision of manners is exploded, and ease is the mode."—"Ease!" said the Colonel, wiping his forehead. "Why, in your days," said Mr. S———, "and I may say in mine too, for I believe there is not much betwixt us, were there not sometimes fantastic modes, which people of rank had brought into use, and which were called genteel because such people practiced them, though the word might not just apply to them in the abstract?"—"I understand you,

S———," said the Colonel, "there were such things; some irregularities that broke out now and then. There were mad-caps of both sexes, that would venture on strange things; but they were in a style somewhat above the canaille: ridiculous enough, I grant you, but not perfectly absurd: coarse, it might be, but not downright vulgar. In all ages, I suppose, people of condition did sometimes entrench themselves behind their titles or their high birth, and committed offences against what lesser folks would call decorum, and yet were allowed to be well bred all the while; were sometimes a little gross, and called it witty; and a little rude, and called it raillery; but 'twas false coinage, and never passed long. Indeed, I have generally remarked, that people did so only because they could not do better; 'tis like pleading privilege for a debt which a man's own funds do not enable him to pay. A great man may perhaps be well bred in a manner which little people do not understand; but, trust me, he is a greater man who is well bred in a manner that every body understands."

26 February 1785

No. 32. Account of the Colonel's Family and Occupations in the Country. Sketch of the Character of His Sister.

I am every day more and more disposed to congratulate myself on this visit to Colonel *Caustic*. Here I find him, with all his good qualities brought forward, with all his failings thrown into the back ground, which only serve (to carry the simile a little farther) to give force and relief to the picture. I am now assured of what before I was willing to believe, that Caustic's spleen is of that sort which is the produce of the warmest philanthropy. As the admirer of painting is most offended with the scrawls of a dauber, as the enthusiast in music is most hurt with the discords of an ill-played instrument; so the lover of mankind, as his own sense of virtue has painted them, when he comes abroad into life, and sees what they really are, feels the disappointment in the severest manner; and he will often indulge in satire beyond the limits of discretion; while indifference or selfishness will be contented to take men as it finds them, and never allow itself to be disquieted with the soreness of disappointed benevolence or the warmth of indignant virtue.

I have likewise made an acquisition of no inconsiderable value in the

acquaintance of Colonel Caustic's sister. His affection for her is of that genuine sort which was to be expected from the view of his character I have
given. The first night of my being here, when Miss Caustic was to retire after supper, her brother rose, drew back the large arm-chair in which she sat
at table with one hand, pulled the bell-string with the other, opened the
parlour-door while she was making her curtesy to me, and then saluted her
as she went out, and bid her good night; and all this with a sort of tender
ceremony which I felt then, and feel still (for it is a thing of custom with
them), as one of the pleasantest pieces of good-breeding I had ever witnessed. "My sister is an excellent woman," said the Colonel, as he shut the
door; "and I don't like her the worse for having something of the primeval
about her. You don't know how much I owe her. When I was a careless
young fellow, living what we called a fashionable life about town, thinking
perhaps, like a puppy as I was, what sort of a coat I should wear, or what sort
of stocking would best show off my leg, or perhaps practicing my salute
before a glass, to enchant the ladies at a review, my sister Peggy, though
several years younger, was here at home, nursing the declining age of one
of the best of mothers, and managing every shilling not only of mine, but
of theirs, to make up a sum for purchasing me a company.[15] Since my
mother's death, and my being settled here, her attentions have been all
transferred to me; my companion in health, my nurse in sickness, with all
those little domestic services which, though they are ciphers in the general
account, a man like me, whose home is so much to him, feels of infinite importance; and there is a manner of doing them, a quiet, unauthoritative,
unbustling way of keeping things right, which is often more important than
the things themselves. Then I am indebted to her for the tolerable terms I
stand in with the world. When it grates harshly on me (and I am old, and
apt perhaps to be a little cross at times), she contrives somehow to smooth
matters between us; and the apology I would not allow from itself, I can
hear from her, knowing, as I do, her worth, and the affection she bears
me.—I were a brute to love her less than I do.

"There is something," continued the Colonel, after a little pause, "in
the circumstance of sex, that mixes a degree of tenderness with our duty to

15. The Colonel refers to a military review. In the eighteenth century military
officers purchased their commissions.

a female, something that claims our protection and our service in a style so different from what the other demands from us;—the very same offices are performed differently;—'tis like grasping a crab-tree, and touching a violet. Whenever I see a man treat a woman not as a woman should be treated, be it a chambermaid or a kitchen-wench, (not to say a wife or a sister, though I have seen such examples,) let him be of what fashion or rank he may, or as polite at other times as he will, I am sure his politeness is not of the right breed. He may have been taught by a dancing-master, at court, or by travel; but still his courtesy is not his own; 'tis borrowed only, and not to be relied on."

Miss Caustic, with all those domestic and household accomplishments which her brother commends, often shows that she has been skilled in more refined ones, though she has now laid them aside, like the dresses of her youth, as unsuitable to her age and situation. She can still talk of music, of poetry, of plays, and of novels; and in conversation with younger people, listens to their discourse on those topics with an interest and a feeling that is particularly pleasing to them. Her own studies, however, are of a more serious cast. Besides those books of devotion which employ her private hours, she reads history for amusement, gardening and medicine by way of business: for she is the physician of the parish, and is thought by the country-folks to be wonderfully skilful. Her brother often jokes her on the number and the wants of her patients. "I don't know, Sister," said he the other morning, "what fees you get; but your patients cost me a great deal of money. I have unfortunately but one recipe, and it is a specific for almost all their diseases."—"I only ask now and then," said she, "the key of your cellar for them, Brother; the key of your purse they will find for themselves. Yet why should we not be apothecaries that way? Poverty is a disease too; and if a little of my cordials, or your money, can cheer the hearts of some who have no other malady"—"It is well bestowed, Sister Peggy; and so we'll continue to practice, though we should now and then be cheated."

"'Tis one of the advantages of the country," said I, "that you get within reach of a certain rank of men, often most virtuous and useful, whom in a town we have no opportunity of knowing at all."—"Why, yes," said Caustic; "but the misfortune is, that those who could do the most for them, seldom see them as they ought. I have heard that every body carries a certain atmosphere of its own along with it, which a change of air does not immediately remove. So there is a certain town-atmosphere which a great man brings with him into the country. He has two or three laced lackeys, and two or three attendants without wages, through whom he sees, and hears, and does every thing; and Poverty, Industry, and Nature, get no nearer than the great gate of his court-yard."—"'Tis but too true," said his Sister. "I have several pensioners who come with heavy hearts from Lord Grubwell's door, though they were once, they say, tenants or workmen of his own; or, as some of them pretend, relations of his grandfather."— "That's the very reason," continued the Colonel; "why will they put the man in mind of his father and grandfather? The fellows deserve a horse-pond for their impertinence."—"Nay, but in truth," replied Miss Caustic, "my Lord knows nothing of the matter. He carries so much of the town at-mosphere, as you call it, about him. He does not rise till eleven, nor break-fast till twelve. Then he has his steward with him for one hour, his architect for another, his layer-out of ground for a third. After this he sometimes gal-lops out for a little exercise, or plays at billiards within doors: dines at a table of twenty covers; sits very late at his bottle; plays cards, except when my Lady chooses dancing, till midnight; and they seldom part till sun-rise."— "And so ends," said the Colonel, "your *Idyllium* on my Lord Grubwell's rural occupations."

We heard the tread of a horse in the court, and presently John entered with a card in his hand; which his master no sooner threw his eyes on, than he said, "But you need not describe, Sister; our friend may see, if he inclines it. That card (I could tell the chaplain's fold at a mile's distance) is my Lord's annual invitation to dinner. Is it not, John?" "—It is my Lord Grub-well's servant, Sir," said John. His master read the card: "*And as he under-stands the Colonel has at present a friend from town with him, he requests that he would present that gentleman his Lordship's compliments, and entreat the honour of his company also.*"—"Here is another card, Sir, for Miss Caus-tic."—"Yes, yes, she always gets a counterpart."—"But I shan't go," said his sister; "her Ladyship has young ladies enough to make fools of; an old woman is not worth the trouble."—"Why then, you must say so," an-swered her brother; "for the chaplain has a note here at the bottom, that an answer is requested. I suppose your great folks now-a-days contract with their *maître d'hôtel* by the head; and so they save half a crown, when one don't set down one's name for a cover."—"But, spite of the half crown, you must go," said the Colonel to me; "you will find food for moralizing; and I shall like my own dinner the better. So return an answer accordingly, Sister; and do you hear, John, give my Lord's servant a slice of cold beef and a tankard of beer in the mean time. It is possible he is fed upon contract too; and for such patients, I believe, Sister Peggy, Dr. Buchan's *Domestic Medicine* recommends cold beef and a tankard."[16]

10 September 1785

No. 33. Relation of a Visit at the House of *Lord Grubwell,* a Neighbour of *Col. Caustic's*

I mentioned in my last Paper, that my friend Colonel Caustic and I had accepted an invitation to dine with his neighbour Lord *Grubwell.* Of that dinner I am now to take the liberty of giving some account to my readers. It is one advantage of that habit of observation, which, as a thinking Lounger, I have acquired, that from most entertainments I can carry something more than the mere dinner away. I remember an old acquaintance of mine, a jolly carbuncle-faced fellow, who used to give an account of a company by the single circumstance of the liquor they could swallow. At such a dinner was one man of three bottles, four of two, six of a bottle and a half, and so on; and as for himself, he kept a sort of journal of what he had *pouched,* as he called it, at every place to which he had been invited during a whole winter. My reckoning is of another sort; I have sometimes carried off from a dinner, one, two, or three characters, swallowed half a dozen anecdotes, and tasted eight or ten insipid things, that were not worth the swallowing. I have one advantage over my old friend; I can digest what, in his phrase, I have *pouched,* without a headache.

When we sat down to dinner at Lord Grubwell's, I found that the table was occupied in some sort by two different parties, one of which belonged to my Lord, and the other to my Lady. At the upper end of my Lord's sat *Mr. Placid,* a man agreeable by profession, who has no corner in his mind, no prominence in his feelings, and, like certain chemical liquors, has the property of coalescing with every thing. He dines with every body

16. William Buchan's popular *Domestic Medicine; or, the Family Physician* (1769) ran through nineteen British editions in the author's lifetime.

that gives a dinner, has seventeen cards for the seven days of the week,[17] cuts up a fowl, tells a story, and hears a story told, with the best grace of any man in the world. Mr. Placid had been brought by my Lord, but seemed inclined to desert to my Lady, or rather to side with both, having a smile on the right cheek for the one, and a simper on the left for the other.

Lord Grubwell being a patron of the fine arts, had at his *board end,* besides the layer out of his grounds, a discarded fiddler from the opera-house, who allowed that *Handel* could compose a tolerable chorus; a painter, who had made what he called fancy-portraits of all the family, who talked a great deal about *Corregio;* a gentleman on one hand of him, who seemed an adept in cookery; and a little blear-eyed man on the other, who was a connoisseur in wine. On horse-flesh, hunting, shooting, cricket, and cock-fighting, we had occasional dissertations, from several young gentlemen at both sides of his end of the table, who, though not directly of his establishment, seemed, from what occurred in conversation, to be pretty constantly in waiting.

Of my Lady's division, the most conspicuous person was a gentleman who sat next her, Sir John ———, who seemed to enjoy the office of her *Cicisbeo,* or *Cavaliere Servente,*[18] as nearly as the custom of this country allows. There was, however, one little difference between him and the Italian Cavaliere, that he did not seem so solicitous to serve as to admire the Lady, the little attentions being rather directed from her, to him. Even his admiration was rather understood than expressed. The gentleman, indeed, to borrow a phrase from the grammarians, appeared to be altogether of the passive mood, and to consider every exertion as vulgar and unbecoming. He spoke mincingly, looked something more delicate than man; had the finest teeth, the whitest hand, and sent a perfume around him at every motion. He had travelled, quoted Italy very often, and called this a *tramontane* country, in which, if it were not for one or two fine women, there would be no possibility of existing.

Besides this male attendant, Lady Grubwell had several female intimates, who seemed to have profited extremely by her patronage and in-

17. Calling or visiting cards were used to convey messages or else simply left to indicate that one had paid a visit.

18. The acknowledged lover or favorite of a married woman, attending to her every desire.

structions, who had learned to talk on all *town* subjects with such ease and confidence, that one could never have supposed they had been bred in the country, and had, as Colonel Caustic informed me, only lost their bashfulness about three weeks before. One or two of them, I could see, were in a professed and particular manner imitators of my Lady, used all her phrases, aped all her gestures, and had their dress made so exactly after her pattern, that the Colonel told me, a blunt country gentleman, who dined there one rainy day, and afterwards passed the night at his house, thought they had got wet to the skin in their way, and had been refitted from her Ladyship's wardrobe. "But he was mistaken," said the Colonel; "they only borrowed a little of her complexion."

The painter had made a picture, of which he was very proud, of my Lady, attended by a group of those young friends, in the character of *Diana*, surrounded by her nymphs, surprised by *Acteon*.[19] My Lady, when she was showing it to me, made me take notice how very like my Lord Acteon was. Sir John, who leaned over her shoulder, put on as broad a smile as his good-breeding would allow, and said it was one of the most monstrous clever things he had ever heard her Ladyship say.

Of my Lord's party there were some young men, brothers and cousins of my Lady's nymphs, who showed the same laudable desire of imitating him, as their kinswomen did of copying her. But each end of the table made now and then interchanges with the other: some of the most promising of my Lord's followers were favoured with the countenance and regard of her Ladyship; while, on the other hand, some of her nymphs drew the particular attention of Acteon, and seemed, like those in the picture, willing to hide his Diana from him. Amidst those different, combined, or mingled parties, I could not help admiring the dexterity of *Placid,* who contrived to divide himself among them with wonderful address. To the landscape-gardener he talked of *clumps* and *swells;* he spoke of harmony to the musician, of colouring to the painter, of hats and feathers to the young ladies, and even conciliated the elevated and unbending Baronet, by appeals to him about the key at *Marseilles,* the *Corso* at *Rome,* and the gallery

19. While bathing, Diana (the Roman goddess of the hunt) was surprised by the hunter Actaeon, whom she punished for having seen her naked by transforming him into a stag, whereupon he was torn apart by his own dogs.

of *Florence*.[20] He was once only a little unfortunate in a reference to Colonel Caustic, which he meant as a compliment to my Lady, "how much more elegant the dress of the Ladies was now-a-days than formerly when they remembered it?" Placid is but very little turned of fifty.

Caustic and I were nearly "mutes and audience to this act."[21] The Colonel, indeed, now and then threw in a word or two of that *dolce piccante,* that sweet and sharp sort in which his politeness contrives to convey his satire. I thought I could discover that the company stood somewhat in awe of him; and even my Lady endeavoured to gain his good-will by a very marked attention. She begged leave to drink his sister's health in a particular manner after dinner, and regretted exceedingly not being favoured with her company. "She hardly ever stirs abroad, my Lady," answered the Colonel; "besides (looking slyly at some of her Ladyship's female friends), she is not young, nor, I am afraid, bashful enough for one of Diana's virgins."

When we returned home in the evening, Caustic began to moralize on the scene of the day. "We were talking," said he to me, "the other morning, when you took up a volume of *Cook's Voyages,* of the advantages and disadvantages arising to newly-discovered countries from our communication with them; of the wants we show them along with the conveniencies of life, the diseases we communicate along with the arts we teach. I can trace a striking analogy between this and the visit of Lord and Lady Grubwell to the savages here, as I am told they often call us.[22] Instead of the plain wholesome fare, the sober manners, the filial, the parental, the family virtues, which some of our households possessed, these great people will inculcate extravagance, dissipation, and neglect of every relative duty; and then, in point of breeding and behaviour, we shall have petulance and inat-

20. References to key sites on the European Grand Tour, including the fifth-century monastery founded by Saint John Cassian, housed in a fortified abbey known as the "key to Marseilles harbor"; the via del Corso, built in ancient Rome to connect the northern gate of the city to the Capitoline Hill; and the Uffizi Gallery in Florence, built by Cosimo de' Medici and opened to the public in 1591.

21. Shakespeare, *Hamlet,* V.ii.287.

22. Colonel Caustic suggests an analogy between the Scots and the "savages" discussed by Captain James Cook in the published accounts of his voyages to the South Pacific in the 1760s and 1770s.

tention, instead of bashful civility, because it is the fashion with fine folks to be *easy;* and rusticity shall be set off with impudence, like a grogram waist-coat with tinsel binding, that only makes its coarseness more disgusting."

"But you must set them right, my good Sir," I replied, "in these par-ticulars. You must tell your neighbours, who may be apt, from some spuri-ous examples, to suppose that every thing contrary to the natural ideas of politeness is polite, that in such an opinion they are perfectly mistaken. Such a caricature is indeed, as in all other imitations, the easiest to be imi-tated; but it is not the real portraiture and likeness of a high-bred man or woman. As good dancing is like a more dignified sort of walk, and as the best dress hangs the easiest on the shape; so the highest good breeding, and the most highly polished fashion, is the nearest to nature, but to nature in its best state, to that *belle nature* which works of taste (and a person of fash-ion is a work of taste) in every department require. It is the same in morals as in demeanour; a real man of fashion has a certain *retenue,* a degree of moderation in every thing, and will not be more wicked or dissipated than there is occasion for; you must therefore signify to that young man who sat near me at Lord Grubwell's, who swore immoderately, was rude to the chaplain, and told us some things of himself for which he ought to have been hanged, that he will not have the honour of going to the devil in the very best company."

"Were I to turn preacher," answered the Colonel, "I would not read your homily. It might be as you say in former times; but in my late excursion to your city, I cannot say I could discover, even in the first company, the high polish you talk of. There was Nature, indeed, such as one may suppose her in places which I have long since forgotten; but as for her beauty or grace, I could perceive but little of it. The world has been often called a *the-atre;* now the theatre of your fashionable world seems to me to have lost the best part of its audience; it is all either the yawn of the side-boxes, or the roar of the upper gallery. There is no *pit* (as I remember the pit); none of that mixture of good-breeding, discernment, taste, and feeling, which con-stitutes an audience, such as a first-rate performer would wish to act his part to. For the simile of the theatre will still hold in this further particular, that a man, to be perfectly well-bred, must have a certain respect and value for his audience, otherwise his exertions will generally be either coarse or fee-ble. Though indeed a perfectly well-bred man will feel that respect even for himself; and were he in a room alone," said Caustic (taking an involuntary step or two, till he got opposite to a mirror that hangs at the upper end of his parlour), "would blush to find himself in a mean or ungraceful attitude, or to indulge a thought gross, illiberal, or ungentlemanlike." "You smile," said Miss Caustic to me; "but I have often told my brother, that he is a very *Oroondates* on that score; and your Edinburgh people may be very well bred, without coming up to his standard."[23] "Nay but," said I, "were I even to give Edinburgh up, it would not affect my position. Edinburgh is but a copy of the larger metropolis; and in every copy the defect I mentioned is apt to take place; and of all qualities I know, this of fashion and good breeding is the most delicate, the most evanescent, if I may be allowed so pedantic a phrase. 'Tis like the flavour of certain liquors, which it is hardly possible to preserve in the removal of them." "Oh! now I understand you," said Caustic, smiling in his turn; "like *Harrowgate-water*, for example, which I am told has spirit at the spring;[24] but when brought hither, I find it, under favour, to have nothing but stink and ill taste remaining."

17 September 1785

23. John Banks's 1677 tragedy *The Rival Kings; or, The Loves of Oroondates and Statira* portrays a Scythian king whose bride is captured by a rival.

24. Mineral water from the fashionable northern English spa town, Harrowgate.

TEN

Leigh Hunt
(1784–1859)

A CLOSE FRIEND OF THE ROMANTIC essayists William Hazlitt and Charles Lamb and the poets John Keats and Percy Bysshe Shelley, James Henry Leigh Hunt strove like a knight of his own imaginary Round Table to defend the value of aesthetics in a growing commercial and industrial society. In the intellectual vanguard of his time, he voiced political cries for liberty as well as cultural opinions in the periodicals he founded and ran with his brothers. These included the liberal weekly *The Examiner* (1808–21) and *The Reflector* (1810–11). In December 1812, he and his brother John, convicted of libeling the Prince Regent in *The Examiner*, were sent to prison for two years. This did not hinder them from continuing publication, however, nor from wallpapering their prison walls, holding occasional dinner parties, or keeping up literary conversation with a group of educated elites.

Hunt's "Round Table" series, first published in *The Examiner* in 1815–17, turns from the public, coffeehouse world of the early periodical essays to the more thematically private space of the dining room, where the Round Table served as a center of conviviality and a symbolic hallmark of the heroic age of Britain under King Arthur. Hunt followed this series with the weekly *Indicator* (1819–21), which ran for seventy-six numbers and was later revived in *The Literary Examiner*. It included poems, short stories, translations, reviews, and essays on subjects from "mists and fogs" to "thieves, ancient and modern." In late 1821, Hunt ill-advisedly accepted an offer to join Shelley and Lord Byron in Italy and found a liberal quarterly that could express opinions more freely than was possible under British censorship. Unfortunately, Shelley was drowned in a boating accident immediately after Hunt's arrival with his family, and the journal, *The Liberal* (1822–23), proved a disappointment. Back in London from 1825, Hunt continued his periodical work unremittingly amid ongoing struggles with poverty. (Dickens later caricatured him as the ne'er-do-well Harold Skim-pole in *Bleak House*.) In the 1830s, his work on *The Tatler,* virtually a one-man enterprise from 4 September 1830 to 13 February 1832, and on *Leigh Hunt's London Journal,* which ran from 2 April 1834 to 27 May 1835, kept him intermittently afloat. In his later years, he found financial relief in an annuity from Sir Percy Shelley, the poet's son, and a Civil List pension from Lord John Russell. Following the deaths of two of his ten children in the mid-forties and of his favorite son, Vincent, in 1852, Hunt's life became increasingly sedentary, and his own health declined. He died two years after his long-suffering, but equally "childlike," wife, Marianne, at the age of seventy-five.

Selections are from Leigh Hunt and William Hazlitt, *The Round Table* (London, 1817), Hunt, *The Indicator* (London, 1820), and Hunt, "The Indicator," in *The Literary Examiner* (London, 1823).

The Round Table
No. 1. Introduction

It has often struck me, in common with other luxurious persons who are fond of reading at breakfast, and who are well-tempered enough, particularly on such occasions, to put up with a little agreeable advice, that there has now been a sufficient distance of time since the publication of our good old periodical works, and a sufficient change in matters worthy of social observation, to warrant the appearance of a similar set of papers.

Upon this design, with the assistance of a few companions, and with all sorts of determinations to be equally instructive and delightful, I am accordingly now entering; and must give the reader to understand, in their name as well as my own, that wishing to be regarded as his companions also, we act as becomes all honest persons under such circumstances, and profess to be no other than what we are: in other words, we assume no fictitious characters, or, what an acquaintance of ours, in his becoming disdain of the original French, would call *names of war.*[1]

A hundred years back, when the mode of living was different from

---

1. Noms de guerre.

what it is now, and taverns and coffee-houses made the persons of the wits familiar to every body, assumptions of this kind may have been necessary. *Captain* Steele, for instance, the *gay* fellow about town, might not always have been listened to with becoming attention or even gravity, especially if he had been a little too inarticulate over night; he therefore put on the wrinkles and privileges of Isaac Bickerstaff, the old gentleman. *Sir Richard* might be a little better, but not perhaps during an election, or after the failure of a fish-pool; and so he retreated into the ancient and impregnable composition of Nestor Ironside.[2]

I do not mean to say, that we have none of the foibles of our illustrious predecessors. It would be odd indeed (to speak candidly, and with that humility which becomes frail beings like men), if our numerous and very eminent virtues had no drawback;—but more on this subject presently. All that I say is, that we have not the same occasion for disguise; and therefore, as we prefer at all times a plain, straight-forward behaviour, and in fact, choose to be as original as we can in our productions, we have avoided the trouble of adding assumed characters to our real ones; and shall talk, just as we think, walk, and take dinner, in our own proper persons. It is true, the want of old age, or of a few patriarchal eccentricities to exercise people's patronage on, and induce their self-love to bear with us, may be a deficiency in our pretensions with some: but we must plainly confess, with whatever mortification, that we are still at a flourishing time of life; and that the trouble and experience, which have passed over our heads, have left our teeth, hair, and eyes, pretty nearly as good as they found them. One of us, (which, by the way, must recommend us to all the married people, and admirers of Agesilaus), was even caught the other day acting the great horse with a boy on his shoulders; and another (which will do as much for us among the bachelors, and give Lord's Ground in particular a lively sense of our turn of thinking) was not a vast while ago counted the second best cricketer in his native town.[3]

2. On Richard Steele's adoption of the pseudonym Isaac Bickerstaff, Esq., see the introduction to chap. 1. When Steele started *The Guardian* in 1713, he adopted the persona of Nestor Ironside, an elderly, well-educated gentleman.

3. "It is a fact also that Agesilaüs was excessively fond of his children, and a story is told of his joining in their childish play. Once, when they were very small, he bestrode a stick, and was playing horse with them in the house, and when he was

On the other hand, as we wish to avoid the solitary and dictatorial manner of the later Essayists, and at the same time are bound to show our readers, that we have something to make up for the want of flapped waist-coats and an instructive decay of the faculties, we hereby inform them, that we are, literally speaking, a small party of friends, who meet once a week at a Round Table to discuss the merits of a leg of mutton and of the subjects upon which we are to write. This we do without any sort of formality, letting the stream of conversation wander through any grounds it pleases, and sometimes retiring into our own respective cogitations, though it must be confessed, very rarely, for we have a lively, worn-visaged fellow among us, who has a trick, when in company, of leaping, as it were, on the top of his troubles, and keeping our spirits in motion with all sorts of pleasant interludes. After dinner, if the weather requires it, we draw round the fire with a biscuit or two, and the remainder of a philosophic bottle of wine; or as we are all passionately fond of music, one of us touches an instrument, in a manner that would make a professor die with laughter to see him using his thumb where he should put his finger, or his finger where he should use his thumb, but nevertheless in such a way as to ravish the rest of us, who know still less than he does. At an Italian air we even think him superior to Tramezzani, though we generally give vent to our feelings on this point in a whisper.[4] We suspect, however, that he overheard us one evening, as he immediately attempted some extraordinary graces, which with all our partiality we own were abominable.

The reader will see, by this account, that we do not mean to be over austere on the score of domestic enjoyments. Then for our accomplishments as writers, one of us is deep in mathematics and the learned languages, another in metaphysics, and a third in poetry; and as for experience, and a proper sympathy with the infirmities of our species, the former of which is absolutely necessary for those who set up to be instructors, and the latter quite as much so to give it a becoming tone and render it lastingly useful,—we shall not break in upon a greater principle by imitating the

---

spied doing this by one of his friends, he entreated him not to tell any one, until he himself should be a father of children"; Plutarch, *Lives* ("Agesilaus"), XXV.5. Lord's Ground was (and still is) a cricket ground.

4. Diomiro Tramezzani, a popular contemporary opera tenor from Portugal.

reckless candour of Rousseau, and make a parade of what other weaknesses we may have,—but for sickness, for ordinary worldly trouble, and in one or two respects, for troubles not very ordinary, few persons perhaps at our time of life can make a handsomer show of infirmities. Of some we shall only say, that they have been common to most men, as well as ourselves, who were not born to estates of their own; but these and others have enabled us to buy, what money might have still kept us poor in,—some good real knowledge, and at bottom of all our egotism, some warm-wishing unaffected humility. Even at school, where there is nothing much to get sick or melancholy with, if indulgent parents are out of the way, we were initiated into experience a little earlier than most people; the tribulations we have fallen into before and after this time are almost innumerable; and we may add, as a specimen of our experience after the fashion of Ulysses, that we have all of us, at separate periods from one another, been in France. I must confess however, for my own part, that I was not of an age to make much use of my travels, having gone thither in my childhood to get rid of one sickness, and just stayed long enough to survive another. It was just before the decrees that altered religious as well as political matters in that country, and almost all that I remember is a good old woman, our landlady, who used to weep bitterly over me, because I should die a heretic and be buried in unconsecrated ground.[5] I have made an exception ever since, out of the whole French nation, in favour of the people at Calais, and was delighted, though not surprised to hear the other day from one of our Round Table, that the women there were all pretty and prepossessing, and still looked as if they could be kind to young heretics.

Of this accomplished and experienced party of ours, circumstances have made me the president; but I wish it to be distinctly understood, that I do not on that account claim any pre-eminence but a nominal one. We shall all choose our own subjects, only open to the suggestions and comments of each other. Correspondents, therefore, (and I must here mention that all persons not actually admitted to the said Table, must write to us in the form of a letter), may address, as they please, either to the President of

5. The French Revolution overthrew the traditional political and religious structures of absolute monarchy with its feudal privileges for the Catholic clergy. The Frenchwoman is concerned for the future state of the author's Protestant soul.

the Round Table; or to the President and his fellows in general, as "Mr. President, Gentlemen of the Round Table;" or to any one of my friends in particular, according to his signature, as "to the member of the Round Table, T. or W." This perhaps will be determined by the nature of the communication; but I was the more anxious to say something on the point, inasmuch as my situation often reminds me of other great men who have sat at the head of tables, round or square, such as Charlemagne with his peers, who were persons of greater prowess than himself; or King Arthur, who in spite of his renown was nothing after all to some of his knights, Launcelot or Tristan for instance; or to give a more familiar example, Robin Hood and his fellows, every one of whom, before he could be admitted into the company, had beaten the captain.

I must not however, before I conclude, pass over King Arthur so slightly, as our Round Table, to a certain degree, is inevitably associated in our minds with his. The name indeed was given to us by one of that sex, who have always been the chief ornaments and promoters of chivalrous institutions; and for my part, when I am sitting at the head of it, with my knights on each side, I can hardly help fancying that I am putting a triumphant finish to the old prophecy, and feeling in me, under an unexpected but more useful character, the revived sprit of that great British Monarch, who was to return again to light from his subterraneous exile, and repair the Round Table in all its glory:

> He is a King yerownid in Fairie
> With scepter and sword, and with his regally
> Shall resort as lord and sovereigne
> Out of Fairie, and reigne in Britaine,
> And repaire againe the old Round Table,
> Among Princes King incomparable. Lydgate.[6]

To this idea, and the long train of romantic associations and inspired works connected with it, we shall sometimes resort in our poetical mo-

6. John Lydgate's *The Fall of Princes* (VIII.3112–18) refers to Merlin's prophecy that King Arthur will one day return to Britain. Hunt drops the penultimate line, "Be prophecie Merlyn set the date."

ments, just as we shall keep the more familiar idea of the dining table before us in our ordinary ones. Nor will it always indeed be absent from our minds during our philosophical and most abstruse speculations; for what have the most chivalrous persons been from the earliest ages, but so many moral re-formers, who encountered error and corruption with various weapons, who brought down brute force however gigantic, who carried light into darkness, and liberty among the imprisoned, and dissipated, with some charm or other about them, the illusions of pleasure?

1 January 1815

No. 6. On Common-Place People

Agreeably to our chivalrous as well as domestic character, and in order to show further in what sort of spirit we shall hereafter confer blame and praise, whom we shall cut up for the benefit of humanity, and to whom ap-ply our healing balsams, we have thought fit, in our present Number, to take the part of a very numerous and ill-treated body of persons, known by the various appellations of common-place people, dull fellows, or people who have nothing to say.

It is perhaps wrong, indeed, to call these persons common-place. Those who are the most vehement in objecting to them have the truest right to the title, however little they may suspect it; but of this more here-after. It is a name by which the others are very commonly known; though they might rather be called persons of simple common sense, and, in fact, have just enough of that valuable quality to inspire them with the very quietness, which brings them into so much contempt.

We need not, however, take any pains to describe a set of people so well known. They are, of course, what none of our readers are, but many are acquainted with. They are the more silent part of companies, and gen-erally the best behaved people at table. They are the best of dumb waiters near the lady of the house. They are always at leisure to help you to good things, if not to say them. They will supply your absence of mind for you while you are talking, and believe you are taking sugar for pepper. Above all, which ought to recommend them to the very hardest of their antago-nists, they are uninquiring laughers at jokes, and most exemplary listeners.

Now, we do not say that these are the very best of companions, or that, when we wished to be particularly amused or informed, we should invite them to our houses, or go to see them at theirs; all we demand is, that they should be kindly and respectfully treated when they are by, and not insolently left out of the pale of discourse, purely because they may not bring with them as much as they find, or say as brilliant things as we imagine we do ourselves.

This is one of the faults of over-civilization. In a stage of society like the present, there is an intellectual as well as personal coxcombry apt to prevail, which leads people to expect from each other a certain dashing turn of mind, and an appearance at least of having ideas, whether they can afford them or not. Their minds endeavour to put on intelligent attitudes, just as their bodies do graceful ones; and every one, who, from conscious modesty, or from not thinking about the matter, does not play the same monkey tricks with his natural deficiency, is set down for a dull fellow, and treated with a sort of scornful resentment for differing with the others. It is equally painful and amusing to see how the latter will look upon an honest fellow of this description, if they happen to find him in a company where they think he has no business. On the first entrance of one of these intolerant men of wisdom, to see, of course, a brilliant friend of his, he concludes that all the party are equally lustrous; but finding, by degrees, no flashes from an unfortunate gentleman on his right, he turns stiffly towards him at the first common-place remark, measures him from head to foot with a kind of wondering indifference, and then falls to stirring his tea with a half-inquiring glance at the rest of the company, just as much as to say, "a fellow not over-burdened, eh?" or, "who the devil has Tom got here?"

Like all who are tyrannically given, and of a bullying turn of mind,— which is by no means confined to those who talk loudest,—these persons are apt to be as obsequious and dumb-stricken before men of whom they have a lofty opinion, as they are otherwise in the case above-mentioned. This, indeed, is not always the case; but you may sometimes find out one of the cast by seeing him waiting with open mouth and impatient eyes for the brilliant things which the great Gentleman to whom he has been introduced is bound to utter. The party, perhaps, are waiting for dinner, and as silent as most Englishmen, not very well known to each other, are upon such occasions. Our hero waits with impatience to hear the celebrated person open his mouth, and is at length gratified; but not hearing very distinctly, asks his next neighbour, in a serious and earnest whisper, what it was.

Pray, Sir, what was it that Mr. W. said?

He says, that it is particularly cold.

Oh—particularly cold.

The Gentleman thinks this no very profound remark for so great a man, but puts on as patient a face as he can, and, refreshing himself with shifting one knee over the other, waits anxiously for the next observation. After a little silence, broken only by a hem or two, and by somebody's begging pardon of a gentleman next him for touching his shoe, Mr. W. is addressed by a friend, and the stranger is all attention.

By the by, W. how did you get home last night?

Oh very well, thank'ye; I couldn't get a coach, but it wasn't very rainy, and I was soon there, and jumped into bed.

Ah—there's nothing like bed after getting one's coat wet.

Nothing, indeed. I had the clothes round me in a twinkling, and in two minutes was as fast as a church.

Here the conversation drops again; and our delighter in intellect cannot hide from himself his disappointment. The description of pulling the clothes round, he thinks, might have been much more piquant; and the simile—as fast as a church—appears to him wonderfully common-place for a man of wit. But such is his misfortune. He has no eyes but for something sparkling or violent; and no more expects to find any thing simple in genius, than any thing tolerable in the want of it.

Persons impatient of other's deficiencies are in fact likely to be equally undiscerning of their merits; and are not aware, in either case, how much they are exposing the deficiencies on their own side. Not only, however, do they get into this dilemma, but what is more, they are lowering their respectability beneath that of the dullest person in the room. They show themselves deficient, not merely in the qualities they miss in him, but in those which he really possesses, such as self-knowledge and good temper. Were they as wise as they pretend to be, they would equal him in these points, and know how to extract something good from them in spite of his deficiency in the other; for intellectual qualities are not the only ones that excite the reflections, or conciliate the regard, of the truly intelligent, of those who can study human nature in all its bearings, and love it or sympathize with it, for all its affections. The best part of pleasure is the communication of it. Why must we be perpetually craving for amusement or information from others, (an appetite which, after all, will seldom be acknowledged,) and never think of bestowing them ourselves? Again, as the best part of pleasure is that we have just mentioned, the best proof of intellectual power is that of extracting fertility from barrenness, or so managing the least cultivated mind, which we may happen to stumble upon, as to win something from it. Setting even this talent aside, there are occasions when it is refreshing to escape from the turmoil and final nothingness of the understanding, and repose upon that contentedness of mediocrity, which seems to have attained its end without the trouble of wisdom. It has often delighted me to observe a profound thinker of my acquaintance, when a good-natured person of ordinary understanding has been present. He is reckoned severe, as it is called, in many of his opinions; and is thought particularly to overrate intellectual qualities in general; and yet it is beautiful to see how he will let down his mind to the other's level, taking pleasure in his harmless enjoyment, and assenting to a thousand truisms, one after another, as familiar to him as his finger-ends. The reason is, that he pierces deeper into the nature of the human being beside him, can make his very deficiencies subservient to his own speculations, and, above all, knows that there is something worth all the knowledge upon earth,— which is happiness and a genial nature. It is thus, that the sunshine of happy faces is reflected upon our own. We may even find a beam of it in every thing that Heaven looks upon. The dullest minds do not vegetate for nothing, any more than the grass in a green lawn. We do not require the trees to talk with us, or get impatient at the monotonous quiet of the fields and hedges. We love them for their contrast to noise and bustle, for their presenting to us something native and elementary, for the peaceful thoughts they suggest to us, and the part they bear in the various beauty of creation.

Is a bird's feather exhibited in company, or a piece of sea-weed, or a shell that contained the stupidest of created beings,—every one is happy to look at it, and the most fastidious pretender in the room will delight to expatiate on its beauty and contrivance. Let this teach him charity and good sense, and inform him, that it is the grossest of all coxcombry, to dwell with

admiration on a piece of insensibility, however beautiful, and find nothing to excite pleasing or profitable reflections in the commonest of his fellow men.
19 March 1815

The Indicator
No. 1. Introduction

There is a bird in the interior of Africa, whose habits would rather seem to belong to the interior of Fairy-land: but they have been well authenticated. It indicates to honey-hunters where the nests of wild bees are to be found. It calls them with a cheerful cry, which they answer; and on finding itself recognized, flies and hovers over a hollow tree containing the honey. While they are occupied in collecting it, the bird goes to a little distance, where he observes all that passes; and the hunters, when they have helped them-selves, take care to leave him his portion of the food. This is the CUCULUS INDICATOR of Linnaeus, otherwise called the moroc, bee cuckoo, or honey bird.

> There he arriving round about doth flie,
> And takes survey with busie, curious eye:
> Now this, now that, he tasteth tenderly.—Spenser.[7]

It is the object of this periodical work to notice any subjects whatso-ever within the range of the Editor's knowledge or reading. He will take them up, as they happen to suggest themselves; and endeavour to point out their essence to the reader, so as at once to be brief and satisfactory. The subjects will chiefly consist of curious recollections of biography; short dis-quisitions on men and things; the most interesting stories in history or fiction told over again, with an eye to their proper appreciation by unvulgar minds; and now and then a few original verses. Indeed the whole matter,

7. The lines are from Spenser, "Muiopotmos; or, The Fate of the Butterflie," ll. 169–73 (with ll. 170 and 172 cut). Hunt is probably mixing up Linnaeus with the Swedish naturalist Andreas Sparrman, who published a "History of the Honey-Guide, or Cuculus Indicator" as part of his "Account of a Journey into Africa from the Cape of Good Hope," in *The Philosophical Transactions of the Royal Society* 67 (1777): 43–47.

whatever the subject may be, will be strictly original, in one sense of the word; and it will be the Editor's aim, as well as a part of his own pleasure, to render it all as entertaining as he can. To the unvulgar he exclusively addresses himself; but he begs it to be particularly understood, that in this description of persons are to be included all those, who without having had a classical education, would have turned it to right account; just as all those are to be excluded, who in spite of that "discipline of humanity" think ill of the nature which they degrade, and vulgarly confound the vulgar with the uneducated.[8]

The INDICATOR will attend to no subject whatsoever of immediate or temporary interest. His business is with the honey in the old woods. The Editor has enough to agitate his spirits during the present eventful times, in another periodical work; and he is willing to be so agitated:[9] but as he is accustomed to use his pen, as habitually as a bird his pinion, and to betake himself with it into the nests and bowers of more lasting speculations, when he has done with public ones, he is determined to keep those haunts of his recreation free from all noise and wrangling, both for his own pleasure and for those who may choose to accompany him.

The INDICATOR will appear every Wednesday morning, at an hour early enough for the breakfast-table; and though the subjects will not be temporary or those of the moment, they will be written as much at the moment as if they were; so that there will still be a certain freshness of intercourse between the Editor and his readers.

DIFFICULTY OF FINDING A NAME
FOR A WORK OF THIS KIND

Never did gossips, when assembled to determine the name of a new-born child, whose family was full of conflicting interests, experience half the

8. "Certainly, *Wife* and *Children*, are a kinde of Discipline of Humanity"; Francis Bacon, "Of Marriage and Single Life" (1625), in Bacon, *The Essayes or Counsels, Civill and Morall*, ed. Michael Kiernan (Cambridge: Harvard University Press, 1985), 26. Hazlitt also uses Bacon's phrase "discipline of humanity" at the start of his essay "On Classical Education," in this volume.

9. Hunt had been working on *The Examiner*, a more politically oriented periodical founded with his brother John, for eleven years (since 1808).

difficulty which an author finds in settling the title for a periodical work. There is generally some paramount uncle, or prodigious third cousin, who is silently understood to have the chief claims, and to the golden lustre of whose face the clouds of hesitation and jealousy gradually give way. But these children of the brain have no godfather ready at hand: and then their single appellation is bound to comprise as many public interests as all the Christian names of a French or a German prince. It is to be modest: it is to be expressive: it is to be new: it is to be striking: it is to have something in it equally intelligible to a man of plain understanding, and surprising for the man of imagination:—in one word, it is to be impossible. How far we have succeeded in the attainment of this happy nonentity, we leave others to judge. There is one good thing however which the hunt after a title is sure to realize; a good deal of despairing mirth. We were visiting a friend the other night, who can do any thing for a book but give it a title; and after many grave and ineffectual attempts to furnish one for the present, the company, after the fashion of Rabelais, and with a chair-shaking merriment which he might have joined in himself, fell to turning a hopeless thing into a jest. It was like that exquisite picture of a set of laughers in Shakespeare:

> One rubbed his elbow, thus; and fleered, and swore
> A better speech was never spoke before:
> Another, with his finger and his thumb,
> Cried "Via! We will do't, come what will come!"
> The third he capered, and cried "All goes well!"
> The fourth turned on the toe, and down he fell.
> With that they all did tumble on the ground,
> With such a zealous laughter, so profound,
> That in this spleen ridiculous, appears,
> To check their laughter, passion's solemn tears.
> *Love's Labour Lost.*[10]

Some of the names had a meaning in their absurdity, such as the Adviser, or Helps for Composing; the Cheap Reflector, or Every Man His Own Look-

---

10. See Shakespeare, *Love's Labor's Lost,* V.ii.109–18; The sixteenth-century French author François Rabelais was known for his ribald humor.

ing-Glass; the Retailer, or Every Man His Own Other Man's Wit; Nonsense, To be Continued. Others were laughable by the mere force of contrast, as the Crocodile, or Pleasing Companion; Chaos, or the Agreeable Miscellany; the Fugitive Guide; the Foot-Soldier, or Flowers of Wit; Bigotry, or the Cheerful Instructor; the Polite Repository of Abuse; Blood, being a Collection of Light Essays. Others were sheer ludicrousness and extravagance, as the Pleasing Ancestor; the Silent Remarker; the Tart; the Leg of Beef by a Layman; the Ingenious Hatband; the Boots of Bliss; the Occasional Diner; the Tooth-ache; Recollections of a Very Unpleasant Nature; Thoughts on Taking up a Pair of Snuffers; Thoughts on a Barouche-Box; Thoughts on a Hill of Considerable Eminence; Meditations on a Pleasing Idea; Materials for Drinking; the Knocker, No. I; the Hippopotamus Entered at Stationers' Hall; the Piano-forte of Paulus Æmilius; the Seven Sleepers at Cards; the Arabian Nights on Horseback: with an infinite number of other mortal murders of common sense, which rose to "push us from our stools,"[11] and which none but the wise or good-natured would ever think of laughing at.

13 October 1819

No. 38. Of Sticks

Among other comparative injuries which we are accustomed to do to the characters of things animate and inanimate, in order to gratify our human vanity, such as calling a rascal a dog (which is a great compliment), and saying that a tyrant makes a beast of himself (which it would be a very good thing, and a lift in the world, if he could), is a habit in which some persons indulge themselves, of calling insipid things and persons STICKS. Such and such a one is said to write a stick; and such another is himself called a stick; a poor stick, a mere stick, a stick of a fellow.

We protest against this injustice done to those genteel, jaunty, useful, and once flourishing sons of a good old stock. Take, for instance, a common cherry stick, which is one of the favourite sort. In the first place, it is a

11. Shakespeare, *Macbeth*, III.vi.81. Stationers' Hall in London administered copyright for all books published in Britain. Paulus Aemilius was a consul in the Roman Empire.

very pleasant substance to look at, the grain running round it in glossy and shadowy rings. Then it is of primeval antiquity, handed down from scion to scion through the most flourishing of genealogical trees. In the third place, it is of Eastern origin; of a stock, which it is possible may have furnished Haroun Al Raschid with a djereed, or Mahomet with a camel-stick, or Xenophon in his famous retreat with fences, or Xerxes with tent-pins, or Alexander with a javelin, or Sardanapalus with tarts, or Solomon with a simile for his mistress's lips, or Jacob with a crook, or Methusalem with shadow, or Zoroaster with mathematical instruments, or the builders of Babel with scaffolding.[12] Lastly, how do you know but that you may have eaten cherries off this very stick; for it was once alive with sap, and rustling with foliage, and powdered with blossoms, and red and laughing with fruit. Where the leathern tassel now hangs, may have dangled a bunch of berries; and instead of the brass ferrel[13] poking in the mud, the tip was growing into the air with its youngest green.

The use of sticks in general is of the very greatest antiquity. It is impossible to conceive a state of society, in which boughs should not be plucked from trees for some purpose of utility or amusement. Savages use clubs, hunters require lances, and shepherds their crooks. Then came the sceptre, which is originally nothing but a staff, or a lance, or a crook, distinguished from others. The Greek word for sceptre signifies also a walking-stick. A mace, however plumped up and disguised with gilding and a heavy crown, is only the same thing in the hands of an inferior ruler; and so are all

12. Harun ar-Rashid (c. 766–809) ruled Islam at the zenith of its empire and was celebrated in *The Thousand and One Nights*. Mahomet (c. 570–632) was the founder of Islam. Xenophon (c. 430–c. 350 B.C.) was an ancient Greek military expert and the author of the *Anabasis*, which described the retreat of the Greek army after its unsuccessful attack on the Persians. Xerxes the Great (c. 519–465 B.C.) was a Persian king who conquered the Greeks and Babylonians, among others. Alexander the Great (356–323 B.C.) was the conqueror of Persia and founder of the largest ancient Western empire. Sardanapalus was a legendary king of Assyria noted for his sensuality. Solomon was the ancient Hebrew king and alleged author of the biblical Song of Songs. Jacob was a shepherd who became the father of the twelve tribes of Israel. Zoroaster (c. first century B.C.) was an ancient Iranian prophet. Methuselah was the oldest man in the Hebrew Bible, who lived to be 969. The builders of Babel, in Genesis 5:21–27, attempted to construct a tower to heaven.

13. That is, ferrule, the cap on the end of a walking stick.

other sticks used in office, from the baton of the Grand Constable of France down to the tipstaff of a constable in Bow-street.[14] As the shepherd's dog is the origin of the gentlest whelp that lies on a hearth-cushion, and of the most pompous barker that jumps about a pair of greys, so the merest stick used by a modern Arcadian, when he is driving his flock to Leadenhall-market with a piece of candle in his hat and No. 554 on his arm, is the first great parent and original of all authoritative staves, from the beadle's cane wherewith he terrifies charity-boys who eat bull's-eyes in church-time, up to the silver mace of the verger; the wands of parishes and governors;[15] the tasselled staff, wherewith the Band-Major so loftily picks out his measured way before the musicians, and which he holds up when they are to cease; the White Staff of the Lord Treasurer; the court-officer emphatically called the Lord Gold Stick; the Bishop's Crozier (Pedum Episcopale) whereby he is supposed to pull back the feet of his straying flock; and the royal and imperial sceptre aforesaid, whose holders, formerly called Shepherds of the People (Ποιμένες Λαῶν) were seditiously said to fleece more than to protect. The Vaulting-Staff, a luxurious instrument of exercise, must have been used in times immemorial for passing streams and rough ground with. It is the ancestor of the staff with which Pilgrims travelled. The Staff and Quarter-Staff of the country Robin Hoods is a remnant of the war-club. So is the Irish Shilelah, which a friend has well defined to be "a stick with two butt-ends." The originals of all these, that are not extant in our own country, may still be seen wherever there are nations uncivilized. The Negro Prince, who asked our countrymen what was said of him in Europe, was surrounded in state with a parcel of ragged fellows with shilelahs over their shoulders,—Lord Old Sticks.[16]

14. A tipstaff is an official's staff with a metal tip or cap. The grand constable of France is the first officer of the crown; Bow Street was the headquarters of the London constabulary, and the constable there was a police officer.

15. Leadenhall market, containing cheesemongers, fishmongers, and butchers, was the destination every Christmas season of numerous flocks of geese, turkeys, and other animals that were driven miles to market by drovers carrying long wands of willow or hazel. Bull's-eyes were a type of caramel cream candy.

16. Shillelaghs are oaken Irish cudgels. Lord Old Sticks alludes to Shakespeare's Falstaff, based on the historical figure of John Oldcastle, suggesting that the scene with the "Negro Prince," though unidentified, is theatrical.

But sticks have been great favourites with civilized as well as un-civilized nations; only the former have used them more for help and ornament. The Greeks were a sceptropherous people. Homer probably used a walking-stick, because he was blind; but we have it on authority that Socrates did. On his first meeting with Xenophon, which was in a narrow passage, he barred up the way with his stick, and asked him in his good-natured manner, where provisions were to be had. Xenophon having told him, he asked again, if he knew where virtue and wisdom were to be had; and this reducing the young man to a non-plus, he said, "Follow me, and learn;" which Xenophon did, and became the great man we have all heard of. The fatherly story of Agesilaus, who was caught amusing his little boy with riding on a stick, and asked his visitor whether he was a father, is too well known for repetition.[17]

There is an illustrious anecdote connected with our subject in Roman history. The highest compliment, which his countrymen thought they could pay to the first Scipio was to call him a walking-stick; for such is the signification of his name.[18] It was given him for the filial zeal with which he used to help his old father about, serving his decrepit age instead of a staff. But the Romans were not remarkable for sentiment. What we hear in general of their sticks, is the thumpings which servants get in their plays; and above all, the famous rods which the lictors carried, and which being actual sticks, must have inflicted horrible dull bruises and malignant stripes.[19] They were pretty things, it must be confessed, to carry before the chief magistrate; just as if the King or the Lord Chancellor were to be preceded by a cat-o'-nine-tails.

Sticks are not at all in such request with modern times as they were. Formerly, we suspect, most of the poorer ranks in England used to carry them, both on account of the prevalence of manly sports, and for security in travelling: for before the invention of posts and mail-coaches, a trip to Mar-

17. Hunt's retelling of the story of Socrates and Xenophon is a relaxed but accurate translation of Diogenes Laertius's "Life of Xenophon," in *Lives,* II.48. Xenophon was a follower of Socrates. For the story of Agesilaus, see n. 3. "Nonplus" is a state of confusion.

18. "Scipio" (related to *sceptrum,* "scepter") means staff.

19. Roman lictors attended the consul or other magistrate, bearing the fasces (bundle of rods with a projecting ax blade) to punish offenders.

lowe or St. Albans was a thing to make a man write his will.[20] As they came to be ornamented, fashion adopted them. The Cavaliers of Charles the First's time were a sticked race, as well as the apostolic divines and puritans, who appear to have carried staves because they read of them among the patriarchs. Charles the First, when at his trial, held out his stick to forbid the Attorney-General's proceeding. There is an interesting little story connected with a stick, which is related of Andrew Marvell's father, (worthy of such a son), and, which as it is little known, we will repeat; though it respects the man more than the machine. He had been visited by a young lady, who in spite of a stormy evening persisted in returning across the Humber, because her family would be alarmed at her absence. The old gentleman, high-hearted and chearful, after vainly trying to dissuade her from perils which he understood better than she, resolved in his gallantry to bear her company. He accordingly walked with her down to the shore, and getting into the boat, threw his stick to a friend, with a request, in a lively tone of voice, that he would preserve it for a keepsake. He then cried out merrily "Ho-hoy for Heaven!" and put off with his visitor. They were drowned.[21]

As commerce increased, exotic sticks grew in request from the Indies. Hence the Bamboo, the Whanghee, the Jambee which makes such a genteel figure under Mr. Lilly's auspices in the Tatler;[22] and our light modern cane, which the Sunday stroller buys at sixpence a piece, with a twist of it at the end for a handle. The physicians, till within the last few score of years, retained among other fopperies which they converted into gravities, the wig and gold-headed cane. The latter had been an indispensible sign royal

20. Saint Albans is about twenty miles northwest of London, and Marlowe Close about fourteen miles from the heart of the city.

21. Andrew Marvell the Elder (c. 1584–1641), a Church of England clergyman and father of the poet, drowned when his boat sank in the Humber River near Hull.

22. The Whangee and Jambee are cane walking sticks from Asia and southeast Asia, respectively. In *Tatler* no. 18, Isaac Bickerstaff directs the attorney Charles Lillie to prepare licenses "to permit the bearer of this cane to pass and repass through the streets and suburbs of London, or any place within ten miles of it, without let or molestation, provided that he does not walk with it under his arm, brandish it in the air, or hang it on a button: in which case it shall be forfeited; and I hereby declare it forfeited, to any one who shall think it safe to take it from him."

of fashion, and was turned to infinite purposes of accomplished gesticulation. One of the most courtly personages in the Rape of the Lock is

> Sir Plume, of amber snuff-box justly vain,
> And the nice conduct of a clouded cane.[23]

Sir Richard Steele, as we have before noticed, is reproached by a busy-body of those times for a habit of jerking his stick against the pavement as he walked. When swords were abolished by Act of Parliament, the tavern-boys took to pinking each other, as injuriously as they could well manage, with their walking-sticks. Macklin the player was tried for his life for poking a man's eye out in this way.[24] Perhaps this helped to bring the stick into disrepute, for the use of it seems to have declined more and more, till it is now confined to old men, and a few among the younger. It is unsuitable to our money-getting mode of rushing hither and thither. Instead of pinking a man's ribs or so, or thrusting out his eye from an excess of the jovial, we break his heart with a bankruptcy.

Canes became so common before the decline of the use of sticks, that whenever a man is beaten with a stick, let it be of what sort it may, it is still common to say that he has had "a caning." Which reminds us of an anecdote more agreeable than surprising; though the patient doubtless thought the reverse. A gentleman, who was remarkable for the amenity of his manners, accompanied by something which a bully might certainly think he might presume upon, found himself compelled to address a person who did not know how to "translate his style," in the following words, which were all delivered in the sweetest tone in the world, with an air of almost hushing gentility:—"Sir,—I am extremely sorry—to be obliged to say,—that you appear to have a very erroneous notion of the manners that become your situation in life;—and I am compelled, with great reluctance, to add,"—(here he became still softer and more delicate) "that if you do not think fit, upon reflection, to alter this very extraordinary conduct towards a gentle-

23. Pope, *The Rape of the Lock*, IV.123–24.
24. The actor Charles Macklin (c. 1699–1797) in a quarrel over a wig on 10 May 1735 poked out the eye of a fellow actor, Thomas Hallam, and the jab proved fatal. He was indicted for manslaughter, although he was not executed and was back to acting by 1741, when he established his fame in the role of Shakespeare's Shylock.

man, I shall be under the necessity of—caning you." The other treated the thing as a joke; and to the delight of the bye-standers, received a very grave drubbing.

There are two eminent threats connected with caning, in the history of Dr. Johnson. One was from himself, when he was told that Foote intended to mimic him on the stage. He replied, that if "the dog" ventured to play his tricks with him, he would step out of the stage-box, chastise him before the audience, and then throw himself upon their candour and common sympathy. Foote desisted, as he had good reason to do. The Doctor would have read him a stout lesson, and then made a speech to the audience as forcible; so that the theatrical annals have to regret, that the subject and Foote's shoulders were not afforded him to expatiate upon. It would have been a fine involuntary piece of acting,—the part of Scipio by Dr. Johnson. The other threat was against the Doctor himself from Macpherson, the compounder of Ossian. It was for denying the authenticity of that work; a provocation the more annoying, inasmuch as he did not seem duly sensible of its merits. Johnson replied to Macpherson's letter by one of contemptuous brevity and pith; and contented himself with carrying about a large stick, with which be intended to repel Macpherson in case of an assault. Had they met, it would have been like "two clouds over the Caspian"; for both were large-built men.[25]

We recollect another bacular Johnsonian anecdote.[26] When he was travelling in Scotland, he lost a huge stick of his in the little tree-less island of Mull. Boswell told him he would recover it; but the Doctor shook his head. "No, no," said he; "let any body in Mull get possession of it, and it will never be restored. Consider, Sir, the value of such a piece of timber here."

The most venerable sticks now surviving, are the smooth amber-

25. Both incidents, regarding the playwright and actor Samuel Foote (1720–77) and the author of the (purportedly) ancient Scottish "Ossian" poems, James MacPherson (1736–96), are recounted in Boswell's *Life of Samuel Johnson* (February 1775). The phrase "two clouds over the Caspian" is loosely quoted from Milton, *Paradise Lost,* II.714–16.

26. "Bacular," like "sceptopherous" above, is a Huntian neologism derived from *bacul* (staff or crozier), approximating *jocular* and pertaining to a rod or to caning. The anecdote appears in Boswell's entry for 16 October 1773 in his *Journal of a Tour to the Hebrides with Samuel Johnson* (1785).

coloured canes in the possession of old ladies. They have sometimes a gold-head, but oftener a crook of ivory. But they have latterly been much displaced by light umbrellas, the handles of which are imitations of them; and these are gradually retreating before the young parasol, especially about town. The old ladies take the wings of the stage-coaches, and are run away with by John Pullen in a style of infinite convenience.[27] The other sticks in use are for the most part of cherry, oak, and crab, and seldom adorned with more than a leathern tassel: often with nothing. Bamboo and other canes do not abound as might be expected from our intercourse with India: but commerce, in this as in other respects, has overshot its mark. People cannot afford to use sticks, any more than bees could in their hives. Of the common sabbatical cane we have already spoken. There is a very sufficing little manual, equally light and lissom, yclept[28] an ebony switch; but we have not seen it often.

That sticks however are not to be despised by the leisurely, any one who has known what it is to want words, or to slice off the head of a thistle, will allow. The utility of the stick seems divisible into three heads; first, to give a general consciousness of power; second, which may be called a part of the first, to help the demeanour; and third, which may be called a part of the second, to assist a man over the gaps of speech, the little awkward intervals, called want of ideas.

Deprive a man of his stick, who is accustomed to carry one, and with what a diminished sense of vigour and gracefulness he issues out of his house. Wanting his stick, he wants himself. His self-possession, like Acres's on the duel-ground, has gone out of his fingers' ends.[29] But restore it him, and how he resumes his energy! If a common walking-stick, he cherishes the top of it with his fingers, putting them out and back again with a fresh desire to feel it in his palm! How he strikes it against the ground, and feels power come back to his arm! How he makes the pavement ring with the ferrel, if in a street; or decapitates the downy thistles aforesaid, if in a field! Then if it be a switch, how firmly he jerks his step at the first infliction of it on the air! How he quivers the point of it as he goes, holding the handle with a straight-dropped arm and a tight grasp! How his foot keeps time to

27. An aptly chosen "Cockney" name.
28. An archaism for "called by the name of."
29. Bob Acres, in Richard Brinsley Sheridan's *The Rivals* (1775), is all bluster and fire until Act V, Scene iii, when his courage fails him in an actual duel.

the switches! How the passengers think he is going to ride, whether he is or not! How he twigs the luckless pieces of lilac or other shrubs, that peep out of a garden railing! And if a sneaking-looking dog is coming by, how he longs to exercise his despotism and his moral sense at once by giving him an invigorating twinge!

But what would certain men of address do without their cane or switch? There is an undoubted Rhabdosophy, Sceptrosophy, or Wisdom of the Stick,[30] besides the famous Divining Rod with which people used to discover treasures and fountains. It supplies a man with inaudible remarks, and an inexpressible number of graces. Sometimes, breathing between his teeth, he will twirl the end of it upon his stretched-out toe; and this means, that he has an infinite number of easy and powerful things to say, if he had a mind. Sometimes, he holds it upright between his knees, and tattoos it against his teeth or under lip; which implies, that he meditates coolly. On other occasions, he switches the side of his boot with it, which announces jauntiness in general. Lastly, if he has not a bon-mot ready in answer to one, he has only to thrust his stick at your ribs, and say "Ah! you rogue!" which sets him above you in an instant, as a sort of patronizing wit, who can dispense with the necessity of joking.

At the same time, to give it its due zest in life, a stick has its inconveniences. If you have yellow gloves on, and drop it in the mud, a too hasty recovery is awkward. To have it stick between the stones of a pavement, is not pleasant; especially if it snap the ferrel off; or more especially if an old gentleman or lady is coming behind you, and after making them start back with winking eyes, it threatens to trip them up. To lose the ferrel on a country road, renders the end liable to the growth of a sordid brush; which, not having a knife with you, or a shop in which to borrow one, goes pounding the wet up against your legs. In a crowded street, you may have the stick driven into a large pane of glass; upon which an unthinking tradesman, utterly indifferent to a chain of events, issues forth and demands twelve shillings and sixpence. But perhaps we have been anticipated on these points by that useful regulator of the philosophy of everyday matters, who wrote a treatise entitled the Miseries of Human Life.[31] We shall only add, that the

30. Hunt coins these terms from the Greek words for rod and staff.

31. James Beresford, *The Miseries of Human Life; or, The Groans of Timothy Testy, and Samuel Sensitive; with a Few Supplementary Sights from Mrs. Testy,* 2 vols. (London, 1806).

stick is never more in the way, than when you meet two ladies, your friends, whose arms you are equally bound and beatified to take. It cannot possibly be held in the usual way, to say nothing of its going against the gown or pelisse: and to carry it over the shoulder, endangers veils and bonnets, besides rendering you liable to the gallant reproaches of the unreflecting; who thinking you must have walked with the ladies from all eternity, instead of the next street, ask you whether you could not leave your stick at home even for two. But see, how situations the most perplexing to an un-reflecting good-will, may change their character before a spirit truly enlightened by the smiles on each side of him. Now is the time, if the fortunate Sceptrosopher wishes to be thought well in a fair bosom. He throws away the stick. The lady smiles and deprecates, and thinks how generously he could protect her without a stick.

It was thus that Sir Walter Raleigh, when he was an aspirant at Elizabeth's court at Greenwich, attending her one day on a walk, in company with other fine spirits of that age, and coming upon a plashy strip of ground, which put her Majesty's princely foot to a non-plus, no sooner saw her dilemma, than he took off a gallant velvet-cloak which he had about him, and throwing it across the mud and dirt, made such a passage for her to go over, as her royal womanhood never forgot.[32]

24 May 1820

The Indicator
No. 77. My Books[33]

There he arriving, round about doth fly.
And takes survey with busie, curious eye,
Now this, now that, he tasteth tenderly.[34]

32. See Thomas Fuller, *The History of the Worthies of England* (London, 1811), 1:287.

33. Hunt continued his popular "Indicator" series in *The Literary Examiner*, numbering the present essay 77 to denote its continuation of the original series, which had been concluded 21 March 1821.

34. See Edmund Spenser, "Muiopotmos; or, The Fate of the Butterflie," ll. 169, 171, 173.

Sitting last winter among my books, and walled round with all the comfort and protection which they and my fire-side could afford me,—to wit, a table of high-piled books at my back, my writing-desk on one side of me, some shelves on the other, and the feeling of the warm fire at my feet,—I began to consider how I loved the authors of those books; how I loved them too, not only for the imaginative pleasures they afforded me, but for their making me love the very books themselves, and delight to be in contact with them. I looked sideways at my Spenser, my Theocritus, and my Arabian Nights; then above them at my Italian Poets; then behind me at my Dryden and Pope, my Romances, and my Boccaccio; then on my left side at my Chaucer, who lay on [my] writing-desk; and thought how natural it was in C. L. to give a kiss to an old folio, as I once saw him do to Chapman's Homer.[35] At the same time I wondered how he could sit in that front room of his with nothing but a few unfeeling tables and chairs, or at best a few engravings in trim frames, instead of putting a couple of arm-chairs into the back room with the books in it, where there is but one window. Would I were there, with both the chairs properly filled and one or two more besides! "We had talk, Sir,"—the only talk capable of making one forget the books. Good God! I could cry like one of the Children in the Wood to think how far I and mine are from home; but this would not be "decent or manly"; so I smile instead, and am philosophic enough to make your heart ache. Besides, I shall love the country I am in more and more, and on the very account for which it angers me at present.

This is confessing a great pain in the midst of my books. I own it; and yet I feel all the pleasure in them which I have expressed.

Take me, my bookshelves, to your arms,
And shield me from the ills of life.[36]

No disparagement to the arms of Stella; but in neither case is pain a reason why we should not have a high enjoyment of the pleasure. I entrench my-

35. C. L. is Charles Lamb. The English poet and dramatist George Chapman had produced famous translations of Homer's *Iliad* (1611) and *Odyssey* (1616).
36. "Snatch me, my Stella, to thy arms, / And screen me from the ills of life"; Samuel Johnson, "The Winter's Walk," ll. 19–20.

self in my books, equally against sorrow and the weather. If the wind comes through a passage, I look about to see how I can fence it off by a better disposition of my moveables: if a melancholy thought is importunate, I give another glance at my Spenser. When I speak of being in contact with my books, I mean it literally. I like to be able to lean my head against them. Living in a southern climate,[37] though in a part sufficiently northern to feel the winter, I was obliged during that season to take some of the books out of the study, and hang them up near the fire-place in the sitting-room, which is the only room that has such a convenience. I therefore walled myself in, as well as I could, in the manner above-mentioned. I took a walk every day, to the astonishment of the Genoese, who used to huddle against a bit of sunny wall, like flies on a chimney-piece. But I did this only that I might so much the more enjoy my *English* evening. The fire was a wood fire instead of a coal; but I imagined myself in the country. I remembered, at the very worst, that one end of my native land was not nearer the other, than England is to Italy.

While writing this article I am in my study again. Like the rooms in all houses in this country, which are not hovels, it is handsome and ornamented. On one side it looks towards a garden and the mountains: on another to the mountains and the sea. What signifies all this? I turn my back upon the sea: I shut up even one of the side windows looking upon the mountains; and retain no prospect but that of the trees. On the right and left of me are book-shelves: a book-case is affectionately open in front of me; and thus kindly enclosed with my books and the green leaves, I write. If all this is too luxurious and effeminate, of all luxuries it is the one that leaves you the most strength. And this is to be said for scholarship in general. It unfits a man for activity—for his bodily part in the world: but it often doubles both the power and the sense of his mental duties: and with much indignation against his body, and more against those who tyrannize over the intellectual claims of mankind, the man of letters, like the magician of old, is prepared to "play the devil" with the great men of this world,[38] in a style that astonishes both the sword and the toga.

I do not like this fine large study. I like elegance; I like room to

---

37. Hunt was living in Italy at the time of writing.
38. Shakespeare, *Richard III,* I.iii.336.

breathe in, and even walk about, when I want to breathe and walk about. I like a great library next my study; but for the study itself, give me a small snug place almost entirely walled with books. There should be only one window in it, looking upon trees. Some prefer a place with few or no books at all; nothing but a chair or a table, like Epictetus:[39] but I should say that these were philosophers, not lovers of books, if I did not recollect that Montaigne was both. He had a study in a round tower, walled as aforesaid. It is true, one forgets one's books while writing: at least they say so. For my part, I think I have them in a sort of sidelong mind's eye; like a second thought, which is none; like a waterfall, or a whispering wind.

I dislike a grand library to study in. I mean an immense apartment, with books all in Museum order, especially wire-safed.[40] I say nothing against the Museum itself, or public libraries. They are capital places to go to, but not to sit in: and talking of this, I hate to read in a public place and in strange company. The jealous silence, the dissatisfied looks of the messengers, the inability to help yourself, the not knowing whether you really ought to trouble the messengers, much less the gentleman in black or brown, who is perhaps half a trustee, with a variety of other jarrings between privacy and publicity, prevent one's settling heartily to work. They say "they manage these things better in France"; and I dare say they do: but I think I should feel still more *distrait* in France,[41] in spite of the benevolence of the servitors, and the generous profusion of pen, ink, and paper. I should feel as if I were doing nothing but interchanging amenities with polite writers.

A grand private library, which the master of the house also makes his study, never looks to me like a real place of books, much less of authorship. I cannot take kindly to it. It is certainly not out of envy; for three parts of the books are generally trash, and I can seldom think of the rest and the

39. According to the Greek Stoic philosopher Epictetus, "You cannot be continually giving attention to both externals and your own governing principle" (*The Discourses as reported by Arrian*, IV.x.25).

40. The British Museum at this time housed the King's Library, consisting of more than 65,000 volumes and 19,000 pamphlets collected by George III and given to the nation by George IV in 1823.

41. See the opening sentence of Laurence Sterne's *A Sentimental Journey* (1768). "Distrait" means distracted.

proprietor together. It reminds me of a fine gentleman, of a collector, of a patron, of Gil Blas and the Marquis of Marialva; of anything but genius and comfort.[42] I have a particular hatred of a round table (not *the* Round Table, for that was a dining one) covered and irradiated with books! and never met with one in the house of a clever man but once. It is the reverse of Montaigne's Round Tower. Instead of bringing the books around you, they all seem turning another way, and eluding your hands.

Conscious of my propriety and comfort in these matters, I take an interest in the book-cases, as well as books of my friends. I long to meddle, and dispose them after my own notions. When they see this confession, they will acknowledge the virtue I have practised. I believe I did mention his book-room to C. L. and I think he told me that he often sat there when alone. It would be hard not to believe him. His library, though not abounding in Greek or Latin (which are the only things to help some persons to an idea of literature) is anything but superficial. The depths of philosophy and poetry are there, the innermost passages of the human heart. It has some Latin, too. It has also a handsome contempt for appearance. It looks like what it is, a selection made at precious intervals from the book-stalls: now a Chaucer at nine and twopence; now a Montaigne or a Sir Thomas Brown at two shillings; now a Jeremy Taylor; a Spinoza; an old English Dramatist, Prior, and Sir Philip Sidney; and the books are "neat as imported." The very perusal of the backs is a "discipline of humanity."[43] There Mr. Southey takes his place again with an old Radical friend: there Jeremy Collier is at peace with Dryden: there the lion, Martin Luther, lies down with the Quaker lamb, Sewell: there Guzman d'Alfarache thinks himself fit company for Sir Charles Grandison, and has his claims admitted.[44] Even the "high

42. The Marquis of Marialva hires Gil Blas as his secretary in Alain-René Lesage's picaresque novel (VII.6–10). See chap. 8, n. 31.

43. For "discipline of humanity," see n. 8; the phrase "neat as imported" is from David Garrick's "Prologue" to *Florizel and Perdita: A Dramatic Pastoral, in Three Acts,* ll. 12–13. Jeremy Taylor was a seventeenth-century Anglican author of sermons; Baruch Spinoza was a seventeenth-century Dutch metaphysician. For Matthew Prior and Philip Sidney see chap. 4, n. 61.

44. Hunt and Hazlitt criticized the poet laureate Robert Southey for reneging on his earlier radical views. Jeremy Collier was a seventeenth-century clergyman opposed to theatrical spectacle, in which Dryden was involved. William Sewel was a

fantastical" Duchess of Newcastle, with her laurel on her head, is received with grave honours, and not the less for declining to trouble herself with the constitutions of her maids.[45] There is an approach to this in the library of W. C. who also includes Italian among his humanities. W H., I believe, has no books, except mine; but he has Shakespeare and Rousseau by heart. N. who though not a book man by profession, is fond of those who are, and who loves his volume enough to read it across the fields, has his library in the common sitting room, which is hospitable. H. R.'s books are all too modern and finely bound, which however is not his fault, for they were left him by will,—not the most kindly act of the testator.[46] Suppose a man were to bequeath us a great japan chest, three feet by four, with an injunction that it was always to stand on the tea-table. I remember borrowing a book of H. R. which, having lost, I replaced with a copy equally well bound. I am not sure I should have been in such haste, even to return the book, had it been a common looking volume; but the splendour of the loss dazzled me into this ostentatious piece of propriety. I set about restoring it as if I had diminished his fortunes; and waived the privilege a friend has to use a man's things as his own. I may venture upon this profligate theory, not only because candour compels me to say that I hold it in higher matters, with Montaigne, but because I have been a meek son in the family of book-losers. I may affirm, upon a moderate calculation, that I have lent and lost in my time, (and I am eight and thirty,) half-a-dozen decent sized libraries,—I mean books enough to fill so many ordinary book cases. I have never complained; and self-love, as well as gratitude, makes me love those who do not complain of me. But like other patient people, I am inclined to burst out now that I grow less strong, now that writing puts a hectic in my cheek.

---

prominent Quaker. Guzmán de Alfarache was the hero of Mateo Alemán's picaresque Spanish novel by that title (translated into English in 1622). Sir Charles Grandison was the eponymous hero of Samuel Richardson's last novel (1753–54).

45. The seventeenth-century Margaret Cavendish, duchess of Newcastle, is described by Hunt's friend Lamb as "somewhat fantastical, and original-brained" in the opening paragraph of "Mackery End, in Hertfordshire." See chap. 12.

46. W. C. is the editor Walter Coulson (1794?–1860); W. H. is William Hazlitt; N. is the musician Vincent Novello (1781–1861); H. R. is Henry Robertson, opera singer and music critic for *The Examiner*. R., below, is the barrister and poet John Hamilton Reynolds (1796–1852), also a close friend of John Keats.

Publicity is nothing now-a-days "between friends." There is R. not H. R. who, in return for breaking a set of my English Poets, makes a point of forgetting me, whenever he has poets in his eye; which is carrying his conscience too far. But W. H. treated me worse; for not content with losing other of said English Poets, together with my Philip Sidney (all in one volume) and divers pieces of Bacon, he vows I never lent them to him; which is "the unkindest cut of all."[47] This comes of being magnanimous. It is a poor thing after all to be "pushed from a level consideration"[48] of one's superiority in matters of provocation. But W. H. is not angry on this occasion, though he is forgetful; and in spite of his offences against me and mine (not to be done away by his good word at intervals). I pardon the irritable patriot and metaphysician, who would give his last penny to an acquaintance, and his last pulse to the good of mankind. Why did he fire up at an idle word from one of the few men, who thought and felt as deeply as himself, and who "died daily" in the same awful cause? But I forgive him, because *he* forgave him; and yet I know not if I can do it for that very reason.[49]

> Come, my friends, my books, and lead me on:
> 'Tis time that I were gone.[50]

I own I borrow books with as much facility as I lend. I cannot see a work that interests me on another person's shelf, without a wish to carry it off: but, I repeat, that I have been much more sinned against than sinning[51]

47. See Shakespeare, *Julius Caesar*, III.ii.181.
48. See Shakespeare, *Henry IV, Part II*, II.i.115–16.
49. Hunt is writing a few months after the death of Percy Bysshe Shelley in a boating accident shortly after Hunt's arrival in Italy. He is criticizing Hazlitt for the latter's accusation in his essay "On Paradox and Common-Place" that Shelley had "a fire in his eye, a fever in his brain, a maggot in his brain" (among other temperamental defects). Hazlitt shared Shelley's desire for governmental reform, but he felt that the poet, though knowledgeable, was immature. In April 1821, Hunt wrote to Hazlitt objecting to his uncongenial remarks as well as to an ironic portrait of himself in Hazlitt's essay "On People with One Idea." Hazlitt wrote back a friendly, dignified, but unrepentant letter in which he expressed affection toward Hunt but refused to hold himself accountable to Shelley. The phrase "die daily" occurs in 1 Corinthians 15:31.
50. Abraham Cowley, "The Motto," ll. 25–26.
51. See Shakespeare, *King Lear*, III.ii.60.

in the article of non-return; and am scrupulous in the article of intention. I never had a felonious intent upon a book but once; and then I shall only say, it was under circumstances so peculiar, that I cannot but look upon the conscience that induced me to restore it, as having sacrificed the spirit of its very self to the letter; and I have a grudge against it accordingly. Some people are unwilling to lend their books. I have a special grudge against them, particularly those who accompany their unwillingness with uneasy professions to the contrary, and smiles like Sir Fretful Plagiary.[52] The friend who helped to spoil my notions of property, or rather to make them too good for the world "as it goes,"[53] taught me also to undervalue my squeamishness in refusing to avail myself of the books of these gentlemen. He showed me how it was doing good to all parties to put an ordinary face on the matter; though I know his own blushed not a little sometimes in doing it, even when the good to be done was for another. I feel in truth, that even when anger inclines me to exercise this privilege of philosophy, it is more out of revenge than contempt. I fear that in allowing myself to borrow books, I sometimes make extremes meet in a very sinful manner, and do it out of a refined revenge. It is like eating a miser's beef at him.

I yield to none in my love of bookstall urbanities. I have spent as happy moments over the stalls (till the woman looked out) as any literary apprentice boy who ought to be moving onwards. But I confess my weakness in liking to see some of my favourite purchases neatly bound. The books I like to have about me most are Spenser, Chaucer, the minor poems of Milton, the Arabian Nights, Theocritus, Plato's Republic, and such old good-natured speculations as Plutarch's Morals. For most of these I love a plain good old binding, never mind how old, provided it wears well; but my Arabian Nights may be bound in as fine and flowery a style as possible, and I should like an engraving to every dozen pages. Book-prints of all sorts, bad and good, take with me as much as when I was a child: and I think some books, such as Prior's Poems, ought always to have portraits of the authors. Prior's airy face with his cap on, is like having his company. From early as-

52. In the opening scene of Sheridan's *The Critic; or, A Tragedy Rehearsed* (1779), Sir Fretful is subjected to "criticism" of his dramatic skills by a friend, at which he must laugh as if diverted.

53. See Byron, *Don Juan*, VIII.711–12: "Without, or with, offence to friends or foes, / I sketch your world exactly as it goes." Hunt's "friend" was the poet Shelley.

sociation, no edition of Milton pleases me so much, as that in which there are pictures of the Devil with brute ears, dressed like a Roman General: nor of Bunyan, as the one containing the print of the Valley of the Shadow of Death, with the Devil whispering in Christian's ear, old Pope sitting by the way side, and

Vanity Fair,
With the Pilgrims suffering there.[54]

I delight in the recollection of the puzzle I used to have with the frontispiece of the Tale of a Tub, of my real horror at the sight of that crawling old man representing Avarice, at the beginning of Enfield's Speaker, the Looking Glass, or some such book; and even of the careless school-boy hats, and the prim stomachers and cottage bonnets, of such golden-age antiquities as the Village School.[55] The oldest and most worn-out wood cut, representing King Pepin, Goody Two Shoes, or the grim Soldan, sitting with three staring blots for his eyes and mouth, his sceptre in one hand, and his other five fingers raised and spread in admiration at the feats of the Gallant London Prentice, cannot raise in me a feeling of ingratitude or disrespect.[56] Cooke's edition of the British Poets and Novelists came out while I was at school: for which reason I never could put up with Suttaby's or Walker's publications, except in the case of such works as the Fairy Tales, which Mr. Cooke did not publish. Besides they are too cramped, thick, and mercenary; and the pictures are all frontispieces. They do not come in at the proper places. It is like having one's pie before dinner. Cooke realized the old woman's beau ideal of a prayer book,—"A little book, with a great deal of matter, and a large type":—for the type was really large for so small a vol-

54. Loosely quoted from John Bunyan, *The Pilgrim's Progress* (1678).
55. Remembrances of Jonathan Swift's prose satire *The Tale of a Tub* (1704), William Enfield's *The Speaker; or, Miscellaneous Pieces, Selected from the Best English Writers* (1774), Abraham Chear's *A Looking-Glass for Children* (1672), and the pseudonymous Dorothy Kilner's *The Village School* (c. 1795).
56. Hunt's "Soldan" (a corruption of "Sultan") or "Great Turk" gives Aurelius, the London Prentice, to his daughter in marriage in the *Famous History of the Valiant London Prentice* (1686); the other popular children's stories to which Hunt refers are *The History of Pepin King of Lilliputia* (c. 1800) and *The History of Little Goody Two-Shoes* (1772).

ume.[57] Shall I ever forget his Collins and his Gray, books at once so superbly ornamented and so inconceivably cheap? Sixpence could procure much before; but never could it procure so much as then, or was at once so much respected, and so little cared for. His artist Kirk was the best artist, except Stothard, that ever designed for periodical works; and I will venture to add (if his name rightly announces his country) the best artist Scotland ever produced, except Wilkie: but he unfortunately had not enough of his country in him to keep him from dying young. His designs for Milton and the Arabian Nights, his female extricated from the water in the Tales of the Genii, and his old hag issuing out of the chest of the Merchant Abadah in the same book, are before me now as vividly as they were then.[58] He possessed elegance and the sense of the beauty in no ordinary degree; though they sometimes played a trick or so of foppery. I shall never forget the gratitude with which I received an odd number of Akenside, value sixpence, one of the set of that poet, which a boarder distributed among three or four of us, "with his mother's compliments." The present might have been more lavish, but I hardly thought of that. I remember my number. It was the one in which there is a picture of the poet on a sofa, with Cupid coming to him, and the words underneath, "Tempt me no more, insidious Love!"[59] The picture and the number appeared to me equally divine. I cannot help thinking to this day, that it is right and natural in a gentleman to sit in a stage dress, on that particular kind of sofa, though on no other, with that exclusive hat and feathers on his head, telling Cupid to begone with a tragedy air. Cowley says, that even when he was "a very young boy at school, instead of his running about on holidays, and playing with his fellows, he was wont to steal from them, and walk into the fields, either alone with a book, or with some one companion, if he could find one of the same

57. Charles Cooke (1759/60–1816) was a publisher best known for his *Pocket Edition . . . of Select British Poets* (including *The Poetical Works of William Collins* and *The Poetical Works of Thomas Gray*) and *Pocket Edition of Select Novels* from the 1790s, which were embellished with engravings. His contemporaries, William Suttaby and John Walker, published similar material.

58. Thomas Kirk (1765?–97), Thomas Stothard (1755–1834), and Sir David Wilkie (1785–1841) were all painters and engravers, the first employed by Cooke. Kirk engraved the designs for Cooke's two-volume *Poetical Works of John Milton* (1796) and his two-volume *Tales of the Genii* (1794) by James Ridley (under the pseudonym Sir Charles Morell), which was modeled on *The Arabian Nights*.

59. Mark Akenside, "Ode. The Complaint" (1772), l. 2.

temper."[60] When I was at school, I had no fields to run into, or I should certainly have gone there; and I must own to having played a great deal; but then I drew my sports as much as possible out of books, playing at Trojan wars, chivalrous encounters with coal-staves, and even at religious mysteries. When I was not at these games, I was either reading in a corner, or walking round the cloisters with a book under one arm, and my friend linked with the other, or with my thoughts. It has since been my fate to realize all the romantic notions I had of a friend at that time, and just as I had embraced him in a distant country, to have him torn from me. This it is that sprinkles the most cheerful of my speculations now with tears, and that must obtain me the reader's pardon for a style unusually chequered and egotistical. No man was a greater lover of books than he. He was rarely to be seen, unless attending to other people's affairs, without a volume of some sort, generally of Plato, or one of the Greek Tragedians. Nor will those who understand the real spirit of his scepticism, be surprised to hear that one of his companions was the Bible. He valued it for the beauty of some of its contents, for the dignity of others, and the curiosity of all; though the philosophy of Solomon he thought *too Epicurean,* and the inconsistencies of other parts afflicted him. His favourite part was the book of Job, which he thought the grandest of tragedies. He projected founding one of his own upon it; and I will undertake to say that Job would have sat in that tragedy, with a patience and a profundity of thought worthy of the original. Being asked on one occasion, what book he would save for himself, if he could save no other? he answered, "The oldest book, the Bible." It was a monument to him of the earliest, most lasting, and most awful aspirations of humanity. But more of this on a fitter occasion.*

    5 July 1823

    *I will mention, however, in this place, that an advantage of a very cunning and vindictive nature was taken of Mr. Shelley's known regard for the Bible, to represent him as having one with him when he was drowned. Nothing was more probable; and it is true, that he had a book in his pocket, the remains of which, at the request of the author of this article, were buried with him: but it was the volume of Mr. Keats's poems, containing Hyperion, of which he was a great admirer. He borrowed it of me when he went away, and knowing how I valued it also, said that he would not let it quit him till he saw me again.

    60. Abraham Cowley, "Of My Self," in Cowley, *The English Writings,* ed. A. R. Waller, 2 vols. (Cambridge: Cambridge University Press, 1905), 2:456.

ELEVEN

William Hazlitt

(1778–1830)

WILLIAM HAZLITT, A MULTIFACETED, much maligned man who was attacked by the conservative press ostensibly for his "vulgarisms and broken English" but really on account of his political and social criticism, made himself into a master of the familiar essay. As the son of an Irish Unitarian clergyman he trained for the ministry, but he lost his taste for the profession while in London. Instead, through the intervention of another Unitarian in training, Samuel Taylor Coleridge, he joined a literary coterie consisting of Leigh Hunt, Charles Lamb, and the poets Wordsworth, Shelley, Robert Southey, and Lord Byron. He explored an alternate career as a painter but finally settled on essay writing, producing works that spice his perennial idealism with dashes of misanthropic irony. In addition to his "Round Table" pieces in *The Examiner,* he published a number of essays in *The Times, The Morning Chronicle,* and *The Examiner* attacking political corruption. He remained to the end, in his own view at least, that rare Romantic who did not sell out by turning Tory—or die tragically in the full flame of youth.

At thirty he married Sarah Stoddart, a friend of Charles and Mary Lamb and the sister of the *Times* editor John Stoddart, but their marriage fell apart after three years. In 1823 his distinguished career as a periodical essayist ran aground when he published his impassioned letters to Sarah Walker, a maid at his lodging house, in the form of a scandalous epistolary romance, *Liber Amorous.* In 1824, he married Isabella Bridgewater, a wealthy widow with whom he toured Europe, but she left him after only one year. Throughout his later life of poverty and sickness, he was preoccupied with a four-volume life of Napoleon Bonaparte (1828–30), a work that gained him no financial recompense but reveals his ongoing commitment to the principles of liberty represented by the French Revolution. Hazlitt also wrote literary criticism, collected in his *Characters of Shake-*

speare's Plays (1817), *Lectures on the English Poets* (1818), *Lectures on the En-glish Comic Writers* (1819), *Dramatic Literature in the Age of Elizabeth* (1821), and *Table-Talk* (1821–22). Perhaps his best-known work, *The Spirit of the Age* (1825), consists of brilliant memoirs of his contemporaries, in-cluding the conservative editor William Gifford, who accused him in *The Quarterly* of making "predatory incursions on taste and common sense."

Selections are from Leigh Hunt and William Hazlitt, *The Round Table* (London, 1817), Hazlitt, *The Plain Speaker* (London, 1826), Hazlitt, *Table-Talk* (London, 1821–22), and *The Monthly Magazine* (1831).

The Round Table
No. 4. On Classical Education

The study of the Classics is less to be regarded as an exercise of the intellect, than as "a discipline of humanity."[1] The peculiar advantage of this mode of education consists not so much in strengthening the understanding, as in softening and refining the taste. It gives men liberal views; it accustoms the mind to take an interest in things foreign to itself; to love virtue for its own sake; to prefer fame to life, and glory to riches; and to fix our thoughts on the remote and permanent, instead of narrow and fleeting objects. It teaches us to believe that there is something really great and excellent in the world, surviving all the shocks of accident and fluctuations of opinion, and raises us above that low and servile fear, which bows only to present power and upstart authority. Rome and Athens filled a place in the history of mankind, which can never be occupied again. They were two cities set on a hill, which could not be hid; all eyes have seen them, and their light shines like a mighty sea-mark into the abyss of time.[2]

> Still green with bays each ancient altar stands,
> Above the reach of sacrilegious hands;

1. Francis Bacon's phrase; see chap. 10, n. 8.
2. See Matthew 5:14–16, the Sermon on the Mount: "Ye are the light of the world. A city that is set on an hill cannot be hid. . . . Let your light so shine before men, that they may see your good works, and glorify your Father which is in heaven."

Secure from flames, from envy's fiercer rage,
Destructive war, and all-involving age.

Hail, bards triumphant, born in happier days,
Immortal heirs of universal praise!
Whose honours with increase of ages grow,
As streams roll down, enlarging as they flow!³

It is this feeling, more than anything else, which produces a marked difference between the study of the ancient and modern languages, and which, from the weight and importance of the consequences attached to the former, stamps every word with a monumental firmness. By conversing with the *mighty dead*,⁴ we imbibe sentiment with knowledge; we become strongly attached to those who can no longer either hurt or serve us, except through the influence which they exert over the mind. We feel the presence of that power which gives immortality to human thoughts and actions, and catch the flame of enthusiasm from all nations and ages.

It is hard to find in minds otherwise formed, either a real love of excellence, or a belief that any excellence exists superior to their own. Every thing is brought down to the vulgar level of their own ideas and pursuits. Persons without education certainly do not want either acuteness or strength of mind in what concerns themselves, or in things immediately within their observation; but they have no power of abstraction, no general standard of taste, or scale of opinion. They see their objects always near, and never in the horizon. Hence arises that egotism which has been remarked as the characteristic of self-taught men, and which degenerates into obstinate prejudice or petulant fickleness of opinion, according to the natural sluggishness or activity of their minds. For they either become blindly bigoted to the first opinions they have struck out for themselves, and inaccessible to conviction; or else (the dupes of their own vanity and shrewdness) are everlasting converts to every crude suggestion that presents itself, and the last opinion is always the true one. Each successive discovery flashes upon them with equal light and evidence, and every new fact overturns their whole system. It is among this class of persons, whose ideas never extend beyond the

3. Alexander Pope, *Essay on Criticism*, ll. 181–84, 189–92.
4. James Thomson, *The Seasons*, from "Winter," l. 432.

feeling of the moment, that we find partizans, who are very honest men, with a total want of principle, and who unite the most hardened effrontery, and intolerance of opinion, to endless inconsistency and self-contradiction.

A celebrated political writer of the present day, who is a great enemy to classical education, is a remarkable instance both of what can and what cannot be done without it.[5]

It has been attempted of late to set up a distinction between the education *of words,* and the education *of things,* and to give the preference in all cases to the latter. But, in the first place, the knowledge of things, or of the realities of life, is not easily to be taught except by things themselves, and, even if it were, is not so absolutely indispensable as it has been supposed. "The world is too much with us, early and late";[6] and the fine dream of our youth is best prolonged among the visionary objects of antiquity. We owe many of our most amiable delusions, and some of our superiority, to the grossness of mere physical existence, to the strength of our associations with words. Language, if it throws a veil over our ideas, adds a softness and refinement to them, like that which the atmosphere gives to naked objects. There can be no true elegance without taste in style. In the next place, we mean absolutely to deny the application of the principle of utility to the present question. By an obvious transposition of ideas, some persons have confounded a knowledge of useful things with useful knowledge. Knowledge is only useful in itself, as it exercises or gives pleasure to the mind: the only knowledge that is of use in a practical sense, is professional knowledge. But knowledge, considered as a branch of general education, can be of use only to the mind of the person acquiring it. If the knowledge of language produces pedants, the other kind of knowledge (which is proposed to be substituted for it) can only produce quacks. There is no question, but that the knowledge of astronomy, of chemistry, and of agriculture, is highly useful to the world, and absolutely necessary to be acquired by persons carry-

5. The radical journalist William Cobbett considered colleges and universities "dens of dunces" and argued that book learning was detrimental to the minds of youths and that "what are called the *learned* languages, operate as a bar to the acquirement of real learning"; *The Weekly Register,* 5 October 1822 and 10 January 1807.

6. See Wordsworth's sonnet, "The world is too much with us, late and soon."

ing on certain professions: but the practical utility of a knowledge of these subjects ends there. For example, it is of the utmost importance to the navigator to know exactly in what degree of longitude and latitude such a rock lies: but to us, sitting here about our Round Table, it is not of the smallest consequence whatever, whether the map-maker has placed it an inch to the right or to the left; we are in no danger of running against it. So the art of making shoes is a highly useful art, and very proper to be known and practised by some body: that is, by the shoemaker. But to pretend that every one else should be thoroughly acquainted with the whole process of this ingenious handicraft, as one branch of useful knowledge, would be preposterous. It is sometimes asked, What is the use of poetry? and we have heard the argument carried on almost like a parody on *Falstaff's* reasoning about Honour.[7] "Can it set a leg? No. Or an arm? No. Or take away the grief of a wound? No. Poetry hath no skill in surgery then? No." It is likely that the most enthusiastic lover of poetry would so far agree to the truth of this statement, that if he had just broken a leg, he would send for a surgeon, instead of a volume of poems from a library. But, "they that are whole need not a physician."[8] The reasoning would be well founded, if we lived in an hospital, and not in the world.

12 February 1815

No. 28. On Imitation

Objects in themselves disagreeable or indifferent, often please in the imitation. A brick-floor, a pewter plate, an ugly cur barking, a Dutch boor smoking or playing at skittles, the inside of a shambles,[9] a fishmonger's or a green-grocer's stall, have been made very interesting as pictures by the fidelity, skill, and spirit, with which they have been copied. One source of the pleasure thus received is undoubtedly the surprise or feeling of admiration, occasioned by the unexpected coincidence between the imitation and the object. The deception, however, not only pleases at first sight, or from mere novelty; but it continues to please upon farther acquaintance, and in

---

7. See Shakespeare, *Henry IV, Part I,* V.i.131–40.
8. See Matthew 9:12.
9. Butchers' market, where the animals were often slaughtered.

proportion to the insight we acquire into the distinctions of nature and of art. By far the most numerous class of connoisseurs are the admirers of pictures of *still life,* which have nothing but the elaborateness of the execution to recommend them. One chief reason, it should seem then, why imitation pleases, is, because, by exciting curiosity, and inviting a comparison between the object and the representation, it opens a new field of inquiry, and leads the attention to a variety of details and distinctions not perceived before. This latter source of the pleasure derived from imitation has never been properly insisted on.

The anatomist is delighted with a coloured plate, conveying the exact appearance of the progress of certain diseases, or of the internal parts and dissections of the human body. We have known a Jennerian Professor[10] as much enraptured with a delineation of the different stages of vaccination, as a florist with a bed of tulips, or an auctioneer with a collection of Indian shells. But in this case, we find that not only the imitation pleases,—the objects themselves give as much pleasure to the professional inquirer, as they would pain to the uninitiated. The learned amateur is struck with the beauty of the coats of the stomach laid bare, or contemplates with eager curiosity the transverse section of the brain, divided on the new Spurzheim principles.[11] It is here, then, the number of the parts, their distinctions, connections, structure, uses; in short, an entire new set of ideas, which occupies the mind of the student, and overcomes the sense of pain and repugnance, which is the only feeling that the sight of a dead and mangled body presents to ordinary men. It is the same in art as in science. The painter of still life, as it is called, takes the same pleasure in the object as the spectator does in the imitation; because by habit he is led to perceive all those distinctions in nature, to which other persons never pay any attention till they are pointed out to them in the picture. The vulgar only see nature as it is reflected to them from art; the painter sees the picture in nature, before he transfers it to the canvas. He refines, he analyses, he remarks fifty things, which escape common eyes; and this affords a distinct source of reflection

10. Edward Jenner (1749–1823) developed the vaccination for smallpox.

11. The phrenology of Johann Gaspar Spurzheim updated the anatomical brain science of Franz Joseph Gall by adding to the number of mental "organs" and systematizing them hierarchically.

and amusement to him, independently of the beauty or grandeur of the objects themselves, or of their connection with other impressions besides those of sight. The charm of the Fine Arts, then, does not consist in any thing peculiar to imitation, even where only imitation is concerned, since *there*, where art exists in the highest perfection, namely, in the mind of the artist, the object excites the same or greater pleasure, before the imitation exists. Imitation renders an object, displeasing in itself, a source of pleasure, not by repetition of the same idea, but by suggesting new ideas, by detecting new properties, and endless shades of difference, just as a close and continued contemplation of the object itself would do. Art shows us nature, divested of the medium of our prejudices. It divides and decompounds objects into a thousand curious parts, which may be full of variety, beauty, and delicacy in themselves, though the object to which they belong may be disagreeable in its general appearance, or by association with other ideas. A painted marigold is inferior to a painted rose only in form and colour: it loses nothing in point of smell. Yellow hair is perfectly beautiful in a picture. To a person lying with his face close to the ground in a summer's day, the blades of spear-grass will appear like tall forest trees, shooting up into the sky; as an insect seen through a microscope is magnified into an elephant. Art is the microscope of the mind, which sharpens the wit as the other does the sight; and converts every object into a little universe in itself.* Art may be said to draw aside the veil from nature. To those who are perfectly unskilled in the practice, unimbued with the principles of art, most objects present only a confused mass. The pursuit of art is liable to be carried to a contrary excess, as where it produces a rage for the *picturesque*. You cannot go a step with a person of this class, but he stops you to point out some choice bit of landscape, or fancied improvement, and teazes you almost to death with the frequency and insignificance of his discoveries!

It is a common opinion, (which may be worth noticing here), that the

---

*In a fruit or flower-piece by [the Dutch painter Jan] Vanhuysum, the minutest details acquire a certain grace and beauty from the delicacy with which they are finished. The eye dwells with a giddy delight on the liquid drops of dew, on the gauze wings of an insect, on the hair and feathers of a bird's nest, the streaked and speckled egg-shells, the fine legs of the little travelling caterpillar. Who will suppose that the painter had not the same pleasure in detecting these nice distinctions in nature, that the critic has in tracing them in the picture?

study of physiognomy has a tendency to make people satirical, and the knowledge of art to make them fastidious in their taste. Knowledge may, indeed, afford a handle to ill-nature; but it takes away the principal temptation to its exercise, by supplying the mind with better resources against *ennui*. Idiots are always mischievous; and the most superficial persons are the most disposed to find fault, because they understand the fewest things. The English are more apt than any other nation to treat foreigners with contempt, because they seldom see any thing but their own dress and manners; and it is only in petty provincial towns that you meet with persons who pride themselves on being satirical. In every country place in England there are one or two persons of this description who keep the whole neighbourhood in terror. It is not to be denied that the study of the *ideal* in art, if separated from the study of nature, may have the effect above stated, of producing dissatisfaction and contempt for everything but itself, as all affectation must; but to the genuine artist, truth, nature, beauty, are almost different names for the same thing.

Imitation interests, then, by exciting a more intense perception of truth, and calling out the powers of observation and comparison: wherever this effect takes place the interest follows of course, with or without the imitation, whether the object is real or artificial. The gardener delights in the streaks of a tulip, or "pansy freak'd with jet";[12] the mineralogist in the varieties of certain strata, because he understands them. Knowledge is pleasure as well as power. A work of art has in this respect no advantage over a work of nature, except inasmuch as it furnishes an additional stimulus to curiosity. Again, natural objects please in proportion as they are uncommon, by fixing the attention more steadily on their beauties or differences. The same principle of the effect of novelty in exciting the attention, may account, perhaps, for the extraordinary discoveries and lies told by travellers, who, opening their eyes for the first time in foreign parts, are startled at every object they meet.

Why the excitement of intellectual activity pleases, is not here the question; but that it does so, is a general and acknowledged law of the human mind. We grow attached to the mathematics only from finding out their truth; and their utility chiefly consists (at present) in the contempla-

12. Milton, *Lycidas*, l. 144.

tive pleasure they afford to the student. Lines, points, angles, squares, and circles are not interesting in themselves; they become so by the power of mind exerted in comprehending their properties and relations. People dispute for ever about Hogarth.[13] The question has not in one respect been fairly stated. The merit of his pictures does not so much depend on the nature of the subject, as on the knowledge displayed of it, on the number of ideas they excite, on the fund of thought and observation contained in them. They are to be looked on as works of science; they gratify our love of truth; they fill up the void of the mind: they are a series of plates of natural history, and also of that most interesting part of natural history, the history of man. The superiority of high art over the common or mechanical consists in combining truth of imitation with beauty and grandeur of subject. The historical painter is superior to the flower-painter, because he combines or ought to combine human interests and passions with the same power of imitating external nature; or, indeed, with greater, for the greatest difficulty of imitation is the power of imitating expression. The difficulty of copying increases with our knowledge of the object; and that again with the interest we take in it. The same argument might be applied to show that the poet and painter of imagination are superior to the mere philosopher or man of science, because they exercise the powers of reason and intellect combined with nature and passion. They treat of the highest categories of the human soul, pleasure and pain.

From the foregoing train of reasoning, we may easily account for the too great tendency of art to run into pedantry and affectation. There is "a pleasure in art which none but artists feel."[14] They see beauty where others see nothing of the sort, in wrinkles, deformity, and old age. They see it in Titian's Schoolmaster as well as in Raphael's Galatea; in the dark shadows of Rembrandt as well as in the splendid colours of Rubens; in an angel's or a butterfly's wing. They see with different eyes from the multitude. But

13. That is, about the value of his work as fine art. Hogarth frequently chose "low" topics to depict in his prints and paintings, e.g., "Gin Lane" and "Beer Street" (1750).

14. Cf. John Dryden, *The Spanish Friar* (1681), ii.2 ("There is a pleasure in being mad which none but madmen know"), frequently adapted, for instance by Cowper in *The Task,* II.285–86 ("There is a pleasure in poetic pains, / Which only poets know").

true genius, though it has new sources of pleasure opened to it, does not lose its sympathy with humanity. It combines truth of imitation with effect, the parts with the whole, the means with the end. The mechanic artist sees only that which nobody else sees, and is conversant only with the technical language and difficulties of his art. A painter, if shown a picture, will generally dwell upon the academic skill displayed in it, and the knowledge of the received rules of composition. A musician, if asked to play a tune, will select that which is the most difficult and the least intelligible. The poet will be struck with the harmony of versification, or the elaborateness of the arrangement in a composition. The conceits in Shakespeare were his greatest delight; and improving upon this perverse method of judging, the German writers, Goethe and Schiller, look upon Werter and The Robbers as the worst of all their works, because they are the most popular. Some artists among ourselves have carried the same principle to a singular excess.* If professors themselves are liable to this kind of pedantry, connoisseurs and dilettanti, who have less sensibility and more affectation, are almost wholly swayed by it. They see nothing in a picture but the execution. They are proud of their knowledge in proportion as it is a secret. The worst judges of pictures in the United Kingdom are, first, picture-dealers; next, perhaps, the Directors of the British Institution; and after them, in all probability, the Members of the Royal Academy.

18 February 1816

No. 29. On Gusto

Gusto in art is power or passion defining any object. It is not so difficult to explain this term in what relates to expression (of which it may be said to be

---

*We here allude particularly to Turner, the ablest landscape painter now living, whose pictures are, however, too much abstractions of aerial perspective, and representations not so properly of the objects of nature as of the medium through which they are seen. They are the triumph of the knowledge of the artist, and of the power of the pencil over the barrenness of the subject. They are pictures of the elements of air, earth, and water. The artist delights to go back to the first chaos of the world, or to that state of things when the waters were separated from the dry land, and light from darkness, but as yet no living thing nor tree bearing fruit was seen upon the face of the earth. All is "without form and void." Some one said of his landscapes that they were *pictures of nothing, and very like.*

the highest degree) as in what relates to things without expression, to the natural appearances of objects, as mere colour or form. In one sense, however, there is hardly any object entirely devoid of expression, without some character of power belonging to it, some precise association with pleasure or pain: and it is in giving this truth of character from the truth of feeling, whether in the highest or the lowest degree, but always in the highest degree of which the subject is capable, that gusto consists.

There is a gusto in the colouring of Titian. Not only do his heads seem to think—his bodies seem to feel. This is what the Italians mean by the *morbidezza* of his flesh-colour. It seems sensitive and alive all over; not merely to have the look and texture of flesh, but the feeling in itself. For example, the limbs of his female figures have a luxurious softness and delicacy, which appears conscious of the pleasure of the beholder. As the objects themselves in nature would produce an impression on the sense, distinct from every other object, and having something divine in it, which the heart owns and the imagination consecrates, the objects in the picture preserve the same impression, absolute, unimpaired, stamped with all the truth of passion, the pride of the eye, and the charm of beauty. Rubens makes his flesh-colour like flowers; Albano's is like ivory;[15] Titian's is like flesh, and like nothing else. It is as different from that of other painters, as the skin is from a piece of white or red drapery thrown over it. The blood circulates here and there, the blue veins just appear, the rest is distinguished throughout only by that sort of tingling sensation to the eye, which the body feels within itself. This is gusto. Vandyke's flesh-colour, though it has great truth and purity, wants gusto. It has not the internal character, the living principle in it. It is a smooth surface, not a warm, moving mass. It is painted without passion, with indifference. The hand only has been concerned. The impression slides off from the eye, and does not, like the tones of Titian's pencil, leave a sting behind it in the mind of the spectator. The eye does not acquire a taste or appetite for what it sees. In a word, gusto in painting is where the impression made on one sense excites by affinity those of another.

Michael Angelo's forms are full of gusto. They every where obtrude the sense of power upon the eye. His limbs convey an idea of muscular

15. The Italian Renaissance painter Francesco Albani (1578–1660).

strength, of moral grandeur, and even of intellectual dignity: they are firm, commanding, broad, and massy, capable of executing with ease the determined purposes of the will. His faces have no other expression than his figures, conscious power and capacity. They appear only to think what they shall do, and to know that they can do it. This is what is meant by saying that his style is hard and masculine. It is the reverse of Correggio's, which is effeminate. That is, the gusto of Michael Angelo consists in expressing energy of will without proportionable sensibility, Correggio's in expressing exquisite sensibility without energy of will. In Correggio's faces as well as figures we see neither bones nor muscles, but then what a soul is there, full of sweetness and of grace—pure, playful, soft, angelical! There is sentiment enough in a hand painted by Correggio to set up a school of history painters. Whenever we look at the hands of Correggio's women or of Raphael's, we always wish to touch them.

Again, Titian's landscapes have a prodigious gusto, both in the colouring and forms. We shall never forget one that we saw many years ago in the Orleans Gallery of Actæon hunting.[16] It had a brown, mellow, autumnal look. The sky was the colour of stone. The winds seemed to sing through the rustling branches of the trees, and already you might hear the twanging of bows resound through the tangled mazes of the wood. Mr. West, we understand, has this landscape. He will know if the description of it is just. The landscape back-ground of the St. Peter Martyr is another well known instance of the power of this great painter to give a romantic interest and an appropriate character to the objects of his pencil, where every circumstance adds to the effect of the scene,—the bold trunks of the tall forest trees, the trailing ground plants, with that cold convent spire rising in the distance, amidst the blue sapphire mountains and the golden sky.[17]

Rubens has a great deal of gusto in his Fauns and Satyrs, and in all that expresses motion, but in nothing else. Rembrandt has it in everything;

16. Titian's *Diana and Actaeon* hung in the Orleans Gallery, an exhibition of Old Masters paintings named for their original owner, the Regent of Orleans, and placed on sale in London in December 1798. For the Roman myth, see chap. 9, n. 19.

17. Benjamin West (1738–1820) was a historical painter under George III and president of the Royal Academy from 1792. Hazlitt saw Titian's *Saint Peter the Martyr* at the Louvre and in Venice; it was destroyed by fire in 1867.

every thing in his pictures has a tangible character. If he puts a diamond in the ear of a burgomaster's wife, it is of the first water; and his furs and stuffs are proof against a Russian winter. Raphael's gusto was only in expression; he had no idea of the character of anything but the human form. The dryness and poverty of his style in other respects is a phenomenon in the art. His trees are like sprigs of grass stuck in a book of botanical specimens. Was it that Raphael never had time to go beyond the walls of Rome? That he was always in the streets, at church, or in the bath? He was not one of the Society of Arcadians.*

Claude's landscapes, perfect as they are, want gusto.[18] This is not easy to explain. They are perfect abstractions of the visible images of things; they speak the visible language of nature truly. They resemble a mirror or a microscope. To the eye only they are more perfect than any other landscapes that ever were or will be painted; they give more of nature, as cognizable by one sense alone; but they lay an equal stress on all visible impressions. They do not interpret one sense by another; they do not distinguish the character of different objects as we are taught, and can only be taught, to distinguish them by their effect on the different senses. That is, his eye wanted imagination: it did not strongly sympathise with his other faculties. He saw the atmosphere, but he did not feel it. He painted the trunk of a tree or a rock in the foreground as smooth—with as complete an abstraction of the gross, tangible impression, as any other part of the picture. His trees are perfectly beautiful, but quite immovable; they have a look of enchantment. In short, his landscapes are unequalled imitations of nature, released from its subjection to the elements, as if all objects were become a delightful fairy vision, and the eye had rarefied and refined away the other senses.

The gusto in the Greek statues is of a very singular kind. The sense of

---

*Raphael not only could not paint a landscape; he could not paint people in a landscape. He could not have painted the heads or the figures, or even the dresses, of the St. Peter Martyr. His figures have always an *in-door* look, that is, a set, determined, voluntary, dramatic character, arising from their own passions, or a watchfulness of those of others, and want that wild uncertainty of expression, which is connected with the accidents of nature and the changes of the elements. He has nothing *romantic* about him.

18. Claude Lorrain (1602–82) was a French Baroque painter who helped define the picturesque landscape.

perfect form nearly occupies the whole mind, and hardly suffers it to dwell on any other feeling. It seems enough for them *to be,* without acting or suffering. Their forms are ideal, spiritual. Their beauty is power. By their beauty they are raised above the frailties of pain or passion; by their beauty they are deified.

The infinite quantity of dramatic invention in Shakespeare takes from his gusto. The power he delights to show is not intense, but discursive. He never insists on anything as much as he might, except a quibble. Milton has great gusto. He repeats his blows twice; grapples with and exhausts his subject. His imagination has a double relish of its objects, an inveterate attachment to the things he describes, and to the words describing them.

> ———Or where Chineses drive
> With sails and wind their *cany* waggons *light.*
> * * * * * * *
> Wild above rule or art, *enormous* bliss.[19]

There is a gusto in Pope's compliments, in Dryden's satires, and Prior's tales; and among prose writers Boccacio and Rabelais had the most of it. We will only mention one other work which appears to us to be full of gusto, and that is the *Beggar's Opera.*[20] If it is not, we are altogether mistaken in our notions on this delicate subject.

26 May 1816

No. 46. On Common-Place Critics

"Nor can I think what thoughts they can conceive."[21]

We have already given some account of common-place people;[22] we shall in this number attempt a description of another class of the community, who

---

19. See Milton, *Paradise Lost,* III.438–39 and V.297.

20. John Gay's comic satire *The Beggar's Opera* (1728) was also the subject of a famous painting by Hogarth.

21. John Dryden, *The Hind and the Panther* (1687), I.315.

22. Leigh Hunt's "On Common-Place People" (1815) in chap. 10 of this volume.

may be called (by way of distinction) common-place critics. The former are a set of people who have no opinions of their own, and do not pretend to have any; the latter are a set of people who have no opinions of their own, but who affect to have one upon every subject you can mention. The former are a very honest, good sort of people, who are contented to pass for what they are; the latter are a very pragmatical, troublesome sort of people, who would pass for what they are not, and try to put off their common-place notions in all companies and on all subjects, as something of their own. They are of both species, the grave and the gay; and it is hard to say which is the most tiresome.

A common-place critic has something to say upon every occasion, and he always tells you either what is not true, or what you knew before, or what is not worth knowing. He is a person who thinks by proxy, and talks by rote. He differs with you, not because he thinks you are in the wrong, but because he thinks somebody else will think so. Nay, it would be well if he stopped here; but he will undertake to misrepresent you by anticipation, lest others should misunderstand you, and will set you right, not only in opinions which you have, but in those which you may be supposed to have. Thus, if you say that *Bottom* the weaver is a character that has not had justice done to it, he shakes his head, is afraid you will be thought extravagant, and wonders you should think the *Midsummer Night's Dream* the finest of all Shakespeare's plays. He judges of matters of taste and reasoning as he does of dress and fashion, by the prevailing tone of good company; and you would as soon persuade him to give up any sentiment that is current there, as to wear the hind part of his coat before. By the best company, of which he is perpetually talking, he means persons who live on their own estates, and other people's ideas. By the opinion of the world, to which he pays and expects you to pay great deference, he means that of a little circle of his own, where he hears and is heard. Again, *good sense* is a phrase constantly in his mouth, by which he does not mean his own sense or that of anybody else, but the opinions of a number of persons who have agreed to take their opinions on trust from others. If any one observes that there is something better than common sense, viz., *uncommon* sense, he thinks this a bad joke. If you object to the opinions of the majority, as often arising from ignorance or prejudice, he appeals from them to the sensible and well-informed; and if you say there may be other persons as sensible and well informed as himself and his friends, he smiles at your presumption. If you attempt to prove anything to him, it is in vain, for he is not thinking of what you say, but of what will be thought of it. The stronger your reasons, the more incorrigible he thinks you; and he looks upon any attempt to expose his gratuitous assumptions as the wandering of a disordered imagination. His notions are like plaster figures cast in a mould, as brittle as they are hollow; but they will break before you can make them give way. In fact, he is the representative of a large part of the community, the shallow, the vain, and indolent, of those who have time to talk, and are not bound to think: and he considers any deviation from the select forms of common-place, or the accredited language of conventional impertinence, as compromising the authority under which he acts in his diplomatic capacity. It is wonderful how this class of people agree with one another; how they herd together in all their opinions; what a tact they have for folly; what an instinct for absurdity; what a sympathy in sentiment; how they find one another out by infallible signs, like Freemasons! The secret of this unanimity and strict accord is, that not any one of them ever admits any opinion that can cost the least effort of mind in arriving at, or of courage in declaring it. Folly is as consistent with itself as wisdom: there is a certain level of thought and sentiment, which the weakest minds, as well as the strongest, find out as best adapted to them; and you as regularly come to the same conclusions, by looking no farther than the surface, as if you dug to the centre of the earth! You know beforehand what a critic of this class will say on almost every subject the first time he sees you, the next time, the time after that, and so on to the end of the chapter. The following list of his opinions may be relied on: it is pretty certain that before you have been in the room with him ten minutes, he will give you to understand that Shakespeare was a great but irregular genius. Again, he thinks it a question whether any one of his plays, if brought out now for the first time, would succeed. He thinks that *Macbeth* would be the most likely, from the music which has been since introduced into it.[23] He has some doubts as to the superiority of the French School over us in

23. Sir William D'Avenant's 1672 production of *Macbeth* introduced music traditionally credited to Matthew Locke, though recently it has been attributed variously to Henry Purcell, John Eccles, and Richard Leveridge.

tragedy,[24] and observes, that Hume and Adam Smith were both of that opinion. He thinks Milton's pedantry a great blemish in his writings, and that *Paradise Lost* has many prosaic passages in it. He conceives that genius does not always imply taste, and that wit and judgment are very different faculties. He considers Dr. Johnson as a great critic and moralist, and that his Dictionary was a work of prodigious erudition and vast industry; but that some of the anecdotes of him in Boswell are trifling. He conceives that Mr. Locke was a very original and profound thinker. He thinks Gibbon's style vigorous but florid. He wonders that the author of *Junius* was never found out.[25] He thinks Pope's translation of the *Iliad* an improvement on the simplicity of the original, which was necessary to fit it to the taste of modern readers. He thinks there is a great deal of grossness in the old comedies; and that there has been a great improvement in the morals of the higher classes since the reign of Charles II. He thinks the reign of Queen Anne the golden period of our literature, but that, upon the whole, we have no English writer equal to Voltaire. He speaks of Boccacio as a very licentious writer, and thinks the wit in Rabelais quite extravagant, though he never read either of them. He cannot get through Spenser's *Fairy Queen,* and pronounces all allegorical poetry tedious. He prefers Smollett to Fielding, and discovers more knowledge of the world in *Gil Blas* than in *Don Quixote.* Richardson he thinks very minute and tedious. He thinks the French Revolution has done a great deal of harm to the cause of liberty; and blames Buonaparte for being so ambitious. He reads the *Edinburgh* and *Quarterly Reviews,* and thinks as they do. He is shy of having an opinion on a new actor or a new singer; for the public do not always agree with the newspapers. He thinks that the moderns have great advantages over the ancients in many respects. He thinks Jeremy Bentham a greater man than Aristotle.[26] He can see no reason why artists of the present day should not paint as well as Raphael or Titian. For instance, he thinks there is something

24. That is, French neoclassical tragedy by the playwrights Pierre Corneille (1609–84), Jean Racine (1639–99), and Molière (1622–73), among others.

25. Junius was the pseudonym, based probably on the Roman patriot Lucius Junius Brutus, of a writer who contributed a series of letters to *The Public Advertiser* from 1769 to 1772.

26. Jeremy Bentham (1748–1832) is known as the father of Utilitarianism.

very elegant and classical in Mr. Westall's drawings. He has no doubt that Sir Joshua Reynolds's Lectures were written by Burke.[27] He considers Horne Tooke's account of the conjunction *That* very ingenious, and holds that no writer can be called elegant who uses the present for the subjunctive mood, who says *If it is* for *If it be*.[28] He thinks Hogarth a great master of low, comic humour; and Cobbett a coarse, vulgar writer. He often talks of men of liberal education, and men without education, as if that made much difference. He judges of people by their pretensions; and pays attention to their opinions according to their dress and rank in life. If he meets with a fool, he does not find him out; and if he meets with any one wiser than himself, he does not know what to make of him. He thinks that manners are of great consequence to the common intercourse of life. He thinks it difficult to prove the existence of any such thing as original genius, or to fix a general standard of taste. He does not think it possible to define what wit is. In religion, his opinions are liberal. He considers all enthusiasm as a degree of madness, particularly to be guarded against by young minds; and believes that truth lies in the middle, between the extremes of right and wrong. He thinks that the object of poetry is to please; and that astronomy is a very pleasing and useful study. He thinks all this, and a great deal more, that amounts to nothing. We wonder we have remembered one half of it—

For true no-meaning puzzles more than wit.[29]

Though he has an aversion to all new ideas, he likes all new plans and matters-of-fact: the new Schools for All, the Penitentiary, the new Bedlam, the new Steam-Boats, the Gas-Lights, the new Patent Blacking; every thing of that sort but the Bible Society. The Society for the Suppression of Vice he thinks a great nuisance, as every honest man must.[30]

27. The English painter Richard Westall (1765–1836). Sir Joshua Reynolds's *Discourses on Art* were delivered at the Royal Academy from 1769 to 1790.
28. John Horne Tooke (1736–1812), a radical political journalist and pamphleteer, was also a philologist who challenged the distinction between refined and vulgar language, influencing Wordsworth's discussion of "the language really spoken by men."
29. Pope's "Epistle to a Lady," l. 114.
30. The "Schools for All" refer to the Romantic interest in school reform and

In a word, a common-place critic is the pedant of polite conversation. He refers to the opinion of Lord M. or Lady G. with the same air of significance that the learned pedant does to the authority of Cicero or Virgil: retails the wisdom of the day, as the anecdote-monger does the wit; and carries about with him the sentiments of people of a certain respectability in life, as the dancing-master does their air, or their valets their clothes.

24 November 1816

The Plain Speaker
No. 20. On Reading Old Books

I hate to read new books. There are twenty or thirty volumes that I have read over and over again, and these are the only ones that I have any desire ever to read at all. It was a long time before I could bring myself to sit down to the Tales of My Landlord, but now that author's works have made a considerable addition to my scanty library. I am told that some of Lady Morgan's are good, and have been recommended to look into Anastasius; but I have not yet ventured upon that task.[31] A lady, the other day, could not refrain from expressing her surprise to a friend, who said he had been reading Delphine: she asked, If it had not been published some time back? Women judge of books as they do of fashions or complexions, which are admired

---

mass education, as espoused by Andrew Bell, among others. The Penitentiary, London's first modern prison, opened in London in 1816; new Bedlam is Bethlehem Royal Hospital (commonly known as Bedlam), which had moved in 1815. Commercial steam navigation began in Britain in 1812; the London and Westminster Chartered Gas-Light and Coke Company was established in 1810; Warren's Blacking (the shoe polish company for which Charles Dickens once worked) began to rival Day and Martin's patent blacking in advertisements around London at this time. The British and Foreign Bible Society was founded in 1804 and the Society for the Suppression of Vice in 1802.

31. Sir Walter Scott's *Tales of My Landlord* (pseudonymously edited by "Jedediah Cleishbotham") was published in four volumes in Edinburgh and London in 1816. The Irish novels of Sydney Owenson (Lady Morgan) included *St. Clair* (1804), *The Novice of St. Dominick* (1804), and *The Wild Irish Girl* (1806). Thomas Hope's *Anastasius; or, Memoirs of a Greek* came out in three volumes in London in 1819.

only "in their newest gloss."[32] That is not my way. I am not one of those who trouble the circulating libraries much, or pester the booksellers for mail-coach copies of standard periodical publications.[33] I cannot say that I am greatly addicted to black-letter, but I profess myself well versed in the marble bindings of Andrew Millar, in the middle of the last century; nor does my taste revolt at Thurloe's State Papers, in Russia leather; or an ample impression of Sir William Temple's Essays, with a portrait after Sir Godfrey Kneller in front.[34] I do not think altogether the worse of a book for having survived the author a generation or two. I have more confidence in the dead than the living. Contemporary writers may generally be divided into two classes—one's friends or one's foes. Of the first we are compelled to think too well, and of the last we are disposed to think too ill, to receive much genuine pleasure from the perusal, or to judge fairly of the merits of either. One candidate for literary fame, who happens to be of our acquaintance, writes finely, and like a man of genius; but unfortunately has a foolish face, which spoils a delicate passage: another inspires us with the highest respect for his personal talents and character, but does not quite come up to our expectations in print. All these contradictions and petty details interrupt the calm current of our reflections. If you want to know what any of the authors were who lived before our time, and are still objects of anxious inquiry, you have only to look into their works. But the dust and smoke and noise of modern literature have nothing in common with the pure, silent air of immortality.

When I take up a work that I have read before (the oftener the better) I know what I have to expect. The satisfaction is not lessened by being anticipated. When the entertainment is altogether new, I sit down to it as I should to a strange dish,—turn and pick out a bit here and there, and am in

32. Shakespeare, *Macbeth*, I.vii.34. Madame de Staël's novel *Delphine* was published in Geneva in 1802.

33. Mail-coach copies are the first to arrive hot off the press, followed by more cheaply transported copies from the same print run.

34. References to typefaces (black letter) and bindings (marble, Russia leather). On the London bookseller Andrew Millar, see chap. 5, n. 4. A seven-volume edition of the state papers of John Thurloe (1616–68), secretary of state during the Interregnum, appeared in 1742. Sir William Temple (1628–99) was an essayist in the style of Montaigne, and Sir Godfrey Kneller (1646–1723) was the leading portrait painter in London; he painted portraits of Richard Steele and other members of the Kit-Cat Club.

doubt what to think of the composition. There is a want of confidence and security to second appetite. New-fangled books are also like made-dishes in this respect, that they are generally little else than hashes and *rifaccimentos*[35] of what has been served up entire and in a more natural state at other times. Besides, in thus turning to a well-known author, there is not only an assurance that my time will not be thrown away, or my palate nauseated with the most insipid or vilest trash, but I shake hands with, and look an old, tried, and valued friend in the face, compare notes, and chat the hours away. It is true, we form dear friendships with such ideal guests—dearer, alas! and more lasting, than those with our most intimate acquaintance. In reading a book which is an old favourite with me (say the first novel I ever read) I not only have the pleasure of imagination and of a critical relish of the work, but the pleasures of memory added to it. It recalls the same feelings and associations which I had in first reading it, and which I can never have again in any other way. Standard productions of this kind are links in the chain of our conscious being. They bind together the different scattered divisions of our personal identity. They are land-marks and guides in our journey through life. They are pegs and loops on which we can hang up, or from which we can take down, at pleasure, the wardrobe of a moral imagination, the relics of our best affections, the tokens and records of our happiest hours. They are "for thoughts and for remembrance!"[36] They are like Fortunatus's Wishing-Cap—they give us the best riches—those of Fancy; and transport us, not over half the globe, but (which is better) over half our lives, at a word's notice![37]

My father Shandy solaced himself with Bruscambille.[38] Give me for this purpose a volume of Peregrine Pickle or Tom Jones. Open either of

35. Remakings or adaptations of literary works, e.g., setting them in modern times.

36. See Shakespeare, *Hamlet*, IV.v.175–77. Although Hazlitt doesn't set it off in quotations, his phrase "wardrobe of a moral imagination," is from Edmund Burke's *Reflections on the Revolution in France* (1790).

37. Fortunatus's wishing-cap had the magical power to transport the wearer to other places; in the playwright Thomas Dekker's version of the story, *Old Fortunatus* (1599), the cap signifies endless riches.

38. Hazlitt assumes a literary paternity in Walter Shandy of Laurence Sterne's *Tristram Shandy*, whose library contained Jean Gracieux, or Bruscambille's, Prologue "upon long noses" (1610).

them any where—at the Memoirs of Lady Vane, or the adventures at the masquerade with Lady Bellaston, or the disputes between Thwackum and Square, or the escape of Molly Seagrim, or the incident of Sophia and her muff, or the edifying prolixity of her aunt's lecture—and there I find the same delightful, busy, bustling scene as ever, and feel myself the same as when I was first introduced into the midst of it. Nay, sometimes the sight of an odd volume of these good old English authors on a stall, or the name lettered on the back among others on the shelves of a library, answers the purpose, revives the whole train of ideas, and sets "the puppets dallying."[39] Twenty years are struck off the list, and I am a child again. A sage philosopher, who was not a very wise man, said, that he should like very well to be young again, if he could take his experience along with him. This ingenious person did not seem to be aware, by the gravity of his remark, that the great advantage of being young is to be without this weight of experience, which he would fain place upon the shoulders of youth, and which never comes too late with years. Oh! what a privilege to be able to let this hump, like Christian's burden, drop from off one's back, and transport one's self, by the help of a little musty duodecimo, to the time when "ignorance was bliss," and when we first got a peep at the rarée-show of the world, through the glass of fiction—gazing at mankind, as we do at wild beasts in a menagerie, through the bars of their cages,—or at curiosities in a museum, that we must not touch![40] For myself, not only are the old ideas of the contents of the work brought back to my mind in all their vividness, but the old associations of the faces and persons of those I then knew, as they were in their life-time—the place where I sat to read the volume, the day when I got it, the feeling of the air, the fields, the sky—return, and all my early impressions with them. This is better to me—those places, those times, those persons, and those feelings that come across me as I retrace the story and devour the page, are to me better far than the wet sheets of the last new novel from the Ballantyne press, to say nothing of the Minerva press in

39. Shakespeare, Hamlet, III.ii.235. Hazlitt is recalling comic scenes from chap. 88 of *The Adventures of Peregrine Pickle* (1751), by Tobias Smollett, and chaps. 13, 4, 5, among others, of Henry Fielding's *Tom Jones* (1749).

40. For Christian's burden see John Bunyan, *Pilgrim's Progress*, I.iii. "Ignorance was bliss" refers to the penultimate line of Thomas Gray's "Ode on a Distant Prospect of Eton College" (1747).

Leadenhall-street.[41] It is like visiting the scenes of early youth. I think of the time "when I was in my father's house, and my path ran down with butter and honey,"—when I was a little, thoughtless child, and had no other wish or care but to con my daily task, and be happy![42] Tom Jones, I remember, was the first work that broke the spell. It came down in numbers once a fortnight, in Cooke's pocket-edition, embellished with cuts.[43] I had hitherto read only in school-books, and a tiresome ecclesiastical history (with the exception of Mrs. Radcliffe's Romance of the Forest): but this had a different relish with it,—"sweet in the mouth," though not "bitter in the belly."[44] It smacked of the world I lived in, and in which I was to live—and showed me groups, "gay creatures" not "of the element," but of the earth; not "living in the clouds," but travelling the same road that I did;[45] some that had passed on before me, and others that might soon overtake me. My heart had palpitated at the thoughts of a boarding-school ball, or gala-day at Midsummer or Christmas: but the world I had found out in Cooke's edition of the British Novelists was to me a dance through life, a perpetual gala-day. The sixpenny numbers of this work regularly contrived to leave off just in the middle of a sentence, and in the nick of a story, where Tom Jones discovers Square behind the blanket; or where Parson Adams, in the inextricable confusion of events, very undesignedly gets to bed to Mrs. Slip-slop. Let me caution the reader against this impression of Joseph Andrews; for there is a picture of Fanny in it which he should not set his heart on, lest he should never meet with any thing like it; or if he should, it would, perhaps, be better for him that he had not. It was just like———
———![46] With what eagerness I used to look forward to the next number,

41. James Ballantyne was the friend and printer of Sir Walter Scott. The Minerva Press was a London publishing house established by William Lane, owner of a circulating library in Leadenhall Street known for its romances and sentimental novels.

42. See Isaiah 7:15–17, alluded to in letter 359 of Samuel Richardson's *Clarissa* (1748).

43. See chap. 10, n. 57; Cooke published a duodecimo, hence "pocket," edition, with woodcuts.

44. Revelation 10:9–10; Anne Radcliffe's 1791 gothic novel.

45. See Milton, *Comus,* ll. 299–301.

46. Perhaps a reference to Hazlitt's maid (and mistress) Sarah Walker.

310 WILLIAM HAZLITT

and open the prints! Ah! never again shall I feel the enthusiastic delight with which I gazed at the figures, and anticipated the story and adventures of Major Bath and Commodore Trunnion, of Trim and my Uncle Toby, of Don Quixote and Sancho and Dapple, of Gil Blas and Dame Lorenza Sephora, of Laura and the fair Lucretia, whose lips open and shut like buds of roses.[47] To what nameless ideas did they give rise, with what airy delights I filled up the outlines, as I hung in silence over the page! Let me still recall them, that they may breathe fresh life into me, and that I may live that birthday of thought and romantic pleasure over again! Talk of the *ideal!* This is the only true ideal—the heavenly tints of Fancy reflected in the bubbles that float upon the spring-tide of human life.

> Oh! Memory! shield me from the world's poor strife,
> And give those scenes thine everlasting life![48]

The paradox with which I set out is, I hope, less startling than it was; the reader will, by this time, have been let into my secret. Much about the same time, or I believe rather earlier, I took a particular satisfaction in reading Chubb's Tracts, and I often think I will get them again to wade through.[49] There is a high gusto of polemical divinity in them; and you fancy that you hear a club of shoemakers at Salisbury, debating a disputable text from one of St. Paul's Epistles in a workmanlike style, with equal shrewdness and pertinacity. I cannot say much for my metaphysical studies, into which I launched shortly after with great ardour, so as to make a toil of a pleasure. I was presently entangled in the briars and thorns of subtle distinctions, of "fate, free-will, fore-knowledge absolute," though I cannot add that "in their wandering mazes I found no end"; for I did arrive at some

47. Leading characters from Fielding's *Tom Jones* and *Joseph Andrews,* Smollett's *Peregrine Pickle,* Sterne's *Tristram Shandy,* Miguel de Cervantes' *Don Quixote* (translated by Smollett), and Alain-René Lesage's *Gil Blas,* published by Cooke in the 1790s.

48. Unidentified. Hazlitt perhaps doesn't remember the author for he mistakenly attributes these lines to Coleridge's play *Remorse* in his essay "My First Acquaintance with Poets."

49. Thomas Chubb, *A Collection of Tracts, on Various Subjects* (London, 1730).

very satisfactory and potent conclusions; nor will I go so far, however un-grateful the subject might seem, as to exclaim with Marlowe's Faustus—"Would I had never seen Wittenberg, never read book"—that is, never studied such authors as Hartley, Hume, Berkeley, &c. Locke's Essay on the Human Understanding is, however, a work from which I never derived ei-ther pleasure or profit; and Hobbes, dry and powerful as he is, I did not read till long afterwards.[50] I read a few poets, which did not much hit my taste, for I would have the reader understand, I am deficient in the faculty of imagination; but I fell early upon French romances and philosophy, and devoured them tooth-and-nail. Many a dainty repast have I made of the New Eloise;—the description of the kiss; the excursion on the water; the letter of St. Preux, recalling the time of their first loves; and the account of Julia's death; these I read over and over again with unspeakable delight and wonder.[51] Some years after, when I met with this work again, I found I had lost nearly my whole relish for it (except some few parts) and was, I re-member, very much mortified with the change in my taste, which I sought to attribute to the smallness and gilt edges of the edition I had bought, and its being perfumed with rose-leaves. Nothing could exceed the gravity, the solemnity with which I carried home and read the Dedication to the Social Contract, with some other pieces of the same author, which I had picked up at a stall in a coarse leathern cover. Of the Confessions I have spoken else-where, and may repeat what I have said—"Sweet is the dew of their mem-ory, and pleasant the balm of their recollection!"[52] Their beauties are not "scattered like stray-gifts o'er the earth," but sown thick on the page, rich and rare. I wish I had never read the Emilius, or read it with less implicit faith. I had no occasion to pamper my natural aversion to affectation or pre-

50. Quotations are from Milton, *Paradise Lost*, II.560–61, and Christopher Marlowe, *Doctor Faustus*, XIV.20–21; David Hartley (1705–57), David Hume (1711–76), and George Berkeley (1685–1753) were British Enlightenment phi-losophers following John Locke (1632–1704) and Thomas Hobbes (1588–1679).

51. Jean-Jacques Rousseau's sentimental novel *Julie; ou, La Nouvelle Héloise* (Julie; or, The New Eloise, 1760) was translated into English in 1773. Below Hazlitt remembers Rousseau's *The Social Contract* (1762), *Confessions* (1782), and *Emile; or, On Education* (1762), i.e., the *Emilius*.

52. Hazlitt quotes from his own essay, "On the Character of Rousseau," no. 32 of *The Round Table*.

tence, by romantic and artificial means. I had better have formed myself on the model of Sir Fopling Flutter.[53] There is a class of persons whose virtues and most shining qualities sink in, and are concealed by, an absorbent ground of modesty and reserve; and such a one I do, without vanity, profess myself.* Now these are the very persons who are likely to attach themselves to the character of Emilius, and of whom it is sure to be the bane. This dull, phlegmatic, retiring humour is not in a fair way to be corrected, but confirmed and rendered desperate, by being in that work held up as an object of imitation, as an example of simplicity and magnanimity—by coming upon us with all the recommendations of novelty, surprise, and superiority to the prejudices of the world—by being stuck upon a pedestal, made amiable, dazzling, a *leurre de dupe!*[54] The reliance on solid worth which it inculcates, the preference of sober truth to gaudy tinsel, hangs like a millstone round the neck of the imagination—"a load to sink a navy"—impedes our progress, and blocks up every prospect in life.[55] A man, to get on, to be successful, conspicuous, applauded, should not retire upon the centre of his conscious resources, but be always at the circumference of appearances. He must envelop himself in a halo of mystery—he must ride in an equipage of opinion—he must walk with a train of self-conceit following him—he must not strip himself to a buff-jerkin, to the doublet and hose of his real merits, but must surround himself with a *cortege* of prejudices, like the signs of the Zodiac—he must seem any thing but what he is, and then he may pass for any thing he pleases. The world loves to be amused by hollow professions, to be deceived by flattering appearances, to live in a state of hallucination; and can forgive every thing but the plain, downright, simple honest truth—such as we see it chalked out in the character of Emilius.— To return from this digression, which is a little out of place here.

Books have in a great measure lost their power over me; nor can I re-

---

*Nearly the same sentiment was wittily and happily expressed by a friend, who had some lottery puffs [advertisements], which he had been employed to write, returned on his hands for their too great severity of thought and classical terseness of style, and who observed on that occasion, that "Modest merit never can succeed!"

53. An allusion to Wordsworth's "Stray Pleasures," ll. 27–28, and to George Etherege's Restoration comedy *The Man of Mode; or, Sir Fopling Flutter* (1676).
54. A deceiving lure.
55. See Shakespeare, *Henry VIII,* III.ii.384.

vive the same interest in them as formerly. I perceive when a thing is good, rather than feel it. It is true,

Marcian Colonna is a dainty book;[56]

and the reading of Mr. Keats's Eve of Saint Agnes lately made me regret that I was not young again. The beautiful and tender images there conjured up, "come like shadows—so depart."[57] The "tiger-moth's wings," which he has spread over his rich poetic blazonry, just flit across my fancy; the gorgeous twilight window which he has painted over again in his verse, to me "blushes" almost in vain "with blood of queens and kings."[58] I know how I should have felt at one time in reading such passages; and that is all. The sharp luscious flavour, the fine *aroma* is fled, and nothing but the stalk, the bran, the husk of literature is left. If any one were to ask me what I read now, I might answer with my Lord Hamlet in the play—"Words, words, words."—"What is the matter?"—"*Nothing!*"[59]—They have scarce a meaning. But it was not always so. There was a time when to my thinking, every word was a flower or a pearl, like those which dropped from the mouth of the little peasant-girl in the Fairy tale, or like those that fall from the great preacher in the Caledonian Chapel![60] I drank of the stream of knowledge that tempted, but did not mock my lips, as of the river of life, freely. How eagerly I slaked my thirst of German sentiment, "as the hart that panteth for the water-springs"; how I bathed and revelled, and added my floods of tears to Goethe's Sorrows of Werter, and to Schiller's Robbers—

56. Hazlitt quotes Charles Lamb, "To the Author of Poems, Published Under the Name of Barry Cornwall [pen name for Bryan Waller Procter]" (1820), l. 5; See Cornwall's *Marcian Colonna: An Italian Tale, with Three Dramatic Scenes and Other Poems* (1820).

57. Shakespeare, *Macbeth,* IV.i.127.

58. Keats, "The Eve of St. Agnes," ll. 213, 216.

59. See Shakespeare, *Hamlet,* II.ii.194–95.

60. A reference to Charles Perrault's fairy tale "Diamonds and Toads." The Scottish divine Edward Irving (1792–1834) enjoyed tremendous success as a preacher at the Caledonian Church in Hatton Garden, London. Hazlitt features him in *The Spirit of the Age.*

Giving my stock of more to that which had too much!

I read, and assented with all my soul to Coleridge's fine Sonnet, beginning—

Schiller! that hour I would have wish'd to die,
If through the shuddering midnight I had sent,
From the dark dungeon of the tow'r time-rent,
That fearful voice, a famish'd father's cry![61]

I believe I may date my insight into the mysteries of poetry from the
commencement of my acquaintance with the authors of the Lyrical Ballads;
at least, my discrimination of the higher sorts—not my predilection for
such writers as Goldsmith or Pope: nor do I imagine they will say I got my
liking for the Novelists, or the comic writers, for the characters of Valentine, Tattle, or Miss Prue, from them.[62] If so, I must have got from them
what they never had themselves. In points where poetic diction and conception are concerned, I may be at a loss, and liable to be imposed upon:
but in forming an estimate of passages relating to common life and manners, I cannot think I am a plagiarist from any man. I there "know my cue
without a prompter."[63] I may say of such studies—*Intus et in cute.*[64] I am
just able to admire those literal touches of observation and description,
which persons of loftier pretensions overlook and despise. I think I comprehend something of the characteristic part of Shakespeare; and in him in-

61. Hazlitt quotes from Psalm 42:1, Shakespeare's *As You Like It* (II.i.48–
49), and Coleridge's "To the Author of 'The Robbers'" (referring to Friedrich
Schiller's 1781 play by that name). Johann Wolfgang von Goethe's sentimental
novel *The Sorrows of Young Werther* (1774) enjoyed immense popularity.
62. References to the *Lyrical Ballads* (1798) by Coleridge and Wordsworth,
the comic characters Timothy Tattle from Addison's *Tatler* no. 165, Miss Prue from
William Congreve's *Love for Love* (1695), and Valentine from Shakespeare's *The Two
Gentlemen of Verona.*
63. See Shakespeare, *Othello,* I.ii.84–85.
64. "Inside and under the skin," from Persius, Satire III.30, suggesting that
the poet must bare himself inside-out to posterity; Rousseau uses the line as the epigraph to his *Confessions.*

deed, all is characteristic, even the nonsense and poetry. I believe it was the celebrated Sir Humphrey Davy[65] who used to say, that Shakespeare was rather a metaphysician than a poet. At any rate, it was not ill said. I wish that I had sooner known the dramatic writers contemporary with Shakespeare; for in looking them over about a year ago, I almost revived my old passion for reading, and my old delight in books, though they were very nearly new to me. The Periodical Essayists I read long ago. The Spectator I liked extremely: but the Tatler took my fancy most. I read the others soon after, the Rambler, the Adventurer, the World, the Connoisseur: I was not sorry to get to the end of them, and have no desire to go regularly through them again. I consider myself a thorough adept in Richardson. I like the longest of his novels best, and think no part of them tedious; nor should I ask to have any thing better to do than to read them from beginning to end, to take them up when I chose, and lay them down when I was tired, in some old family mansion in the country, till every word and syllable relating to the bright Clarissa, the divine Clementina, the beautiful Pamela,[66] "with every trick and line of their sweet favour," were once more "graven in my heart's tables."* I have a sneaking kindness for Mackenzie's Julia de Roubigné—for the deserted mansion, and straggling gilliflowers on the mouldering garden-wall; and still more for his Man of Feeling; not that it is better, nor so good; but at the time I read it, I sometimes thought of the heroine, Miss Walton, and of Miss———together, and "that ligament, fine

---

*During the peace of Amiens, a young English officer, of the name of Lovelace, was presented at Buonaparte's levee. Instead of the usual question, "Where have you served, Sir?" the First Consul immediately addressed him, "I perceive your name, Sir, is the same as that of the hero of Richardson's Romance!" Here was a Consul. The young man's uncle, who was called Lovelace, told me this anecdote while we were stopping together at Calais. I had also been thinking that his was the same name as that of the hero of Richardson's Romance. This is one of my reasons for liking Buonaparte.

65. The English chemist Humphry Davy (1778–1829) was a friend of Coleridge and a poet himself.

66. Hazlitt eulogizes Samuel Richardson's characters Clarissa Harlowe (and Lovelace from the same novel), Pamela Andrews, and Clementina (from *Sir Charles Grandison*, 1753); he quotes Shakespeare, *All's Well That Ends Well*, I.i.95, and Proverbs 3:3.

as it was, was never broken!"[67] One of the poets that I have always read with most pleasure, and can wander about in for ever with a sort of voluptuous indolence, is Spenser; and I like Chaucer even better. The only writer among the Italians I can pretend to any knowledge of, is Boccacio, and of him I cannot express half my admiration. His story of the Hawk I could read and think of from day to day,[68] just as I would look at a picture of Titian's!

I remember, as long ago as the year 1798, going to a neighbouring town (Shrewsbury, where Farquhar has laid the plot of his Recruiting Officer) and bringing home with me, "at one proud swoop,"[69] a copy of Milton's Paradise Lost, and another of Burke's Reflections on the French Revolution—both which I have still; and I still recollect, when I see the covers, the pleasure with which I dipped into them as I returned with my double prize. I was set up for one while. That time is past "with all its giddy raptures": but I am still anxious to preserve its memory, "embalmed with odours."[70] With respect to the first of these works, I would be permitted to remark here in passing, that it is a sufficient answer to the German criticism which has since been started against the character of Satan (viz. that it is not one of disgusting deformity, or pure, defecated malice) to say that Milton has there drawn, not the abstract principle of evil, not a devil incarnate, but a fallen angel. This is the scriptural account, and the poet has followed it. We may safely retain such passages as that well-known one—

————His form had not yet lost
All her original brightness; nor appear'd
Less than archangel ruin'd; and the excess
Of glory obscur'd————

67. Laurence Sterne, Tristram Shandy, VI.x. Hazlitt recalls Henry Mackenzie's sentimental novel The Man of Feeling (1771) and his epistolary Julia de Roubigné (1777).

68. Giovanni Boccaccio's tale "Currado's Cook" from The Decameron (5th day, 9th story).

69. See Shakespeare, Macbeth, IV.iii.220. George Farquhar's The Recruiting Officer was performed at Drury Lane Theatre in 1706.

70. See Wordsworth, "Lines Composed a Few Miles Above Tintern Abbey," ll. 83–85; Milton, Paradise Lost, II.842–43.

for the theory, which is opposed to them, "falls flat upon the grunsel edge, and shames its worshippers."[71] Let us hear no more then of this monkish cant, and bigotted outcry for the restoration of the horns and tail of the devil! Again, as to the other work, Burke's Reflections, I took a particular pride and pleasure in it, and read it to myself and others for months afterwards. I had reason for my prejudice in favour of this author. To understand an adversary is some praise: to admire him is more. I thought I did both: I knew I did one. From the first time I ever cast my eyes on any thing of Burke's (which was an extract from his Letter to a Noble Lord in a three-times a week paper, The St. James's Chronicle, in 1796), I said to myself, "This is true eloquence: this is a man pouring out his mind on paper." All other style seemed to me pedantic and impertinent. Dr. Johnson's was walking on stilts; and even Junius's (who was at that time a favourite with me) with all his terseness, shrunk up into little antithetic points and well-trimmed sentences.[72] But Burke's style was forked and playful as the lightning, crested like the serpent. He delivered plain things on a plain ground; but when he rose, there was no end of his flights and circumgyrations—and in this very Letter, "he, like an eagle in a dove-cot, fluttered *his* Volscians" (the Duke of Bedford and the Earl of Lauderdale)* "in Corioli."[73] I did not care for his doctrines. I was then, and am still, proof against their contagion; but I admired the author, and was considered as not a very staunch partisan of the opposite side, though I thought myself that an abstract proposition was one thing—a masterly transition, a brilliant metaphor, another. I conceived too that he might be wrong in his main argument, and yet deliver fifty truths in arriving at a false conclusion. I remember Coleridge assuring me, as a poetical and political set-off to my sceptical admiration, that Wordsworth had written an Essay on Marriage,[74] which, for manly thought and nervous expression, he deemed incomparably superior. As I had not, at that time, seen any specimens of Mr. Wordsworth's prose

*He is there called "Citizen Lauderdale." Is this the present Earl? [It was in fact the same James Maitland, eighth Earl of Lauderdale.]

71. See Milton, *Paradise Lost,* I.591–94 and 460–61.

72. For Junius see n. 25.

73. See Shakespeare, *Coriolanus,* V.vi.115–16. Hazlitt's note refers to Burke's *Letter to a Noble Lord*.

74. This essay is not known to be extant.

style, I could not venture my doubts on the subject. If there are greater prose-writers than Burke, they either lie out of my course of study, or are beyond my sphere of comprehension. I am too old to be a convert to a new mythology of genius. The niches are occupied, the tables are full. If such is still my admiration of this man's misapplied powers, what must it have been at a time when I myself was in vain trying, year after year, to write a single Essay, nay, a single page or sentence; when I regarded the wonders of his pen with the longing eyes of one who was dumb and a changeling; and when, to be able to convey the slightest conception of my meaning to others in words, was the height of an almost hopeless ambition! But I never measured others' excellences by my own defects: though a sense of my own incapacity, and of the steep, impassable ascent from me to them, made me regard them with greater awe and fondness. I have thus run through most of my early studies and favourite authors, some of whom I have since criticised more at large. Whether those observations will survive me, I neither know nor do I much care: but to the works themselves, "worthy of all acceptation,"[75] and to the feelings they have always excited in me since I could distinguish a meaning in language, nothing shall ever prevent me from looking back with gratitude and triumph. To have lived in the cultivation of an intimacy with such works, and to have familiarly relished such names, is not to have lived quite in vain.

There are other authors whom I have never read, and yet whom I have frequently had a great desire to read, from some circumstance relating to them. Among these is Lord Clarendon's History of the Grand Rebellion, after which I have a hankering, from hearing it spoken of by good judges—from my interest in the events, and knowledge of the characters from other sources, and from having seen fine portraits of most of them. I like to read a well-penned character, and Clarendon is said to have been a master in this way. I should like to read Froissart's Chronicles, Hollinshed and Stowe, and Fuller's Worthies.[76] I intend, whenever I can, to read Beau-

75. I Timothy 1:15.

76. Edward Hyde, first Earl of Clarendon, *The History of the Grand Rebellion, Containing the Most Remarkable Transactions from the Beginning of the Reign of King Charles I to the Happy Restoration* (1717); Jean Froissart's *Chronicles* (1523), Raphael Holinshed's *Chronicles of England, Scotland, and Ireland* (1587), John Stow's *A Summarye of the Chronicles of England* (1570), and Thomas Fuller's *The Worthies of England* (1592) were all well-known histories.

mont and Fletcher all through. There are fifty-two of their plays, and I have only read a dozen or fourteen of them. A Wife for a Month, and Thierry and Theodoret, are, I am told, delicious, and I can believe it. I should like to read the speeches in Thucydides, and Guicciardini's History of Florence, and Don Quixote in the original. I have often thought of reading the Loves of Persiles and Sigismunda, and the Galatea of the same author. But I somehow reserve them like "another Yarrow."[77] I should also like to read the last new novel (if I could be sure it was so) of the author of Waverley: no one would be more glad than I to find it the best!

February 1821

Table-Talk
No. 24. On Familiar Style

It is not easy to write a familiar style. Many people mistake a familiar for a vulgar style, and suppose that to write without affectation is to write at random. On the contrary, there is nothing that requires more precision, and, if I may so say, purity of expression, than the style I am speaking of. It utterly rejects not only all unmeaning pomp, but all low, cant phrases, and loose, unconnected, *slipshod* allusions. It is not to take the first word that offers, but the best word in common use; it is not to throw words together in any combinations we please, but to follow and avail ourselves of the true idiom of the language. To write a genuine familiar or truly English style, is to write as any one would speak in common conversation, who had a thorough command and choice of words, or who could discourse with ease, force, and perspicuity, setting aside all pedantic and oratorical flourishes. Or to give another illustration, to write naturally is the same thing in regard to common conversation, as to read naturally is in regard to common speech. It does not follow that it is an easy thing to give the true accent and inflection to the words you utter, because you do not attempt to rise above the

77. References to the seventeenth-century playwrights Francis Beaumont and John Fletcher, the speeches in Thucydides' fifth-century B.C. *History of the Peloponnesian War,* Francesco Guicciardini's *History of Florence* (1508–10), Cervantes' *Don Quixote, Los Trabajos de Persiles and Sigismunda,* and *La Galatea,* and Wordsworth, "Yarrow Unvisited," l. 56, from *Memorials of a Tour in Scotland* (1803). Hazlitt goes on to anticipate the next anonymously published novel by Sir Walter Scott.

level of ordinary life and colloquial speaking. You do not assume indeed the solemnity of the pulpit, or the tone of stage-declamation: neither are you at liberty to gabble on at a venture, without emphasis or discretion, or to resort to vulgar dialect or clownish pronunciation. You must steer a middle course. You are tied down to a given and appropriate articulation, which is determined by the habitual associations between sense and sound, and which you can only hit by entering into the author's meaning, as you must find the proper words and style to express yourself by fixing your thoughts on the subject you have to write about. Any one may mouth out a passage with a theatrical cadence, or get upon stilts to tell his thoughts: but to write or speak with propriety and simplicity is a more difficult task. Thus it is easy to affect a pompous style, to use a word twice as big as the thing you want to express: it is not so easy to pitch upon the very word that exactly fits it. Out of eight or ten words equally common, equally intelligible, with nearly equal pretensions, it is a matter of some nicety and discrimination to pick out the very one, the preferableness of which is scarcely perceptible, but decisive. The reason why I object to Dr. Johnson's style is, that there is no discrimination, no selection, no variety in it. He uses none but "tall, opaque words," taken from the "first row of the rubric":[78] words with the greatest number of syllables, or Latin phrases with merely English terminations. If a fine style depended on this sort of arbitrary pretension, it would be fair to judge of an author's elegance by the measurement of his words, and the substitution of foreign circumlocutions (with no precise associations) for the mother-tongue.* How simple it is to be dignified without ease, to be pompous without meaning! Surely, it is but a mechanical rule for avoiding what is low to be always pedantic and affected. It is clear you cannot use a vulgar English word, if you never use a common English word at all. A fine tact is shown in adhering to those which are perfectly common, and yet never falling into any expressions which are debased by disgusting circumstances, or which owe their signification and point to technical or profes-

*I have heard of such a thing as an author, who makes it a rule never to admit a monosyllable into his vapid verse. Yet the charm and sweetness of Marlow's lines depended often on their being made up almost entirely of monosyllables.

78. See Sterne, *Tristram Shandy*, III.xx; Shakespeare, *Hamlet*, II.ii.421 (as adapted by Alexander Pope from the 1676 quarto for David Garrick).

sional allusions. A truly natural or familiar style can never be quaint or vulgar, for this reason, that it is of universal force and applicability, and that quaintness and vulgarity arise out of the immediate connection of certain words with coarse and disagreeable, or with confined ideas. The last form what we understand by *cant* or *slang* phrases. To give an example of what is not very clear in the general statement. I should say that the phrase *To cut with a knife,* or *To cut a piece of wood,* is perfectly free from vulgarity, because it is perfectly common: but to *cut an acquaintance* is not quite unexceptionable, because it is not perfectly common or intelligible, and has hardly yet escaped out of the limits of slang phraseology. I should hardly therefore use the word in this sense without putting it in italics as a license of expression, to be received *cum grano salis.*[79] All provincial or byephrases come under the same mark of reprobation—all such as the writer transfers to the page from his fire-side or a particular *coterie,* or that he invents for his own sole use and convenience. I conceive that words are like money, not the worse for being common, but that it is the stamp of custom alone that gives them circulation or value. I am fastidious in this respect, and would almost as soon coin the currency of the realm as counterfeit the King's English. I never invented or gave a new and unauthorised meaning to any word but one single one (the term *impersonal* applied to feelings) and that was in an abstruse metaphysical discussion to express a very difficult distinction. I have been (I know) loudly accused of revelling in vulgarisms and broken English.[80] I cannot speak to that point: but so far I

79. With a grain of salt.

80. On the term "impersonal" see Hazlitt's *Essay on the Principles of Human Action.* His "vulgarisms and broken English" refer to a series of essays in *Blackwood's* and *The Quarterly.* In an article entitled "Hazlitt Cross-Questioned," John Lockhart and John Wilson, writing under the pseudonym "Z," portrayed Hazlitt as an intellectual fraud (much like Keats, whom they also associated with the "Cockney School" of Leigh Hunt) in *Blackwood's Edinburgh Magazine* of August 1818 (the same issue in which "Z" scathingly reviewed Keats's *Endymion*). Hazlitt wrote "A Reply to Z" (sent to Archibald Constable but never published) and, hearing about the reply and receiving a legal summons, William Blackwood privately paid Hazlitt £100 and expenses to make up for the insult. The conservative editor William Gifford attacked Hazlitt's *Lectures on the English Poets* in *The Quarterly Review* of July 1818, to which Hazlitt responded with the biting "Letter to William Gifford, Esq.," printed privately in 1819. Desiring the last word, Gifford then con-

plead guilty to the determined use of acknowledged idioms and common elliptical expressions. I am not sure that the critics in question know the one from the other, that is, can distinguish any medium between formal pedantry and the most barbarous solecism. As an author, I endeavour to employ plain words and popular modes of construction, as were I a chapman and dealer, I should common weights and measures.

The proper force of words lies not in the words themselves, but in their application. A word may be a fine-sounding word, of an unusual length, and very imposing from its learning and novelty, and yet in the connection in which it is introduced, may be quite pointless and irrelevant. It is not pomp or pretension, but the adaptation of the expression to the idea that clenches a writer's meaning: as it is not the size or glossiness of the materials, but their being fitted each to its place, that gives strength to the arch; or as the pegs and nails are as necessary to the support of the building as the larger timbers, and more so than the mere showy, unsubstantial ornaments. I hate any thing that occupies more space than it is worth. I hate to see a load of band-boxes go along the street, and I hate to see a parcel of big words without any thing in them. A person who does not deliberately dispose of all his thoughts alike in cumbrous draperies and flimsy disguises, may strike out twenty varieties of familiar every-day language, each coming somewhat nearer to the feeling he wants to convey, and at last not hit upon that particular and only one, which may be said to be identical with the exact impression in his mind. This would seem to show that Mr. Cobbett is hardly right in saying that the first word that occurs is always the best.[81] It may be a very good one; and yet a better may present itself on reflection or from time to time. It should be suggested naturally, however, and spontaneously, from a fresh and lively conception of the subject. We seldom succeed by trying at improvement, or by merely substituting one word for another that we are not satisfied with, as we cannot recollect the name of a place or person by merely plaguing ourselves about it. We wander farther from the point by persisting in a wrong scent; but it starts up accidentally in

demned Hazlitt's *Political Essays* in *The Quarterly* of July 1819. After that the critics seem to have lost their taste for blood and left him alone. Hazlitt printed a condensed version of his letter to Gifford in *The Spirit of the Age*.

81. See n. 5 and William Cobbett's *A Grammar of the English Language*.

the memory when we least expected it, by touching some link in the chain of previous association.

There are those who hoard up and make a cautious display of nothing but rich and rare phraseology; ancient medals, obscure coins, and Spanish pieces of eight. They are very curious to inspect; but I myself would neither offer nor take them in the course of exchange. A sprinkling of archaisms is not amiss; but a tissue of obsolete expressions is more fit *for keep than wear.* I do not say I would not use any phrase that had been brought into fashion before the middle or end of the last century; but I should be shy of using any that had not been employed by any approved author during the whole of that time. Words, like clothes, get old-fashioned, or mean and ridiculous, when they have been for some time laid aside. Mr. Lamb is the only imitator of old English style I can read with pleasure; and he is so thoroughly imbued with the spirit of his authors, that the idea of imitation is almost done away. There is an inward unction, a marrowy vein both in the thought and feeling, an intuition, deep and lively, of his subject, that carries off any quaintness or awkwardness arising from an antiquated style and dress. The matter is completely his own, though the manner is assumed. Perhaps his ideas are altogether so marked and individual, as to require their point and pungency to be neutralised by the affectation of a singular but traditional form of conveyance. Tricked out in the prevailing costume, they would probably seem more startling and out of the way. The old English authors, Burton, Fuller, Coryate, Sir Thomas Brown, are a kind of mediators between us and the more eccentric and whimsical modern, reconciling us to his peculiarities.[82] I do not however know how far this is the case or not, till he condescends to write like one of us. I must confess that what I like best of his papers under the signature of Elia (still I do not presume, amidst such excellence, to decide what is most excellent) is the account of *Mrs. Battle's Opinions on Whist,* which is also the most free from obsolete allusions and turns of expression—

82. Robert Burton (1577–1640, author of *Anatomy of Melancholy*), the poet and theologian Thomas Fuller (1608–61), the writer and traveler Thomas Coryate (1577–1617), and Sir Thomas Brown (1605–82, author of *Religio Medici*) were all favorites of Charles Lamb.

A well of native English undefiled.[83]

To those acquainted with his admitted prototypes, these Essays of the ingenious and highly gifted author have the same sort of charm and relish, that Erasmus's Colloquies or a fine piece of modern Latin have to the classical scholar.[84] Certainly, I do not know any borrowed pencil that has more power or felicity of execution than the one of which I have here been speaking.

It is as easy to write a gaudy style without ideas, as it is to spread a pallet of shewy colours, or to smear in a flaunting transparency. "What do you read?"—"Words, words, words."—"What is the matter?"—"*Nothing*," it might be answered.[85] The florid style is the reverse of the familiar. The last is employed as an unvarnished medium to convey ideas; the first is resorted to as a spangled veil to conceal the want of them. When there is nothing to be set down but words, it costs little to have them fine. Look through the dictionary, and cull out a *florilegium*, rival the *tulippomania*.[86] *Rouge* high enough, and never mind the natural complexion. The vulgar, who are not in the secret, will admire the look of preternatural health and vigour; and the fashionable, who regard only appearances, will be delighted with the imposition. Keep to your sounding generalities, your tinkling phrases, and all will be well. Swell out an unmeaning truism to a perfect tympany of style. A thought, a distinction is the rock on which all this brittle cargo of verbiage splits at once. Such writers have merely *verbal* imaginations, that retain nothing but words. Or their puny thoughts have dragon-wings, all green and gold.

They soar far above the vulgar failing of the *Sermo humi obrepens*[87]— their most ordinary speech is never short of an hyperbole, splendid, impos-

83. Spenser, *The Faerie Queene*, IV.ii.32. For Lamb's Elia essays, see chap. 12.
84. Erasmus, *Familiarium colloquiorum formulae* (1519).
85. See n. 59.
86. A *florilegium* is a literary collection of abstracts or anthology; *tulipomania* refers to a craze for tulips that raged in Holland from 1634 to 1637—when a tulip could cost as much as a house and many people who invested money lost fortunes—and stands for any large economic bubble.
87. For a similar concept, see Horace, *Epistles*, II.i.250–51: "Discourse that creeps along the ground." Cf. *Ars Poetica*, 28.

ing, vague, incomprehensible, magniloquent, a cento of sounding common-places. If some of us, whose "ambition is more lowly," pry a little too narrowly into nooks and corners to pick up a number of "unconsidered trifles,"[88] they never once direct their eyes or lift their hands to seize on any but the most gorgeous, tarnished, thread-bare patch-work set of phrases, the left-off finery of poetic extravagance, transmitted down through successive generations of barren pretenders. If they criticise actors and actresses, a huddled phantasmagoria of feathers, spangles, floods of light, and oceans of sound float before their morbid sense, which they paint in the style of Ancient Pistol.[89] Not a glimpse can you get of the merits or defects of the performers: they are hidden in a profusion of barbarous epithets and wilful rhodomontade. Our hypercritics are not thinking of these little fantoccini beings—

That strut and fret their hour upon the stage—

but of tall phantoms of words, abstractions, *genera* and *species,* sweeping clauses, periods that unite the Poles, forced alliterations, astounding antitheses—

And on their pens *Fustian* sits plumed.[90]

If they describe kings and queens, it is an Eastern pageant. The Coronation at either House is nothing to it. We get at four repeated images—a curtain, a throne, a sceptre, and a foot-stool. These are with them the wardrobe of a lofty imagination; and they turn their servile strains to servile uses. Do we read a description of pictures? It is not a reflection of tones and hues which "nature's own sweet and cunning hand laid on," but piles of precious stones, rubies, pearls, emeralds, Golconda's mines, and all the blazonry of

88. See Shakespeare, *The Tempest,* I.ii.486–87, and *The Winter's Tale,* IV.iii.26.

89. A blustering comic character who serves as ensign under Falstaff in Shakespeare's *Henry IV, Part I* and *Henry V.*

90. See Shakespeare, *Macbeth,* V.v.24, and Milton, *Paradise Lost,* IV.988–89 ("and on his Crest / Sat horror Plum'd"). Fantoccini are Italian puppets moved by strings or mechanical devices.

art.[91] Such persons are in fact besotted with words, and their brains are turned with the glittering, but empty and sterile phantoms of things. Personifications, capital letters, seas of sunbeams, visions of glory, shining inscriptions, the figures of a transparency, Britannia with her shield, or Hope leaning on an anchor, make up their stock in trade. They may be considered as *hieroglyphical* writers. Images stand out in their minds isolated and important merely in themselves, without any ground-work of feeling—there is no context in their imaginations. Words affect them in the same way, by the mere sound, that is, by their possible, not by their actual application to the subject in hand. They are fascinated by first appearances, and have no sense of consequences. Nothing more is meant by them than meets the ear: they understand or feel nothing more than meets their eye. The web and texture of the universe, and of the heart of man, is a mystery to them: they have no faculty that strikes a chord in unison with it. They cannot get beyond the daubings of fancy, the varnish of sentiment. Objects are not linked to feelings, words to things, but images revolve in splendid mockery, words represent themselves in their strange rhapsodies. The categories of such a mind are pride and ignorance—pride in outside show, to which they sacrifice every thing, and ignorance of the true worth and hidden structure both of words and things. With a sovereign contempt for what is familiar and natural, they are the slaves of vulgar affectation—of a routine of high-flown phrases. Scorning to imitate realities, they are unable to invent any thing, to strike out one original idea. They are not copyists of nature, it is true: but they are the poorest of all plagiarists, the plagiarists of words. All is far-fetched, dear-bought, artificial, oriental in subject and allusion: all is mechanical, conventional, vapid, formal, pedantic in style and execution. They startle and confound the understanding of the reader, by the remoteness and obscurity of their illustrations: they soothe the ear by the monotony of the same everlasting round of circuitous metaphors. They are the *mock-school* in poetry and prose. They flounder about between fustian in expression, and bathos in sentiment. They tantalise the fancy, but never reach the head nor touch the heart. Their Temple of Fame is like a shadowy structure

91. Shakespeare, *Twelfth Night*, I.v.229. Hazlitt alludes again to Edmund Burke's well-known phrase "wardrobe of a moral imagination," from *Reflections on the Revolution in France* (1790). The Golconda diamond mines of India were famous.

raised by Dulness to Vanity, or like Cowper's description of the Empress of Russia's palace of ice, as "worthless as in shew 'twas glittering"—

It smiled, and it was cold![92]

15 June 1822

The Monthly Magazine
The Letter-Bell

Complaints are frequently made of the vanity and shortness of human life, when, if we examine its smallest details, they present a world by themselves. The most trifling objects, retraced with the eye of memory, assume the vividness, the delicacy, and importance of insects seen through a magnifying glass. There is no end of the brilliancy or the variety. The habitual feeling of the love of life may be compared to "one entire and perfect chrysolite,"[93] which, if analyzed, breaks into a thousand shining fragments. Ask the sum-total of the value of human life, and we are puzzled with the length of the account, and the multiplicity of items in it: take any one of them apart, and it is wonderful what matter for reflection will be found in it! As I write this, the *Letter-Bell* passes:[94] it has a lively, pleasant sound with it, and not only fills the street with its importunate clamour, but rings clear through the length of many half-forgotten years. It strikes upon the ear, it vibrates to the brain, it wakes me from the dream of time, it flings me back upon my first entrance into life, the period of my first coming up to town, when all around was strange, uncertain, adverse—a hubbub of confused noises, a chaos of shifting objects—and when this sound alone, startling me with the recollection of a letter I had to send to the friends I had lately left,

92. "The Temple of Fame" is the title of a 1715 poem by Alexander Pope; Dulness and Vanity were standard eighteenth-century poetic personifications suggestive of Pope's *The Dunciad* (1728) and Johnson's "Vanity of Human Wishes" (1749). See William Cowper, *The Task* (1785), V.173–76.

93. Shakespeare, *Othello*, V.ii.152.

94. In Hazlitt's London, letters could be delivered between six and twelve times per day. The letter-bell signaled the passing of a courier on his rounds (postboxes were not placed on street corners for another twenty-one years). See nn. 110, 111.

brought me as it were to myself, made me feel that I had links still connecting me with the universe, and gave me hope and patience to persevere. At that loud-tinkling, interrupted sound (now and then), the long line of blue hills near the place where I was brought up waves in the horizon, a golden sunset hovers over them, the dwarf-oaks rustle their red leaves in the evening-breeze, and the road from ——— to ———, by which I first set out on my journey through life, stares me in the face as plain, but from time and change not less visionary and mysterious, than the pictures in the *Pilgrim's Progress*.[95] I should notice, that at this time the light of the French Revolution circled my head like a glory, though dabbled with drops of crimson gore: I walked confident and cheerful by its side—

> And by the vision splendid
> Was on my way attended.

It rose then in the east: it has again risen in the west. Two suns in one day, two triumphs of liberty in one age, is a miracle which I hope the Laureate will hail in appropriate verse. Or may not Mr. Wordsworth give a different turn to the fine passage, beginning—

> What, though the radiance which was once so bright,
> Be now for ever vanished from my sight;
> Though nothing can bring back the hour
> Of glory in the grass, of splendour in the flower? [96]

95. The road from Wem (within sight of the blue-topped Welsh mountains) to Shrewsbury; Hazlitt had left his parents and sister in September 1793 to attend the Unitarian New College in Hackney, London, where he met Samuel Taylor Coleridge, then in training for a Unitarian ministry in Shrewsbury. Hazlitt compares his journey to that of John Bunyan's Christian in *Pilgrim's Progress* (1678), which appeared in many illustrated editions.

96. Wordsworth, "Ode, Intimations of Immortality from Recollections of Early Childhood," ll. 73–74, 175–78. Robert Southey was poet laureate at the time the essay was written, though Hazlitt is remembering the French Revolution (September 1793) when the Reign of Terror had just begun in Paris and the guillotine had yet to do much of its bloody work. Southey had not yet renounced his idealism and sympathy with the Revolution.

For is it not brought back, "like morn risen on mid-*night*"; and may he not yet greet the yellow light shining on the evening bank with eyes of youth, of genius, and freedom, as of yore?[97] No, never! But what would not these persons give for the unbroken integrity of their early opinions—for one un-shackled, uncontaminated strain—one *Io pæan* to Liberty[98]—one burst of indignation against tyrants and sycophants, who subject other countries to slavery by force, and prepare their own for it by servile sophistry, as we see the huge serpent lick over its trembling, helpless victim with its slime and poison, before it devours it! On every stanza so penned would be written the word RECREANT! Every taunt, every reproach, every note of exultation at restored light and freedom, would recall to them how their hearts failed them in the Valley of the Shadow of Death. And what shall we say to *him*—the sleep-walker, the dreamer, the sophist, the word-hunter, the craver after sympathy, but still vulnerable to truth, accessible to opinion, because not sordid or mechanical?[99] The Bourbons being no longer tied about his neck, he may perhaps recover his original liberty of speculating; so that we may apply to him the lines about his own *Ancient Mariner*—

> And from his neck so free
> The Albatross fell off, and sank
> Like lead into the sea.[100]

This is the reason I can write an article on the *Letter-Bell,* and other such subjects; I have never given the lie to my own soul. If I have felt any im-pression once, I feel it more strongly a second time; and I have no wish to revile and discard my best thoughts. There is at least a thorough *keeping* in what I write—not a line that betrays a principle or disguises a feeling. If my wealth is small, it all goes to enrich the same heap; and trifles in this way ac-cumulate to a tolerable sum. Or if the Letter-Bell does not lead me a dance into the country, it fixes me in the thick of my town recollections, I know not how long ago. It was a kind of alarm to break off from my work when

97. An allusion to Adam's description of Raphael to Eve in Milton's *Paradise Lost,* V.310–11: "another Morn / Ris'n on mid-noon."

98. "Let us rejoice."

99. Hazlitt has now switched his criticism to Coleridge.

100. Coleridge, *The Rime of the Ancient Mariner* (1834), ll. 289–91.

there happened to be company to dinner or when I was going to the play. *That* was going to the play, indeed, when I went twice a year, and had not been more than half a dozen times in my life. Even the idea that any one else in the house was going, was a sort of reflected enjoyment, and conjured up a lively anticipation of the scene. I remember a Miss D———, a maiden lady from Wales (who in her youth was to have been married to an earl), tantalized me greatly in this way, by talking all day of going to see Mrs. Siddons's "airs and graces" at night in some favourite part;[101] and when the Letter-Bell announced that the time was approaching, and its last receding sound lingered on the ear, or was lost in silence, how anxious and uneasy I became, lest she and her companion should not be in time to get good places—lest the curtain should draw up before they arrived—and lest I should lose one line or look in the intelligent report which I should hear the next morning! The punctuating of time at that early period—every thing that gives it an articulate voice—seems of the utmost consequence; for we do not know what scenes in the *ideal* world may run out of them: a world of interest may hang upon every instant, and we can hardly sustain the weight of future years which are contained in embryo in the most minute and inconsiderable passing events. How often have I put off writing a letter till it was too late! How often had to run after the postman with it—now missing, now recovering, the sound of his bell—breathless, angry with my-self—then hearing the welcome sound come full round a corner—and see-ing the scarlet costume which set all my fears and self-reproaches at rest! I do not recollect having ever repented giving a letter to the postman, or wishing to retrieve it after he had once deposited it in his bag. What I have once set my hand to, I take the consequences of, and have been always pretty much of the same humour in this respect. I am not like the person who, having sent off a letter to his mistress, who resided a hundred and twenty miles in the country, and disapproving, on second thoughts, of some expressions contained in it, took a post-chaise and four to follow and intercept it the next morning. At other times, I have sat and watched the decaying embers in a little *back* painting-room (just as the wintry day de-clined), and brooded over the half-finished copy of a Rembrandt, or a land-

101. The British actress Sarah Siddons (1755–1831) specialized in tragic roles.

scape by Vangoyen,[102] placing it where it might catch a dim gleam of light from the fire; while the Letter-Bell was the only sound that drew my thoughts to the world without, and reminded me that I had a task to perform in it. As to that landscape, methinks I see it now—

> The slow canal, the yellow-blossomed vale,
> The willow-tufted bank, the gliding sail.[103]

There was a windmill, too, with a poor low clay-built cottage beside it: how delighted I was when I had made the tremulous, undulating reflection in the water, and saw the dull canvas become a lucid mirror of the commonest features of nature! Certainly, painting gives one a strong interest in nature and humanity (it is not the *dandy-school* of morals or sentiment)—

> While with an eye made quiet by the power
> Of harmony and the deep power of joy,
> We see into the life of things.[104]

Perhaps there is no part of a painter's life (if we must tell "the secrets of the prison-house")[105] in which he has more enjoyment of himself and his art, than that in which after his work is over, and with furtive sidelong glances at what he has done, he is employed in washing his brushes and cleaning his pallet for the day. Afterwards, when he gets a servant in livery to do this for him, he may have other and more ostensible sources of satisfaction— greater splendour, wealth, or fame; but he will not be so wholly in his art, nor will his art have such a hold on him as when he was too poor to transfer its meanest drudgery to others—too humble to despise aught that had to do with the object of his glory and his pride, with that on which all his projects of ambition or pleasure were founded. "Entire affection scorneth nicer

---

102. The Dutch baroque painter Jan Van Goyen (1596–1666), a contemporary of Rembrandt's.

103. Oliver Goldsmith, "The Traveller," ll. 293–94.

104. Wordsworth, "Lines, Composed a Few Miles Above Tintern Abbey," ll. 47–49.

105. Shakespeare, *Hamlet*, I.v.14.

hands."[106] When the professor is above this mechanical part of his business, it may have become a *stalking-horse* to other worldly schemes, but is no longer his *hobby-horse* and the delight of his inmost thoughts—

His shame in crowds, his solitary pride![107]

I used sometimes to hurry through this part of my occupation, while the Letter-Bell (which was my dinner-bell) summoned me to the fraternal board, where youth and hope

Made good digestion wait on appetite
And health on both—[108]

or oftener I put it off till after dinner, that I might loiter longer and with more luxurious indolence over it, and connect it with the thoughts of my next day's labours.

The dustman's-bell, with its heavy, monotonous noise, and the brisk, lively tinkle of the muffin-bell, have something in them, but not much. They will bear dilating upon with the utmost licence of inventive prose. All things are not alike *conductors* to the imagination. A learned Scotch professor found fault with an ingenious friend and arch-critic for cultivating a rookery on his grounds: the professor declared "he would as soon think of encouraging a *froggery*." This was barbarous as it was senseless. Strange, that a country that has produced the Scotch novels and Gertrude of Wyoming should want sentiment![109]

The postman's double knock at the door the next morning is "more germain to the matter."[110] How that knock often goes to the heart! We dis-

106. See Spenser, *The Faerie Queene*, I.viii.40.

107. Oliver Goldsmith, "The Deserted Village," l. 412.

108. See Shakespeare, *Macbeth*, III.iv.37–38.

109. Referring to the historical novels of Sir Walter Scott and Thomas Campbell's 1809 poem *Gertrude of Wyoming*.

110. Shakespeare, *Hamlet*, V.ii.120. Londoners received their mail from letter carriers, also called bellmen since they rang their bell along a set route to collect letters in the evening, after the receiving houses (official drop-off location for letters) closed. Throughout the eighteenth century, in the two-penny post region (Lon-

tinguish to a nicety the arrival of the Two-penny or the General Post. The summons of the latter is louder and heavier, as bringing news from a greater distance, and as, the longer it has been delayed, fraught with a deeper interest. We catch the sound of what is to be paid—eight-pence, nine-pence, a shilling—and our hopes generally rise with the postage. How we are provoked at the delay in getting change—at the servant who does not hear the door! Then if the postman passes, and we do not hear the expected knock, what a pang is there! It is like the silence of death—of hope! We think he does it on purpose, and enjoys all the misery of our suspense. I have sometimes walked out to see the Mail-Coach pass, by which I had sent a letter, or to meet it when I expected one. I never see a Mail-Coach, for this reason, but I look at it as the bearer of glad tidings—the messenger of fate. I have reason to say so.—The finest sight in the metropolis is that of the Mail-Coaches setting off from Piccadilly. The horses paw the ground, and are impatient to be gone, as if conscious of the precious burden they convey. There is a peculiar secresy and despatch, significant and full of meaning, in all the proceedings concerning them. Even the outside passengers have an erect and supercilious air, as if proof against the accidents of the journey.[111] In fact, it seems indifferent whether they are to encounter the summer's heat or winter's cold, since they are borne through the air in a winged chariot. The Mail-Carts drive up; the transfer of packages is made; and, at a signal given, they start off, bearing the irrevocable scrolls that give wings to thought, and that bind or sever hearts for ever. How we hate the Putney and Brentford stages that draw up in a line after they are gone![112] Some

don, Westminster, and the Borough of Southwark), deliveries were made several times per day. Charles II opened the General Post Office in 1660. Charles I established the first public mail service in 1635, with postage paid by the recipient.

111. Beginning in 1784, mail to outlying regions went in the evenings by mail coach, a carriage drawn by four horses to carry packages and mail, with seating for four people inside and more outside on the roof with the driver. Before that time, mounted carriers had ridden from post to post with the mail. Mail coaches, however, did not last long after the advent of the railway in the early nineteenth century. (De Quincey remembers them nostalgically in "The English Mail-Coach, or the Glory of Motion," 1849.)

112. Hazlitt refers to Putney, a district in the London Borough of Wandsworth; Brentford, a suburb in the Borough of Hounslow; and, below, Land's End, the most westerly tip of the English mainland.

persons think the sublimest object in nature is a ship launched on the bottom of the ocean: but give me, for my private satisfaction, the Mail-Coaches that pour down Piccadilly of an evening, tear up the pavement, and devour the way before them to the Land's-End!

In Cowper's time, Mail-Coaches were hardly set up; but he has beautifully described the coming in of the Post-Boy:

> Hark! 'tis the twanging horn o'er yonder bridge,
> That with its wearisome but needful length
> Bestrides the wintry flood, in which the moon
> Sees her unwrinkled face reflected bright:—
> He comes, the herald of a noisy world,
> With spattered boots, strapped waist, and frozen locks;
> News from all nations lumbering at his back.
> True to his charge, the close-packed load behind,
> Yet careless what he brings, his one concern
> Is to conduct it to the destined inn;
> And having dropped the expected bag, pass on.
> He whistles as he goes, light-hearted wretch!
> Cold and yet cheerful; messenger of grief
> Perhaps to thousands, and of joy to some;
> To him indifferent whether grief or joy.
> Houses in ashes and the fall of stocks,
> Births, deaths, and marriages, epistles wet
> With tears that trickled down the writer's cheeks
> Fast as the periods from his fluent quill,
> Or charged with amorous sighs of absent swains
> Or nymphs responsive, equally affect
> His horse and him, unconscious of them all.[113]

And yet, notwithstanding this, and so many other passages that seem like the very marrow of our being, Lord Byron denies that Cowper was a poet![114]—The Mail-Coach is an improvement on the Post-Boy; but I fear

113. William Cowper, *The Task*, IV.1–22.
114. See Byron's *Letter to John Murray Esqre.* (1821).

it will hardly bear so poetical a description. The picturesque and dramatic do not keep pace with the useful and mechanical. The telegraphs that lately communicated the intelligence of a new revolution to all France within a few hours, are a wonderful contrivance; but they are less striking and appalling than the beacon-fires (mentioned by Æschylus), which, lighted from hill-top to hill-top, announced the taking of Troy and the return of Agamemnon.[115]

March 1831

115. In Aeschylus, *Agamemnon,* ll. 281–316, Clytemnestra describes lighting the beacon fires that carried the news of the fall of Troy. The new revolution in France was the July 1830 revolution.

TWELVE

Charles Lamb

(1775–1834)

CHARLES LAMB WAS A FRIEND OF the "Lake poets" Wordsworth and Coleridge, though he identified with city tastes and occupations. His first essay in *The London Magazine* was signed "The Londoner" (1802), though he achieved almost mythic status with his essays published under the pseudonym "Elia" from 1820 through 1825. Behind the humor and metaphorical whimsy of the essays, however, lay a terrible buried truth: the brutal murder of his mother by his beloved sister Mary, who in a fit of insanity grabbed a kitchen knife and turned the afternoon of 22 September 1796 into Lamb's never-ending "day of horrors." In order to save Mary from confinement at Bedlam, Charles took official responsibility for her. Their shared life together as old bachelor and old maid set the pattern for the life of "double singleness" that Elia shares with his fictional cousin Bridget. Despite repeated relapses during which Mary had to be sent back into confinement, the siblings were extremely close, as we see in self-portraits like "Mackery End, in Hertfordshire" and "Old China."

Lamb, despite his stutter, was a gifted conversationalist, and many of his bons mots have been recorded. Like Hunt he was a bit of the gastronome, and his essays show appreciation for the pleasures of good living. Yet Lamb had to squeeze his life as a man of letters and bon vivant into another life of full-time drudgery as an employee for the British East India Company, where he worked as an accounting clerk from 1792 until his retirement in 1825. Ironically, Lamb's retired leisure slowed down his pace of writing, and except for penning a few minor contributions to *The New Monthly Magazine,* he spent his time poring over the tattered volumes of his cherished library, attending art exhibitions, and visiting the British Museum. His love of the seventeenth-century English writers influenced his own antiquated, highly original prose style.

Selections are from Charles Lamb, *Elia: Essays Which Have Appeared Under That Signature in "The London Magazine"* (London, 1823) and *The Last Essays of Elia: Being a Sequel to Essays Published Under That Name* (London, 1833).

Essays of Elia
Christ's Hospital Five and Thirty Years Ago

In Mr. Lamb's "Works,"[1] published a year or two since, I find a magnificent eulogy on my old school, such as it was, or now appears to him to have been, between the years 1782 and 1789.* It happens, very oddly, that my own standing at Christ's was nearly corresponding with his; and, with all gratitude to him for his enthusiasm for the cloisters, I think he has contrived to bring together whatever can be said in praise of them, dropping all the other side of the argument most ingeniously.

I remember L. at school; and can well recollect that he had some peculiar advantages, which I and others of his schoolfellows had not. His friends lived in town, and were near at hand; and he had the privilege of going to see them, almost as often as he wished, through some invidious distinction, which was denied to us. The present worthy sub-treasurer to the Inner Temple can explain how that happened.[2] He had his tea and hot rolls in a morning, while we were battening upon our quarter of a penny loaf— our *crug*—moistened with attenuated small beer, in wooden piggins,[3] smacking of the pitched leathern jack it was poured from. Our Monday's milk porritch, blue and tasteless, and the pease soup of Saturday, coarse and choking, were enriched for him with a slice of "extraordinary bread and butter," from the hot-loaf of the Temple. The Wednesday's mess of millet,

---

*Recollections of Christ's Hospital.

1. The narrative is told from the perspective of Elia, with a focus on Samuel Taylor Coleridge's experiences at Christ's Hospital (from the archaic sense of hospice or lodging), a boarding school established by Edward VI for the education of poor children, where Lamb and Coleridge were schoolfellows.

2. Randal Norris, subtreasurer from 1801 of the Inner Temple, knew Lamb's patron Samuel Salt.

3. Wooden scoops or cups with a handle on the side for drinking; a "jack" was a leather bottle or tankard.

somewhat less repugnant—(we had three banyan to four meat days in the week)—was endeared to his palate with a lump of double-refined, and a smack of ginger (to make it go down the more glibly) or the fragrant cinnamon.[4] In lieu of our *half-pickled* Sundays, or *quite fresh* boiled beef on Thursdays (strong as *caro equina*), with detestable marigolds floating in the pail to poison the broth—our scanty mutton crags on Fridays—and rather more savoury, but grudging, portions of the same flesh, rotten-roasted or rare, on the Tuesdays (the only dish which excited our appetites, and disappointed our stomachs, in almost equal proportion)—he had his hot plate of roast veal, or the more tempting griskin (exotics unknown to our palates), cooked in the paternal kitchen (a great thing), and brought him daily by his maid or aunt! I remember the good old relative (in whom love forbade pride) squatting down upon some odd stone in a by-nook of the cloisters, disclosing the viands (of higher regale than those cates which the ravens ministered to the Tishbite); and the contending passions of L. at the unfolding.[5] There was love for the bringer; shame for the thing brought, and the manner of its bringing; sympathy for those who were too many to share in it; and, at top of all, hunger (eldest, strongest of the passions!) predominant, breaking down the stony fences of shame, and awkwardness, and a troubling over-consciousness.

I was a poor friendless boy. My parents, and those who should care for me, were far away. Those few acquaintances of theirs, which they could reckon upon being kind to me in the great city, after a little forced notice, which they had the grace to take of me on my first arrival in town, soon grew tired of my holiday visits. They seemed to them to recur too often, though I thought them few enough; and, one after another, they all failed me, and I felt myself alone among six hundred playmates.

O the cruelty of separating a poor lad from his early homestead! The yearnings which I used to have towards it in those unfledged years! How, in my dreams, would my native town (far in the west) come back, with its

4. A banyan day, from the Indian banyan tree under which the Buddha sat, was a no-meat day; millet is a cereal; "double-refined" refers to sugar. Below *caro equina* means horseflesh, served surreptitiously in charity schools of the eighteenth century as a cheap meat; griskin is the lean part of a loin of pork.
5. In 1 Kings 17 ravens feed Elijah (the Tishbite) on "bread and flesh," here described as "cates" (choice foods).

church, and trees, and faces! How I would wake weeping, and in the anguish of my heart exclaim upon sweet Calne in Wiltshire![6]

To this late hour of my life, I trace impressions left by the recollection of those friendless holidays. The long warm days of summer never return but they bring with them a gloom from the haunting memory of those *whole-day-leaves*, when, by some strange arrangement, we were turned out, for the live-long day, upon our own hands, whether we had friends to go to, or none. I remember those bathing-excursions to the New-River, which L. recalls with such relish, better, I think, than he can—for he was a home-seeking lad, and did not much care for such water-pastimes: how merrily we would sally forth into the fields; and strip under the first warmth of the sun; and wanton like young dace in the streams; getting us appetites for noon, which those of us that were pennyless (our scanty morning crust long since exhausted) had not the means of allaying—while the cattle, and the birds, and the fishes, were at feed about us, and we had nothing to satisfy our cravings—the very beauty of the day, and the exercise of the pastime, and the sense of liberty, setting a keener edge upon them! How faint and languid, finally, we would return, towards nightfall, to our desired morsel, half-rejoicing, half-reluctant, that the hours of our uneasy liberty had expired!

It was worse in the days of winter, to go prowling about the streets objectless—shivering at cold windows of print-shops, to extract a little amusement; or haply, as a last resort, in the hope of a little novelty, to pay a fifty-times repeated visit (where our individual faces should be as well known to the warden as those of his own charges) to the Lions in the Tower[7]—to whose levée, by courtesy immemorial, we had a prescriptive title to admission.

L.'s governor (so we called the patron who presented us to the foundation) lived in a manner under his paternal roof.[8] Any complaint which he

6. Out of sequence: Coleridge lived with his friends John and Mary Morgan in the market town of Calne in Wiltshire later in life (in 1815, when he dictated *Biographia Literaria*).

7. A Royal Menagerie was established at the Tower of London in the thirteenth century.

8. Samuel Salt, a member of Parliament and bencher of the Inner Temple for whom Lamb's father (John Lamb) worked as a clerk and valet, obtained Lamb's entrance to Christ's Hospital, where he remained from the age of eight to fifteen.

had to make was sure of being attended to. This was understood at Christ's, and was an effectual screen to him against the severity of masters, or worse tyranny of the monitors. The oppressions of these young brutes are heart-sickening to call to recollection. I have been called out of my bed, and *waked for the purpose,* in the coldest winter nights—and this not once, but night after night—in my shirt, to receive the discipline of a leathern thong, with eleven other sufferers, because it pleased my callow overseer, when there has been any talking heard after we were gone to bed, to make the six last beds in the dormitory, where the youngest children of us slept, answerable for an offence they neither dared to commit, nor had the power to hinder. The same execrable tyranny drove the younger part of us from the fires, when our feet were perishing with snow; and, under the cruelest penalties, forbad the indulgence of a drink of water, when we lay in sleepless summer nights, fevered with the season, and the day's sports.

There was one H———, who, I learned, in after days, was seen expiating some maturer offence in the hulks. (Do I flatter myself in fancying that this might be the planter of that name, who suffered—at Nevis, I think, or St. Kits,—some few years since?[9] My friend Tobin was the benevolent instrument of bringing him to the gallows.) This petty Nero actually branded a boy, who had offended him, with a red hot iron; and nearly starved forty of us, with exacting contributions, to the one half of our bread, to pamper a young ass, which, incredible as it may seem, with the connivance of the nurse's daughter (a young flame of his) he had contrived to smuggle in, and keep upon the leads of the *ward,*[10] as they called our dormitories. This game went on for better than a week, till the foolish beast, not able to fare well but he must cry roast meat—happier than Caligula's minion, could he have kept his own counsel—but, foolisher, alas! than any of his species in the fables—waxing fat, and kicking, in the fulness of bread, one unlucky minute would needs proclaim his good fortune to the world below; and, laying out his simple throat, blew such a

9. H—— may refer to Arthur William Hodge, who was hanged in the West Indies in 1811; the "hulks" refer to any sailing vessel used as a prison. Nevis and Saint Christopher's, islands in the British West Indies, served as a stopover in the transportation route from Britain to the Americas. James Webbe Tobin (1767–1814) became a planter in the West Indies.

10. A metaphorical use of leads, or leash.

ram's horn blast, as (toppling down the walls of his own Jericho) set concealment any longer at defiance.[11] The client was dismissed, with certain attentions, to Smith-field; but I never understood that the patron underwent any censure on the occasion. This was in the stewardship of L.'s admired Perry.[12]

Under the same *facile* administration, can L. have forgotten the cool impunity with which the nurses used to carry away openly, in open platters, for their own tables, one out of two of every hot joint, which the careful matron had been seeing scrupulously weighed out for our dinners? These things were daily practised in that magnificent apartment, which L. (grown connoisseur since, we presume) praises so highly for the grand paintings "by Verrio, and others," with which it is "hung round and adorned."[13] But the sight of sleek well-fed blue-coat boys in pictures was, at that time, I believe, little consolatory to him, or us, the living ones, who saw the better part of our provisions carried away before our faces by harpies; and ourselves reduced (with the Trojan in the hall of Dido)

To feed our mind with idle portraiture.[14]

L. has recorded the repugnance of the school to *gags*, or the fat of fresh beef boiled; and sets it down to some superstition. But these unctuous morsels are never grateful to young palates (children are universally fat-haters) and in strong, coarse, boiled meats, *unsalted*, are detestable. A *gag-eater* in our time was equivalent to a *goul*, and held in equal detestation. ———[15] suffered under the imputation.

11. The Roman historian Suetonius reports that the third Roman emperor, Caligula, appointed his horse (Incitatus) to the senate and tried to make him a consul. In Deuteronomy 32:15, "Iesurun waxed fat, and kicked"; in Joshua 6, the walls of Jericho are toppled by the cry of the people incited by the clamor of the rams' horns blown by Joshua and his priests.

12. John Perry was steward at Christ's Hospital from 1761 to 1785.

13. A reference to Lamb's earlier essay on Christ's Hospital.

14. See Virgil, *Aeneid*, I.464; for the scene in which the harpies eat or befoul the daily feast spread before Aeneas and his men, see III.247–57.

15. The identity of this student is so taboo that Lamb gives no initial preceding the dash.

————'Twas said,
He ate strange flesh.[16]

He was observed, after dinner, carefully to gather up the remnants
left at his table (not many, nor very choice fragments, you may credit me)
and, in an especial manner, these disreputable morsels, which he would
convey away, and secretly stow in the settle that stood at his bed-side. None
saw when he ate them. It was rumoured that he privately devoured them in
the night. He was watched, but no traces of such midnight practices were
discoverable. Some reported, that, on leave-days, he had been seen to carry
out of the bounds a large blue check handkerchief, full of something. This
then must be the accursed thing.[17] Conjecture next was at work to imagine
how he could dispose of it. Some said he sold it to the beggars. This belief
generally prevailed. He went about moping. None spake to.him. No one
would play with him. He was excommunicated; put out of the pale of the
school. He was too powerful a boy to be beaten, but he underwent every
mode of that negative punishment, which is more grievous than many
stripes. Still he persevered. At length he was observed by two of his school-
fellows, who were determined to get at the secret, and had traced him one
leave-day for that purpose, to enter a large worn-out building, such as there
exist specimens of in Chancery-lane, which are let out to various scales of
pauperism with open door, and a common staircase. After him they silently
slunk in, and followed by stealth up four flights, and saw him tap at a poor
wicket, which was opened by an aged woman, meanly clad. Suspicion was
now ripened into certainty. The informers had secured their victim. They
had him in their toils. Accusation was formally preferred, and retribution
most signal was looked for. Mr. Hathaway,[18] the then steward (for this happened a little after my time), with that patient sagacity which tempered all
his conduct, determined to investigate the matter, before he proceeded to
sentence. The result was, that the supposed mendicants, the receivers or

16. See Shakespeare, *Antony and Cleopatra*, I.iv.66–68.
17. The accursed thing stolen by Achan in Joshua 7:13 is "a goodly Baby-
lonish garment, and 200 shekels of silver, and a wedge of gold 50 shekels in weight."
A settle is a wooden bench with a high back, arms, and, typically, storage under the
seat.
18. Perry's successor Matthias Hathaway was steward from 1790 to 1813.

purchasers of the mysterious scraps, turned out to be the parents of ———,
an honest couple come to decay, whom this seasonable supply had, in all
probability, saved from mendicancy; and that this young stork, at the expense of his own good name, had all this while been only feeding the old
birds! The governors on this occasion, much to their honour, voted a present relief to the family of ———, and presented him with a silver medal.
The lesson which the steward read upon RASH JUDGMENT, on the occasion
of publicly delivering the medal to ———, I believe, would not be lost
upon his auditory. I had left school then, but I well remember ———. He
was a tall, shambling youth, with a cast in his eye, not at all calculated to
conciliate hostile prejudices. I have since seen him carrying a baker's basket.
I think I heard he did not do quite so well by himself, as he had done by the
old folks.

I was a hypochondriac lad; and the sight of a boy in fetters, upon
the day of my first putting on the blue clothes, was not exactly fitted to assuage the natural terrors of initiation. I was of tender years, barely turned of
seven; and had only read of such things in books, or seen them but in
dreams. I was told he had *run away*. This was the punishment for the first
offence. As a novice I was soon after taken to see the dungeons. These were
little, square, Bedlam cells, where a boy could just lie at his length upon
straw and a blanket—a mattress, I think, was afterwards substituted—with
a peep of light, let in askance, from a prison-orifice at top, barely enough to
read by. Here the poor boy was locked in by himself all day, without sight of
any but the porter who brought him his bread and water—who *might not
speak to him;* or of the beadle, who came twice a week to call him out to receive his periodical chastisement, which was almost welcome, because it
separated him for a brief interval from solitude: and here he was shut up by
himself *of nights,* out of the reach of any sound, to suffer whatever horrors
the weak nerves, and superstition incident to his time of life, might subject
him to.* This was the penalty for the second offence. Wouldst thou like,
reader, to see what became of him in the next degree?

*One or two instances of lunacy, or attempted suicide, accordingly, at length
convinced the governors of the impolicy of this part of the sentence, and the midnight torture of the spirits was dispensed with.—This fancy of dungeons for children was a sprout of [Sir Robert] Howard's brain; for which (saving the reverence
due to Holy Paul) methinks, I could willingly spit upon his statue.

The culprit, who had been a third time an offender, and whose expulsion was at this time deemed irreversible, was brought forth, as at some solemn *auto da fe,* arrayed in uncouth and most appalling attire—all trace of his late "watchet weeds" carefully effaced, he was exposed in a jacket, resembling those which London lamplighters formerly delighted in, with a cap of the same.[19] The effect of this divestiture was such as the ingenious devisers of it could have anticipated. With his pale and frighted features, it was as if some of those disfigurements in Dante had seized upon him.[20] In this disguisement he was brought into the hall (*L.'s favourite state-room*), where awaited him the whole number of his school-fellows, whose joint lessons and sports he was thenceforth to share no more; the awful presence of the steward, to be seen for the last time; of the executioner beadle, clad in his state robe for the occasion; and of two faces more, of direr import, because never but in these extremities visible. These were governors; two of whom, by choice, or charter, were always accustomed to officiate at these *Ultima Supplicia;*[21] not to mitigate (so at least we understood it), but to enforce the uttermost stripe. Old Bamber Gascoigne, and Peter Aubert, I remember, were colleagues on one occasion, when the beadle turning rather pale, a glass of brandy was ordered to prepare him for the mysteries. The scourging was, after the old Roman fashion, long and stately. The lictor accompanied the criminal quite round the hall. We were generally too faint with attending to the previous disgusting circumstances, to make accurate report with our eyes of the degree of corporal suffering inflicted. Report, of course, gave out the back knotty and livid. After scourging, he was made over, in his *San Benito,* to his friends, if he had any (but commonly such poor runagates were friendless), or to his parish officer, who, to enhance the effect of the scene, had his station allotted to him on the outside of the hall gate.[22]

19. An auto-da-fé was an execution under the Inquisition; "watchet weeds" grow on Gallia's shore in William Collins's brief pastoral ode "The Manners" (1747).

20. A reference to "l'ombre triste smozzicate" (the sad, mutilated shades) of Dante's *Inferno,* XXIX.6.

21. "Final punishments"; Seneca, *De ira,* 1.6.3.

22. The San Benito was a yellow robe worn by victims of the Inquisition. A runagate is a deserter, fugitive, or runaway.

These solemn pageantries were not played off so often as to spoil the general mirth of the community. We had plenty of exercise and recreation *after* school hours; and, for myself, I must confess, that I was never happier, than *in* them. The Upper and the Lower Grammar Schools were held in the same room; and an imaginary line only divided their bounds. Their character was as different as that of the inhabitants on the two sides of the Pyrennees. The Rev. James Boyer was the Upper Master; but the Rev. Matthew Field presided over that portion of the apartment, of which I had the good fortune to be a member. We lived a life as careless as birds. We talked and did just what we pleased, and nobody molested us. We carried an accidence, or a grammar, for form; but, for any trouble it gave us, we might take two years in getting through the verbs deponent, and another two in forgetting all that we had learned about them. There was now and then the formality of saying a lesson, but if you had not learned it, a brush across the shoulders (just enough to disturb a fly) was the sole remonstrance. Field never used the rod; and in truth he wielded the cane with no great good will—holding it "like a dancer."[23] It looked in his hands rather like an emblem than an instrument of authority; and an emblem, too, he was ashamed of. He was a good easy man, that did not care to ruffle his own peace, nor perhaps set any great consideration upon the value of juvenile time. He came among us, now and then, but often stayed away whole days from us; and when he came, it made no difference to us—he had his private room to retire to, the short time he stayed, to be out of the sound of our noise. Our mirth and uproar went on. We had classics of our own, without being beholden to "insolent Greece or haughty Rome," that passed current among us—Peter Wilkins—the Adventures of the Hon. Capt. Robert Boyle—the Fortunate Blue Coat Boy—and the like.[24] Or we cultivated a turn for me-

23. See Shakespeare, *Antony and Cleopatra*, III.xi.35–36. Accidence is the part of grammar that deals with the inflections of words; verbs deponent in Latin and Greek are passive in form but active in meaning. Caning was a standard punishment for mistakes in class as well as for graver offences.

24. The phrase is from Ben Jonson's praise of Shakespeare in "To the Memory of My Beloved, The Author, Mr. William Shakespeare," (1623), l. 39. The boys spend their time reading adventure stories involving love, rough escapes, and action on the high seas, e.g., William Rufus Chetwood, *The Voyages and Adventures of Captain Robert Boyle* (1726); Robert Paltock, *The Life and Adventures of Peter*

chanic or scientific operations; making little sun-dials of paper; or weaving those ingenious parentheses, called *cat-cradles;* or making dry peas to dance upon the end of a tin pipe; or studying the art military over that laudable game "French and English," and a hundred other such devices to pass away the time—mixing the useful with the agreeable—as would have made the souls of Rousseau and John Locke chuckle to have seen us.[25]

Matthew Field belonged to that class of modest divines who affect to mix in equal proportion the *gentleman,* the *scholar,* and the *Christian;* but, I know not how, the first ingredient is generally found to be the predominating dose in the composition. He was engaged in gay parties, or with his courtly bow at some episcopal levée, when he should have been attending upon us. He had for many years the classical charge of a hundred children, during the four or five first years of their education; and his very highest form seldom proceeded further than two or three of the introductory fables of Phædrus.[26] How things were suffered to go on thus, I cannot guess. Boyer, who was the proper person to have remedied these abuses, always affected, perhaps felt, a delicacy in interfering in a province not strictly his own. I have not been without my suspicions, that he was not altogether displeased at the contrast we presented to his end of the school. We were a sort of Helots to his young Spartans.[27] He would sometimes, with ironic deference, send to borrow a rod of the Under Master, and then, with sardonic grin, observe to one of his upper boys, "how neat and fresh the twigs looked." While his pale students were battering their brains over Xenophon and Plato, with a silence as deep as that enjoined by the Samite, we were enjoying ourselves at our ease in our little Goshen. [28] We saw a little into the

---

Wilkins (1751); and *The Fortunate Blue-Coat Boy; or, Memoirs of the Life and Happy Adventures of Mr. Benjamin Templeman; Formerly a Scholar in Christ's Hospital,* by "an Orphanotrophian" (1770).

25. Jean-Jacques Rousseau and John Locke expounded philosophies of education in *Emile* (1762) and *Some Thoughts Concerning Education* (1692), respectively.

26. A dialogue by Plato.

27. Plutarch's *Lives* ("Lycurgus"), XXVIII.4, records that the Spartans "were harsh and cruel to the Helots," the slave caste of Sparta.

28. The Samite is Pythagoras, who required his followers to keep silent for five years. God promises that he will spare the land of Goshen (where his people dwell) in Exodus 8:22.

secrets of his discipline, and the prospect did but the more reconcile us to our lot. His thunders rolled innocuous for us; his storms came near, but never touched us; contrary to Gideon's miracle, while all around were drenched, our fleece was dry.[29] His boys turned out the better scholars; we, I suspect, have the advantage in temper. His pupils cannot speak of him without something of terror allaying their gratitude; the remembrance of Field comes back with all the soothing images of indolence, and summer slumbers, and work like play, and innocent idleness, and Elysian exemptions, and life itself a "playing holiday."[30]

Though sufficiently removed from the jurisdiction of Boyer, we were near enough (as I have said) to understand a little of his system. We occasionally heard sounds of the *Ululantes*,[31] and caught glances of Tartarus. B. was a rabid pedant. His English style was crampt to barbarism. His Easter anthems (for his duty obliged him to those periodical flights) were grating as scrannel pipes.* He would laugh, ay, and heartily, but then it must be at Flaccus's quibble about *Rex*—or at the *tristis severitas in vultu*, or *inspicere in patinas*, of Terence—thin jests, which at their first broaching could hardly have had *vis* enough to move a Roman muscle.[32] He had two

---

*In this and every thing B. was the antipodes of his co-adjutor. While the former was digging his brains for crude anthems, worth a pig-nut, F. would be recreating his gentlemanly fancy in the more flowery walks of the Muses. A little dramatic effusion of his, under the name of Vertumnus and Pomona, is not yet forgotten by the chroniclers of that sort of literature. It was accepted by Garrick, but the town did not give it their sanction. B. used to say of it, in a way of half-compliment, half-irony, that it was *too classical for representation.*

29. Lamb alludes to Abraham Cowley's "The Complaint": "One of old *Gideons* Miracles was shown, / For every Tree, and every Herb around, / With Pearly dew was crown'd, . . . And nothing but the Muses Fleece was dry" (IV.7–12).

30. Shakespeare, *Henry IV, Part I*, I.ii.201–2.

31. Howling sufferers glimpsed by Aeneas in Book VI of the *Aeneid* on the fiery road to Tartarus, or Hell.

32. Elia compares Boyer's vocal cords to the pastoral "scrannel pipes of wretched straw" used by church prelates in Milton's *Lycidas*, l. 124. See Horace: "The Greek Persius, now soused with Italian vinegar, cries out: 'By the great gods, I implore you, O Brutus, since it is in your line to take off "kings," why not behead this Rex?'" (*Satires*, I.vii.32–35). The "thin jests" are Terence, *Andria* (The Girl from Andros), V.i: "Tristis severitas inest in vultu" (a grave severity in his face); and

wigs, both pedantic, but of differing omen. The one serene, smiling, fresh powdered, betokening a mild day. The other, an old discoloured, unkempt, angry caxon,[33] denoting frequent and bloody execution. Woe to the school, when he made his morning appearance in his *passy,* or *passionate wig.* No comet expounded surer. J. B. had a heavy hand. I have known him double his knotty fist at a poor trembling child (the maternal milk hardly dry upon its lips) with a "Sirrah, do you presume to set your wits at me?" Nothing was more common than to see him make a head-long entry into the school-room, from his inner recess, or library, and, with turbulent eye, singling out a lad, roar out, "Od's my life, Sirrah," (his favourite adjuration) "I have a great mind to whip you,"—then, with as sudden a retracting impulse, fling back into his lair—and, after a cooling lapse of some minutes (during which all but the culprit had totally forgotten the context) drive headlong out again, piecing out his imperfect sense, as if it had been some Devil's Litany, with the expletory yell—"*and I WILL, too.*" In his gentler moods, when the *rabidus furor* was assuaged, he had resort to an ingenious method, peculiar, for what I have heard, to himself, of whipping the boy, and reading the Debates,[34] at the same time; a paragraph, and a lash between; which in those times, when parliamentary oratory was most at a height and flourishing in these realms, was not calculated to impress the patient with a veneration for the diffuser graces of rhetoric.

Once, and but once, the uplifted rod was known to fall ineffectual from his hand—when droll squinting W——— having been caught putting the inside of the master's desk to a use for which the architect had clearly not designed it, to justify himself, with great simplicity averred, that *he did not know that the thing had been forewarned.* This exquisite irrecognition of any law antecedent to the *oral* or *declaratory,* struck so irresistibly upon the fancy of all who heard it (the pedagogue himself not excepted) that remission was unavoidable.

L. has given credit to B.'s great merits as an instructor. Coleridge,

---

Adelphoi (The Brothers), III.iii: "in patinas . . . inspicere" (look into the dishes [as a mirror]). *Vis* is force.

33. A type of wig.

34. The Latin phrase, from Gaius Valerius Catullus, *Poems,* LXIII.38, means "delirious madness." *The Parliamentary Debates* was published beginning in 1803 as a record of parliamentary speeches.

in his literary life, has pronounced a more intelligible and ample encomium on them. The author of the Country Spectator doubts not to compare him with the ablest teachers of antiquity.[35] Perhaps we cannot dismiss him better than with the pious ejaculation of C. when he heard that his old master was on his death-bed—"Poor J.B.!—may all his faults be forgiven; and may he be wafted to bliss by little cherub boys, all head and wings, with no *bottoms* to reproach his sublunary infirmities."

Under him were many good and sound scholars bred. First Grecian of my time was Lancelot Pepys Stevens, kindest of boys and men, since Co-grammar-master (and inseparable companion) with Dr. T———e.[36] What an edifying spectacle did this brace of friends present to those who remembered the anti-socialities of their predecessors! You never met the one by chance in the street without a wonder, which was quickly dissipated by the almost immediate sub-appearance of the other. Generally arm in arm, these kindly coadjutors lightened for each other the toilsome duties of their profession, and when, in advanced age, one found it convenient to retire, the other was not long in discovering that it suited him to lay down the fasces also.[37] Oh, it is pleasant, as it is rare, to find the same arm linked in yours at forty, which at thirteen helped it to turn over the *Cicero De Amicitia,* or some tale of Antique Friendship, which the young heart even then was burning to anticipate! Co-Grecian with S. was Th—, who has since executed with ability various diplomatic functions at the Northern courts.[38] Th— was a tall, dark, saturnine youth, sparing of speech, with raven locks. Thomas Fanshaw Middleton followed him (now Bishop of Calcutta) a scholar and a gentleman in his teens. He has the reputation of an excellent

35. Thomas Fanshaw Middleton published *The Country Spectator* (1792–93) and *The Doctrine of the Greek Article* (1813). Coleridge discusses Boyer in the opening chapter of *Biographia Literaria* (1817).

36. L. P. Stephens (1766–1833) became Under Grammar Master at the school, and Arthur William Trollope (1768–1827) succeeded Boyer as Upper Grammar Master.

37. The "fasces" were a bundle of rods, often enclosing an ax, carried by Roman officials as a symbol of power, signifying here the disciplinary birch rod.

38. Cicero's *De amicitia* (On Friendship) was part of the curriculum; S. is Henry Scott, who was in school with Lamb (1780–89) and whom he notes died in Bedlam; Th— is the diplomat Sir Edward Thornton (1766–1852). A Grecian was one of two students sent annually to Cambridge with a scholarship.

critic; and is author (besides the Country Spectator) of a Treatise on the Greek Article, against Sharpe. M. is said to bear his mitre high in India, where the *regni novitas*[39] (I dare say) sufficiently justifies the bearing. A humility quite as primitive as that of Jewel or Hooker might not be exactly fitted to impress the minds of those Anglo-Asiatic diocesans with a reverence for home institutions, and the church which those fathers watered. The manners of M. at school, though firm, were mild, and unassuming. Next to M. (if not senior to him) was Richards, author of the Aboriginal Britons, the most spirited of the Oxford Prize Poems; a pale, studious Grecian.[40] Then followed poor S———, ill-fated M———! of these the Muse is silent.

> Finding some of Edward's race
> Unhappy, pass their annals by.[41]

Come back into memory, like as thou wert in the day-spring of thy fancies, with hope like a fiery column before thee—the dark pillar not yet turned—Samuel Taylor Coleridge—Logician, Metaphysician, Bard! How have I seen the casual passer through the Cloisters stand still, entranced with admiration (while he weighed the disproportion between the *speech* and the *garb* of the young Mirandula), to hear thee unfold, in thy deep and sweet intonations, the mysteries of Jamblichus, or Plotinus (for even in those years thou waxedst not pale at such philosophic draughts), or reciting Homer in his Greek, or Pindar—while the walls of the old Grey Friars re-echoed to the accents of the *inspired charity-boy!*[42] Many were the "wit-

39. "New rulers"; Virgil, *Aeneid,* I.563.

40. M. is John Maunde (c. 1770–1813), who was expelled from Christ's Hospital in 1789, was imprisoned for four years in Paris during the Revolution, and subsequently settled down as a cleric and scholar. Bishop John Jewel's *Apology of the Church of England* (1562) outlined the founding principles of the Reformed Church of England under Elizabeth I. See chap. 8, n. 21, on his protégé Hooker. George Richards's poem "Aboriginal Britons" won a prize in 1791; he later became Vicar of Bampton, in Devon.

41. Matthew Prior, "Carmen Seculare" (1700).

42. Iamblichus and Plotinus were Neoplatonic philosophers; Mirandula was Giovanni Pico della Mirandola (1463–94), an Italian nobleman and friend of Lorenzo de' Medici. Christ's Church was also known as Christ's Church Greyfriars, and Coleridge was the inspired charity boy.

combats," (to dally awhile with the words of old Fuller,) between him and C. V. Le G———, "which two I behold like a Spanish great galleon, and an English man of war; Master Coleridge, like the former, was built far higher in learning, solid, but slow in his performances. C. V. L., with the English man of war, lesser in bulk, but lighter in sailing, could turn with all tides, tack about, and take advantage of all winds, by the quickness of his wit and invention."[43]

Nor shall thou, their compeer, be quickly forgotten, Allen, with the cordial smile, and still more cordial laugh, with which thou wert wont to make the old Cloisters shake, in thy cognition of some poignant jest of theirs; or the anticipation of some more material, and, peradventure, practical one, of thine own. Extinct are those smiles, with that beautiful countenance, with which (for thou wert the *Nireus formosus* of the school), in the days of thy maturer waggery, thou didst disarm the wrath of infuriated town-damsel, who, incensed by provoking pinch, turning tigress-like round, suddenly converted by thy angel-look, exchanged the half-formed terrible "*bl*———," for a gentler greeting—"*bless thy handsome face!*"[44]

Next follow two, who ought to be now alive, and the friends of Elia— the junior Le G———and F———; who impelled, the former by a roving temper, the latter by too quick a sense of neglect—ill capable of enduring the slights poor Sizars are sometimes subject to in our seats of learning— exchanged their Alma Mater for the camp; perishing, one by climate, and one on the plains of Salamanca:[45] Le G———, sanguine, volatile, sweet-natured; F——— dogged, faithful, anticipative of insult, warm-hearted, with something of the old Roman height about him.

Fine, frank-hearted Fr———, the present master of Hertford, with

---

43. Lamb refers to the "wit-combats" between Shakespeare and Jonson as described in Thomas P. Fuller's *The History of the Worthies of England* (1811), 2:414– 15. C . V. Le G—— was the clergyman Charles Valentine Le Grice (1773–1858).

44. The journalist and army surgeon Robert Allen (1772–1805) is compared to the beautiful Nerius described in Homer's *Iliad*, II.673. The expletive is probably "blast you."

45. Samuel Le Grice and Robert Favell became soldiers; the former lost his life in the West Indies, the latter was killed at Salamanca during the Peninsular War in 1812. Sizars were students of limited means who received financial assistance at Cambridge University and Trinity College, Dublin. Lamb applies the term to students at Christ's.

Marmaduke T———, mildest of Missionaries—and both my good friends still—close the catalogue of Grecians in my time.[46]

November 1820

The Two Races of Men

The human species, according to the best theory I can form of it, is composed of two distinct races, *the men who borrow,* and *the men who lend.* To these two original diversities may be reduced all those impertinent classifications of Gothic and Celtic tribes, white men, black men, red men. All the dwellers upon earth, "Parthians, and Medes, and Elamites," flock hither, and do naturally fall in with one or other of these primary distinctions.[47] The infinite superiority of the former, which I choose to designate as the *great race,* is discernible in their figure, port, and a certain instinctive sovereignty. The latter are born degraded. "He shall serve his brethren."[48] There is something in the air of one of this cast, lean and suspicious; contrasting with the open, trusting, generous manners of the other.

Observe who have been the greatest borrowers of all ages—Alcibiades—Falstaff—Sir Richard Steele—our late incomparable Brinsley—what a family likeness in all four![49]

What a careless, even deportment hath your borrower! what rosy gills! what a beautiful reliance on Providence doth he manifest, taking no more thought than lilies! What contempt for money, accounting it (yours and mine especially) no better than dross! What a liberal confounding of those pedantic distinctions of *meum* and *tuum!* or rather, what a noble simplification of language (beyond Tooke), resolving these supposed opposites into one clear, intelligible pronoun adjective![50] What near ap-

46. Rev. Frederick William Franklin, master of the Hertford branch of the school from 1801 to 1827, and Marmaduke Thompson, an Anglican missionary in Madras.

47. In Acts 2:9, "Parthians, and Medes, and Elamites" gathered at Pentecost.

48. Genesis 9:25.

49. Shakespeare's characters Alcibiades from *Timon of Athens* and Falstaff from the *Henry IV* plays; the essayist Richard Steele; the dramatist Richard Brinsley Sheridan.

50. "*Meum* and *tuum*": mine and yours. The philologist and politician John Horne Tooke wrote *Epea Pteroenta; or, The Diversions of Purley* (1786–1805).

proaches doth he make to the primitive *community,* to the extent of one half of the principle at least! He is the true taxer who "calleth all the world up to be taxed"; and the distance is as vast between him and *one of us,* as subsisted betwixt the Augustan Majesty and the poorest obolary Jew that paid it tribute-pittance at Jerusalem![51] His exactions, too, have such a cheerful, voluntary air! So far removed from your sour parochial or state-gatherers, those ink-horn varlets, who carry their want of welcome in their faces! He cometh to you with a smile, and troubleth you with no receipt; confining himself to no set season. Every day is his Candlemas, or his Feast of Holy Michael. He applieth the *lene tormentum* of a pleasant look to your purse, which to that gentle warmth expands her silken leaves, as naturally as the cloak of the traveller, for which sun and wind contended![52] He is the true Propontic which never ebbeth![53] The sea which taketh handsomely at each man's hand. In vain the victim, whom he delighteth to honour, struggles with destiny; he is in the net. Lend therefore cheerfully, O man ordained to lend—that thou lose not in the end, with thy worldly penny, the reversion promised.[54] Combine not preposterously in thine own person the penalties of Lazarus and of Dives!—but, when thou seest the proper authority coming, meet it smilingly, as it were half-way.[55] Come, a handsome sacrifice! See how light *he* makes of it! Strain not courtesies with a noble enemy.

Reflections like the foregoing were forced upon my mind by the death of my old friend, Ralph Bigod, Esq., who departed this life on Wednesday evening; dying, as he had lived, without much trouble. He boasted himself a descendant from mighty ancestors of that name, who heretofore held ducal dignities in this realm. In his actions and sentiments

51. A reference to Luke 2:1, wherein Caesar Augustus declares that "all the world should be taxed"; *obolary* means "impoverished."

52. *Lene tormentum* (pleasant compulsion) is from Horace, *Odes,* III.xxi.13. The traveler is from Aesop's fable "The Wind and the Sun," in which the North Wind and the sun compete to make a traveler remove his cloak; the sun wins. Candlemas was the traditional day on which rents were due and taxes collected. The apostle Matthew was formerly a tax collector.

53. See Shakespeare, *Othello,* III.iii.456–59. Propontis is the ancient name for the Sea of Marmara, connecting the Black Sea with the Aegean.

54. See Proverbs 19:17.

55. A reference to Luke 16:19–31, in which Lazarus, a poor man covered with sores, begs from the rich man Dives, who refuses his request and winds up in hell tormented by flames, while Lazarus is taken into Abraham's bosom in heaven.

he belied not the stock to which he pretended. Early in life he found himself invested with ample revenues; which, with that noble disinterestedness which I have noticed as inherent in men of the *great race,* he took almost immediate measures entirely to dissipate and bring to nothing: for there is something revolting in the idea of a king holding a private purse; and the thoughts of Bigod were all regal. Thus furnished, by the very act of disfurnishment; getting rid of the cumbersome luggage of riches, more apt (as one sings)

> To slacken virtue, and abate her edge,
> Than prompt her to do aught may merit praise,

he set forth, like some Alexander, upon his great enterprise, "borrowing and to borrow!"[56]

In his periegesis, or triumphant progress throughout this island, it has been calculated that he laid a tithe part of the inhabitants under contribution.[57] I reject this estimate as greatly exaggerated: but having had the honour of accompanying my friend, divers times, in his perambulations about this vast city, I own I was greatly struck at first with the prodigious number of faces we met, who claimed a sort of respectful acquaintance with us. He was one day so obliging as to explain the phenomenon. It seems, these were his tributaries; feeders of his exchequer; gentlemen, his good friends (as he was pleased to express himself), to whom he had occasionally been beholden for a loan. Their multitudes did no way disconcert him. He rather took a pride in numbering them; and, with Comus, seemed pleased to be "stocked with so fair a herd."[58]

With such sources, it was a wonder how he contrived to keep his treasury always empty. He did it by force of an aphorism, which he had often in his mouth, that "money kept longer than three days stinks."[59] So he made

56. Milton, *Paradise Regained,* II.455–56. The first horseman of the Apocalypse in Revelation 6:2 rides out "conquering, and to conquer."

57. The second-century Greek writer Pausanias recorded his *periegesis,* a geographical tour of Greece.

58. See Milton, *Comus,* ll. 151–53.

59. Adapted from the popular wisdom that guests, like fish, begin to stink after three days.

use of it while it was fresh. A good part he drank away (for he was an excellent toss-pot), some he gave away, the rest he threw away, literally tossing and hurling it violently from him—as boys do burrs, or as if it had been infectious, into ponds, or ditches, or deep holes, inscrutable cavities of the earth; or he would bury it (where he would never seek it again) by a river's side under some bank, which (he would facetiously observe) paid no interest—but out away from him it must go peremptorily, as Hagar's offspring into the wilderness, while it was sweet.[60] He never missed it. The streams were perennial which fed his fisc.[61] When new supplies became necessary, the first person that had the felicity to fall in with him, friend or stranger, was sure to contribute to the deficiency. For Bigod had an *undeniable* way with him. He had a cheerful, open exterior, a quick jovial eye, a bald forehead, just touched with grey (*cana fides*).[62] He anticipated no excuse, and found none. And, waiving for a while my theory as to the *great race,* I would put it to the most untheorising reader, who may at times have disposable coin in his pocket, whether it is not more repugnant to the kindliness of his nature to refuse such a one as I am describing, than to say *no* to a poor petitionary rogue (your bastard borrower), who, by his mumping visnomy,[63] tells you, that he expects nothing better; and, therefore, whose preconceived notions and expectations you do in reality so much less shock in the refusal.

When I think of this man; his fiery glow of heart; his swell of feeling; how magnificent, how *ideal* he was; how great at the midnight hour; and when I compare with him the companions with whom I have associated since, I grudge the saving of a few idle ducats, and think that I am fallen into the society of *lenders,* and *little men.*

To one like Elia, whose treasures are rather cased in leather covers than closed in iron coffers, there is a class of alienators more formidable than that which I have touched upon; I mean your *borrowers of books—*those mutilators of collections, spoilers of the symmetry of shelves, and cre-

60. See Genesis 21, in which Hagar and her son (by Abraham) Ishmael are forced to wander in the wilderness.

61. The public treasury of Rome.

62. "Hoary faith or honor," from Virgil, *Aeneid,* I.292.

63. Miserable expression.

ators of odd volumes. There is Comberbatch, matchless in his depredations![64]

That foul gap in the bottom shelf facing you, like a great eye-tooth knocked out (you are now with me in my little back study in Bloomsbury, reader!) with the huge Switzer-like tomes on each side (like the Guildhall giants, in their reformed posture, guardant of nothing) once held the tallest of my folios, *Opera Bonaventuræ,* choice and massy divinity, to which its two supporters (school divinity also, but of a lesser calibre,—Bellarmine, and Holy Thomas), showed but as dwarfs,—itself an Ascapart!—*that* Comberbatch abstracted upon the faith of a theory he holds, which is more easy, I confess, for me to suffer by than to refute, namely, that "the title to property in a book (my Bonaventure, for instance), is in exact ratio to the claimant's powers of understanding and appreciating the same."[65] Should he go on acting upon this theory, which of our shelves is safe?

The slight vacuum in the left-hand case—two shelves from the ceiling—scarcely distinguishable but by the quick eye of a loser—was whilom the commodious resting-place of Brown on Urn Burial.[66] C. will hardly allege that he knows more about that treatise than I do, who introduced it to him, and was indeed the first (of the moderns) to discover its beauties—but so have I known a foolish lover to praise his mistress in the presence of a rival more qualified to carry her off than himself. Just below, Dodsley's dramas want their fourth volume, where Vittoria Corombona is![67] The remainder nine are as distasteful as Priam's refuse sons, when the Fates *borrowed* Hector.[68] Here stood the Anatomy of Melancholy, in sober state.

---

64. Silas Tomkyn Comberbache was the name Coleridge assumed when he left Cambridge and enlisted in the Fifteenth or King's Regiment of Light Dragoons.

65. Ascupart was the giant made to serve as a slave in Michael Drayton's *Poly-Olbion,* II.368–69. The Guildhall giants Gog and Magog, recarved in wood by Captain Richard Saunders in 1708, replaced those lost in the Great Fire of London (1666). Lamb refers to his editions of theological works by Saint Bonaventure, Cardinal Robert Bellarmine (1542–1621), and Saint Thomas Aquinas.

66. Sir Thomas Browne's *Hydriotaphia; or, Urn Burial* (1658).

67. John Webster's *The White Devil; or, Vittoria Corombona* (1780).

68. In Homer's *Iliad,* XXIV.486 ff., after Achilles kills Priam's son Hector in

There loitered the Complete Angler; quiet as in life, by some stream side. In yonder nook, John Buncle, a widower-volume, with "eyes closed," mourns his ravished mate.[69]

One justice I must do my friend, that if he sometimes, like the sea, sweeps away a treasure, at another time, sea-like, he throws up as rich an equivalent to match it. I have a small under-collection of this nature (my friend's gatherings in his various calls), picked up, he has forgotten at what odd places, and deposited with as little memory as mine. I take in these or-phans, the twice-deserted. These proselytes of the gate are welcome as the true Hebrews.[70] There they stand in conjunction; natives, and naturalised. The latter seem as little disposed to inquire out their true lineage as I am. I charge no warehouse-room for these deodands,[71] nor shall ever put myself to the ungentlemanly trouble of advertising a sale of them to pay expenses.

To lose a volume to C. carries some sense and meaning in it. You are sure that he will make one hearty meal on your viands, if he can give no ac-count of the platter after it. But what moved thee, wayward, spiteful K.,[72] to be so importunate to carry off with thee, in spite of tears and adjurations to thee to forbear, the Letters of that princely woman, the thrice noble Margaret Newcastle?—knowing at the time, and knowing that I knew also, thou most assuredly wouldst never turn over one leaf of the illustrious folio: what but the mere spirit of contradiction, and childish love of getting the better of thy friend? Then, worst cut of all! to transport it with thee to the Gallican land—

---

battle, the Trojan king enters the Greek camp by night to plead with Achilles for the return of his body, which he values more than his remaining sons.

69. Robert Burton's *Anatomy of Melancholy* (1621) and Izaak Walton's *The Compleat Angler* (1653) were favorite books of Lamb's. Thomas Armory's novel *The Life and Opinions of John Buncle, Esq.*, was published in two volumes in 1756 and 1766. Because he is missing one volume, Lamb describes his widower volume mourning its mate like the fictional John Buncle, who mourns the deaths of a suc-cession of wives with his "eyes shut" (for his most beautiful wife, for a full ten days).

70. Proselytes of the gate were strangers to Israel, or religious converts to Ju-daism.

71. Things forfeit to God or the Crown under Old English law.

72. The dramatist James Kenney (1780–1849), whom the Lambs visited in France in 1822.

Unworthy land to harbour such a sweetness,
A virtue in which all ennobling thoughts dwelt,
Pure thoughts, kind thoughts, high thoughts, her sex's wonder![73]

—hadst thou not thy play-books, and books of jests and fancies, about thee, to keep thee merry, even as thou keepest all companies with thy quips and mirthful tales? Child of the Green-room, it was unkindly done of thee. Thy wife, too, that part-French, better-part Englishwoman!—that *she* could fix upon no other treatise to bear away, in kindly token of remembering us, than the works of Fulke Greville, Lord Brook—of which no Frenchman, nor woman of France, Italy, or England, was ever by nature constituted to comprehend a tittle! *Was there not Zimmerman on Solitude?*[74]

Reader, if haply thou art blessed with a moderate collection, be shy of showing it; or if thy heart overfloweth to lend them, lend thy books; but let it be to such a one as S. T. C.—he will return them (generally anticipating the time appointed) with usury; enriched with annotations, tripling their value. I have had experience. Many are these precious MSS. of his—(in *matter* oftentimes, and almost in *quantity* not unfrequently, vying with the originals)—in no very clerkly hand—legible in my Daniel; in old Burton; in Sir Thomas Browne; and those abstruser cogitations of the Greville, now, alas! wandering in Pagan lands. I counsel thee, shut not thy heart, nor thy library, against S. T. C.

December 1820

Mackery End, in Hertfordshire

Bridget Elia has been my housekeeper for many a long year. I have obligations to Bridget, extending beyond the period of memory. We house together, old bachelor and maid, in a sort of double singleness; with such tolerable comfort, upon the whole, that I, for one, find in myself no sort of

73. Lamb owned at least two works by the poet, philosopher, and playwright Margaret Cavendish, Duchess of Newcastle: a 1656 folio of *Nature's Pictures* and a 1671 folio of *The World's Olio.* The lines of verse have been ascribed to Lamb.

74. Fulke Greville, or Lord Brook (1554–1628), was an English poet. Various translations of Johann Georg Zimmerman's *On Solitude; or, The Effects of Occasional Retirement* appeared in London from 1797 on.

disposition to go out upon the mountains, with the rash king's offspring, to bewail my celibacy. We agree pretty well in our tastes and habits—yet so, as "with a difference."[75] We are generally in harmony, with occasional bicker-ings—as it should be among near relations. Our sympathies are rather un-derstood, than expressed; and once, upon my dissembling a tone in my voice more kind than ordinary, my cousin burst into tears, and complained that I was altered. We are both great readers in different directions. While I am hanging over (for the thousandth time) some passage in old Burton, or one of his strange contemporaries, she is abstracted in some modern tale, or adventure, whereof our common reading-table is daily fed with assiduously fresh supplies. Narrative teazes me. I have little concern in the progress of events. She must have a story—well, ill, or indifferently told—so there be life stirring in it, and plenty of good or evil accidents. The fluctuations of fortune in fiction—and almost in real life—have ceased to interest, or op-erate but dully upon me. Out-of-the-way humours and opinions—heads with some diverting twist in them—the oddities of authorship please me most. My cousin has a native disrelish of any thing that sounds odd or bizarre. Nothing goes down with her, that is quaint, irregular, or out of the road of common sympathy. She "holds Nature more clever." I can pardon her blindness to the beautiful obliquities of the Religio Medici; but she must apologise to me for certain disrespectful insinuations, which she has been pleased to throw out latterly, touching the intellectuals of a dear favourite of mine, of the last century but one—the thrice noble, chaste, and virtuous,—but again somewhat fantastical, and original-brain'd, generous Margaret Newcastle.[76]

It has been the lot of my cousin, oftener perhaps than I could have wished, to have had for her associates and mine, free-thinkers—leaders, and disciples, of novel philosophies and systems; but she neither wrangles with, nor accepts, their opinions. That which was good and venerable to her,

75. See Ophelia: "O you must wear your rue/with a difference"; Shake-speare, *Hamlet*, IV.v.181–82. The "rash king's offspring" is Jephthah's daughter in Judges 11:37.

76. John Gay, "Epitaph of Bye-Words," l. 4. Lamb refers to his favorite books, *Religio Medici* (1643) by Sir Thomas Brown and *Description of a New World, Called the Burning-World* (1666) by Margaret Cavendish, Duchess of Newcastle. "Old Burton" is Robert Burton, author of *Anatomy of Melancholy* (1621).

when a child, retains its authority over her mind still. She never juggles or plays tricks with her understanding.

We are both of us inclined to be a little too positive; and I have observed the result of our disputes to be almost uniformly this—that in matters of fact, dates, and circumstances, it turns out, that I was in the right, and my cousin in the wrong. But where we have differed upon moral points; upon something proper to be done, or let alone; whatever heat of opposition, or steadiness of conviction, I set out with, I am sure always, in the long run, to be brought over to her way of thinking.

I must touch upon the foibles of my kinswoman with a gentle hand, for Bridget does not like to be told of her faults. She hath an awkward trick (to say no worse of it) of reading in company: at which times she will answer *yes* or *no* to a question, without fully understanding its purport—which is provoking, and derogatory in the highest degree to the dignity of the putter of the said question. Her presence of mind is equal to the most pressing trials of life, but will sometimes desert her upon trifling occasions. When the purpose requires it, and is a thing of moment, she can speak to it greatly; but in matters which are not stuff of the conscience,[77] she hath been known sometimes to let slip a word less seasonably.

Her education in youth was not much attended to; and she happily missed all that train of female garniture, which passeth by the name of accomplishments. She was tumbled early, by accident or design, into a spacious closet of good old English reading, without much selection or prohibition, and browsed at will upon that fair and wholesome pasturage.[78] Had I twenty girls, they should be brought up exactly in this fashion. I know not whether their chance in wedlock might not be diminished by it; but I can answer for it, that it makes (if the worst come to the worst) most incomparable old maids.

In a season of distress, she is the truest comforter; but in the teazing accidents, and minor perplexities, which do not call out the *will* to meet them, she sometimes maketh matters worse by an excess of participation. If she does not always divide your trouble, upon the pleasanter occasions of life she is sure always to treble your satisfaction. She is excellent to be at a play with, or upon a visit; but best, when she goes a journey with you.

77. See Shakespeare, *Othello*, I.ii.2.
78. A library belonging to Samuel Salt; see n. 8.

We made an excursion together a few summers since, into Hertford-shire, to beat up the quarters of some of our less-known relations in that fine corn country.

The oldest thing I remember is Mackery End; or Mackarel End, as it is spelt, perhaps more properly, in some old maps of Hertfordshire; a farm-house, delightfully situated within a gentle walk from Wheathampstead. I can just remember having been there, on a visit to a great-aunt, when I was a child, under the care of Bridget; who, as I have said, is older than myself by some ten years. I wish that I could throw into a heap the remainder of our joint existences, that we might share them in equal division. But that is impossible. The house was at that time in the occupation of a substantial yeoman, who had married my grandmother's sister. His name was Glad-man. My grandmother was a Bruton, married to a Field. The Gladmans and the Brutons are still flourishing in that part of the county, but the Fields are almost extinct. More than forty years had elapsed since the visit I speak of; and, for the greater portion of that period, we had lost sight of the other two branches also. Who or what sort of persons inherited Mackery End— kindred or strange folk—we were afraid almost to conjecture, but deter-mined some day to explore.

By somewhat a circuitous route, taking the noble park at Luton in our way from Saint Alban's, we arrived at the spot of our anxious curiosity about noon. The sight of the old farm-house, though every trace of it was effaced from my recollection, affected me with a pleasure which I had not experi-enced for many a year. For though *I* had forgotten it, *we* had never forgotten being there together, and we had been talking about Mackery End all our lives, till memory on my part became mocked with a phantom of itself, and I thought I knew the aspect of a place, which, when present, O how unlike it was to *that*, which I had conjured up so many times instead of it!

Still the air breathed balmily about it; the season was in the "heart of June," and I could say with the poet,

> But thou, that didst appear so fair
> To fond imagination,
> Dost rival in the light of day
> Her delicate creation![79]

79. Wordsworth, "Yarrow Visited," ll. 41–44. "Heart of June" is from Ben Jonson's "Epithalamion" (1640) for Jerome Weston, l. 16.

Bridget's was more a waking bliss than mine,[80] for she easily remembered her old acquaintance again—some altered features, of course, a little grudged at. At first, indeed, she was ready to disbelieve for joy; but the scene soon re-confirmed itself in her affections—and she traversed every out-post of the old mansion, to the wood-house, the orchard, the place where the pigeon-house had stood (house and birds were alike flown) with a breathless impatience of recognition, which was more pardonable perhaps than decorous at the age of fifty odd. But Bridget in some things is behind her years.

The only thing left was to get into the house—and that was a difficulty which to me singly would have been insurmountable; for I am terribly shy in making myself known to strangers and out-of-date kinsfolk. Love, stronger than scruple, winged my cousin in without me; but she soon returned with a creature that might have sat to a sculptor for the image of Welcome. It was the youngest of the Gladmans; who, by marriage with a Bruton, had become mistress of the old mansion. A comely brood are the Brutons. Six of them, females, were noted as the handsomest young women in the county. But this adopted Bruton, in my mind, was better than they all—more comely. She was born too late to have remembered me. She just recollected in early life to have had her cousin Bridget once pointed out to her, climbing a style. But the name of kindred, and of cousinship, was enough. Those slender ties, that prove slight as gossamer in the rending atmosphere of a metropolis, bind faster, as we found it, in hearty, homely, loving Hertfordshire. In five minutes we were as thoroughly acquainted as if we had been born and bred up together; were familiar, even to the calling each other by our Christian names. So Christians should call one another. To have seen Bridget, and her—it was like the meeting of the two scriptural cousins![81] There was a grace and dignity, an amplitude of form and stature, answering to her mind, in this farmer's wife, which would have shined in a palace—or so we thought it. We were made welcome by husband and wife equally—we, and our friend that was with us—I had almost forgotten him—but B. F. will not so soon forget that

80. "Waking bliss" is from Milton, *Comus,* ll. 263–64.
81. The Virgin Mary and Saint Elizabeth, who meet in Juda in the house of Zacharias in Luke 1:39–40.

meeting, if peradventure he shall read this on the far distant shores where the Kangaroo haunts.[82] The fatted calf was made ready, or rather was already so, as if in anticipation of our coming; and, after an appropriate glass of native wine, never let me forget with what honest pride this hospitable cousin made us proceed to Wheathampstead, to introduce us (as some new-found rarity) to her mother and sister Gladmans, who did indeed know something more of us, at a time when she almost knew nothing. With what corresponding kindness we were received by them also—how Bridget's memory, exalted by the occasion, warmed into a thousand half-obliterated recollections of things and persons, to my utter astonishment, and her own—and to the astoundment of B. F. who sat by, almost the only thing that was not a cousin there,—old effaced images of more than half-forgotten names and circumstances still crowding back upon her, as words written in lemon come out upon exposure to a friendly warmth,—when I forget all this, then may my country cousins forget me; and Bridget no more remember, that in the days of weakling infancy I was her tender charge—as I have been her care in foolish manhood since—in those pretty pastoral walks, long ago, about Mackery End, in Hertfordshire.

July 1821

Dream-Children; A Reverie

Children love to listen to stories about their elders, when *they* were children; to stretch their imagination to the conception of a traditionary great-uncle, or grandame, whom they never saw. It was in this spirit that my little ones crept about me the other evening to hear about their great-grandmother Field, who lived in a great house in Norfolk (a hundred times bigger than that in which they and papa lived) which had been the scene—so at least it was generally believed in that part of the country—of the tragic incidents which they had lately become familiar with from the ballad of the Children in the Wood. Certain it is that the whole story of the children and their cruel uncle was to be seen fairly carved out in wood upon the chim-

---

82. Lamb's friend Barron Field (1786–1846) was serving as a judge on the Supreme Court of the Civil Judicature in New South Wales, Australia, at the time this essay was written.

ney-piece of the great hall, the whole story down to the Robin Red-breasts,[83] till a foolish rich person pulled it down to set up a marble one of modern invention in its stead, with no story upon it. Here Alice put out one of her dear mother's looks, too tender to be called upbraiding. Then I went on to say, how religious and how good their great-grandmother Field was, how beloved and respected by every body, though she was not indeed the mistress of this great house, but had only the charge of it (and yet in some respects she might be said to be the mistress of it too) committed to her by the owner, who preferred living in a newer and more fashionable mansion which he had purchased somewhere in the adjoining county; but still she lived in it in a manner as if it had been her own, and kept up the dignity of the great house in a sort while she lived, which afterwards came to decay, and was nearly pulled down, and all its old ornaments stripped and carried away to the owner's other house, where they were set up, and looked as awkward as if some one were to carry away the old tombs they had seen lately at the Abbey, and stick them up in Lady C.'s tawdry gilt drawing-room. Here John smiled, as much as to say, "that would be foolish indeed." And then I told how, when she came to die, her funeral was attended by a concourse of all the poor, and some of the gentry too, of the neighbour-hood for many miles round, to show their respect for her memory, because she had been such a good and religious woman; so good indeed that she knew all the Psaltery by heart, ay, and a great part of the Testament besides. Here little Alice spread her hands. Then I told what a tall, upright, graceful person their great-grandmother Field once was; and how in her youth she was esteemed the best dancer—here Alice's little right foot played an involuntary movement, till, upon my looking grave, it desisted—the best dancer, I was saying, in the county, till a cruel disease, called a cancer, came, and bowed her down with pain; but it could never bend her good spirits, or make them stoop, but they were still upright, because she was so good and religious. Then I told how she was used to sleep by herself in a lone chamber of the great lone house; and how she believed that an apparition of two

83. In the fairy tale "The Children of the Wood" (also known as "The Babes in the Wood") a brother and sister are left to the care of a cruel uncle who hires an assassin to kill them so that he can inherit their wealth; although one of the murderers relents and kills his companion instead, the children are found dead in the woods, their bodies having been covered with leaves by a robin.

infants was to be seen at midnight gliding up and down the great staircase near where she slept, but she said "those innocents would do her no harm"; and how frightened I used to be, though in those days I had my maid to sleep with me, because I was never half so good or religious as she—and yet I never saw the infants. Here John expanded all his eye-brows and tried to look courageous. Then I told how good she was to all her grand-children, having us to the great-house in the holydays, where I in particular used to spend many hours by myself, in gazing upon the old busts of the Twelve Caesars, that had been Emperors of Rome, till the old marble heads would seem to live again, or I to be turned into marble with them; how I never could be tired with roaming about that huge mansion, with its vast empty rooms, with their worn-out hangings, fluttering tapestry, and carved oaken pannels, with the gilding almost rubbed out—sometimes in the spacious old-fashioned gardens, which I had almost to myself, unless when now and then a solitary gardening man would cross me—and how the nectarines and peaches hung upon the walls, without my ever offering to pluck them, because they were forbidden fruit, unless now and then,—and because I had more pleasure in strolling about among the old melancholy-looking yew trees, or the firs, and picking up the red berries, and the fir apples, which were good for nothing but to look at—or in lying about upon the fresh grass, with all the fine garden smells around me—or basking in the or-angery, till I could almost fancy myself ripening too along with the oranges and the limes in that grateful warmth—or in watching the dace that darted to and fro in the fish-pond, at the bottom of the garden, with here and there a great sulky pike hanging midway down the water in silent state, as if it mocked at their impertinent friskings,—I had more pleasure in these busy-idle diversions than in all the sweet flavours of peaches, nectarines, or-anges, and such like common baits of children. Here John slyly deposited back upon the plate a bunch of grapes, which, not unobserved by Alice, he had meditated dividing with her, and both seemed willing to relinquish them for the present as irrelevant. Then in somewhat a more heightened tone, I told how, though their great-grandmother Field loved all her grand-children, yet in an especial manner she might be said to love their uncle, John L———, because he was so handsome and spirited a youth, and a king to the rest of us; and, instead of moping about in solitary corners, like some of us, he would mount the most mettlesome horse he could get, when but an imp no bigger than themselves, and make it carry him half over the county in a morning, and join the hunters when there were any out—and yet he loved the old great house and gardens too, but had too much spirit to be always pent up within their boundaries—and how their uncle grew up to man's estate as brave as he was handsome, to the admiration of every body, but of their great-grandmother Field most especially; and how he used to carry me upon his back when I was a lame-footed boy—for he was a good bit older than me—many a mile when I could not walk for pain; and how in after life he became lame-footed too, and I did not always (I fear) make allowances enough for him when he was impatient, and in pain, nor remember sufficiently how considerate he had been to me when I was lame-footed; and how when he died, though he had not been dead an hour, it seemed as if he had died a great while ago, such a distance there is betwixt life and death; and how I bore his death as I thought pretty well at first, but afterwards it haunted and haunted me; and though I did not cry or take it to heart as some do, and as I think he would have done if I had died, yet I missed him all day long, and knew not till then how much I had loved him. I missed his kindness, and I missed his crossness, and wished him to be alive again, to be quarrelling with him (for we quarreled sometimes), rather than not have him again, and was as uneasy without him, as he their poor uncle must have been when the doctor took off his limb. Here the children fell a crying, and asked if their little mourning which they had on was not for uncle John, and they looked up, and prayed me not to go on about their uncle, but to tell them some stories about their pretty dead mother. Then I told how for seven long years, in hope sometimes, sometimes in despair, yet persisting ever, I courted the fair Alice W—n; and, as much as children could understand, I explained to them what coyness, and difficulty, and denial meant in maidens—when suddenly, turning to Alice, the soul of the first Alice looked out at her eyes with such a reality of re-presentment, that I became in doubt which of them stood there before me, or whose that bright hair was; and while I stood gazing, both the children gradually grew fainter to my view, receding, and still receding till nothing at last but two mournful features were seen in the uttermost distance, which, without speech, strangely impressed upon me the effects of speech; "We are not of Alice, nor of thee, nor are we children at all. The children of Alice call Bartrum father. We are nothing; less than nothing, and dreams. We are only what might have been, and must wait upon the tedious shores of Lethe millions of ages before we have existence, and a name"[84]—and immediately awaking, I found myself quietly seated in my bachelor arm-chair, where I had fallen asleep, with the faithful Bridget unchanged by my side—but John L. (or James Elia) was gone for ever.

January 1822

Detached Thoughts on Books and Reading

> To mind the inside of a book is to entertain one's self
> with the forced product of another man's brain.
> Now I think a man of quality and breeding may be
> much amused with the natural sprouts of his own.
> *Lord Foppington in the Relapse.*[85]

An ingenious acquaintance of my own was so much struck with this bright sally of his Lordship, that he has left off reading altogether, to the great improvement of his originality. At the hazard of losing some credit on this head, I must confess that I dedicate no inconsiderable portion of my time to other people's thoughts. I dream away my life in others' speculations. I love to lose myself in other men's minds. When I am not walking, I am reading; I cannot sit and think. Books think for me.

I have no repugnances. Shaftesbury is not too genteel for me, nor Jonathan Wild too low.[86] I can read any thing which I call a *book*. There are things in that shape which I cannot allow for such.

In this catalogue of *books which are no books—biblia a-biblia—*I reckon Court Calendars, Directories, Pocket Books, Draught Boards

84. In Virgil, *Aeneid*, VI.748–51, the dead in the underworld wait on the shores of Lethe (river of forgetfulness) for a thousand years before they are sent back, unremembering, into new bodies. "John L—" is Charles and Mary Lamb's older brother, John Lamb, a clerk in the South-Sea House; he was the favorite of his mother "as the deformed child is frequently the dearest," according to Lamb's friend Procter (Barry Cornwall) in *Charles Lamb: A Memoir* (1886).

85. Spoken by Lord Foppington in Act II of Sir John Vanbrugh's *The Relapse; or, Virtue in Danger* (1696).

86. The philosopher Anthony Ashley Cooper, third Earl of Shaftesbury (1671–1713) and Henry Fielding's 1743 novel *The Life of Jonathan Wild the Great.*

bound and lettered at the back, Scientific Treatises, Almanacks, Statutes at Large; the works of Hume, Gibbon, Robertson, Beattie, Soame Jenyns, and, generally, all those volumes which "no gentleman's library should be without"; the Histories of Flavius Josephus (that learned Jew), and Paley's Moral Philosophy.[87] With these exceptions, I can read almost any thing. I bless my stars for a taste so catholic, so unexcluding.

I confess that it moves my spleen to see these *things in books' clothing* perched upon shelves, like false saints, usurpers of true shrines, intruders into the sanctuary, thrusting out the legitimate occupants. To reach down a well-bound semblance of a volume, and hope it is some kind-hearted play-book, then, opening what "seem its leaves,"[88] to come bolt upon a withering Population Essay. To expect a Steele, or a Farquhar, and find— Adam Smith. To view a well-arranged assortment of blockheaded Ency-clopaedias (Anglicanas or Metropolitanas) set out in an array of Russia, or Morocco, when a tithe of that good leather would comfortably re-clothe my shivering folios; would renovate Paracelsus himself, and enable old Ray-mund Lully to look like himself again in the world. I never see these impos-tors, but I long to strip them, to warm my ragged veterans in their spoils.[89]

To be strong-backed and neat-bound is the desideratum of a volume. Magnificence comes after. This, when it can be afforded, is not to be lav-ished upon all kinds of books indiscriminately. I would not dress a set of Magazines, for instance, in full suit. The dishabille, or half-binding (with Russia backs ever) is *our* costume. A Shakespeare, or a Milton (unless the first editions), it were mere foppery to trick out in gay apparel. The posses-sion of them confers no distinction. The exterior of them (the things them-selves being so common), strange to say, raises no sweet emotions, no tick-

87. Lamb rejects as *biblia a biblia* works by the Scottish philosophers David Hume (1711–76) and James Beattie (1735–1803); the historians Edward Gibbon (1737–94), William Robertson (1721–93), and Flavius Josephus (37–100); and the theologians Soame Jenyns (1704–87) and William Paley (1743–1805).

88. See Milton, *Paradise Lost*, II.672–73; the population essay is Thomas Malthus's *An Essay on the Principle of Population* (1798).

89. Lamb contrasts the comic essayist Richard Steele and dramatist George Farquhar with the moral philosopher and economist Adam Smith. Paracelsus was a Swiss alchemist of the Renaissance; Raymond Lully was a medieval Spanish philoso-pher. Russia and Morocco were expensive leather bindings.

ling sense of property in the owner. Thomson's Seasons, again, looks best (I maintain it) a little torn, and dog's-eared. How beautiful to a genuine lover of reading are the sullied leaves, and worn out appearance, nay, the very odour (beyond Russia), if we would not forget kind feelings in fastidiousness, of an old "Circulating Library" Tom Jones, or Vicar of Wakefield! How they speak of the thousand thumbs, that have turned over their pages with delight!—of the lone sempstress, whom they may have cheered (milliner, or harder-working mantua-maker) after her long day's needletoil, running far into midnight, when she has snatched an hour, ill spared from sleep, to steep her cares, as in some Lethean cup, in spelling out their enchanting contents! Who would have them a whit less soiled? What better condition could we desire to see them in?

In some respects the better a book is, the less it demands from binding. Fielding, Smollet, Sterne, and all that class of perpetually self-reproductive volumes—Great Nature's Stereotypes—we see them individually perish with less regret, because we know the copies of them to be "eterne." But where a book is at once both good and rare—where the individual is almost the species, and when *that* perishes,

> We know not where is that Promethean torch
> That can its light relumine—

such a book, for instance, as the Life of the Duke of Newcastle, by his Duchess—no casket is rich enough, no casing sufficiently durable, to honour and keep safe such a jewel.[90]

Not only rare volumes of this description, which seem hopeless ever to be reprinted; but old editions of writers, such as Sir Philip Sydney, Bishop Taylor, Milton in his prose-works, Fuller—of whom we *have* reprints, yet the books themselves, though they go about, and are talked of here and there, we know, have not endenizened themselves (nor possibly ever will) in the national heart, so as to become stock books—it is good to possess these in durable and costly covers. I do not care for a First Folio of Shakespeare. I rather prefer the common editions of Rowe and Tonson,

90. On "eterne" see Shakespeare, *Macbeth*, III.ii.39. The lines are loosely quoted from Shakespeare, *Othello*, V.ii.12–13. On the Duchess of Newcastle see n. 73.

without notes, and with *plates,* which, being so execrably bad, serve as maps, or modest remembrancers, to the text; and without pretending to any supposable emulation with it, are so much better than the Shakespeare gallery *engravings,* which *did.*[91] I have a community of feeling with my countrymen about his Plays, and I like those editions of him best, which have been oftenest tumbled about and handled. On the contrary, I cannot read Beaumont and Fletcher but in Folio. The Octavo editions are painful to look at. I have no sympathy with them. If they were as much read as the current editions of the other poet, I should prefer them in that shape to the older one. I do not know a more heartless sight than the reprint of the Anatomy of Melancholy. What need was there of unearthing the bones of that fantastic old great man, to expose them in a winding-sheet of the newest fashion to modern censure? what hapless stationer could dream of Burton ever becoming popular? The wretched Malone could not do worse, when he bribed the sexton of Stratford church to let him white-wash the painted effigy of old Shakespeare, which stood there, in rude but lively fashion depicted, to the very colour of the cheek, the eye, the eye-brow, hair, the very dress he used to wear—the only authentic testimony we had, however imperfect, of these curious parts and parcels of him.[92] They covered him over with a coat of white paint. By ———, if I had been a justice of peace for Warwickshire, I would have clapt both commentator and sexton fast in the stocks, for a pair of meddling sacrilegious varlets.

I think I see them at their work—these sapient trouble-tombs.

Shall I be thought fantastical, if I confess, that the names of some of our poets sound sweeter, and have a finer relish to the ear—to mine, at least—than that of Milton or of Shakespeare? It may be, that the latter are more staled and rung upon in common discourse. The sweetest names, and

---

91. Jacob Tonson was an eighteenth-century publisher for whom the playwright Nicholas Rowe produced an edition of Shakespeare (1709). A nine-volume folio of engravings from John Boydell's Shakespeare Gallery was published in 1802.

92. References are to the Renaissance playwrights Francis Beaumont and John Fletcher; Robert Burton's *Anatomy of Melancholy* (1621), and the eighteenth-century Shakespeare critic Edmund Malone, who persuaded the Vicar of Stratford-on-Avon to whitewash the bust of the poet in the chancel of the church in 1793.

which carry a perfume in the mention, are, Kit Marlowe, Drayton, Drummond of Hawthornden, and Cowley.[93]

Much depends upon *when* and *where* you read a book. In the five or six impatient minutes, before the dinner is quite ready, who would think of taking up the Fairy Queen for a stop-gap, or a volume of Bishop Andrewes' sermons?[94]

Milton almost requires a solemn service of music to be played before you enter upon him. But he brings his music, to which, who listens, had need bring docile thoughts, and purged ears.

Winter evenings—the world shut out—with less of ceremony the gentle Shakespeare enters. At such a season, the Tempest, or his own Winter's Tale—

These two poets you cannot avoid reading aloud—to yourself, or (as it chances) to some single person listening. More than one—and it degenerates into an audience.

Books of quick interest, that hurry on for incidents, are for the eye to glide over only. It will not do to read them out. I could never listen to even the better kind of modern novels without extreme irksomeness.

A newspaper, read out, is intolerable. In some of the Bank offices it is the custom (to save so much individual time) for one of the clerks—who is the best scholar—to commence upon the Times, or the Chronicle, and recite its entire contents aloud *pro bono publico*. With every advantage of lungs and elocution, the effect is singularly vapid. In barbers' shops and public-houses a fellow will get up, and spell out a paragraph, which he communicates as some discovery. Another follows with *his* selection. So the entire journal transpires at length by piece-meal. Seldom-readers are slow readers, and, without this expedient no one in the company would probably ever travel through the contents of a whole paper.

Newspapers always excite curiosity. No one ever lays one down without a feeling of disappointment.

93. The Renaissance poets Christopher Marlowe, Michael Drayton, William Drummond of Hawthornden, and Abraham Cowley.
94. Edmund Spenser, *The Faerie Queene,* and Lancelot Andrewes, Bishop of Winchester (1555–1626).

What an eternal time that gentleman in black, at Nando's,[95] keeps the paper! I am sick of hearing the waiter bawling out incessantly, "the Chronicle is in hand, Sir."

Coming in to an inn at night—having ordered your supper—what can be more delightful than to find lying in the window-seat, left there time out of mind by the carelessness of some former guest—two or three numbers of the old Town and Country Magazine, with its amusing *tête-à-tête* pictures—"The Royal Lover and Lady G———"; "The Melting Platonic and the old Beau,"—and such like antiquated scandal? Would you exchange it—at that time, and in that place—for a better book?

Poor Tobin, who latterly fell blind, did not regret it so much for the weightier kinds of reading—the Paradise Lost, or Comus, he could have *read* to him—but he missed the pleasure of skimming over with his own eye a magazine, or a light pamphlet.

I should not care to be caught in the serious avenues of some cathedral alone, and reading *Candide*.[96]

I do not remember a more whimsical surprise than having been once detected—by a familiar damsel—reclined at my ease upon the grass, on Primrose Hill (her Cythera), reading—*Pamela*.[97] There was nothing in the book to make a man seriously ashamed at the exposure; but as she seated herself down by me, and seemed determined to read in company, I could have wished it had been—any other book. We read on very sociably for a few pages; and, not finding the author much to her taste, she got up, and—went away. Gentle casuist, I leave it to thee to conjecture, whether the blush (for there was one between us) was the property of the nymph or the swain in this dilemma. From me you shall never get the secret.

I am not much a friend to out-of-doors reading. I cannot settle my spirits to it. I knew a Unitarian minister, who was generally to be seen upon Snow-hill (as yet Skinner's-street *was not*), between the hours of ten and eleven in the morning, studying a volume of Lardner. I own this to have

95. A coffeehouse on Fleet Street near the Inner Temple.
96. Voltaire's 1759 satire of philosophical optimism pokes fun at religion and theologians, among other matters.
97. Samuel Richardson's *Pamela; or, Virtue Rewarded* (1740), a popular sentimental novel, described the attempted seduction of a virtuous servant by her master. Cythera was a Greek island sacred to Venus.

been a strain of abstraction beyond my reach. I used to admire how he si-
dled along, keeping clear of secular contacts. An illiterate encounter with a
porter's knot, or a bread basket, would have quickly put to flight all the theology I am master of, and have left me worse than indifferent to the five
points.[98]

There is a class of street-readers, whom I can never contemplate without affection—the poor gentry, who, not having wherewithal to buy or
hire a book, filch a little learning at the open stalls—the owner, with his
hard eye, casting envious looks at them all the while, and thinking when
they will have done. Venturing tenderly, page after page, expecting every
moment when he shall interpose his interdict, and yet unable to deny themselves the gratification, they "snatch a fearful joy." Martin B———, in this
way, by daily fragments, got through two volumes of Clarissa, when the
stall-keeper damped his laudable ambition, by asking him (it was in his
younger days) whether he meant to purchase the work. M. declares, that
under no circumstances of his life did he ever peruse a book with half the
satisfaction which he took in those uneasy snatches.[99] A quaint poetess of
our day has moralised upon this subject in two very touching but homely
stanzas.

> I saw a boy with eager eye
> Open a book upon a stall,
> And read, as he'd devour it all;
> Which when the stall-man did espy,
> Soon to the boy I heard him call,
> "You, Sir, you never buy a book,
> Therefore in one you shall not look."

98. References to the Unitarian theologian Nathaniel Lardner (1684–1768)
and the five points of Calvinist doctrine: original sin, predestination, irresistible
grace, limited atonement, and perseverance of the saints. Snow Hill was the steep,
winding thoroughfare between Holborn (Westminster) and the City of London,
historically associated with the death of John Bunyan and altered in 1802 to create
Skinner Street.

99. Thomas Gray, "Ode on a Distant Prospect of Eton College" l. 40. Martin B—— was Martin Charles Burney, nephew of the novelist Frances Burney.
Clarissa (1748) by Samuel Richardson was originally published in seven volumes.

The boy pass'd slowly on, and with a sigh
He wish'd he never had been taught to read,
Then of the old churl's books he should have had no need.

Of sufferings the poor have many,
Which never can the rich annoy:
I soon perceiv'd another boy,
Who look'd as if he'd not had any
Food, for that day at least—enjoy
The sight of cold meat in a tavern larder.
This boy's case, then thought I, is surely harder,
Thus hungry, longing, thus without a penny,
Beholding choice of dainty-dressed meat:
No wonder if he wish he ne'er had learn'd to eat.[100]

July 1822

Old China

I have an almost feminine partiality for old china. When I go to see any great house, I inquire for the china-closet, and next for the picture gallery. I cannot defend the order of preference, but by saying, that we have all some taste or other, of too ancient a date to admit of our remembering distinctly that it was an acquired one. I can call to mind the first play, and the first exhibition, that I was taken to; but I am not conscious of a time when china jars and saucers were introduced into my imagination.

I had no repugnance then—why should I now have?—to those little, lawless, azure-tinctured grotesques, that under the notion of men and women, float about, uncircumscribed by any element, in that world before perspective—a china tea-cup.

I like to see my old friends—whom distance cannot diminish—figuring up in the air (so they appear to our optics), yet on *terra firma* still—for so we must in courtesy interpret that speck of deeper blue, which the decorous artist, to prevent absurdity, has made to spring up beneath their sandals.

100. Mary Lamb, "The Two Boys," *Poetry for Children* (1809).

I love the men with women's faces, and the women, if possible, with still more womanish expressions.

Here is a young and courtly Mandarin, handing tea to a lady from a salver—two miles off. See how distance seems to set off respect! And here the same lady, or another—for likeness is identity on tea-cups—is stepping into a little fairy boat, moored on the hither side of this calm garden river, with a dainty mincing foot, which in a right angle of incidence (as angles go in our world) must infallibly land her in the midst of a flowery mead—a furlong off on the other side of the same strange stream!

Farther on—if far or near can be predicated of their world—see horses, trees, pagodas, dancing the hays.[101]

Here—a cow and rabbit couchant, and co-extensive—so objects show, seen through the lucid atmosphere of fine Cathay.[102]

I was pointing out to my cousin last evening, over our Hyson, (which we are old fashioned enough to drink unmixed still of an afternoon) some of these *speciosa miracula* upon a set of extraordinary old blue china (a recent purchase) which we were now for the first time using;[103] and could not help remarking, how favourable circumstances had been to us of late years, that we could afford to please the eye sometimes with trifles of this sort—when a passing sentiment seemed to over-shade the brows of my companion. I am quick at detecting these summer clouds in Bridget.

"I wish the good old times would come again," she said, "when we were not quite so rich. I do not mean, that I want to be poor; but there was a middle state";—so she was pleased to ramble on,—"in which I am sure we were a great deal happier. A purchase is but a purchase, now that you have money enough and to spare. Formerly it used to be a triumph. When we coveted a cheap luxury (and, O! how much ado I had to get you to consent in those times!) we were used to have a debate two or three days before, and to weigh the *for* and *against,* and think what we might spare it out

---

101. The "hays," an Old English dance, would have been out of place amid pagodas.

102. China.

103. Hyson is Chinese green tea. *Speciosa miracula* ("shining wonders") is a phrase used by Horace in *Ars poetica* (The Art of Poetry), l. 144, to describe the wonders of the *Odyssey*.

of, and what saving we could hit upon, that should be an equivalent. A thing was worth buying then, when we felt the money that we paid for it.

"Do you remember the brown suit, which you made to hang upon you, till all your friends cried shame upon you, it grew so thread-bare—and all because of that folio Beaumont and Fletcher, which you dragged home late at night from Barker's in Covent-garden?[104] Do you remember how we eyed it for weeks before we could make up our minds to the purchase, and had not come to a determination till it was near ten o'clock of the Saturday night, when you set off from Islington, fearing you should be too late—and when the old bookseller with some grumbling opened his shop, and by the twinkling taper (for he was setting bed-wards) lighted out the relic from his dusty treasures—and when you lugged it home, wishing it were twice as cumbersome—and when you presented it to me—and when we were exploring the perfectness of it (*collating* you called it)—and while I was repairing some of the loose leaves with paste, which your impatience would not suffer to be left till day-break—was there no pleasure in being a poor man? or can those neat black clothes which you wear now, and are so careful to keep brushed, since we have become rich and finical, give you half the honest vanity, with which you flaunted it about in that over-worn suit— your old corbeau[105]—for four or five weeks longer than you should have done, to pacify your conscience for the mighty sum of fifteen—or sixteen shillings was it?—a great affair we thought it then—which you had lavished on the old folio. Now you can afford to buy any book that pleases you, but I do not see that you ever bring me home any nice old purchases now.

"When you came home with twenty apologies for laying out a less number of shillings upon that print after Lionardo, which we christened the 'Lady Blanch';[106] when you looked at the purchase, and thought of the

104. The Elizabethan dramatists Francis Beaumont and John Fletcher were among Lamb's favorite authors. Barker's bookshop was at 20 Great Russell Street, over which the Lambs lived in 1817 (by which time it had become a brazier's) in Covent Garden.

105. A draper's term, from the French word for raven.

106. Leonardo's "Modesty and Vanity" (called by the Lambs "Lady Blanche and the Abbess") was also the subject of an 1804 poem by Mary Lamb entitled "Lines Suggested by a Picture of Two Females by Lionardo da Vinci." Colnaghi was a print seller on Cockspur Street.

money—and thought of the money, and looked again at the picture—was there no pleasure in being a poor man? Now, you have nothing to do but to walk into Colnaghi's, and buy a wilderness of Lionardos. Yet do you?

"Then, do you remember our pleasant walks to Enfield, and Potter's Bar, and Waltham, when we had a holyday—holydays, and all other fun, are gone, now we are rich—and the little hand-basket in which I used to deposit our day's fare of savory cold lamb and salad—and how you would pry about at noon-tide for some decent house, where we might go in, and produce our store—only paying for the ale that you must call for—and speculate upon the looks of the landlady, and whether she was likely to allow us a table-cloth—and wish for such another honest hostess, as Izaak Walton has described many a one on the pleasant banks of the Lea, when he went a fishing—and sometimes they would prove obliging enough, and sometimes they would look grudgingly upon us—but we had cheerful looks still for one another, and would eat our plain food savorily, scarcely grudging Piscator his Trout Hall?[107] Now, when we go out a day's pleasuring, which is seldom moreover, we *ride* part of the way—and go into a fine inn, and order the best of dinners, never debating the expense—which, after all, never has half the relish of those chance country snaps, when we were at the mercy of uncertain usage, and a precarious welcome.

"You are too proud to see a play anywhere now but in the pit. Do you remember where it was we used to sit, when we saw the battle of Hexham, and the surrender of Calais, and Bannister and Mrs. Bland in the Children in the Wood—when we squeezed out our shillings a-piece to sit three or four times in a season in the one-shilling gallery—where you felt all the time that you ought not to have brought me—and more strongly I felt obligation to you for having brought me—and the pleasure was the better for a little shame—and when the curtain drew up, what cared we for our place in the house, or what mattered it where we were sitting, when our thoughts were with Rosalind in Arden, or with Viola at the Court of Il-lyria?[108] You used to say, that the gallery was the best place of all for enjoy-

107. In the second chapter of Izaak Walton's *Compleat Angler*, Piscador proposes to lodge with his friends at Trout-Hall.

108. The musical dramas *The Battle of Hexham; or, Days of Old* (1789) and *The Surrender of Calais* (1791) were by George Colman the Younger. *The Children*

ing a play socially—that the relish of such exhibitions must be in proportion to the infrequency of going—that the company we met there, not being in general readers of plays, were obliged to attend the more, and did attend, to what was going on, on the stage—because a word lost would have been a chasm, which it was impossible for them to fill up. With such reflections we consoled our pride then—and I appeal to you, whether, as a woman, I met generally with less attention and accommodation, than I have done since in more expensive situations in the house? The getting in indeed, and the crowding up those inconvenient staircases, was bad enough,—but there was still a law of civility to women recognised to quite as great an extent as we ever found in the other passages—and how a little difficulty overcome heightened the snug seat, and the play, afterwards! Now we can only pay our money, and walk in. You cannot see, you say, in the galleries now. I am sure we saw, and heard too, well enough then—but sight, and all, I think, is gone with our poverty.

"There was pleasure in eating strawberries, before they became quite common—in the first dish of peas, while they were yet dear—to have them for a nice supper, a treat. What treat can we have now? If we were to treat ourselves now—that is, to have dainties a little above our means, it would be selfish and wicked. It is the very little more that we allow ourselves beyond what the actual poor can get at, that makes what I call a treat—when two people living together, as we have done, now and then indulge themselves in a cheap luxury, which both like; while each apologises, and is willing to take both halves of the blame to his single share. I see no harm in people making much of themselves in that sense of the word. It may give them a hint how to make much of others. But now—what I mean by the word—we never do make much of ourselves. None but the poor can do it. I do not mean the veriest poor of all, but persons as we were, just above poverty.

"I know what you were going to say, that it is mighty pleasant at the end of the year to make all meet—and much ado we used to have every

---

in the Wood was by Thomas Morton. Lamb discusses the actors Maria Theresa Bland and Jack Bannister in his essay "On Some of the Old Actors" (1822). Rosalind and Viola are Shakespeare's heroines in *As You Like It* and *Twelfth Night*, respectively.

Thirty-first Night of December to account for our exceedings—many a long face did you make over your puzzled accounts, and in contriving to make it out how we had spent so much—or that we had not spent so much—or that it was impossible we should spend so much next year—and still we found our slender capital decreasing—but then, betwixt ways, and projects, and compromises of one sort or another, and talk of curtailing this charge, and doing without that for the future—and the hope that youth brings, and laughing spirits (in which you were never poor till now,) we pocketed up our loss, and in conclusion, with "lusty brimmers" (as you used to quote it out of *hearty cheerful Mr. Cotton,* as you called him), we used to welcome in the "coming guest."[109] Now we have no reckoning at all at the end of the old year—no flattering promises about the new year doing better for us."

Bridget is so sparing of her speech on most occasions, that when she gets into a rhetorical vein, I am careful how I interrupt it. I could not help, however, smiling at the phantom of wealth which her dear imagination had conjured up out of a clear income of poor ——— hundred pounds a year. "It is true we were happier when we were poorer, but we were also younger, my cousin. I am afraid we must put up with the excess, for if we were to shake the superflux into the sea, we should not much mend ourselves. That we had much to struggle with, as we grew up together, we have reason to be most thankful. It strengthened, and knit our compact closer. We could never have been what we have been to each other, if we had always had the sufficiency which you now complain of. The resisting power—those natural dilations of the youthful spirit, which circumstances cannot straiten—with us are long since passed away. Competence to age is supplementary youth; a sorry supplement indeed, but I fear the best that is to be had. We must ride, where we formerly walked: live better, and lie softer—and shall be wise to do so—than we had means to do in those good old days you speak of. Yet could those days return—could you and I once more walk our thirty miles a-day—could Bannister and Mrs. Bland again be young, and you and I be young to see them—could the good old one shilling gallery days return—they are dreams, my cousin, now—but could you and I at this

109. "Then let us welcome the new guest, / With lusty Brimmers of the best"; Charles Cotton, "The New Year" (1689), ll. 49–50.

moment, instead of this quiet argument, by our well-carpeted fire-side, sitting on this luxurious sofa—be once more struggling up those inconvenient stair-cases, pushed about, and squeezed, and elbowed by the poorest rabble of poor gallery scramblers—could I once more hear those anxious shrieks of yours—and the delicious *Thank God, we are safe,* which always followed when the topmost stair, conquered, let in the first light of the whole cheerful theatre down beneath us—I know not the fathom line that ever touched a descent so deep as I would be willing to bury more wealth in than Croesus had, or the great Jew R——— is supposed to have, to purchase it.[110] And now do just look at that merry little Chinese waiter holding an umbrella, big enough for a bed-tester, over the head of that pretty insipid half-Madona-ish chit of a lady in that very blue summer-house."

March 1823

Captain Jackson

Among the deaths in our obituary for this month, I observe with concern "At his cottage on the Bath road, Captain Jackson." The name and attribution are common enough; but a feeling like reproach persuades me, that this could have been no other in fact than my dear old friend, who some five-and-twenty years ago rented a tenement, which he was pleased to dignify with the appellation here used, about a mile from Westbourn Green. Alack, how good men, and the good turns they do us, slide out of memory, and are recalled but by the surprise of some such sad memento as that which now lies before us!

He whom I mean was a retired half-pay officer, with a wife and two grown-up daughters, whom he maintained with the port and notions of gentlewomen upon that slender professional allowance. Comely girls they were too.

And was I in danger of forgetting this man?—his cheerful suppers—the noble tone of hospitality, when first you set your foot in *the cottage*—the anxious ministerings about you, where little or nothing (God knows) was to be ministered. Althea's horn in a poor platter—the power of self-en-

110. King Croesus (b. 595) of Lydia was proverbial for his wealth, as was the financier Nathan Meyer Rothschild (1777–1836).

chantment, by which, in his magnificent wishes to entertain you, he multiplied his means to bounties.[111]

You saw with your bodily eyes indeed what seemed a bare scrag—cold savings from the foregone meal—remnant hardly sufficient to send a mendicant from the door contented. But in the copious will—the revelling imagination of your host—the "mind, the mind, Master Shallow," whole beeves were spread before you—hecatombs—no end appeared to the profusion.[112]

It was the widow's cruse—the loaves and fishes;[113] carving could not lessen nor helping diminish it—the stamina were left—the elemental bone still flourished, divested of its accidents.

"Let us live while we can," methinks I hear the open-handed creature exclaim; "while we have, let us not want," "here is plenty left"; "want for nothing"—with many more such hospitable sayings, the spurs of appetite, and old concomitants of smoking boards, and feast-oppressed chargers. Then sliding a slender ratio of Single Gloucester upon his wife's plate, or the daughter's, he would convey the remanent rind into his own, with a merry quirk of "the nearer the bone," &c., and declaring that he universally preferred the outside. For we had our table distinctions, you are to know, and some of us in a manner sat above the salt.[114] None but his guest or guests dreamed of tasting flesh luxuries at night, the fragments were *verè hospitibus sacra*.[115] But of one thing or another there was always enough,

---

111. The Greek goddess Amalthea raised Zeus on the milk of a goat and was rewarded with the goat's magic horn, known as the horn of plenty, or cornucopia.

112. See Justice Shallow in Shakespeare, *Henry IV, Part II*, V.iii.29–30. *Beeves* is the plural of beef (from cow, bull, or ox); in ancient Greece, a hecatomb was a sacrificial offering of a hundred cattle, hence, a great many.

113. The miraculous never-failing oil cruse (small earthenware pot or jar for liquids) and barrel of meal that sustained the widow, her son, and the prophet Elijah in 1 Kings 17:10–16; the feeding of the five thousand with seven loaves and "a few little fishes" in Matthew 15:32–38.

114. To sit above the salt is to sit in a place of distinction at table. Single Gloucester is a cheese. "The nearer the bone, the sweeter the flesh" is a saying by the early church father Bartholomaeus Anglicus in *De proprietatibus rerum* (On the Properties of Things).

115. "Truly sacred to the guests."

and leavings: only he would sometimes finish the remainder crust, to show that he wished no savings.

Wine he had none; nor, except on very rare occasions, spirits; but the sensation of wine was there. Some thin kind of ale I remember—"British beverage," he would say! "Push about, my boys"; "Drink to your sweet-hearts, girls." At every meagre draught a toast must ensue, or a song. All the forms of good liquor were there, with none of the effects wanting. Shut your eyes, and you would swear a capacious bowl of punch was foaming in the centre, with beams of generous Port or Madeira radiating to it from each of the table corners. You got flustered, without knowing whence; tipsy upon words; and reeled under the potency of his unperforming Bacchana-lian encouragements.

We had our songs—"Why, Soldiers, Why"—and the "British Gren-adiers"—in which last we were all obliged to bear chorus. Both the daugh-ters sang. Their proficiency was a nightly theme—the masters he had given them—the "no-expence" which he spared to accomplish them in a science "so necessary to young women." But then—they could not sing "without the instrument."

Sacred, and by me, never-to-be violated, Secrets of Poverty! Should I disclose your honest aims at grandeur, your makeshift efforts of mag-nificence? Sleep, sleep, with all thy broken keys, if one of the bunch be ex-tant; thrummed by a thousand ancestral thumbs; dear, cracked spinnet of dearer Louisa! Without mention of mine, be dumb, thou thin accompanier of her thinner warble! A veil be spread over the dear delighted face of the well-deluded father, who now haply listening to cherubic notes, scarce feels sincerer pleasure than when she awakened thy time-shaken chords respon-sive to the twitterings of that slender image of a voice.

We were not without our literary talk either. It did not extend far, but as far as it went, it was good. It was bottomed well; had good grounds to go upon. In *the cottage* was a room, which tradition authenticated to have been the same in which Glover, in his occasional retirements, had penned the greater part of his Leonidas.[116] This circumstance was nightly quoted, though none of the present inmates, that I could discover, appeared ever to

116. The poet Richard Glover (1712–85), author of the blank verse epic *Leonidas* (1737).

have met with the poem in question. But that was no matter. Glover had written there, and the anecdote was pressed into the account of the family importance. It diffused a learned air through the apartment, the little side casement of which (the poet's study window), opening upon a superb view as far as to the pretty spire of Harrow, over domains and patrimonial acres, not a rood nor square yard whereof our host could call his own, yet gave occasion to an immoderate expansion of—vanity shall I call it?—in his bosom, as he showed them in a glowing summer evening. It was all his, he took it all in, and communicated rich portions of it to his guests. It was a part of his largess, his hospitality; it was going over his grounds; he was lord for the time of showing them, and you the implicit lookers-up to his magnificence.

He was a juggler, who threw mists before your eyes—you had no time to detect his fallacies. He would say "hand me the *silver* sugar tongs"; and, before you could discover it was a single spoon, and that *plated*, he would disturb and captivate your imagination by a misnomer of "the urn" for a tea kettle; or by calling a homely bench a sofa. Rich men direct you to their furniture, poor ones divert you from it; he neither did one nor the other, but by simply assuming that everything was handsome about him, you were positively at a demur what you did, or did not see, at *the cottage*. With nothing to live on, he seemed to live on everything. He had a stock of wealth in his mind; not that which is properly termed *Content,* for in truth he was not to be *contained* at all, but overflowed all bounds by the force of a magnificent self-delusion.

Enthusiasm is catching; and even his wife, a sober native of North Britain, who generally saw things more as they were, was not proof against the continual collision of his credulity. Her daughters were rational and discreet young women; in the main, perhaps, not insensible to their true circumstances. I have seen them assume a thoughtful air at times. But such was the preponderating opulence of his fancy, that I am persuaded, not for any half hour together, did they ever look their own prospects fairly in the face. There was no resisting the vortex of his temperament. His riotous imagination conjured up handsome settlements before their eyes, which kept them up in the eye of the world too, and seem at last to have realised themselves; for they both have married since, I am told, more than respectably.

It is long since, and my memory waxes dim on some subjects, or I should wish to convey some notion of the manner in which the pleasant creature described the circumstances of his own wedding-day. I faintly remember something of a chaise and four, in which he made his entry into Glasgow on that morning to fetch the bride home, or carry her thither, I forget which. It so completely made out the stanza of the old ballad—

When we came down through Glasgow town,
We were a comely sight to see;
My love was clad in black velvet,
And I myself in cramasie.[117]

I suppose it was the only occasion, upon which his own actual splendour at all corresponded with the world's notions on that subject. In homely cart, or travelling caravan, by whatever humble vehicle they chanced to be transported in less prosperous days, the ride through Glasgow came back upon his fancy, not as a humiliating contrast, but as a fair occasion for reverting to that one day's state. It seemed an "equipage etern" from which no power of fate or fortune, once mounted, had power thereafter to dislodge him.

There is some merit in putting a handsome face upon indigent circumstances. To bully and swagger away the sense of them before strangers, may be not always discommendable. Tibbs, and Bobadil, even when detected, have more of our admiration than contempt.[118] But for a man to put the cheat upon himself; to play the Bobadil at home; and, steeped in poverty up to the lips, to fancy himself all the while chin-deep in riches, is a strain of constitutional philosophy, and a mastery over fortune, which was reserved for my old friend Captain Jackson.

November 1824

117. Lamb regularizes "Waly, Waly," an anonymous seventeenth-century ballad in a Scottish dialect; *cramasie* means crimson.

118. Beau Tibbs in Goldsmith's *The Citizen of the World* (1760–61) is a portrait of vain (though impoverished) affectation. In Ben Jonson's *Every Man in His Humour* (1598), Captain Bobadill is a man in his cups—a gentlemanly, ruffianly sort of swearer.

The Superannuated Man

Sera tamen respexit
Libertas.   VIRGIL.

A Clerk I was in London gay.
O'Keefe.[119]

If peradventure, Reader, it has been thy lot to waste the golden years of thy life—thy shining youth—in the irksome confinement of an office; to have thy prison days prolonged through middle age down to decrepitude and silver hairs, without hope of release or respite; to have lived to forget that there are such things as holidays, or to remember them but as the prerogatives of childhood; then, and then only, will you be able to appreciate my deliverance.

It is now six and thirty years since I took my seat at the desk in Mincing-lane. Melancholy was the transition at fourteen from the abundant play-time, and the frequently-intervening vacations of school days, to the eight, nine, and sometimes ten hours a-day attendance at a counting-house. But time partially reconciles us to anything. I gradually became content—doggedly contented, as wild animals in cages.

It is true I had my Sundays to myself; but Sundays, admirable as the institution of them is for purposes of worship, are for that very reason the very worst adapted for days of unbending and recreation. In particular, there is a gloom for me attendant upon a city Sunday, a weight in the air. I miss the cheerful cries of London, the music, and the ballad-singers—the buzz and stirring murmur of the streets. Those eternal bells depress me. The closed shops repel me. Prints, pictures, all the glittering and endless succession of knacks and gewgaws, and ostentatiously displayed wares of tradesmen, which make a week-day saunter through the less busy parts of the metropolis so delightful—are shut out. No book-stalls deliciously to idle over—No busy faces to recreate the idle man who contemplates them ever passing by—the very face of business a charm by contrast to his tem-

119. "Freedom, who, though late, yet cast her eyes upon me in my sloth—"; Virgil, *Eclogues,* I.27; the second epigraph is from George Colman the Younger's "Inkle and Yarico: An Opera, in Three Acts" (1787), III.i. A superannuated man is someone who is retired on a pension.

porary relaxation from it. Nothing to be seen but unhappy countenances— or half-happy at best—of emancipated 'prentices and little tradesfolks, with here and there a servant maid that has got leave to go out, who, slaving all the week, with the habit has lost almost the capacity of enjoying a free hour; and livelily expressing the hollowness of a day's pleasuring. The very strollers in the fields on that day look anything but comfortable.

But besides Sundays I had a day at Easter, and a day at Christmas, with a full week in the summer to go and air myself in my native fields of Hertfordshire. This last was a great indulgence; and the prospect of its recurrence, I believe, alone kept me up through the year, and made my durance tolerable. But when the week came round, did the glittering phantom of the distance keep touch with me? or rather was it not a series of seven uneasy days, spent in restless pursuit of pleasure, and a wearisome anxiety to find out how to make the most of them? Where was the quiet, where the promised rest? Before I had a taste of it, it was vanished. I was at the desk again, counting upon the fifty-one tedious weeks that must intervene before such another snatch would come. Still the prospect of its coming threw something of an illumination upon the darker side of my captivity. Without it, as I have said, I could scarcely have sustained my thraldom.

Independently of the rigours of attendance, I have ever been haunted with a sense (perhaps a mere caprice) of incapacity for business. This, during my latter years, had increased to such a degree, that it was visible in all the lines of my countenance. My health and my good spirits flagged. I had perpetually a dread of some crisis, to which I should be found unequal. Besides my daylight servitude, I served over again all night in my sleep, and would awake with terrors of imaginary false entries, errors in my accounts, and the like. I was fifty years of age, and no prospect or emancipation presented itself. I had grown to my desk, as it were; and the wood had entered into my soul.

My fellows in the office would sometimes rally me upon the trouble legible in my countenance; but I did not know that it had raised the suspicions of any of my employers, when, on the 5th of last month, a day ever to be remembered by me, L———, the junior partner in the firm, calling me on one side, directly taxed me with my bad looks, and frankly inquired the cause of them. So taxed, I honestly made confession of my infirmity, and added that I was afraid I should eventually be obliged to resign his service.

He spoke some words of course to hearten me, and there the matter rested. A whole week I remained labouring under the impression that I had acted imprudently in my disclosure; that I had foolishly given a handle against myself, and had been anticipating my own dismissal. A week passed in this manner, the most anxious one, I verily believe, in my whole life, when on the evening of the 12th of April, just as I was about quitting my desk to go home (it might be about eight o'clock) I received an awful summons to attend the presence of the whole assembled firm in the formidable back parlour. I thought, now my time is surely come, I have done for myself, I am going to be told that they have no longer occasion for me. L———, I could see, smiled at the terror I was in, which was a little relief to me, when to my utter astonishment B———, the eldest partner, began a formal harangue to me on the length of my services, my very meritorious conduct during the whole of the time (the deuce, thought I, how did he find out that? I protest I never had the confidence to think as much). He went on to descant on the expediency of retiring at a certain time of life (how my heart panted!) and asking me a few questions as to the amount of my own property, of which I have a little, ended with a proposal, to which his three partners nodded a grave assent, that I should accept from the house, which I had served so well, a pension for life to the amount of two-thirds of my accustomed salary—a magnificent offer! I do not know what I answered between surprise and gratitude, but it was understood that I accepted their proposal, and I was told that I was free from that hour to leave their service. I stammered out a bow, and at just ten minutes after eight I went home— for ever. This noble benefit—gratitude forbids me to conceal their names— I owe to the kindness of the most munificent firm in the world—the house of Boldero, Merryweather, Bosanquet, and Lacy.

Esto perpetua![120]

For the first day or two I felt stunned, overwhelmed. I could only apprehend my felicity; I was too confused to taste it sincerely. I wandered about, thinking I was happy, and knowing that I was not. I was in the condition of a prisoner in the old Bastile, suddenly let loose after a forty years' confinement. I could scarce trust myself with myself. It was like passing out of Time into Eternity—for it is a sort of Eternity for a man to have his Time

120. "Let it endure forever." (The names of Lamb's liberators are disguised.)

all to himself. It seemed to me that I had more time on my hands than I could ever manage. From a poor man, poor in Time, I was suddenly lifted up into a vast revenue; I could see no end of my possessions; I wanted some steward, or judicious bailiff, to manage my estates in Time for me. And here let me caution persons grown old in active business, not lightly, nor without weighing their own resources, to forego their customary employment all at once, for there may be danger in it. I feel it by myself, but I know that my resources are sufficient; and now that those first giddy raptures have subsided, I have a quiet home-feeling of the blessedness of my condition. I am in no hurry. Having all holidays, I am as though I had none. If Time hung heavy upon me, I could walk it away; but I do *not* walk all day long, as I used to do in those old transient holidays, thirty miles a day, to make the most of them. If Time were troublesome, I could read it away, but I do *not* read in that violent measure, with which, having no Time my own but candlelight Time, I used to weary out my head and eyesight in by-gone winters. I walk, read or scribble (as now) just when the fit seizes me. I no longer hunt after pleasure; I let it come to me. I am like the man

　　　　———That's born, and has his years come to him,
　　In some green desart.[121]

"Years," you will say! "what is this superannuated simpleton calculating upon? He has already told us, he is past fifty."

I have indeed lived nominally fifty years, but deduct out of them the hours which I have lived to other people, and not to myself, and you will find me still a young fellow. For *that* is the only true Time, which a man can properly call his own, that which he has all to himself; the rest, though in some sense he may be said to live it, is other people's time, not his. The remnant of my poor days, long or short, is at least multiplied for me three-fold. My ten next years, if I stretch so far, will be as long as any preceding thirty. 'Tis a fair rule-of-three sum.[122]

　　121. See Thomas Middleton, *Hengist, King of Kent; or, The Mayor of Queens-borough*, I.i.102–3.
　　122. The rule of three in mathematics is a way to find the fourth term of a proportion when the other three are known.

Among the strange fantasies which beset me at the commencement of my freedom, and of which all traces are not yet gone, one was, that a vast tract of time had intervened since I quitted the Counting House. I could not conceive of it as an affair of yesterday. The partners, and the clerks, with whom I had for so many years, and for so many hours in each day of the year, been closely associated—being suddenly removed from them—they seemed as dead to me. There is a fine passage, which may serve to illustrate this fancy, in a Tragedy by Sir Robert Howard, speaking of a friend's death:

> ————'Twas but just now he went away;
> I have not since had time to shed a tear;
> And yet the distance does the same appear
> As if he had been a thousand years from me.
> Time takes no measure in Eternity.[123]

To dissipate this awkward feeling, I have been fain to go among them once or twice since; to visit my old desk-fellows—my co-brethren of the quill—that I had left below in the state militant. Not all the kindness with which they received me could quite restore to me that pleasant familiarity, which I had heretofore enjoyed among them. We cracked some of our old jokes, but methought they went off but faintly. My old desk; the peg where I hung my hat, were appropriated to another. I knew it must be, but I could not take it kindly. D————l take me, if I did not feel some remorse—beast, if I had not,—at quitting my old compeers, the faithful partners of my toils for six and thirty years, that smoothed for me with their jokes and conundrums the ruggedness of my professional road. Had it been so rugged then after all? or was I a coward simply? Well, it is too late to repent; and I also know, that these suggestions are a common fallacy of the mind on such occasions. But my heart smote me. I had violently broken the bands betwixt us. It was at least not courteous. I shall be some time before I get quite reconciled to the separation. Farewell, old cronies, yet not for long, for again and again I will come among ye, if I shall have your leave. Farewell Ch————, dry, sarcastic, and friendly! Do————, mild, slow to move, and

123. Spoken by Verginia near the end of Act V of Sir Robert Howard's *The Vestal-Virgin; or, The Roman Ladies* (1665).

gentlemanly! Pl———, officious to do, and to volunteer, good services!—
and thou, thou dreary pile, fit mansion for a Gresham or a Whittington of
old, stately House of Merchants;[124] with thy labyrinthine passages, and
light-excluding, pent-up offices, where candles for one half the year supplied the place of the sun's light; unhealthy contributor to my weal, stern
fosterer of my living, farewell! In thee remain, and not in the obscure collection of some wandering bookseller, my "works!" There let them rest, as
I do from my labours, piled on thy massy shelves, more MSS. in folio than
ever Aquinas left, and full as useful! My mantle I bequeath among ye.

A fortnight has passed since the date of my first communication. At
that period I was approaching to tranquillity, but had not reached it. I
boasted of a calm indeed, but it was comparative only. Something of the
first flutter was left; an unsettling sense of novelty; the dazzle to weak eyes
of unaccustomed light. I missed my old chains, forsooth, as if they had been
some necessary part of my apparel. I was a poor Carthusian,[125] from strict
cellular discipline suddenly by some revolution returned upon the world. I
am now as if I had never been other than my own master. It is natural to me
to go where I please, to do what I please. I find myself at eleven o'clock in
the day in Bond-street, and it seems to me that I have been sauntering there
at that very hour for years past. I digress into Soho, to explore a book-stall.
Methinks I have been thirty years a collector. There is nothing strange
nor new in it. I find myself before a fine picture in a morning. Was it ever
otherwise? What is become of Fish-street Hill? Where is Fenchurch-street?
Stones of old Mincing-lane which I have worn with my daily pilgrimage for
six and thirty years, to the footsteps of what toil-worn clerk are your everlasting flints now vocal?[126] I indent the gayer flags of Pall Mall. It is Change

124. References are to the former Lord Mayors of London Richard (Dick)
Whittington (1350–1423), Sir Richard Gresham (1485?–1549), and his brother Sir
John Gresham (d. 1556). E. V. Lucas identifies the unnamed men as John Chambers
(an old Christ's Hospitaller), Henry Dodwell, and W. D. Plumley. The business was
the British East India Company (or House) where Lamb worked as an accounting
clerk.

125. The Carthusian monks were the highest and strictest order of the Roman
Catholic Church.

126. See Shakespeare, *Romeo and Juliet*, II.v.17.

time, and I am strangely among the Elgin marbles.[127] It was no hyperbole when I ventured to compare the change in my condition to a passing into another world. Time stands still in a manner to me. I have lost all distinction of season. I do not know the day of the week, or of the month. Each day used to be individually felt by me in its reference to the foreign post days; in its distance from, or propinquity to, the next Sunday. I had my Wednesday feelings, my Saturday nights' sensations. The genius of each day was upon me distinctly during the whole of it, affecting my appetite, spirits, &c. The phantom of the next day, with the dreary five to follow, sat as a load upon my poor Sabbath recreations. What charm has washed that Ethiop white? What is gone of Black Monday? All days are the same. Sunday itself—that unfortunate failure of a holyday as it too often proved, what with my sense of its fugitiveness, and over-care to get the greatest quantity of pleasure out of it—is melted down into a week day. I can spare to go to church now, without grudging the huge cantle[128] which it used to seem to cut out of the holyday. I have Time for everything. I can visit a sick friend. I can interrupt the man of much occupation when he is busiest. I can insult over him with an invitation to take a day's pleasure with me to Windsor this fine May-morning. It is Lucretian pleasure to behold the poor drudges, whom I have left behind in the world, carking and caring; like horses in a mill, drudging on in the same eternal round—and what is it all for?[129] A man can never have too much Time to himself, nor too little to do. Had I a little son, I would christen him NOTHING-TO-DO; he should do nothing. Man, I verily believe, is out of his element as long as he is operative. I am altogether for the life contemplative. Will no kindly earthquake come and swallow up those accursed cotton mills? Take me that lumber of a desk there, and bowl it down

As low as to the fiends.[130]

127. The Elgin Marbles were classical sculptures from the Parthenon brought to Britain by Lord Elgin in the early nineteenth century.

128. Corner or other sliced-off portion.

129. Lucretius suggests that it is pleasant "to gaze from shore upon another's great tribulation"; *De rerum natura* (On the Nature of Things), II.1.

130. Shakespeare, *Hamlet*, II.ii.500.

I am no longer * * * * * *, clerk to the Firm of &c. I am Retired Leisure. I am to be met with in trim gardens. I am already come to be known by my vacant face and careless gesture, perambulating at no fixed pace, nor with any settled purpose. I walk about; not to and from. They tell me, a certain *cum dignitate* air, that has been buried so long with my other good parts, has begun to shoot forth in my person. I grow into gentility perceptibly. When I take up a newspaper, it is to read the state of the opera. *Opus operatum est.*[131] I have done all that I came into this world to do. I have worked task work, and have the rest of the day to myself.

May 1825

131. The work is finished; *otium cum dignitate* means "ease with dignity."

THIRTEEN

Thomas De Quincey
(1785–1859)

THOMAS DE QUINCEY, A MEMBER of the triumvirate of Romantic essayists in the familiar style that also includes Hazlitt and Lamb, was a shy, sensitive, romantically minded youth who could write and speak Greek fluently by the age of fifteen. In 1802 he ran away from Manchester Grammar School for a four-month walking tour of Wales, surviving on an allowance of a guinea a week from his uncle. After the uncle became frustrated with De Quincey's lack of communication, he withdrew the stipend, and De Quincy borrowed money to travel to London, where he lived near starvation on the streets, an experience that endangered his already frail health. As he later recalled, his first encounter with opium was due to stomach upset (much as his friend Coleridge's had been). The concept of addiction had not yet been formulated, and the drug was readily available at druggists' shops. In 1803 he left London for Worcester College, Oxford, where he led a reclusive existence on a meager income and began in earnest his lifelong career as an opium eater.

After four years De Quincey left Oxford without a degree and cultivated friendships with Lamb, Wordsworth, Coleridge, and Southey. He followed the poets to Grasmere, settling down next to them in the Lake District amid his own mountains of books. In 1821 he sold some translations of German authors and contracted his "Confessions of an English Opium Eater" with *The London Magazine*, where Lamb and Hazlitt also published. Seven years later he left the Lakes for Edinburgh, where he contributed pieces to *Blackwood's Magazine*, *Knight's Quarterly Magazine*, *Tait's Magazine*, and the *Edinburgh Literary Gazette*. He married Margaret Simpson (mother of his illegitimate son, William Pensen) in February 1817 and fathered a family of four more sons and three daughters. After Margaret's death in 1827, he retreated further into his books, living out his remaining years as a scholar and gentleman.

Selections are excerpted from Thomas De Quincey, "Confessions of an English Opium Eater," *The London Magazine* (1821).

Confessions of an English Opium Eater
Preliminary Confessions

These preliminary confessions, or introductory narrative of the youthful adventures which laid the foundation of the writer's habit of opium-eating in after-life, it has been judged proper to premise, for three several reasons:

1. As forestalling that question, and giving it a satisfactory answer, which else would painfully obtrude itself in the course of the Opium-Confessions—"How came any reasonable being to subject himself to such a yoke of misery, voluntarily to incur a captivity so servile, and knowingly to fetter himself with such a seven-fold chain?"[1]—a question which, if not somewhere plausibly resolved, could hardly fail, by the indignation which it would be apt to raise as against an act of wanton folly, to interfere with that degree of sympathy which is necessary in any case to an author's purposes.

2. As furnishing a key to some parts of that tremendous scenery which afterwards peopled the dreams of the Opium-eater.

3. As creating some previous interest of a personal sort in the confessing subject, apart from the matter of the confessions, which cannot fail to render the confessions themselves more interesting. If a man "whose talk is of oxen," should become an Opium-eater, the probability is, that (if he is not too dull to dream at all)—he will dream about oxen: whereas, in the case before him, the reader will find that the Opium-eater boasteth himself to be a philosopher; and accordingly, that the phantasmagoria of his dreams (waking or sleeping, day-dreams or night-dreams) is suitable to one who in that character,

Humani nihil a se alienum putat.[2]

1. See Genesis 4:15, where God warns that if anyone kills Cain, Cain shall be avenged sevenfold.
2. "I am a man, I hold that what affects another man affects me"; Terence, *Heauton Timorumenos* (The Self-Tormentor), I.i.77. For "whose talk is of oxen," see *Ecclesiasticus* 38:25 in the Apocrypha.

For amongst the conditions which he deems indispensable to the sustaining of any claim to the title of philosopher, is not merely the possession of a superb intellect in its *analytic* functions (in which part of the pretension, however, England can for some generations show but few claimants; at least, he is not aware of any known candidate for this honour who can be styled emphatically a *subtle thinker,* with the exception of *Samuel Taylor Coleridge,* and in a narrower department of thought, with the recent illustrious exception* of *David Ricardo*)³—but also on such a constitution of the *moral* faculties, as shall give him an inner eye and power of intuition for the vision and the mysteries of our human nature: *that* constitution of faculties, in short, which (amongst all the generations of men that from the beginning of time have deployed into life, as it were, upon this planet) our English poets have possessed in the highest degree—and Scottish Professors in the lowest.†

I have often been asked, how I first came to be a regular opium-eater; and have suffered, very unjustly, in the opinion of my acquaintance, from being reputed to have brought upon myself all the sufferings which I shall have to record, by a long course of indulgence in this practice purely for the sake of creating an artificial state of pleasurable excitement. This, however, is a misrepresentation of my case. True it is, that for nearly ten years I did

---

*A third exception might perhaps have been added: and my reason for not adding that exception is chiefly because it was only in his juvenile efforts that the writer whom I allude to, expressly addressed himself to philosophical themes [William Hazlitt, who published *An Essay on the Principles of Human Action* in 1803]; his riper powers having been all dedicated (on very excusable and very intelligent grounds, under the present direction of the popular mind in England) to criticism and the Fine Arts. This reason apart, however, I doubt whether he is not rather to be considered an acute thinker than a subtle one. It is, besides, a great drawback on his mastery over philosophical subjects, that he has obviously not had the advantage of a regular scholastic education: he has not read Plato in his youth (which most likely was only his misfortune); but neither has he read Kant in his manhood (which is his fault).

†I disclaim any allusion to *existing* professors, of whom indeed I know only one. [John Wilson, professor of moral philosophy at Edinburgh University and a leading contributor to *Blackwood's Magazine* under the pseudonym "Christopher North."]

3. David Ricardo was the author of *Principles of Political Economy and Taxation* (1817).

occasionally take opium, for the sake of the exquisite pleasure it gave me: but, so long as I took it with this view, I was effectually protected from all material bad consequences, by the necessity of interposing long intervals between the several acts of indulgence, in order to renew the pleasurable sensations. It was not for the purpose of creating pleasure, but of mitigating pain in the severest degree, that I first began to use opium as an article of daily diet. In the twenty-eighth year of my age, a most painful affection of the stomach, which I had first experienced about ten years before, attacked me in great strength. This affection had originally been caused by extremities of hunger, suffered in my boyish days. During the season of hope and redundant happiness which succeeded (that is, from eighteen to twenty-four) it had slumbered: for the three following years it had revived at intervals: and now, under unfavourable circumstances, from depression of spirits, it attacked me with a violence that yielded to no remedies but opium. As the youthful sufferings, which first produced this derangement of the stomach, were interesting in themselves, and in the circumstances that attended them, I shall here briefly retrace them.

My father died, when I was about seven years old, and left me to the care of four guardians. I was sent to various schools, great and small; and was very early distinguished for my classical attainments, especially for my knowledge of Greek. At thirteen, I wrote Greek with ease; and at fifteen my command of that language was so great, that I not only composed Greek verses in lyric metres, but could converse in Greek fluently, and without embarrassment—an accomplishment which I have not since met with in any scholar of my times, and which, in my case, was owing to the practice of daily reading off the newspapers into the best Greek I could furnish *extempore:* for the necessity of ransacking my memory and invention, for all sorts and combinations of periphrastic expressions, as equivalents for modern ideas, images, relations of things, &c. gave me a compass of diction which would never have been called out by a dull translation of moral essays, &c. "That boy," said one of my masters, pointing the attention of a stranger to me, "that boy could harangue an Athenian mob, better than you or I could address an English one."

. . .

I contrived, by means which I must omit for want of room, to transfer myself to London. And now began the latter and fiercer stage of my long-sufferings; without using a disproportionate expression I might say, of my agony. For I now suffered, for upwards of sixteen weeks, the physical anguish of hunger in various degrees of intensity; but as bitter, perhaps, as ever any human being can have suffered who has survived it. I would not needlessly harass my reader's feelings, by a detail of all that I endured: for extremities such as these, under any circumstances of heaviest misconduct or guilt, cannot be contemplated, even in description, without a rueful pity that is painful to the natural goodness of the human heart. Let it suffice, at least on this occasion, to say, that a few fragments of bread from the break-fast-table of one individual (who supposed me to be ill, but did not know of my being in utter want), and these at uncertain intervals, constituted my whole support. During the former part of my sufferings (that is, generally in Wales, and always for the first two months in London) I was houseless, and very seldom slept under a roof. To this constant exposure to the open air I ascribe it mainly, that I did not sink under my torments. Latterly, how-ever, when colder and more inclement weather came on, and when, from the length of my sufferings, I had begun to sink into a more languishing condition, it was, no doubt, fortunate for me, that the same person to whose breakfast-table I had access, allowed me to sleep in a large unoccu-pied house, of which he was tenant. Unoccupied, I call it, for there was no household or establishment in it; nor any furniture, indeed, except a table, and a few chairs. But I found, on taking possession of my new quarters, that the house already contained one single inmate, a poor friendless child, ap-parently ten years old; but she seemed hunger-bitten; and sufferings of that sort often make children look older than they are. From this forlorn child I learned, that she had slept and lived there alone, for some time before I came: and great joy the poor creature expressed, when she found that I was, in future, to be her companion through the hours of darkness. The house was large; and, from the want of furniture, the noise of the rats made a prodigious echoing on the spacious stair-case and hall; and, amidst the real fleshly ills of cold, and, I fear, hunger, the forsaken child had found leisure to suffer still more (it appeared) from the self-created one of ghosts. I promised her protection against all ghosts whatsoever: but, alas! I could of-fer her no other assistance. We lay upon the floor, with a bundle of cursed law papers for a pillow: but with no other covering than a sort of large horseman's cloak: afterwards, however, we discovered, in a garret, an old sopha-cover, a small piece of rug, and some fragments of other articles, which added a little to our warmth. The poor child crept close to me for warmth, and for security against her ghostly enemies. When I was not more than usually ill, I took her into my arms, so that, in general, she was tolerably warm, and often slept when I could not: for, during the last two months of my sufferings, I slept much in the day-time, and was apt to fall into transient dozings at all hours. But my sleep distressed me more than my watching: for, besides the tumultuousness of my dreams (which were only not so awful as those which I shall have to describe hereafter as produced by opium), my sleep was never more than what is called *dog-sleep;*[4] so that I could hear myself moaning, and was often, as it seemed to me, wakened suddenly by my own voice; and, about this time, a hideous sensation began to haunt me as soon as I fell into a slumber, which has since returned upon me, at different periods of my life, viz. a sort of twitching (I know not where, but apparently about the region of the stomach), which compelled me violently to throw out my feet for the sake of relieving it. This sensation coming on as soon as I began to sleep, and the effort to relieve it constantly awaking me, at length I slept only from exhaustion; and from increasing weakness (as I said before) I was constantly falling asleep, and constantly awaking. Meantime, the master of the house sometimes came in upon us suddenly, and very early, sometimes not till ten o'clock, sometimes not at all. He was in constant fear of bailiffs: improving on the plan of Cromwell, every night he slept in a different quarter of London;[5] and I observed that he never failed to examine, through a private window, the appearance of those who knocked at the door, before he would allow it to be opened. He breakfasted alone: indeed, his tea equipage would hardly have admitted of his hazarding an invitation to a second person—any more than the quantity of esculent *matériel,*[6] which, for the most part, was little more than a roll, or a few biscuits, which he had bought on his road from the place where he had slept. Or, if he *had* asked a party, as I once learnedly and facetiously ob-

4. Fitful naps.

5. Oliver Cromwell "rarely lodged two nights together in one chamber" for fear of assassination, according to Edward, Earl of Clarendon, *History of the Rebellion* (1849), 6:100. The landlord was afraid that the bailiffs would arrest him for debt.

6. Edible matter.

served to him—the several members of it must have *stood* in the relation to each other (not *sat* in any relation whatever) of succession, as the metaphysicians have it, and not of co-existence; in the relation of parts of time, and not of the parts of space. During his breakfast, I generally contrived a reason for lounging in; and, with an air of as much indifference as I could assume, took up such fragments as he had left—sometimes, indeed, there were none at all. In doing this, I committed no robbery except upon the man himself, who was thus obliged (I believe) now and then to send out at noon for an extra biscuit; for, as to the poor child, *she* was never admitted into his study (if I may give that name to his chief depository of parchments, law writings, &c.); that room was to her the Blue-beard room of the house, being regularly locked on his departure to dinner, about six o'clock, which usually was his final departure for the night.[7] Whether this child were an illegitimate daughter of Mr. ———, or only a servant, I could not ascertain; she did not herself know; but certainly she was treated altogether as a menial servant. No sooner did Mr. ——— make his appearance, than she went below stairs, brushed his shoes, coat, &c.; and, except when she was summoned to run an errand, she never emerged from the dismal Tartarus of the kitchens, &c. to the upper air, until my welcome knock at night called up her little trembling footsteps to the front door. Of her life during the day-time, however, I knew little but what I gathered from her own account at night; for, as soon as the hours of business commenced, I saw that my absence would be acceptable; and, in general, therefore, I went off and sat in the parks, or elsewhere, until night-fall.

But who, and what, meantime, was the master of the house himself? Reader, he was one of those anomalous practitioners in lower departments of the law, who—what shall I say?—who, on prudential reasons, or from necessity, deny themselves all indulgence in the luxury of too delicate a conscience: (a periphrasis which might be abridged considerably, but *that* I leave to the reader's taste:) in many walks of life, a conscience is a more expensive encumbrance, than a wife or a carriage; and just as people talk of "laying down" their carriages, so I suppose my friend, Mr. ——— had "laid

7. In Charles Perrault's fairy-tale, Bluebeard's wife is forbidden to enter a certain room in his castle, which contained the bodies of his previous wives, whom he had murdered.

down" his conscience for a time; meaning, doubtless, to resume it as soon as he could afford it. The inner economy of such a man's daily life would present a most strange picture, if I could allow myself to amuse the reader at his expense. Even with my limited opportunities for observing what went on, I saw many scenes of London intrigues, and complex chicanery, "cycle and epicycle, orb in orb,"[8] at which I sometimes smile to this day—and at which I smiled then, in spite of my misery. My situation, however, at that time, gave me little experience, in my own person, of any qualities in Mr. ————'s character but such as did him honour; and of his whole strange composition, I must forget every thing but that towards me he was obliging, and, to the extent of his power, generous.

That power was not, indeed, very extensive; however, in common with the rats, I sat rent free; and, as Dr. Johnson has recorded, that he never but once in his life had as much wall-fruit as he could eat,[9] so let me be grateful, that on that single occasion I had as large a choice of apartments in a London mansion as I could possibly desire. Except the Blue-beard room, which the poor child believed to be haunted, all others, from the attics to the cellars, were at our service; "the world was all before us";[10] and we pitched our tent for the night in any spot we chose. This house I have already described as a large one; it stands in a conspicuous situation, and in a well-known part of London. Many of my readers will have passed it, I doubt not, within a few hours of reading this. For myself, I never fail to visit it when business draws me to London; about ten o'clock, this very night, August 15, 1821, being my birth-day—I turned aside from my evening walk, down Oxford-street, purposely to take a glance at it: it is now occupied by a respectable family; and, by the lights in the front drawing-room, I observed a domestic party, assembled perhaps at tea, and apparently cheerful and gay. Marvellous contrast in my eyes to the darkness—cold—silence—and desolation of that same house eighteen years ago, when its nightly occupants were one famishing scholar, and a neglected child. Her, by the bye, in after years, I vainly endeavoured to trace. Apart from her sit-

8. Milton, *Paradise Lost*, VIII.84.

9. See Hester Lynch Piozzi's *Anecdotes of the Late Samuel Johnson* (London, 1786), 103. Wall-fruit comes from trees trained to grow up against a wall.

10. Adapted from the final lines of Milton's *Paradise Lost*, on the expulsion of Adam and Eve from Eden.

uation, she was not what would be called an interesting child: she was neither pretty, nor quick in understanding, nor remarkably pleasing in manners. But, thank God! even in those years I needed not the embellishments
of novel-accessaries to conciliate my affections; plain human nature, in its
humblest and most homely apparel, was enough for me: and I loved the
child because she was my partner in wretchedness. If she is now living, she
is probably a mother, with children of her own; but, as I have said, I could
never trace her.

This I regret, but another person there was at that time, whom I have
since sought to trace with far deeper earnestness, and with far deeper sorrow at my failure. This person was a young woman, and one of that unhappy class who subsist upon the wages of prostitution. I feel no shame, nor
have any reason to feel it, in avowing, that I was then on familiar and
friendly terms with many women in that unfortunate condition. The reader
needs neither smile at this avowal, nor frown. For, not to remind my classical readers of the old Latin proverb—"*Sine Cerere,*" &c., it may well be
supposed that in the existing state of my purse, my connexion with such
women could not have been an impure one.[11] But the truth is, that at no
time of my life have I been a person to hold myself polluted by the touch or
approach of any creature that wore a human shape: on the contrary, from
my very earliest youth it has been my pride to converse familiarly, *more So-
cratico,*[12] with all human beings, man, woman, and child, that chance
might fling in my way: a practice which is friendly to the knowledge of human nature, to good feelings, and to that frankness of address which becomes a man who would be thought a philosopher. For a philosopher
should not see with the eyes of the poor limitary creature calling himself a
man of the world, and filled with narrow and self-regarding prejudices of
birth and education, but should look upon himself as a Catholic creature,
and as standing in an equal relation to high and low—to educated and
uneducated, to the guilty and the innocent. Being myself at that time of necessity a peripatetic, or a walker of the streets, I naturally fell in more frequently with those female peripatetics who are technically called Street-

11. To the Latin phrase, "Without Ceres [Roman goddess of agriculture,
hence bread, food] and without Bacchus [god of wine]," Byron added, "Venus will
not long attack us"; *Don Juan,* II.1352.

12. By the Socratic method: question and answer to arrive at truth.

walkers. Many of these women had occasionally taken my part against watchmen who wished to drive me off the steps of houses where I was sitting. But one amongst them, the one on whose account I have at all introduced this subject—yet no! let me not class thee, Oh noble minded Ann ———, with that order of women; let me find, if it be possible, some gentler name to designate the condition of her to whose bounty and compassion, ministering to my necessities when all the world had forsaken me, I owe it that I am at this time alive.—For many weeks I had walked at nights with this poor friendless girl up and down Oxford Street, or had rested with her on steps and under the shelter of porticos. She could not be so old as myself: she told me, indeed, that she had not completed her sixteenth year. By such questions as my interest about her prompted, I had gradually drawn forth her simple history. Hers was a case of ordinary occurrence (as I have since had reason to think), and one in which, if London beneficence had better adapted its arrangements to meet it, the power of the law might oftener be interposed to protect, and to avenge. But the stream of London charity flows in a channel which, though deep and mighty, is yet noiseless and underground; not obvious or readily accessible to poor houseless wanderers: and it cannot be denied that the outside air and frame-work of London society is harsh, cruel, and repulsive. In any case, however, I saw that part of her injuries might easily have been redressed: and I urged her often and earnestly to lay her complaint before a magistrate: friendless as she was, I assured her that she would meet with immediate attention; and that English justice, which was no respecter of persons, would speedily and amply avenge her on the brutal ruffian who had plundered her little property. She promised me often that she would; but she delayed taking the steps I pointed out from time to time: for she was timid and dejected to a degree which showed how deeply sorrow had taken hold of her young heart: and perhaps she thought justly that the most upright judge, and the most righteous tribunals, could do nothing to repair her heaviest wrongs. Something, however, would perhaps have been done: for it had been settled between us at length, but unhappily on the very last time but one that I was ever to see her, that in a day or two we should go together before a magistrate, and that I should speak on her behalf. This little service it was destined, however, that I should never realise. Meantime, that which she rendered to me, and which was greater than I could ever have repaid her, was this: one night, when we were pacing slowly along Oxford Street, and after a day when I had felt more than usually ill and faint, I requested her to turn off with me into Soho Square: thither we went; and we sat down on the steps of a house, which, to this hour, I never pass without a pang of grief, and an inner act of homage to the spirit of that unhappy girl, in memory of the noble action which she there performed. Suddenly, as we sat, I grew much worse: I had been leaning my head against her bosom; and all at once I sank from her arms and fell backwards on the steps. From the sensations I then had, I felt an inner conviction of the liveliest kind that without some powerful and reviving stimulus, I should either have died on the spot—or should at least have sunk to a point of exhaustion, from which all reascent under my friendless circumstances would soon have become hopeless. Then it was, at this crisis of my fate, that my poor orphan companion—who had herself met with little but injuries in this world—stretched out a saving hand to me. Uttering a cry of terror, but without a moment's delay, she ran off into Oxford Street, and in less time than could be imagined, returned to me with a glass of port wine and spices, that acted upon my empty stomach (which at that time would have rejected all solid food) with an instantaneous power of restoration: and for this glass the generous girl without a murmur paid out of her own humble purse at a time—be it remembered!—when she had scarcely wherewithal to purchase the bare necessaries of life, and when she could have no reason to expect that I should ever be able to reimburse her. ——— Oh! youthful benefactress! how often in succeeding years, standing in solitary places, and thinking of thee with grief of heart and perfect love, how often have I wished that, as in ancient times the curse of a father was believed to have a supernatural power, and to pursue its object with a fatal necessity of self-fulfilment,—even so the benediction of a heart oppressed with gratitude, might have a like prerogative; might have power given to it from above to chase—to haunt—to waylay—to overtake—to pursue thee into the central darkness of a London brothel, or (if it were possible) into the darkness of the grave—there to awaken thee with an authentic message of peace and forgiveness, and of final reconciliation!

. . .

Meantime, what had become of poor Ann? For her I have reserved my concluding words: according to our agreement, I sought her daily, and waited for her every night, so long as I stayed in London, at the corner of Titchfield-street. I inquired for her of every one who was likely to know her; and, during the last hours of my stay in London, I put into activity every means of tracing her that my knowledge of London suggested, and the limited extent of my power made possible. The street where she had lodged I knew, but not the house; and I remembered at last some account which she had given me of ill treatment from her landlord, which made it probable that she had quitted those lodgings before we parted. She had few acquaintance; most people, besides, thought that the earnestness of my inquiries arose from motives which moved their laughter, or their slight regard; and others, thinking I was in chase of a girl who had robbed me of some trifles, were naturally and excusably indisposed to give me any clue to her, if, indeed, they had any to give. Finally, as my despairing resource, on the day I left London I put into the hands of the only person who (I was sure) must know Ann by sight, from having been in company with us once or twice, an address to ——— in ——— shire, at that time the residence of my family. But, to this hour, I have never heard a syllable about her. This, amongst such troubles as most men meet with in this life, has been my heaviest affliction. If she lived, doubtless we must have been sometimes in search of each other, at the very same moment, through the mighty labyrinths of London; perhaps, even within a few feet of each other—a barrier no wider in a London street, often amounting in the end to a separation for eternity! During some years, I hoped that she did live; and I suppose that, in the literal and unrhetorical use of the word *myriad,* I may say that on my different visits to London, I have looked into many, many myriads of female faces, in the hope of meeting her. I should know her again amongst a thousand, if I saw her for a moment; for, though not handsome, she had a sweet expression of countenance, and a peculiar and graceful carriage of the head. I sought her, I have said, in hope. So it was for years; but now I should fear to see her; and her cough, which grieved me when I parted with her, is now my consolation. I now wish to see her no longer, but think of her, more gladly, as one long since laid in the grave; in the grave, I would hope, of a Magdalen; taken away, before injuries and cruelty had blotted out and transfigured her ingenuous nature, or the brutalities of ruffians had completed the ruin they had begun.

September 1821

So then, Oxford-street, stony-hearted step-mother! thou that listenest to the sighs of orphans, and drinkest the tears of children, at length I was dismissed from thee: the time was come at last that I no more should pace in anguish thy never-ending terraces; no more should dream, and wake in captivity to the pangs of hunger. Successors, too many, to myself and Ann, have, doubtless, since then trodden in our footsteps—inheritors of our calamities: other orphans than Ann have sighed: tears have been shed by other children: and thou, Oxford-street, hast since, doubtless, echoed to the groans of innumerable hearts. For myself, however, the storm which I had outlived seemed to have been the pledge of a long fair-weather; the premature sufferings which I had paid down, to have been accepted as a ransom for many years to come, as a price of long immunity from sorrow: and if again I walked in London, a solitary and contemplative man (as oftentimes I did), I walked for the most part in serenity and peace of mind. And, although it is true that the calamities of my noviciate in London had struck root so deeply in my bodily constitution that afterwards they shot up and flourished afresh, and grew into a noxious umbrage that has overshadowed and darkened my latter years, yet these second assaults of suffering were met with a fortitude more confirmed, with the resources of a maturer intellect, and with alleviations from sympathising affection—how deep and tender!

Thus, however, with whatsoever alleviations, years that were far asunder were bound together by subtle links of suffering derived from a common root. And herein I notice an instance of the short-sightedness of human desires, that oftentimes on moonlight nights, during my first mournful abode in London, my consolation was (if such it could be thought) to gaze from Oxford-street up every avenue in succession which pierces through the heart of Marylebone to the fields and the woods; for that, said I, travelling with my eyes up the long vistas which lay part in light and part in shade, "*that* is the road to the North, and therefore to ———, and if I had the wings of a dove, *that* way I would fly for comfort."[13] Thus I said, and thus I wished, in my blindness; yet, even in that very northern re-

13. The blank should be filled in with "Wordsworth," who lived at Grasmere and whom De Quincey remembers in his *Recollections of the Lakes and the Lake Poets* (1823). The quotation alludes to Psalm 55:6.

gion it was, even in that very valley, nay, in that very house to which my erroneous wishes pointed, that this second birth of my sufferings began; and
that they again threatened to besiege the citadel of life and hope. There it
was, that for years I was persecuted by visions as ugly, and as ghastly phantoms as ever haunted the couch of an Orestes:[14] and in this unhappier than
he, that sleep, which comes to all as a respite and a restoration, and to him
especially, as a blessed* balm for his wounded heart and his haunted brain,
visited me as my bitterest scourge. Thus blind was I in my desires; yet, if a
veil interposes between the dim-sightedness of man and his future calamities, the same veil hides from him their alleviations; and a grief which had
not been feared is met by consolations which had not been hoped. I, therefore, who participated, as it were, in the troubles of Orestes (excepting only
in his agitated conscience), participated no less in all his supports: my Eu-
menides, like his, were at my bed-feet, and stared in upon me through the
curtains: but, watching by my pillow, or defrauding herself of sleep to bear
me company through the heavy watches of the night, sat my Electra: for
thou, beloved M., dear companion of my later years, thou wast my Electra![15] and neither in nobility of mind nor in long-suffering affection,
wouldst permit that a Grecian sister should excel an English wife. For thou
thoughtst not much to stoop to humble offices of kindness, and to servile†
ministrations of tenderest affection; to wipe away for years the unwhole-
some dews upon the forehead, or to refresh the lips when parched and baked
with fever; nor, even when thy own peaceful slumbers had by long sympathy
become infected with the spectacle of my dread contest with phantoms and
shadowy enemies that oftentimes bade me "sleep no more!"[16]—not even
then, didst thou utter a complaint or any murmur, nor withdraw thy angelic

*ὦ φίλον ὕπνου θέλγητρον ἐπίκουρον νόσου ["O sleep's enchantment, friend
and helper against sickness"; Euripides, *Orestes*, l. 211].

†ἡδὺ δούλευμα [sweet slavery]. *Eurip. Orest.* [l. 221].

14. Here and in De Quincey's notes the references are to Euripides' *Orestes*.
In the tragedy, Orestes, having murdered his mother, Clytemnestra, to avenge his
father, Agamemnon (whom she murdered), is tormented by the Furies (Eu-
menides).

15. M. is Margaret Simpson, the mother of De Quincey's eight children.
Electra was Orestes' sister, who urged him to murder his mother and comforted
him when he was tormented by the Furies.

16. Shakespeare, *Macbeth*, II.ii.33.

smiles, nor shrink from thy service of love more than Electra did of old. For she too, though she was a Grecian woman, and the daughter of the king* of men, yet wept sometimes, and hid her face† in her robe.

But these troubles are past: and thou wilt read these records of a period so dolorous to us both as the legend of some hideous dream that can return no more. Meantime, I am again in London: and again I pace the terraces of Oxford-street by night: and oftentimes, when I am oppressed by anxieties that demand all my philosophy and the comfort of thy presence to support, and yet remember that I am separated from thee by three hundred miles, and the length of three dreary months, I look up the streets that run northwards from Oxford-street, upon moonlight nights, and recollect my youthful ejaculation of anguish; and remembering that thou art sitting alone in that same valley, and mistress of that very house to which my heart turned in its blindness nineteen years ago, I think that, though blind indeed, and scattered to the winds of late, the promptings of my heart may yet have had reference to a remoter time, and may be justified if read in another meaning: and, if I could allow myself to descend again to the impotent wishes of childhood, I should again say to myself, as I look to the north, "Oh, that I had the wings of a dove—" and with how just a confidence in thy good and gracious nature might I add the other half of my early ejaculation—"And *that* way I would fly for comfort."

The Pleasures of Opium

It is so long since I first took opium, that if it had been a trifling incident in my life, I might have forgotten its date: but cardinal events are not to be

---

*ἄναξ ἀνδρῶν Ἀγαμέμνων ["the king of men, Agamemnon"; Homer, *Iliad*, X.64].

†ὄμμα θεὶς ἔισω πέπλον ["covering your head with your garments"; Euripides," *Orestes*, l. 280]. The scholar will know that throughout this passage I refer to the early scenes of the Orestes; one of the most beautiful exhibitions of the domestic affections which even the dramas of Euripides can furnish. To the English reader, it may be necessary to say, that the situation at the opening of the drama is that of a brother attended only by his sister during the demoniacal possession of a suffering conscience (or, in the mythology of the play, haunted by furies), and in circumstances of immediate danger from enemies, and of desertion or cold regard from nominal friends.

forgotten; and from circumstances connected with it, I remember that it must be referred to the autumn of 1804. During that season I was in London, having come thither for the first time since my entrance at college. And my introduction to opium arose in the following way. From an early age I had been accustomed to wash my head in cold water at least once a day: being suddenly seized with tooth-ache, I attributed it to some relaxation caused by an accidental intermission of that practice; jumped out of bed; plunged my head into a basin of cold water; and with hair thus wetted went to sleep. The next morning, as I need hardly say, I awoke with excruciating rheumatic pains of the head and face, from which I had hardly any respite for about twenty days. On the twenty-first day, I think it was, and on a Sunday, that I went out into the streets; rather to run away, if possible, from my torments, than with any distinct purpose. By accident I met a college acquaintance who recommended opium. Opium! dread agent of unimaginable pleasure and pain! I had heard of it as I had of manna or of Ambrosia, but no further: how unmeaning a sound was it at that time! what solemn chords does it now strike upon my heart! what heart-quaking vibrations of sad and happy remembrances! Reverting for a moment to these, I feel a mystic importance attached to the minutest circumstances connected with the place and the time, and the man (if man he was) that first laid open to me the Paradise of Opium-eaters. It was a Sunday afternoon, wet and cheerless: and a duller spectacle this earth of ours has not to show than a rainy Sunday in London.[17] My road homewards lay through Oxford-street; and near "the stately Pantheon," (as Mr. Wordsworth has obligingly called it)[18] I saw a druggist's shop. The druggist—unconscious minister of celestial pleasures!—as if in sympathy with the rainy Sunday, looked dull and stupid, just as any mortal druggist might be expected to look on a Sunday: and, when I asked for the tincture of opium, he gave it to me as any other man might do: and furthermore, out of my shilling, returned me what seemed to be real copper halfpence, taken out of a real wooden drawer. Nevertheless, in spite of such indications of humanity, he has ever since existed in my mind as the beatific vision of an immortal drug-

17. An inversion of the first line of Wordsworth's "Composed Upon Westminster Bridge, Sept. 3, 1802": "Earth has not anything to show more fair."
18. From line 3 of "The Power of Music."

gist, sent down to earth on a special mission to myself. And it confirms me in this way of considering him, that, when I next came up to London, I sought him near the stately Pantheon, and found him not: and thus to me, who knew not his name (if indeed he had one) he seemed rather to have vanished from Oxford-street than to have removed in any bodily fashion. The reader may choose to think of him as, possibly, no more than a sublunary druggist: it may be so: but my faith is better: I believe him to have evanesced,* or evaporated. So unwillingly would I connect any mortal remembrances with that hour, and place, and creature, that first brought me acquainted with the celestial drug.

Arrived at my lodgings, it may be supposed that I lost not a moment in taking the quantity prescribed. I was necessarily ignorant of the whole art and mystery of opium-taking: and, what I took, I took under every disadvantage. But I took it: and in an hour, oh! Heavens! what a revulsion! what an upheaving, from its lowest depths, of the inner spirit! what an apocalypse of the world within me! That my pains had vanished, was now a trifle in my eyes: this negative effect was swallowed up in the immensity of those positive effects which had opened before me—in the abyss of divine enjoyment thus suddenly revealed. Here was a panacea—a φάρμακον νηπενθές for all human woes:[19] here was the secret of happiness, about which philosophers had disputed for so many ages, at once discovered: happiness might now be bought for a penny, and carried in the waistcoat pocket: portable ecstacies might be had corked up in a pint bottle: and peace of mind could be sent down in gallons by the mail coach.

. . .

Evanesced: this way of going off the stage of life appears to have been well known in the 17th century, but at that time to have been considered a peculiar privilege of blood-royal, and by no means allowed to druggists. For about the year 1686, a poet of rather ominous name (and who, by the bye, did ample justice to his name), viz. Mr *Flat-man,* in speaking of the death of Charles II, expresses his surprise that any prince should commit so absurd an act as dying; because, says he, "Kings should disdain to die, and only *disappear.*" They should abscond, that is, into the other world. [See Thomas Flatman's Pindaric ode "On the Death of Our Late Sovereign Lord King Charles II" (1685).]

19. The Greek phrase, meaning "an anodyne of forgetfulness," is loosely adapted from Homer's *Odyssey,* IV.220–21.

Paint me, then, a room seventeen feet by twelve, and not more than seven and a half feet high. This, reader, is somewhat ambitiously styled, in my family, the drawing-room: but, being contrived "a double debt to pay,"[20] it is also, and more justly, termed the library; for it happens that books are the only article of property in which I am richer than my neighbours. Of these, I have about five thousand, collected gradually since my eighteenth year. Therefore, painter, put as many as you can into this room. Make it populous with books: and, furthermore, paint me a good fire; and furniture, plain and modest, befitting the unpretending cottage of a scholar. And near the fire, paint me a tea-table; and (as it is clear that no creature can come to see one such a stormy night,) place only two cups and saucers on the tea-tray; and, if you know how to paint such a thing symbolically or otherwise, paint me an eternal tea-pot—eternal *à parte ante* and *à parte post;*[21] for I usually drink tea from eight o'clock at night to four o'clock in the morning. And, as it is very unpleasant to make tea, or to pour it out for oneself, paint me a lovely young woman, sitting at the table. Paint her arms like Aurora's, and her smiles like Hebe's:[22]—But no, dear M., not even in jest let me insinuate that thy power to illuminate my cottage rests upon a tenure so perishable as mere personal beauty; or that the witchcraft of angelic smiles lies within the empire of any earthly pencil. Pass, then, my good painter, to something more within its power: and the next article brought forward should naturally be myself—a picture of the Opium-eater, with his "little golden receptacle of the pernicious drug,"[23] lying beside

20. Goldsmith, *The Deserted Village,* l. 229.

21. See sermon 54, "On Eternity" in John Wesley, *Sermons on Several Occasions* (1771). The Latin phrases mean an eternity before and after (this life).

22. Aurora is the Roman goddess of dawn; Hebe is the Greek goddess of youth and cup-bearer to the gods.

23. De Quincey derisively lifts a phrase from Thomas Hope's novel *Anastasius; or, Memoirs of a Greek* (London, 1819), 1:232–33: "The old man here fell back into his apathy, but I was roused effectually. I resolved to renounce the slow poison of whose havock my neighbour was so woeful a specimen; and, in order not even to preserve a memento of the sin I abjured, presented him, as a reward for his advice, with the little golden receptacle of the pernicious drug which I used to carry. He took the bauble without appearing sensible of the gift; while I, running into the middle of the square, pronounced, with outstretched hands, against the execrable market where insanity was sold by the ounce, an elaborate and solemn malediction."

him on the table. As to the opium, I have no objection to see a picture of *that*, though I would rather see the original: you may paint it, if you choose; but I apprize you, that no "little" receptacle would, even in 1816, answer *my* purpose, who was at a distance from the "stately Pantheon," and all druggists (mortal or otherwise). No: you may as well paint the real receptacle, which was not of gold, but of glass, and as much like a wine-decanter as possible. Into this you may put a quart of ruby-colored laudanum:[24] that, and a book of German metaphysics placed by its side, will sufficiently attest my being in the neighbourhood; but, as to myself,—there I demur. I admit that, naturally, I ought to occupy the foreground of the picture; that being the hero of the piece, or (if you choose) the criminal at the bar, my body should be had into court. This seems reasonable: but why should I confess, on this point, to a painter? or why confess at all? If the public (into whose private ear I am confidentially whispering my confessions, and not into my painter's) should chance to have framed some agreeable picture for itself, of the Opium-eater's exterior,—should have ascribed to him, romantically, an elegant person, or a handsome face, why should I barbarously tear from it so pleasing a delusion—pleasing both to the public and to me? No: paint me, if at all, according to your own fancy: and, as a painter's fancy should teem with beautiful creations, I cannot fail, in that way, to be a gainer. And now, reader, we have run through all the ten categories of my condition, as it stood about 1816–17: up to the middle of which latter year I judge myself to have been a happy man: and the elements of that happiness I have endeavoured to place before you, in the above sketch of the interior of a scholar's library, in a cottage among the mountains, on a stormy winter evening.

. . .

October 1821

24. An alcoholic solution with morphine, prepared from opium and formerly used as an over-the-counter narcotic painkiller.

Chronology

1660   The Restoration: after a decade of civil war, Charles II is restored to the throne. French tastes begin to influence culture, as the Puritans' influence wanes; the theaters reopen.

1665   The second Anglo-Dutch War breaks out on 4 March (lasting through July 1667). The Great Plague kills a fifth of London's population.

1666   The Great Fire of London wipes out a large portion of the city and population but ends the plague.

1667   Milton publishes *Paradise Lost* in ten books.

1670   John Dryden becomes England's first poet laureate.

1672   The third Anglo-Dutch War begins (lasting until 1674).

1674   Nicolas Boileau-Despréaux produces the first French translation of Longinus's treatise *On the Sublime*. The Theatre Royal, Drury Lane, designed by Christopher Wren, opens.

1678   John Bunyan publishes *The Pilgrim's Progress;* Milton's twelve-book *Paradise Lost* appears.

1685   The Catholic James II succeeds his brother Charles II, inciting political rebellions and power struggles.

1687   Isaac Newton defines the principles of modern physics in his *Principia*.

1688   The "Glorious Revolution": Prince William of Orange invades England with his wife, Mary, the Protestant daughter of James II, and the two become joint rulers.

1690   John Locke's *An Essay Concerning Human Understanding* defines the mind as a product of empirical experience.

1694   The Bank of England is founded. Queen Mary dies, but William III takes over the crown.

1701   The War of the Spanish Succession begins, pitting France, Bourbon Spain, Savoy, Cologne, and Bavaria against Austria, the Dutch Republic, and Portugal. (It lasts until 1714.)

1702   Queen Anne, the second daughter of James II, succeeds William III.

1704   The Duke of Marlborough leads English and Dutch troops to victory over France in the Battle of Blenheim, assisted by Austrian forces; the English capture Gibraltar as part of the War of the Spanish Succession. Jonathan Swift satirizes religious and literary excesses in *A Tale of a Tub*.

1707   The Act of Union unites England and Scotland into the kingdom of Great Britain.

1709   Richard Steele begins publication of *The Tatler* thrice weekly, starting 12 April (through 2 January 1711).

1710   The Whig ministry falls when Tories are elected to power.

1711   Joseph Addison and Richard Steele commence publication of *The Spectator,* issued every day but Sunday, starting 1 March (through 20 December 1712).

1712   The Stamp Act imposes a tax on newspapers. Joseph Addison's politically timely tragedy *Cato* opens to great acclaim at Drury Lane.

1713   Steele publishes *The Guardian* and becomes a Whig member of Parliament.

1714   Steele is expelled from Parliament on a charge of sedition. George I of Hanover succeeds Queen Anne. The War of the Spanish Succession ends, terminating France's hegemony over continental Europe and beginning European concern with a balance of power, mentioned in the 1713 Treaty of Utrecht. The second run of *The Spectator* begins, printed thrice-weekly from 18 July through 20 December.

1715   The first Jacobite uprising: James Stuart, the Old Pretender and son of James II, fails to recapture the throne from the Hanoverian George I. Louis XIV of France dies.

1719   Eliza Haywood publishes her scandalous novel *Love in Excess,* and Daniel Defoe publishes *Robinson Crusoe*. Addison dies at age forty-seven and is buried in Westminster Abbey.

1720   The speculative South Sea Bubble bursts, causing the stock market to crash.

1721   Robert Walpole becomes prime minister.

1722   Richard Steele's last major work, the comedy *The Conscious Lovers,* is staged.

1727   George II succeeds to the throne. Spain decides to recapture Gibraltar, triggering the Anglo-Spanish War, which lasts until 1729, with Britain still in control of Gibraltar.

1728   Alexander Pope publishes *The Dunciad,* mocking leading figures of the Republic of Letters. John Gay's musical comedy *The Beggar's Opera* is staged at Drury Lane.

1733   Covent Garden Theatre opens.

1737   The Theater Licensing Act imposes censorship on drama, under the office of the Lord Chamberlain.

1739   David Hume publishes the first volumes of *A Treatise of Human Nature.*

1740   Samuel Richardson's *Pamela* initiates the epistolary novel tradition.

1742   David Garrick takes over management of Drury Lane Theatre (through 1776).

1744   Alexander Pope dies. Eliza Haywood begins publication of *The Female Spectator* (through May 1746).

1745   The second Jacobite uprising, led by Charles Edward Stuart ("Bonnie Prince Charlie"), the son of James Stuart, who also fails to recapture the throne. Jonathan Swift dies and is buried in Westminster Abbey, signaling the end of the golden age of Augustan letters.

1749   Henry Fielding publishes *The History of Tom Jones, a Foundling.*

1750   Samuel Johnson begins bi-weekly publication of *The Rambler* (through March 1752). Elizabeth Montagu founds the Bluestocking Club.

1752   Henry Fielding publishes *The Covent Garden Journal,* bi-weekly and then weekly, from 4 January to 25 November.

1753   William Hogarth outlines his aesthetic principles in *The Analysis of Beauty.*

1754   On 31 January, the satirists George Colman and Bonnell Thornton begin weekly publication of *The Connoisseur* (through 31 September 1756). The Seven Years' War breaks out, involving the major powers in Europe and ending France's power in the Americas.

1755   Samuel Johnson publishes his dictionary of the English language.

1758   Dr. Johnson commences weekly publication of "The Idler" in *The Universal Chronicle* (through April 1760).

1759   Oliver Goldsmith publishes *The Bee* in weekly numbers, Adam Smith publishes *The Theory of Moral Sentiments,* Laurence Sterne publishes the first two volumes (of nine) of *Tristram Shandy,* and Voltaire publishes *Candide.* The British Museum opens to the public.

1760   George III succeeds to the throne; he is the first Hanoverian born in England with English as his native language.

1762   Jean-Jacques Rousseau outlines principles of liberty in *The Social Contract.*

1764   Wolfgang Amadeus Mozart moves to London (through 30 July 1765), writing his first two symphonies and performing regularly at concerts. Dr. Johnson founds his "Club" of literary and cultural elites.

1769   Sir Joshua Reynolds begins delivering his "Discourses on Art" at the Royal Academy.

1771   Henry Mackenzie publishes *The Man of Feeling.*

1774   Sarah Siddons, at age twenty, causes a sensation with her role as Lady Macbeth.

1775   The American Revolutionary War begins (lasting through 1783). Samuel Johnson publishes *A Journey to the Western Islands of Scotland,* a trip undertaken in company with James Boswell.

1776   Adam Smith publishes *The Wealth of Nations,* outlining laissez-faire economic theory; Edward Gibbon begins publishing *The Decline and Fall of the Roman Empire.*

1777   In October, Boswell commences monthly publication of "The Hypochondriack" in *The London Magazine* (through August 1783).

1779   Henry Mackenzie and his Mirror Club publish their periodical, *The Mirror,* in Edinburgh starting 23 January (through 27 May 1780).

1782   Samuel Taylor Coleridge joins Charles Lamb at Christ's Hospital School, London.

1784   Samuel Johnson dies and is buried in Westminster Abbey.

1785   Henry Mackenzie and friends publish *The Lounger,* starting 6 February (through 6 January 1787). William Cowper publishes his long poem in conversational style, *The Task.*

1788   George III suffers his first bout of madness (followed by others in 1801, 1803, and 1810).

1789   The storming of the Bastille prison initiates the French Revolution.

1790   Edmund Burke publishes his *Reflections on the Revolution in France,* initiating a pamphlet war and Mary Wollstonecraft's response, *A Vindication of the Rights of Men.*

1791   Boswell publishes his landmark biography, *The Life of Samuel Johnson.*

1793   Louis XVI is beheaded, beginning the Reign of Terror in Paris. Britain declares war on France.

1794   Habeas corpus is suspended in Britain, signaling a reactionary regime.

1797   Charles Lamb's sister Mary, in a fit of insanity, murders their mother.

1799   Napoleon becomes first Consul of the French Republic.

1800   Wordsworth outlines the principles of a new kind of poetry in the "Preface" to *Lyrical Ballads.*

1802   The Treaty of Amiens heralds a year of peace between Britain and France.

1804   Napoleon becomes emperor of France.

1808   Leigh and John Hunt found *The Examiner* and criticize British wartime policy.

1810   George Augustus Frederick, Prince of Wales (later George IV), is made regent, inaugurating the decade-long Regency period.

1812   Lord Byron becomes an overnight sensation with the first two cantos of *Childe Harold's Pilgrimage.*

1813   Robert Southey is appointed poet laureate. In January Leigh and John Hunt are indicted for libel against the Prince Regent and spend two years in prison. Jane Austen publishes *Pride and Prejudice.*

1814   Walter Scott publishes *Waverley,* a best-selling tale about the Jacobite uprising. Jane Austen publishes *Mansfield Park.*

1815   The Duke of Wellington, commanding the forces of Britain, Prussia, and the Russian Empire, defeats Napoleon at Waterloo, ending the Napoleonic Wars.

1818   Mary Shelley's *Frankenstein* and William Hazlitt's *Lectures on the English Poets* are published.

1819   Hunt begins publication of *The Indicator* (through 1821).

1820   George IV becomes king of Britain. John Keats publishes his last volume of poems. Charles Lamb begins a series of essays under the pseudonym "Elia" in *The London Magazine.*

1821   Thomas De Quincey publishes "Confessions of an English Opium Eater" in *The London Magazine.*

1822   Percy Bysshe Shelley drowns off the coast of Lerici.

1823   Hazlitt publishes the scandalous *Liber Amoris.*

1830   William IV succeeds to the throne, and the battle for parliamentary reform begins. Alfred Tennyson publishes his first volume of poems.

1832   The Reform Act begins to enfranchise the middle classes.

1837   Queen Victoria succeeds to the throne. Charles Dickens begins serial publication of *The Pickwick Papers,* the first of his many best-selling novels.

Glossary of Places

BRITISH MUSEUM   Opened in 1759 to the public in Montagu House in Bloomsbury, the museum houses antiquities, curiosities of natural history, and the royal libraries.

BUTTON'S COFFEE-HOUSE   Located on Russell Street near Will's and Tom's Coffee-houses, this was a successor to Will's and a center for wits and literary life after the death of Dryden, until Addison's death and Steele's retirement from London.

CAT AND FIDDLE   This coffeehouse, originally owned by the mutton-pie maker Christopher Kat, was where the Kit-Cat Club met at the end of William and Mary's reign to promote Whig policy and the arts.

CHILD'S COFFEE-HOUSE   A favored Tory resort in Saint Paul's Church-yard, Child's was patronized by doctors, both medical and philosophical.

COCOA-TREE   A popular chocolate house on Saint James's Street, it was the Tory response to the Whigs' Saint James's during the reign of Queen Anne.

COVENT GARDEN THEATRE   Now an opera house, the theater opened in 1732 on Bow Street, a strip of coffeehouses and gin shops, as a venue for plays, pantomimes, and opera.

DICK'S COFFEE-HOUSE   Situated on Fleet Street, Dick's was frequented by students of law (or Templars) during the reign of George II.

DRURY LANE THEATRE   This theater opened in 1663 under Charles II as the Theatre Royal; it was destroyed by fire in 1672 and rebuilt two years later on Drury Lane, where it remains.

GRAECIAN   The oldest of the better-known coffeehouses, the Graecian was located in Devereaux Court on the Strand and patronized by antiquarians, philosophers, and lawyers.

GROSVENOR SQUARE   This district in Mayfair was popular among the aristocracy during the Georgian period.

HANOVER SQUARE   Like Grosvenor Square, this was a garden square in the fashionable district of Mayfair.

HAY-MARKET THEATRE   Opened in 1720 as the Theatre Royal Haymarket, it was closed temporarily in 1737 when Henry Fielding staged a series of political satires, prompting the Theatre Licensing Act.

HYDE PARK   Formerly the royal hunting grounds, the park was opened to the public in 1637 under Charles I.

INNER TEMPLE   Along with Middle Temple, Lincoln's Inn, and Gray's Inn, this is one of the Inns of Court, located in the general vicinity of the Royal Courts of Justice.

JONATHAN'S COFFEE-HOUSE   Founded in Exchange Alley around 1680, it was a center of political conversation and commercial speculation from stock-trading to lotteries.

LLOYD'S COFFEE-HOUSE   Founded on Lombard Street the 1680s, it was a haunt for wine merchants, shipbrokers, insurance men, and other financiers.

LORD'S GROUND   This cricket ground, located in Saint John's Wood, is still operative.

MALL   South of Saint James's Palace, the Mall was a long, tree-lined avenue, fashionable for promenading.

NANDO'S COFFEE-HOUSE   Located in an ornate building on Fleet Street near Inner Temple Gate, it was a popular site for legal and literary conversation.

OLD BAILEY   The central criminal court in London, it is located at the corner of Bailey and Newgate Streets near the prison.

RANELAGH   Richard, Viscount Ranelagh, opened these pleasure grounds, featuring gardens and a rotunda for concerts, balls, masquerades, fireworks, regattas, and other amusements, in 1742 in Chelsea.

RING   A railed-off riding circle in the northern half of Hyde Park, the Ring was a favorite spot for gallants and ladies of fashion to see and be seen.

ROSAMOND'S POND   In the southwest corner of Saint James's Park, this was a popular place for romantic encounters until 1770, when it was filled in.

ROYAL EXCHANGE   Commonly known as "the Change," it was founded in 1565 as a center of commercial activity for London merchants.

SAINT GILES   A working-class area in central London characterized by poorly built tenements, this is where many indigents scraped by as needlewomen, chairmen, street-hawkers, and the like.

SAINT JAMES'S COFFEE-HOUSE   The preferred haunt of Whigs from the reign of Queen Anne through George III, it was located near Saint James's Palace.

SAINT JAMES'S PARK   The oldest and most ornamental of central London's royal parks, it was landscaped during the reign of Charles II.

TOM'S COFFEE-HOUSE   Located opposite Button's on Russell Street, it was a gathering place for cards and conversation among nobility, statesmen, gentry, and literati from Queen Anne's day through George III's.

WESTMINSTER ABBEY   Located near the Houses of Parliament, the abbey is the site of coronations and other national ceremonies and the burial place of many British historical and cultural figures.

WHITE'S CHOCOLATE-HOUSE   This gathering spot, more famous for its gaming than its chocolate, opened on Saint James's Street in 1693 to courtiers and other pleasure-seekers.

WILL'S COFFEE-HOUSE   This coffeehouse, founded by William Unwin on Russell Street in Covent Garden and made famous by John Dryden's patronage in the 1690s, was a leading resort for wits, poets, and dramatists until 1713, when fashion shifted across the street to Button's.

Glossary of Terms

ANCIENTS   Persons or works of Greek or Roman antiquity

BAND-BOX   Lightweight container for apparel, especially hats

BASHAW   Pasha, or high-ranking officer in the Ottoman Empire

BEADLE   Church warden who wields a stick to keep order

BEAUX   Gallant young men, courtiers

BENCHER   Magistrate, judge

BILLS OF MORTALITY   Weekly list of christenings and deaths published in
the newspaper

BLOT   Vulnerable piece in backgammon

BON MOT   Witticism

BOX   Private seat in a theater

BRILLIANT   Gem

BUCK   Dandy, dashing fellow

BUSINESS   Everyday activity, employment

CANAILLE   Masses, mob

CANARY   Sweet wine from the Canary Islands

CANT   Dogma or jargon

CARRIAGE   Posture, deportment; alternately, postage

CATHOLIC   Broad or universal

CENTO   Literary work composed of quotations from other authors

CHAIRMAN   Sedan-chair bearer

CHANGE, THE   The Royal Exchange

CHAPMAN   Peddlar (from *chap*, "cheap")

CHARGER   Platter

CHEAPEN   To bargain for, ask the price of, bid for

CHIMERICAL   Illusory, fantastical

CIPHER   Zero

CIT   City dweller or middle-class person aspiring to higher status

CLOSET   Private room or study

COINER   One who coins counterfeit money

CONCORD   Agreement, harmony of thought or sentiment

CONDITION   Rank or quality

CONSORT   Partner, spousal or parental

COQUET   Flirt

CORAL   Teething ring

COUNTRY, THE   Provinces or rural areas

COXCOMB   Dandy, fop

DAB   Expert

DAMASCENE   Small plum

DAUBER   Inartistic painter

DEMONSTRATION   Philosophical or scientific proof

DEPENDING   In progress

DIGEST   To arrange, organize, classify

DISTICH   Verse couplet

DIVINE   Clergyman

DRAWER   One who draws liquor for customers, a tapster

DRAYMAN   Person who delivers beer for a brewery

DROPSY   Disease characterized by an accumulation of fluid in the joints

DUNGHILL-COCK   Domestic fowl

DUSTMAN   Garbage collector

DUTCH MAIL   News, particularly political or military, from the Continent

EQUIPAGE   Horse-drawn carriage with servants

EXPATIATE   To range freely, elaborate discursively

FABRIC   Construction

FETCH   Artifice, stratagem, subterfuge

FIGURE   Appearance, as in "to make a good figure"

FLAMBEAU   Torch or torch bearer

FOND   Affectionate, foolish

FREEHOLDER   Landowner

FRIENDS   Relatives; alternately, Quakers

FURBELOW   Flounce on a woman's dress

GALLANTRY   Amorous intrigue

GALLERY   Balcony seating in the theater

GAMING   Gambling

GENIUS   Natural abilities or aptitude

GEWGAW   Showy or worthless object

GOTHIC   Overly elaborate

GRAVEL   Urinary condition

GRUB STREET   Associated with literary hack writing

HACKNEY   Coach, or boat, for hire

HEAVY   Dull, slow-witted

HEMISTICH   Half a verse

HOB OR NOB   To drink together and take turns toasting

HOUSE   Business establishment

INNER TEMPLE   London residence of civil law students

INTELLIGENCE   News, chiefly military or political

JOINTURE   Financial provisions made for a woman at the time of her marriage

KEEPING   Harmony or proportion in painting; alternately, financially supporting a mistress

KNACK   Knick-knack, an object more for ornament than for use

LAUDANUM   Liquid opium, readily available in the nineteenth century as a painkiller

LICTOR   Roman official who carried fasces (bundle of rods) to punish offenders

LEVÉE   Reception or assembly

LOVER   Suitor

LOW   Vulgar, plebian

LUCUBRATION   Midnight study, thoughts produced by candlelight

MAGAZINE   Storehouse or supply of merchandise

MAKE LOVE   To court or woo

MAN   Servant

MARRIAGE ARTICLES   Legal contract stipulating property ownership and behavior between a married couple

MECHANIC   Manual laborer, artisan

MODERNS   Contemporary authors, artists

MUSKIN   Pretty face

NICE   Discerning, fastidious

NINE STOPS   Holes in a pipe to regulate pitch

NON-PLUS   State of being confused or disconcerted

ORDINARY   Tavern or eating-house serving public meals

PANACHE   Tuft of feathers on a headdress

PARTS   Natural abilities

PATCH   Piece of silk used to cover facial blemishes

PELISSE   Woman's cloak reaching to the ankles

PENSIONER   Person on a stipend

PERIOD   Sentence of several clauses arranged with rhetorical finesse

PERRIWIG   Wig used for fashion or professional purposes

PHYSIC   Medicine

PINK   To pierce or nick someone with a sword

PIT   Cheapest section of a theater, which has only standing room

PLAYER   Actor

POLITE   Refined, cultivated

POSIE   Legend or motto

PRECEPTOR   Teacher

PRIG   Vague term of dislike or disrespect

PROFESSOR   An artist; one who professes an art

QUADRATE   To square with, agree

QUALITY   Person(s) of high social rank

RAKE   Libertine, dissipated man of fashion

RECLAIM   To protest

RHODOMONTADE   Vain, empty boasting

ROLLER   Kind of stocking

ROSTRAL CROWNS   Honorific military adornment

ROUT   Large evening party or reception

SCRAG   Piece of lean or bony meat

SENSIBLE   Sensitive, having acute power of sensation

SHAMBLES   Butcher's slaughterhouse

SHARPER   Swindler, one who cheats at gambling

SMART   Fashionable, witty

SMATTERER   Dabbler with only superficial knowledge of a matter

SMOCK-FACED   Pale

SNUFFY   Contemptuous

SOUNDING   Resounding, impressive

SPANISH   Wine or snuff of Spanish origin

SQUABB   Ottoman

STALKING-HORSE   False pretext concealing real intentions

STILE   Steps allowing passage over a fence

STOMACHER   V-shaped piece of decorative cloth worn over the chest and stomach

SUBSCRIPTION   Agreement to purchase printed matter before publication

SUPERANNUATED   Retired on a pension

SWITCH   Slender, flexible shoot from a tree used for riding

SWORD-KNOT   Tassel or ribbon tied to the hilt of a sword

SYLLABUB   Creamy dessert flavored with white wine or sherry

TAW   Game played with marbles

TEMPLAR   Lawyer or law student residing at the Inner Temple

TIPPET   Scarf or accoutrement dangling from a sleeve, hood, or headdress

TOSS-POT   Drunkard

TOWN   City, usually London (in Mackenzie, Edinburgh)

TRANSPORT   Condition of being swept away by emotion; alternately, to banish overseas

TYMPANY   Physiological term referring to a swelling of the abdomen with air or gas

VERGER   Church officer who bears a staff before the bishop

VIRTUOSO   Natural-history buff, collector of curiosities

VISNOMY   Face, countenance

WANT   Lack

WEEDS   Garments

WHIST   Popular card game

WOMAN   Servant